DECOLONIZING THE SODOMITE

Decolonizing the Sodomite

QUEER TROPES OF SEXUALITY IN COLONIAL ANDEAN CULTURE

Michael J. Horswell

UNIVERSITY OF TEXAS PRESS
Austin

Requests for permission to reproduce material from this work
should be sent to Permissions, University of Texas Press, P.O. Box
7819, Austin, TX 78713-7819.
www.utexas.edu/utpress/about/bpermission.html

♾ The paper used in this book meets the minimum requirements of
ANSI/NISO Z39.4-1992 (R1997) (Permanence of Paper).

LIBRARY OF CONGRESS CATALOGING-IN-PUBLICATION DATA
Horswell, Michael J. (Michael Jenkins), 1965–
Decolonizing the sodomite : queer tropes of sexuality in colonial
Andean culture / by Michael J. Horswell. — 1st ed.
    p.   cm.
Includes bibliographical references and index.

ISBN 978-0-292-71267-6

  1. Homosexuality, Male—Andes Region—History.
2. Homosexuality, Male—Spain—History.   3. Sex customs—Andes
Region—History.   4. Sex customs—Spain—History.   5. Indians of
South America—Andes Region—Sexual behavior.   6. Indians of
South America—Colonization—Andes Region.   7. Incas—Sexual
behavior.   8. Indian gays—Andes Region—History.   9. Indian
gays—Andes Region—Sexual behavior.   10. Spain—Colonies—
America.   11. Spain—Foreign relations—Andes Region.
12. Andes Region—Foreign relations—Spain.   I. Title.
HQ76.3.A65H67   2005
306.76′6′08998323—dc22

                                                              2005020852

In memory of my mother, Bette B. Horswell;
my father, James R. Horswell;
and my grandmother, "Granny B.,"
Katie Sue Black

CONTENTS

ACKNOWLEDGMENTS

From my first steps down the Inca trail near Cuzco, Peru, some seventeen years ago, I was captivated by the beauty and serenity of the Andes, and by the vibrancy and warmth of the people who welcomed me into their homes and lives. As all Andeanists know, once you begin exploring the richness of the civilization that thrives there to this day, it is impossible to stop going back. Ironically, one of my first and most indelible experiences in Cuzco was the time I spent being chased by an aggressively amorous transvestite, who had taken a liking to me, a naïve gringo backpacker looking to practice his Spanish and to learn a few Quechua words in a late-night *peña*. Whether that night had anything to do with my choosing the topic of this book as my doctoral research project many years later I do not know. Perhaps a subliminal memory of her triggered the curiosity that led me to question the presence of so many references to transvested "sodomites" in the colonial chronicles and histories I read in graduate school.

My journey into Latin American studies began before that fateful trip, thanks to the inspiration and mentoring of several teachers in South Carolina. I would never have thought of studying Spanish and Latin American literature were it not for the early inspiration of my high school Spanish teacher, Rosemary Hunt. At Wofford College, Prof. Susan Griswold continued the encouragement that led to my living and studying in Spain and Argentina. Prof. Walt Hudgins inspired me to value the pursuit of knowledge and helped shape the social consciousness that informs this project. My intellectual development in the study of Latin American literature and culture blossomed under the tutelage of several professors who taught at the University of Maryland during my time as a graduate student, including Jorge Aguilar-Mora, Louise Fothergill-Payne, José Emilio Pacheco, José Rabasa, and Javier Sanjinés.

I owe a special debt of gratitude to Regina Harrison, the director of my doctoral dissertation and the person instrumental in my specialization in the Andean region. Professor Harrison's love for the Andes and scholarly integrity inspired me in myriad ways. Her diligent and patient guidance throughout my doctoral program made me a better researcher, writer, and teacher. I am grateful for her continued support and friendship.

In Peru, at the Centro de Estudios Regionales Andinos Bartolomé de las Casas, I wish to recognize the assistance of Henrique Urbano, Juan Carlos Godenzzi, and the faculty and librarians at the Colegio Andino, above all, Irene Silverblatt, Bruce Mannheim, and Isabel Iriarte. My Quechua teachers in Cuzco, Janet and Claudio Vengoa, in addition to introducing me to the nuances of the language, shared their rich cultural heritage and beautiful singing voices. Doña María's flavorful cooking and *huayno* dancing made my stays in Cuzco all the more enjoyable. It was at her table that I truly began to grasp the warmth and depth of the Andean people.

I was fortunate to have the financial support of several institutions to carry out research over the years, including the National Security Education Program fellowship, the U.S. Department of Education Foreign Language and Area Studies fellowship, and Florida Atlantic University's Dorothy F. Schmidt College of Arts and Letters summer research grant.

I thank the many readers who have made invaluable suggestions at different stages of this project, including Virginia Bell, Carmen Benito-Vessels, Karen Christian, Carlos Iván DeGregori, Kimberley Gauderman, Max Kirsch, William Leap, José Antonio Mazzotti, Phyllis Peres, José Rabasa, Simon Richter, Peter Sigal, Doris Sommer, Gustavo Verdesio, and the anonymous readers for the University of Texas Press. I appreciate my two graduate assistants, John Colhouer and Fernanda Márquez, for their help with many details. My colleagues at Florida Atlantic University have been especially supportive of my research, from helping with translations of arcane words, to giving career advice, to simply being an understanding sounding board in moments of frustration. Many thanks go to Nora Erro-Peralta, Yolanda Gamboa, Martha Mendoza, Carmen Chávez, Luis Duno-Gottberg, Anthony Tamburri, and Myriam Ruthenberg.

I am also very grateful for the support of the editorial staff at the University of Texas Press, especially Theresa May, for stewarding this project from start to finish. I am grateful for Allison Faust's, Leslie Tingle's, and Nancy Bryan's expertise in preparing the manuscript for production. My special thanks go to my copy editor, Kathy Bork, for her keen eye and rigorous attention to detail.

Finally, none of this would have been possible or worthwhile without the support and companionship of my family and friends. I am grateful for everyone's patience and love throughout this process. I would never have finished this project without my dear friend Lynda Klich's constant encouragement, friendship, brainstorming, and editing. My sister, Patti, has always been there for me, even traveling to Peru with George to see me while I was doing research in Cuzco and climbing the Inca trail. I dedicate this book to my parents and grandmother, for the life they gave me, and for their love, which nurtures me still.

DECOLONIZING THE SODOMITE

INTRODUCTION

Transculturating Tropes of Sexuality, Tinkuy, *and* Third Gender *in the Andes*

The chieftains and settlers [from Carabaya] bring a chuqui
chinchay, an animal painted in all the colors. They say that it
was the apo [deity] of the jaguars, under whose protection were
the hermaphrodites, or Indians of two genders. [Los curacas y
mitmais (de Carabaya) trae a chuqui chinchay, animal muy
pintado de todos colores. Dizen que era apo de los otorongos,
en cuya guarda da a los ermofraditas yndios de dos naturas.]
—SANTACRUZ PACHACUTI,
Relación de antigüedades deste reyno del Perú

These ruinous people are all sodomites . . . there is not a chief
among them who does not carry with him four or five gallant
pages. He keeps these as concubines. [Es gente muy bellaca son
todos someticos no ay principal que no trayga quatro o cinco
pajes muy galanes. Estos tiene por mancebos.]
—JUAN RUIZ DE ARCE, *Relación de servicios en Indias*

In the late fifteenth century there was a crisis in the suc-
cession of Inca rulers in Tawantinsuyu—a *pachacuti* (cataclysmic change)
that became a liminal moment in the cultural reproduction of the Andean
social body and in the transition of Inca imperial bodies from one generation to another.[1] As recounted in the first epigraph above, to mediate the tension created during this time of change, the Inca summoned
to Cuzco a queer figure, the *chuqui chinchay,* or the *apo de los otorongos,* a
mountain deity of the jaguars who was the patron of dual-gendered indigenous peoples.[2] While we do not know precisely why the *chuqui chinchay* was called to Cuzco that day, we can now appreciate that this apo was
a revered figure in Andean culture, and its human *huacsas,* or ritual atten-

dants—third-gendered subjects—were vital actors in Andean ceremonies. These *quariwarmi* (men-women) shamans mediated between the symmetrically dualistic spheres of Andean cosmology and daily life by performing rituals that at times required same-sex erotic practices. Their transvested attire served as a visible sign of a third space that negotiated between the masculine and the feminine, the present and the past, the living and the dead. Their shamanic presence invoked the androgynous creative force often represented in Andean mythology.

The third gender's body was a sign in a semiotic system that privileged representation and communication on a corporeal plane rather than on the written page. The Andeans' collective memory depended on oral transmission and interpretation aided by mnemonic devices such as *quipus* (multicolored knotted cords used to record historical and other data in the Andes), textiles, natural topography, rituals, monumental architecture, ceramics, and sculpture. Above all, this memory depended on the people who performed their culture's ritualized history rather than on print technology and standardized alphabets, a significant cultural difference that would have far-reaching effects when the Spanish invasion, another *pachacuti*, was unleashed in the Andes. The impermanence of the human body and its vestments reflected the relative fragility of Andean cultural memory. When sacred figures like the *chuqui chinchay* and its third-gender ritualists are inscribed as diabolical and deviant subjects in Spanish colonial writings, scholars are presented with a challenge.

The Spanish "Conquest" and colonization of the Andes was recorded for posterity in the legendary "books of the brave," narratives that created the infamous "lettered cities" (ciudades letradas) in the shadows of the "darker side" of Renaissance humanism.[3] These familiar metaphors for Spanish literary hegemony in the Americas have in common an assumed masculinity of the writing subject, a masculinity often naturalized in the original colonial texts, later historiographies, and literary criticism. The relationship between colonial literature and the dominant masculine subject personified by the Renaissance's ideal man—one of arms and letters—finds its roots in Iberian medieval culture and literature. This subjectivity was central to shaping the colonial narratives that tried to make sense of the invasion, colonization, and indigenous resistance in the first century after Francisco Pizarro penetrated the west coast of South America. Yet, the "brave," "lettered" men of the time, some more or less touched by the nascent humanist philosophies, expressed an implicit instability of Spanish male sexuality in their writings, an instability revealed in performative discursive iterations of the ideal masculine subject once again under siege by a cultural Other, this time by the indigenous Americans rather than the Christians' Moorish rivals in Iberia.

From the beginning of the "Encounter" and Conquest of the Americas, indigenous gender and sexual difference, like that embodied in the third-gender ritual specialists, challenged Spanish concepts of masculinity and femininity. The chroniclers, missionaries, civil servants, and historians of the period reacted to these differences by inscribing them in the colonial discourse through what I consider tropes of sexuality and through distorted interpretative testimonies. Such tropes are important markers for the places of enunciation shaped by the Spanish writing subjects who employed them.[4] I argue, however, that these tropes also left traces of pre-Columbian cultural values and subjectivities that can be recovered through careful readings and reconstructions from the fragments of colonial discourse.

This book has a double objective: to interrogate the performative nature of these tropes of sexuality found in early colonial texts; and to recover the subaltern knowledge of the colonized third-gender subjects misrepresented by the rhetorical figures. I contend that Andean cultural memory of what became subaltern knowledge was recorded through ritual performances deemed anathema to the cultural values that informed Spanish colonial discourse. The public use of the body, outside the context of the vestiges of medieval Christian religiosity, was viewed by the Spanish as a debased, effeminate activity and therefore idolatrous or sinful. The Andean body, a site of cultural memory, became subjugated to a masculinized, lettered discourse or incorporated into Spanish-sanctioned Christian religious performances, such as Corpus Christi celebrations. From the Spanish perspective, ritual cultural reproduction through the body was a dangerous indigenous resistance, and the traces of this sacred rituality were viewed as a heretical counterdiscourse that sometimes pitted the feminine and androgynous against the masculine.

In Spanish culture, the feminine and the androgyne were contemptible, whereas in Andean culture the feminine was understood as complementary and reciprocal to the male. The tensions between the feminine and the masculine were ritually negotiated in order to reenact the originary, utopian, androgynous whole represented in Andean mythology. The symmetrical balance between the masculine and the feminine was at times arbitrated through the corporal performances of third-gender ritualists, most often represented as debased, lascivious sodomites by Spanish tropes of sexuality. Transvested Andeans introduced a crisis into the Spanish patriarchal paradigm because the third gender's symbolic rupture of the gender binary served the purpose of creating harmony and complementarity between the sexes and invoked the power and privilege of the androgynous creative force.

This challenge to Spanish gender and sexual norms invited a counteroffensive in various arenas of colonial culture: historiography, civil law, ecclesiastical literature, and religious art and performance. These strands of colonial discourse conspired in the near erasure and eventual transculturation of third-gender ritual subjectivity.

The Spanish effort to eliminate the ritual attendant, represented in this study by the third-gendered *ipa* or *orua,* who interpreted and transmitted cultural knowledge, was an attempt to destroy part of the people's memory and understanding of the cosmos.[5] In the first Spanish chronicles of the conquest of Tawantinsuyu we find references to the cultural misunderstanding and misinterpretation of enigmatic third-gender figures, commonly referred to by the Spanish as sodomites, and the call for their extermination. Juan Ruiz de Arce's comment in his version of Francisco Pizarro's first foray on the coast of South America, which serves as the second epigraph to this introduction, sets the stage for the next hundred years of acculturation of indigenous gender and sexuality. His equation of same-sex sexuality and lasciviousness reflects medieval patriarchal values and an abjection of the feminine that informed the subjectivities of the conquistadores in the Americas. His mention of "ruinous" peoples whose leaders were so corrupt as to keep male concubines begins the discourse of abjection that obfuscated the complexities of the indigenous gender culture. Julia Kristeva has defined the abject as that which "disturbs identity, system, order. What does not respect borders, positions, rules" (*Powers of Horror,* 11). I argue that, just as in the Iberian Peninsula the feminine was figured as a disturbance of the masculine "order" and a threat to the "borders" that the male Spanish subject patrolled in his performance of gender identity, in the Andes same-sex sexuality and the third-gender subject threatened these "rules" and put into question the patriarchal "system" constructed on the basis of dual gender categories.[6]

It is important to locate this analysis in the transatlantic context of the early-modern period; to understand this first wave of globalization in the Americas and its effects on indigenous gender culture requires a constant crisscrossing of the oceans to comprehend what values and tropes traveled to the periphery of the Spanish empire in the Americas and, in turn, what perceptions and revaluations returned to the metropolis. I trace the roots of the abjection of the feminine to the Iberian Peninsula by reading tropes of sexuality in canonical literary texts and by pursuing how the subjugation of the feminine manifested in the persecution of same-sex sexuality. Without an appreciation of the history of the deep-rooted instability of Spanish masculinity, one cannot understand the anxiety expressed in the chronicles and histories of the Andes related to sacred and profane same-sex sexuality and ritual performances of the feminine and androgynous sphere of Andean culture. As the transculturation of the Andes unfolds, this anxiety is absorbed by the first-generation ladino and mestizo writers, further obscuring our understanding of pre-Hispanic indigenous gender and sexuality.[7] Transculturated tropes of sexuality cross back to the peninsula in a venerable transatlantic text, one produced in Renaissance Spain by an Andean mestizo who would become one of the cultural mediators between his mother's Inca heritage and his father's Spanish ancestry. The celebrated Inca Garcilaso de la Vega brings us full circle from the originary Iberian gender anxiety of the cultural Other I analyze in *El poema del mio Cid* to the mestizo's unique form of self-censure and sacrifice of his "queer" Inca ancestors, as expressed in his seminal *Comentarios reales.*

To reconstruct the nearly shattered subjectivity of third gender in the colonial discourse of the Andes is to elicit a reflection of the subject based on the distorted image of the abject Other both in and of that discourse. How do we make the image whole when the language that reflects its fragments is the very same that broke the illusion of wholeness in the first place? How do we read for subjectivities in the profane, frozen word-images of an outsider's mirror when those same subjects were inscribed in their culture's collective memory through ritual, sacred performances in an oral tradition? To make sense of the fragmented colonial accounts of the cross-dressed "temple sodomites" encountered in colonial readings is to embark on a multidisciplinary cultural study of gender and sexuality in the pre-Hispanic and colonial Andes. To comprehend the representation of colonized subjectivities marked by processes of marginalization in hegemonic discourses requires an inquiry into the gender and sexual culture of both the invader and the invaded.

I begin by relocating third-gender subjectivities from the margins of colonial scholarship to the center and suggest that, from this new vantage point, all readers, regardless of their subject positions, might hear a questioning of the gender and sexual binaries that have historically marginalized what might be understood as a "queer" identity. This is not to situate this project only or even primarily in the recent academic trend of queer studies, but it is to bring aspects of queer theory to colonial Andean studies in order to enact a claim to space in the historical and theoretical record.[8] It is in this spirit that I place the Andean third gender at the center of this research, as a subjectivity that once served a ceremonial role in Andean culture and that later put into question the colonizing gender binaries that marginalized his/her once-sacred subjectivity. It is to restore the maligned subject to his/her historically vital third space, a space that mediated between absolute binaries. Restoring him/her to this third space requires a new reading strategy for colonial Andean texts. As I explain more fully below, this approach leads me to reconceptualize transculturation as a process that produces alterity, as a dynamic "third space" in the continuous stream of cultural reproduction in which queer subjects are produced. This "queering" of the term "transculturation" is formulated from Andean philosophy and narrative practice; I wish to think from an Andean paradigm of cultural reproduction in order to reinvigorate a theoretical construct born in the Caribbean and used throughout the continent to its near exhaustion.

TRANSCULTURATION: A QUEER, THIRD SPACE

The concept of transculturation has undergone an intense theoretical revision in the last few years. The term speaks to a multifaceted process in which hegemonic cultures influence subjugated ones, in which subjugated cultures give up old and acquire new values and meanings, and in which completely new cultural forms are created.[9] Fernando Ortiz is credited with coining the term transculturation in his 1940 study *Cuban Counterpoint: Tobacco and Sugar*. His neologism was intended to replace the popular sociological word acculturation, which for Ortiz, signified "the process of transition from one culture to another, and its manifold social repercussions" (98). Ortiz believed that the social and cultural processes that formed twentieth-century Cuban culture were much more complex, and as his thorough analysis of Cuban historical development suggests, "the real history of Cuba is the history of its intermeshed transculturations" (ibid.), which included the mixing of many races and ethnicities, from the originary Taínos to the Spanish, African, Asian, and Anglo immigrants. Defending his neologism, Ortiz explains:

> I am of the opinion that the word transculturation better
> expresses the different phases of the process of transition from
> one culture to another because this does not consist merely
> in acquiring another culture, which is what the English word
> acculturation really implies, but the process also necessarily

> involves the loss or uprooting of a previous culture, which
> could be described as a deculturation. In addition it carries the
> idea of the consequent creation of new cultural phenomena,
> which could be called neoculturation. In the end, as the school
> of Malinowski's followers maintains, the result of every union
> of cultures is similar to that of the reproductive process be-
> tween individuals: the offspring always has something of both
> parents but is always different from each of them.
>
> (Ibid., 102–103)

This process, however, is not an equal exchange of cultural values, as Ortiz's somewhat idealized description of *mestizaje* might lead us to believe. Due to the violent and persistent nature of colonial practices, the early and intermediate stages of transculturation can be characterized as "acculturation" and "deculturation," as Ortiz understands the terms, while in simultaneous and later stages the strategies of resistance and accommodation of the marginalized culture begin to affect the dominant, invasive culture, which leads to new cultural forms in the "contact zone," or neocultures.

Ortiz's foundational metaphor equates the cultural reproductive process with human procreation. Sylvia Spitta, in her reconsideration of the term, observes how Ortiz "tends to overlook imbalances of power" (*Between Two Waters,* 6). She points out that in "his appeal to the family and to relations between the sexes as a model for transculturation, women and men, mothers and fathers, although physiologically different, are assumed to be equal. Women and men, however, are never equal when it comes to power — particularly in a colonial context based on the violence of one race over another and one gender over another" (ibid.). As Walter Mignolo has observed, Ortiz's conceptualization was deeply connected to questions of nationality and did not address coloniality (*Local Histories/Global Designs,* 16). Ortiz's priority was to characterize the unique cultural history of his nation through a concept of miscegenation that privileged biological and reproductive metaphors.

To this critique I would add that Ortiz's heterosexist paradigm must be challenged, for a model of cultural reproduction should not implicitly exclude those subjects that do not conform to hegemonic forms of sexuality. Normative metaphors do not convey the complexity and heterogeneity of cultural reproduction. As we will see in this study, for example, same-sex practices and transgendering were ritually important in the Andean re-

gion's cultural reproduction. Furthermore, as the third-gender subjects became marginalized and resemanticized in the process of colonization, they
began to signify sites of transculturation in the form of what I characterize as queer tropes of sexuality. To ignore the gender and sexual bias inherent in Ortiz's metaphor is to disseminate a theoretical term that replicates
the same ideology of exclusion that critics seek to challenge in the colonial
and postcolonial culture of the Americas. The task at hand is to understand
how and why the representation of gender and sexuality changed, and what
ideological affinities made its representation such a conflictive issue; therefore, it is necessary to analyze issues of transculturation from a perspective
that holds no identity markers as essential or naturalized.

I argue that the process of transculturation produces and is produced
by queer subjectivities. The word *queer* as I use it throughout this study
purposefully evokes the most common meanings of the term, both its traditional denotation as something "odd, singular, strange, doubtful, suspicious, eccentric" and its currently more fashionable, activist, and academic
meaning as that which is transgressively marginal to normative gender and
sexual culture. The production of "culturally queer," that is, eccentric, singular subjectivities is central to the process. The various subjects produced
and reproduced are consistently marginal to both the hegemonic and the
subjugated cultures. The subjects of transculturation often find themselves
in third spaces, neither of the originary nor of the new, invading culture. Homi Bhabha has observed that colonial discourse not only represses
native voices through its myriad strands of colonial authority, but also creates hybrid subjects who are of neither the native nor the dominant culture, but are in liminal positions between the two (*Location of Culture,* 36–
39). Thus, they embody and articulate difference in contested "third spaces,"
particularly in colonial, postcolonial, and neocolonial "contact zones." This
difference is often considered unorthodox, and the vanguard of these new
third spaces is anything but "natural" sons and daughters of cultural procreation, as Ortiz's metaphor might imply. A more radical conception of the
queerness of transculturated subjects opens our readings and understanding of cultural reproduction to include those social actors whose queer
gender and sexuality both distinguished them in their originary culture
and increasingly marginalized them in their transculturated one. To recognize the queer aspects of cultural reproduction is to affirm the Otherness
subjects must assume or disavow in the metamorphoses they undergo and
create.

Gloria Anzaldúa began writing about the material and psychic border-
lands of this third space in her influential *Borderlands/La Frontera,* in which

she goes back to the colonial writings of Mexico to recuperate terms from Nahuatl and the Mesoamerican cultures of her ancestors. The terms *nepantla* and *nepantlismo,* first defined by Anzaldúa as "torn between ways" (ibid., 100), is taken from an indigenous scribe's self-description during the sixteenth century. While *nepantla* is also theorized as the liminal geographic space of the U.S. Southwest, in between the two spaces of Mesoamerica and the United States, Anzaldúa increasingly understands the concept to be a psychic space of transformation in which new subjects are agents in the creation of their new realities. *Nepantleras* create new forms of language, new cultural relations, and new values that express in-between states of being, in the intersections of gender, ethnicity, class, race, sexuality, and geographic displacement. Anzaldúa first employed the term in her development of the notion of a mestiza consciousness whose place is that intense, ambiguous third space of liminality and creativity: "In attempting to work out a synthesis, the self has added a third element which is greater than the sum of its several parts. The third element is a new consciousness —a mestiza consciousness—and though it is a source of intense pain, its energy comes from continual creative motion that keeps breaking down the unitary aspect of each new paradigm" (ibid., 101–102). The third space of *nepantlismo* yields alternative histories that give voice to subaltern subjects' *conocimiento,* or knowledge. Anzaldúa defines *conocimiento* as "an epistemology that tries to encompass all the dimensions of life, both inner —mental, emotional, instinctive, imaginal, spiritual, bodily realms—and outer—social, political, lived experiences" (*Entrevistas,* 177). Her work adds to our understanding of transculturation because she unflinchingly goes to the heart, the interior workings, of the metamorphoses of cultural change and the hybrid identities that emerge from the painful processes, mediated by power, that produce *conocimiento.*

I will argue that, in the Andes, this process was often performed by subjects who embodied this third space at ritually significant moments and represented *conocimiento* crucial to transitional periods in their societies. This is the knowledge that was nearly erased by the Spanish Conquest and colonization, but that remains embedded in both the writings and the cultural practices of some Andean, mestizo, and Spanish writers and performers. My recovery of what had become subaltern knowledge and practice in the case of the third-gender ritual roles in Andean culture can be understood as a *conocimiento* that informs alternative, queer ways of cultural reproduction.

The power relations that inform this obscuring of subaltern knowledge determine which cultural values and activities—queer and otherwise—

continue to be reproduced and which are "sacrificed." Walter Mignolo has contributed to the theorization of subaltern knowledge and the relationship between difference—what I am characterizing as queer subjects—and colonial power. He recognizes that

> colonial difference is the space where coloniality of power is enacted. It is also the space where the restitution of subaltern knowledge is taking place and where border thinking is emerging. The colonial difference is the space where local histories inventing and implementing global designs meet local histories, the space in which global designs have to be adapted, adopted, rejected, integrated, or ignored. The colonial difference is, finally, the physical as well as the imaginary location where the coloniality of power is at work in the confrontation of two kinds of local histories displayed in different spaces and times across the planet.
>
> (*Local Histories/Global Designs,* ix)

While Mignolo is addressing how the "coloniality of power" has permeated the myriad spaces of the global culture, both the classic center and the periphery, in the late twentieth century, his conceptualization of subaltern knowledge, border thinking, and the relationship between local and global discourses is rooted in the sixteenth- and seventeenth-century writings of colonial Mexico and the Andes. Like Anzaldúa, Mignolo is intrigued by the notion of "*nepantla*"; he glosses "estamos nepantla" from the Nahuatl as "to be or feel in between" (ibid., x) and understands the unique voice that emerges in the context of colonial difference as one that expresses a "border gnosis," or *conocimiento.* Mignolo helps us appreciate the dialogic nature of the "fractured enunciations" that emerge from the subaltern spaces of coloniality. His emphasis on the semiotics of coloniality guides us to focus on issues of representation, and not on racial, genetic miscegenation, in our analysis of colonial discourse (or semiosis, as he prefers). "Transculturation" as a critical term is useful insofar as it serves as "a principle to produce descriptions that changes the principle in which similar descriptions have been made up to the point of its introduction in cultures of scholarship's vocabulary" (ibid., 16).

This stress on "descriptions" might risk locating projects like mine in a Eurocentric logocentrism if it were not for Mignolo's concomitant insistence that our analysis be grounded in a "pluritopic hermeneutics." This understanding of colonial semiosis frames my approach to the subaltern knowledge found in the representations of the body, particularly the queer corporeal signs that signify important *conocimiento,* or "border gnosis," in the colonial Andes. Furthermore, my attention to the specificity of culturally performed bodies and their myriad representations in the fractured enunciations of subaltern coloniality reminds us to pay closer attention to the agency of those participating in the processes of transculturation.

In other words, the "transculturators," as Ángel Rama named the vanguards of neoculturations in Latin America, are agents in the course of cultural change.[10] These subjects cannot be blindly celebrated, as much criticism related to hybridity and mestizaje has tended to do. Instead, a more nuanced reading of the effects of transculturation on all social actors is needed, especially as this relates to the sexually queer aspects of the culture. Some culturally queer transculturators I consider, like Inca Garcilaso de la Vega, for example, contributed to the marginalization of the newly colonized, sexually queer, despite their traditional role in cultural reproduction of their originary culture. I will focus on this phenomenon in order to further interrogate cultural hybridity and its relationship to the sexual heterogeneity of Andean culture and to the larger theme of what Rama calls the "selection" process undertaken by the transculturators.

Alberto Moreiras problematizes this selection process by reminding us that transculturation works like a "war machine, which feeds on cultural difference, whose primary function is the reduction of the possibilities of radical heterogeneity" ("José María Arguedas," 218; all translations are mine unless otherwise noted). This reductive "war machine" can be "understood as a systematic part of the Western productionist ideology or metaphysics, which still retains a strong colonizing power in relation to alternative symbolic fields in culture" (ibid., 218–219). Moreiras's insight into the colonizing erasure of all that does not enter into a certain productive model of transculturation provides a framework within which to examine how colonial discourse reduced indigenous sexual heterogeneity to forms and practices acceptable to the orthodox Catholicism and humanism of the early-modern period. This war machine may have reached its finale in the work of José María Arguedas, as Moreiras concludes, but I will argue that it began in the Andes with Inca Garcilaso's colonial hybrid, the *Comentarios reales,* an early constituent of the lettered city.

However powerful the social dynamic of transculturation is, we cannot lose sight of Rama's original observations, which privileged the agency of the transculturators (*Transculturación narrativa,* 38–39). It was through a process of "cultural plasticity" that "donors" and "receptors" of culture selected and invented cultural components from which the neocultures would be fashioned. I will explore how the indigenous and mestizo writers contributed to the silencing of third gender as either a resistant, contestatory strategy of survival, on the one hand, and how, on the other hand, they encoded the third-gender *conocimiento* in order to preserve it, as in the case of culturally queer, indigenous ladino writer Santa Cruz Pachacuti Yamqui. To recover the cultural value of this pre-Hispanic diversity is a challenge that requires a "pluritopic hermeneutic" that underscores the traces of orality and, by extension, subaltern discourse in colonial texts. My intention is to highlight the sexual heterogeneity of pre-Hispanic and early colonial Andean culture, often lost in lettered accounts but found between the lines of the transcribed and transculturated oral accounts that are both historical sources and transculturating agents in that process. Understanding how the sexual Other is treated in the colonial texts offers us insight into the workings of colonial subjectivization and subaltern hybridity as well as a better appreciation of the performative nature of alterity represented by tropes of sexuality.

TRANSCULTURATING TROPES OF SEXUALITY

Spanish colonial discourse is marked by a series of what I will name "transculturating tropes of sexuality."[11] If "troping is the soul of discourse," as White has asserted (*Tropics of Discourse*, 3), then it is crucial to understand how certain gender and sexual tropes play a part in the transformation of subjectivities to whom the figures of speech refer. It is through analysis of this "troping" that we can come to understand how Spanish and, later, mestizo and indigenous writers used the power of their imaginations and the weight of traditional tropes in the interpretation of Andean culture. Since the 1980's, the primary fields of knowledge making up colonial studies have undergone a fundamental transformation related to the epistemological shift known broadly as poststructuralism. History, anthropology, and literary criticism have converged in their increasing distrust of language as representing "reality" and making "truth claims."[12] What before was a tacit acceptance of the transparency of language has entered into question; the polysemous nature of signs, the ideology that informs writing, and the complexity of the contexts involved underscore the inherent opacity of language. The challenge for my project and any analysis of colonial historiography is identified by Hayden White in his discussion of the problems with narrative translation of knowing into telling: "If we view narration and narrativity as the instruments with which the conflicting claims of the imaginary and the real are mediated, arbitrated, or resolved in a discourse, we begin to comprehend both the appeal of narrative and the grounds for refusing it" (*Content of the Form*, 4).

In the case of the chronicles, *relaciones*, and histories that constitute the primary sources of this study, I examine how the Spanish and mestizo writers narrativize the gender and sexuality of indigenous Andeans. I problematize how the resulting narratives infuse events and observations in the contact zone with significance intelligible to the Spanish but alien to the indigenous culture. We will come to understand that the truth claims imbedded in the texts are related to colonial authority that legitimizes their writing in the first place and respond to what White calls the latent desire to moralize the observed reality (*Content of the Form*, 14). Each chronicler or historian I analyze must be understood in the context of his place of enunciation; his relationship with authority and tradition must be foregrounded. The writer's subjectivity is crucial to an understanding of his narrative, since, in White's words, "the more historically self-conscious the writer of any form of historiography, the more the question of the social system and the law that sustains it, the authority of this law and its justification, and threats to the law occupy his attention" (ibid., 13).

To understand this desire to moralize, it is necessary to examine the tradition from which the chroniclers and historians emerge; therefore, my study begins with a reading of peninsular Spanish literature, which will provide a background to the primary research. Subsequently, each writer's relationship with the colonial apparatus will be closely examined to detect its influence in the representation of Andean gender culture. Much of the corpus of colonial discourse has characteristics of protoethnography insofar as the writers attempt to represent the Other in the newly encountered Andean cultures. But, as James Clifford reminds us in his critique of twentieth-century ethnographies, those representations are often more analogous to inventions of cultures than transparent representations (Clifford and Marcus, *Writing Culture*, 2).

Integral to the "invention" of the Andes is reproduction of tropes of sexuality in colonial discourse.[13] Ultimately, this troping operates to stereotype the cultural Other, who, in Bhabha's terms, becomes "fixed" through the repetition of a stereotypical representation, which especially concerns us in this study because of the way the discourses of power inscribe the Other's difference on the body. Bhabha reminds us that "the construction of colonial subjects in discourse, and the exercise of colonial power through discourse, demands an articulation of forms of difference—racial and sexual" (*Location of Culture,* 67). While much attention has been paid to the racial stereotypes of colonial discourse, it is also important to examine the sexual differentiation of the Other and its rhetorical relationship with colonial power. In addition, the problematic relationship between this rhetorical Othering in the dominant colonial discourse and the emerging contestatory voices of mestizo and indigenous writers suggests that sexual tropes played a significant role in colonial processes of subjectivization and transculturation.

Jonathan Goldberg was one of the first to identify sodomy as a colonial discursive trope and to call for further scholarship on its employment in colonial texts:

> This history needs to be retold in as unpresuming and discriminating a fashion as possible in order to uncover the density of the concept of sodomy and to understand the work it is put to do; but also to recognize that sodomy, "that utterly confused category," as Foucault memorably put it, identifies neither persons nor acts with any coherence or specificity. This is one reason why the term can be mobilized—precisely because it is incapable of precise definition; but this is also how the bankruptcy of the term, and what has been done in its name, can be uncovered.
>
> ("Sodomy in the New World," 46)

This "sodomy trope" is characterized by the various "mobilizations" of the ambiguous terms and idioms that signify "sodomy." As Goldberg recognizes in the sodomy trope and Bhabha has theorized for colonial stereotypes in general, it is the "ambiguity" of the signifying tropes that invests them with power: "For it is the force of ambivalence that gives the colonial stereotype its currency: ensures its repeatability in changing historical and discursive conjunctures; informs its strategies of individualization and marginalization; produces that effect of probabilistic truth and predictability which, for the stereotype, must always be in excess of what can be empirically proved or logically construed" (Bhabha, *Location of Culture,* 66). This ambivalence will be underscored in my "genealogy" of the term *sodomite* and its many derivatives.

Asunción Lavrin, concentrating primarily on colonial Mexico's heterosexual relations and marriage, offers a definition, derived from "moral theologians" of the times, of the so-called sins against nature, though she does not specify these sources: "Sodomy or sin contra naturam was the copulation of two persons of the same sex. It also applied, however, to any form of sex between man and woman, married or not, contravening the physical position accepted by the church as 'natural'" (*Sexuality and Marriage*, 51). Regina Harrison's definition of sodomy in the Andean colonial context is more precise and relevant to this project, since it is taken from a sixteenth-century Peruvian catechism ("'True' Confessions," 20). This definition also suggests that the term was employed to represent several "unnatural" acts, including "bestiality, homosexuality, or unnatural heterosexual acts" (ibid.).

I will be analyzing passages that speak to sex acts between males and third-gender subjects, or what colonial writers speculated to be same-sex activity among unspecified "*sodomitas,*" while emphasizing how the sodomy trope transculturates performative notions of Andean gender culture.[14] I am reading "sodomy" as a discursive marker for sites of cultural difference that elicited the wrath of moralizing Spanish colonizers and as transculturated phantasms reiterated in the discourse. The meaning of these tropes was ideologically charged to justify conquest, massacre, and colonization, as Goldberg suggests. Those subjects that did not conform to hegemonic discourses of cultural foundation, especially those that betrayed a binary gender system, were demonized through a rhetoric of Christian morality. The Andean public performance of a third-gender subjectivity disrupted the Spanish semiotics of masculinity. The transvested so-called sodomites were unintelligible subjects who mis-signified, perverting the orthodox signification of sexuality, given that the Spanish marginalized the sexual Other deemed effeminate or sodomitical.

The resemanticization of third-gender subjects into sodomites, which became tropes of colonial discourse, resulted from a process of transculturation that involved the representation of their roles in the writing of both the invading and the invaded. I will trace how these tropes found their way into both the civil legal discourse, which controlled the native populations, and the texts of ecclesiastical literature and religious performance, which were the tools of evangelization.

Implicit in this understanding of historical discourse is the privileged role writing technologies played in the colonization of the Americas.[15] The Spanish imposed what Michel de Certeau has called a "scriptural economy" in which the Americas became the colonists' "blank page" to be filled with an ordering of the disparate linguistic fragments that formed the indigenous culture, the object of the colonial subject's writing (*Practice of Everyday Life,* 134). Hegemonic authority and law are inscribed on the body of the indigenous; Spanish morality "engraves itself on parchments made from the skin of its subjects" (ibid., 140), whose bodies are "defined, delimited, and articulated by what writes [them]" (ibid., 139). The native bodies discussed in this study are the sites of this scriptural violence as the colonial discourse moves toward the formation of a social body in which codes purge undesirable elements. I argue that the sodomy trope not only stereotypes the Other but also functions as a "speech act" in its active denunciation of sacred and profane aspects of indigenous sexuality, which leads to its near disappearance from culture. This speech act has the unique characteristic of being one that "dare[s] not speak its name"; that is, at times it is a silent speech act because of the medieval Christian legacy that prohibited the mere speaking of the word *sodomy.* My analysis of the *Doctrina christiana,* the first book published and printed in Peru, will demonstrate how code words and phrases were substituted in sermons, confession manuals, and catechisms to represent the moral censure of the silent speech act.

What de Certeau calls the "machinery of representation" operates in two ways: "The first seeks primarily to *remove* something excessive, diseased, or unaesthetic from the body, or else to *add* to the body what it lacks" (*Practice of Everyday Life,* 147, original emphasis). Spaniards saw third-gender subjects as dangerously "excessive" within a scriptural economy in which a dimorphic gender system was privileged. To remove these excesses, their bodies were inscribed as morally diseased and degenerative to the colonial social body. The second operation, according to de Certeau, is "making the body tell the code" (ibid., 148); in our case, the indigenous come to believe and practice the colonial law inscribed on their bodies. Through my study of civil codes, questionnaires, and disciplinary practices, I will explore the ways colonial discourse inscribed Spanish laws of masculinity and heterosexuality on colonized Andean bodies. This revelation requires us to reconsider Michel Foucault's assertion that sex is a product of nineteenth-century European discourse and rethink the colonial contact zone in the Americas as one of the earlier spaces in which bodies were regulated and sexuality was registered as a possible threat to proto-state apparatuses.

In the course of a century, Andean gender culture was reinscribed not only by the colonizers, but also by the mestizos and indigenous peoples who had become incorporated into the scriptural economy, an important element of Andean transculturation that is marked by indigenous resistance and adaptation. As de Certeau clarifies, "*normative* discourse 'operates' only if it has already become a *story,* a text articulated on something real and speaking in its name, i.e. a law made into a story and historicized, recounted by bodies" (ibid., 149, original emphasis). We will explore the ways in which normative discourse on gender and sexuality, beginning with the peninsular tradition, transformed, and was transformed by, indigenous Andean bodies.[16] It is time to read the normative story in a new way, to decode how the sexually queer bodies of the Andes performed vital roles in the cultural reproduction of their society while undergoing the scriptural violence of the Spanish tropes of sexuality.

MEDIATING THE *TINKUY:* THIRD GENDER IN THE ANDES

The new reading I propose is grounded in an Andean epistemology of gender and sexuality that is revealed in part by taking into consideration several Andean notions of narrativization and cultural reproduction as well as Andean philosophical principles. I will explore the relationship between the Quechua concepts of *tinkuy* and *yanantin* and the role that third-gender subjects play in community rituals. *Tinkuy* is essentially the joining together of complementary opposites through a process of ritual mediation; similarly, *yanantin* is an expression of dualistic symmetry of inclusion.[17]

My interest in *tinkuy* is twofold. First, I will argue that we incorporate the aesthetic and structural importance of the concept into our reading practices when approaching indigenous Andean texts. Anthropologists have interpreted many contemporary ritual performances through the lenses of *tinkuy.* Can we benefit from this paradigm when approaching historical texts transcribed from the Andean oral tradition? I use a *tinkuy* reading strategy in order to better understand the Quechua language mythology found in the *Huarochirí Manuscript.* I uncover two threads of narrative, which I bring together and understand reciprocally and complementarily in order to explicate pre-Hispanic gender culture. This approach, in turn, helps me explain how the presence of third gender, which invoked the androgynous primordial whole, was ritually vital in order to bring gendered opposites into harmony and symmetry in different ceremonial contexts. I am using *tinkuy* as a metaphor, one with deep resonances in a culture of highly abstract thought and symmetrical aesthetic and social organization.

Verónica Cereceda has shown how this symmetry and mediation are expressed in the quintessential Andean text: the woven textile. Her insightful analysis of *talegas,* woven bags from a traditional Chilean Aymara community, reveals in weaving what I discuss in terms of other aspects of Andean culture: mediation of difference is achieved through negotiations of symmetrical binaries.[18] Cereceda describes the *talega:* "The design of the *talegas* is formed mostly through longish bands, their colors those of the natural hues of alpaca and llama fleeces. At a closer view, one notices that the colors of the bands are repeated, two by two, in such a way that each has its pair on the opposite half of the bag, but since the number of bands is always odd, one of them remains without a pair, and sometimes it acts as a central axis" ("Semiology of Andean Textiles," 152). This singular band, without a mate, is conspicuous in a world of complementary pairs. A question will arise throughout this book: What does a third space signify in Andean culture? Discussing the center of the textile composition, the middle axis dividing the two sides of the *talega,* Cereceda remarks: "This odd band, found at the center of the *talegas,* is called a *chhima,* which means 'heart' in the Aymara spoken in Isluga. This heart is both the meeting place and the separating line of the two sides. It plays the ambivalent role of separator, creating two halves, and simultaneously it is the nexus, the common 'territory'" (ibid.). The center is thus defined as a point of articulation within the woven space—an axis, always sharp, that divides the bag lengthwise in the direction of the warp threads. This in-between space in the *talega,* known as the "heart" of the composition, is suggestive of how a third space can be a "point of articulation."

Andean ladino writers, I argue, symbolically embodied this "heart" space, the *chhima* or *chaupi* between cultures.[19] I will use the term *chaupi* throughout this study to invoke this notion of in-between positioning, both as a way of characterizing colonial indigenous, ladino writers and as a way of explaining the symbolic positioning of third-gender ritualists. In Quechua, the one among paired things, but without a pair, is the *chhullu,* an idea I return to in later discussions.[20] Symbolically, the third-gender ritual attendants, *chhullus* embodied, formed the chaupi that separated the two complements brought together in a metaphorical or, at times, an actual *tinkuy.* Did they at times represent the heart of ritual mediation? I argue that, through this "queer" union, one in which the odd, unpaired ritualist facilitates the joining of opposites, culture was reproduced.

Through this understanding of the *chaupi* position embodied by third-gender ritualists in *tinkuy,* I bring to the foreground the performative role third gender played (and continues to enact) in what has previously been described and studied as a binary gender system. Irene Silverblatt's *Moon, Sun, and Witches* provides us with one of the most complete histories of the gender systems and their evolutions in the Andes. Her analysis of colonial historiography and archival records reveals deeply ingrained daily practices as well as frequent sacred rituals that indicate that women in the pre-Columbian Andes had access to material resources and supernatural power.[21]

While Silverblatt's scholarship, as well as subsequent studies, suggests that gender complementarity is the fundamental basis for human interaction and cultural reproduction in the Andes, research on this structure has not fully considered third-gender subjects, which populated the Andes alongside the *acllas* ("chosen women"), Incas, and other Andean peoples. While Silverblatt posits the female's divine relationship with earth/female deities and discusses the material positions of women in the conquest politics of the pre-Hispanic and colonial Andes, I strive to account for female expression of agency in the pre-Inca conquest politics of gendered prestige hierarchies, a theme that I take up in my discussion of the Huarochirí myths. This recuperation of feminine agency informs my theoretical construction of *tinkuy* as both a reading strategy and a mode of cultural reproduction. Without an appreciation of the symbolic, performative role of the feminine and the androgyne, we cannot fully understand the complexities of Andean gender culture and the negotiation of complementarity in ritual and quotidian contexts.

While the feminist movement in the fields of anthropology and literary studies has moved decidedly toward theorizing a break from the traditional categorizing of gender in direct relation to biological sex, other research has sharpened the focus on those subjects of ethnographies that do not seem to fit neatly in either a male or a female gender designation. Traditionally, ethnographies discussed these variations in terms of homosexuality and cross-dressing. Evelyn Blackwood edited the first volume of anthropology to study homosexuality, *The Many Faces of Homosexuality,* and changed the focus from treating homosexual acts as deviant individual behavior to emphasizing institutional and cultural patterns of that behavior. The contributing researchers avoided imposing Western prejudices in sexology and psychoanalysis on the non-Western cultures under study.

It became readily evident, however, that consideration of these non-Western cultures required a revision of assumptions concerning a binary gender system in addition to a better understanding of sexuality. Thomas Laqueur's *Making Sex* took a step toward breaking the traditional understanding of a dimorphic sex model by proposing that from the Greeks to the eighteenth century the West actually had a single-sex model and that the female body was culturally constructed as incomplete and inferior relative to a male point of reference. That the West at one point posited the existence of only one sex opens us to the notion that both sex and gender are contingent constructs. Scholars have now begun to reexamine passages in ethnographies that suggest a more diverse population of sexes and genders throughout the world. From this scholarship has emerged the term "third gender."

As Gilbert Herdt argues in his introduction to *Third Sex/Third Gender,* to speak of third genders is not to say there are three genders instead of two, but it is to break with the sex and gender bipolarity that has, until recently, dominated Western popular and scientific thought. Herdt follows sociologist George Simmel in viewing the presence of just two categories as creating an intrinsic relationship of potential oppositional conflict. Herdt claims "third" as "emblematic of other possible combinations that transcend dimorphism" (*Third Sex/Third Gender,* 20). The essays in Herdt's volume strive to unravel the multiple discourses that construct gender identities around human propensities to "categorize things into twos, threes, or other structures of the mind" (ibid.). Theorizing beyond sexual dimorphism is a gesture toward thinking about infinite rather than finite numbers of gender categories. "Third gender," then, becomes a metonymic signifier for those gendered subjectivities that fall outside the classic dimorphic gender categories but whose intelligibility depends on cultural specificity. Therefore, each third-gender subject can be meaningfully discussed only within the context of his or her gender culture. While third-gender presence seems to be widespread in many forms in a variety of geographic locales, research related to the Americas is the most relevant as an introduction to how I will theorize third gender in the Andes.

Will Roscoe's articles—"How to Become a Berdache" and "Gender Diversity in Native North America"—and book—*Changing Ones*—work toward establishing that what the traditional ethnographic literature long identified as "berdache" is in many cases the manifestation of a third-gender designation within specific native cultures.[22] His work also gives an extensive review of berdache studies.[23] As Roscoe explains, *berdache* is the term anthropology adopted from colonial discourse in the Americas to refer to men who dress like and adopt the roles of women in native societies. Male berdache have been documented in nearly 150 North American societies, while female berdache (females who take on the lifeways of males) appear in half as many groups (*Changing Ones,* 330). Because the Western colonial chroniclers, nineteenth-century ethnographers, and, later, anthropologists did not have linguistic or cultural categories that corresponded to the berdache subjectivity, naming it became a problem and usually resulted in misnomers such as the term *berdache* itself, which was originally a Persian and Arabic name for the younger male partner in a same-sex erotic relationship (ibid., 331).

In the different discourses alluded to above, these subjectivities have been variously named "hermaphrodite," "sodomite," "effeminate," and, more recently, "homosexual" and "transsexual." Each of these terms misrepresents the berdache in its own way, some expressing bodily confusions, others inscribing the native subject in Christian or psychosexual discourses, and all ignoring the often-sacred roles these subjects performed. In this book, I have opted to use the term third gender except when the specific indigenous word for the subjectivity in question is known. I employ the term berdache only when discussing other researchers' use of the term and do not adopt the term "Two-Spirit," whose cultural specificity relates directly to the contemporary North American Native American community and issues of self-identification. I make this distinction because, as we will see, third gender in the Andes does not always approximate the subjectivity of berdache as it has been articulated in other cultures. Moreover, my study is as much about a symbolic, spatial concept as it is about actual subjects who represent the idea of *chaupi* mediation.

Walter Williams's *The Spirit and the Flesh* was the first book-length study devoted to revising Western knowledge of the berdache in native North America. Combining archival research with field investigations, Williams reconstructed a more integral understanding of berdache roles in native societies, calling particular attention to their often-sacred status in many ethnic groups. While Williams tended to romanticize the berdache in utopian terms, his study did open the way to further, more culturally specific, study of the topic.

Roscoe followed Williams's Pan-American survey with a detailed ethnohistory of the Zuni berdache, *The Zuni Man-Woman*. Since the publication of this study, Roscoe has used the burgeoning literature on the subject to research, as noted above, the commonalities between the berdache in different North American native societies.[24] This consensus does not necessarily predict that we will find the same gender constructs in the Andes; indeed, I restrain from making explicit comparisons in my analysis of the Andean context in order to respect the cultural specificity of Andean gender culture. It is instructive, however, to have a sense of third gender in other American cultures so that the reader will have at least one other point of reference, albeit contested, in addition to the European tradition.

First, male berdache are known to have had productive specialization in the areas of crafts and domestic work, including the care of children, and they are often marked as overachievers in their occupations ("How to Become a Berdache," 334). Second, berdache often enjoy supernatural sanction and fulfill religious functions in their communities. Due to their reputations in both these aspects, berdache are integrated members of society (ibid., 335). Gender variation in relation to the culture's norms for male and female genders varies; berdache often cross-dress or dress completely differently from either males or females (ibid., 334). Their sexuality also varies, from exclusively same-sex (male biological sex) relationships to bisexual and heterosexual partnerings. Their sexual activity ranges from casual encounters to long-term relationships (ibid., 335). Roscoe notes that, increasingly, scholars are abandoning "deterministic hypotheses concerning the 'cause' of berdache behavior" (ibid., 336). The trend is to recover the berdache's agency in taking on social roles, rather than accepting biased discourses' "practices [that] predetermine and overdetermine berdaches as objects of action, never the subjects" (ibid., 336). (I will return to this point below.) Finally, some berdache are increasingly categorized as third genders. Rather than conceptualize them as crossing genders or in terms of sexual object choice (homosexual), third-gender theory posits them as "a separate gender within a multiple gender, gender system" (ibid., 38).

The fundamental strength of Roscoe's methodology is its combination of fieldwork in current Native American communities with archival research, extensive collaboration with a host of researchers, and an engagement of the traditional historiography and ethnography with a critical skepticism. I have used the few anthropological or ethnographic accounts available to help reconstruct the historical figure, and I hope this study will encourage future research on contemporary Andean gender culture to include a consideration of gender and sexual diversity. Fritz Villasante Sullca is one of the few Peruvian anthropologists to address this topic in his fieldwork, though several contemporary ethnographers mention aspects of third-gender performance in passing, but not in the terms of my study (Allen, Bolin, Franquemont, Isbell). Villasante's research on the role of sexuality and humor in Paucartambo's festival in honor of the Mamacha del Carmen is helpful in understanding how gender liminality continues to be performed today. I discuss the transculturation of third gender in Andean colonial ecclesiastical literature and reflect on Villasante's research as further evidence of the mutability of performative ritual identities in the Andes.

"Third gender" is a controversial term. In a critique of its use, "Romancing the Transgender Native," Towle and Morgan discuss the abuse of the term in its transference from anthropological literature to "popular American writing by and about transgendered people" (469). The title of their article speaks to one of the principal pitfalls of its use. Whereas I believe it is nearly impossible to reliably recover the "lived experience" of the subjects who performed third gender in the pre-Hispanic and colonial Andes, one should no more "celebrate" their roles in ritual contexts than celebrate human sacrifice victims, for example. My book attempts to recover their roles and, moreover, the symbolic signification they represent, in order to understand Andean notions of gender and sexuality and their eventual transculturation in colonial discourse. Without romanticizing the roles of third genders, I hope to open a dialogue on the place of gender liminality in our understanding of broader cultural patterns in the Andes. As Towle and Morgan advise, studies of third gender "should center on the meanings, ideologies, disputes, and practices that situate gender dynamics in specific historical and cultural contexts" (ibid., 471). I use the term in its metonymic capacity because, as we shall see, there are multiple manifestations of gender liminality that mediate between the gendered spheres of Andean culture. Again, Towle and Morgan insightfully remind us of the potential "reductionism and exclusionism" of the term, which can erase the very difference some anthropologists wish to highlight (ibid., 484–485).

My use of *third gender* works in the opposite direction—toward expansion and inclusion—in the sense that gender liminality in the Andes is not about "breaking binaries" conceived as naturalized notions of masculinity and femininity, but about negotiating gender difference to create a complementary pairing, an invocation of an androgynous whole. To get there, Andeans conceive of themselves on a gender continuum in temporal performances of gender that are not fixed in time and space. To understand these complexities, third-gender subjects must be studied with cultural specificity.[25]

Richard Trexler's *Sex and Conquest* is the most sustained analysis of the Latin American berdache.[26] Trexler reconstructs a Pan-American identity and argues that the berdache was a product of a pre-Hispanic gender ideology that sexually objectified defeated or otherwise subjugated males in ways that magnified the masculine power of the conqueror. These cultural patterns, he contends, remarkably approximated the early-modern, European treatment of same-sex behavior and effeminized dependency. While this characterization may hold true for other parts of the Americas that Trexler analyzes, I assert that the Andean versions of this historical subjectivity had culturally distinct meanings that transcended European notions of effeminacy as dependency and degeneracy, especially in ritual contexts.

Trexler's notion of the berdache as a "dependent," and therefore demeaned, subject does not concur with a more nuanced reading of the native gender culture of the Andes.

My demonstration of how third-gender peoples fit into the native societies and performed sacred ritual duties and specialized productive roles reconstructs third-gender subjectivity from an Andean paradigm of gender culture and stresses the differences between this epistemology and early-modern European notions of degradation of the feminine. My approach does not efface issues of power that Trexler stresses in his reconstruction of berdache; indeed, the performance of any subject position is conditioned by structures of power. Whereas Trexler privileges masculine power as the determining agent in berdache subjectivity by linking fragmentary evidence across myriad cultures of the Americas, I emphasize the culturally specific role the feminine and the androgyne played in the performance of subjectivity in the Andes. My approach does not ignore masculinity, an equally and, at times, more dominant force in the Andes. Rather, I seek to understand how gender liminality mediated between the masculine and the feminine by invoking the mythic, androgynous whole. Rather than work with essentialist notions of masculinity and femininity, I posit the performativity of these categories in a symbolic system in which the androgyne, not the phallus, may be the "universal signifier."

A PERFORMATIVE APPROACH TO
TRANSCULTURATED THIRD GENDER

My approach to third gender in the pre-Columbian and colonial Andes underscores the performativity of the third-gender subjectivity within a context of transculturation. In tracing the textual representation of gender and sexuality in premodern Iberian culture, and later in Andean colonial culture, I problematize notions of a "natural," inherent, or essential gender and sexuality in the peninsula and Andean region by interrogating their discursive constructedness. As Diana Fuss has pointed out, however, there is no need for us to be caught between false theoretical binaries; even for those who maintain that there is no prediscursive gender or sexuality, that all manifestations of identity are constructs of a given discourse, a reading begins at some point in time, which implies starting from an essence (*Essentially Speaking*, 3–4). While a constructionist reading strategy often resorts to a historicism that is itself an essentialized version of the social process, and while there are essentialist aspects of psychological and deconstruction theories as well, as Fuss indicates, the critic must accept, in terms dating to Locke, "nominal essence," that is, that identities are "merely a linguistic convenience, a classificatory fiction we need to categorize and label" (ibid., 4). Similar to Spivak's "strategic essentialism," this conception of identity enables an identity politics based on unstable identity categories, for example, man or woman. Strategic essentialism is also helpful in the theorization of subjectivity.

Judith Butler's conception of gender performativity suggests that discursive subjectivities are agents of their gendered selves (*Gender Trouble,* 147), agents that reiterate culturally constructed imitations of an imagined original gender. Any substance to a gendered identity, that is, its essence, is actually a phantasm, a mere appearance of substance that has acquired the illusion of essence through its repetition in discourse. Individuals imitate the phantasms in "performances" that pass as gendered identities. Butler has clarified her position in *Bodies That Matter* by emphasizing the discursive nature of the human body, which is as much a cultural construct as gender itself. Therefore, the body is "sexed" through cultural norms; in the West, for example, sexual dimorphism cannot be taken as a naturalized condition for, as recent scholarship reveals, the body has at times been considered as a single-sexed entity (Laqueur), a position that reiterates progress in the field of anthropology toward understanding the instability of bodies and genders.

Also important for my understanding of the representation of third-gender subjectivities in colonial discourse is Butler's assertion that "the subject is constituted through the force of exclusion and abjection, one which produces a constitutive outside to the subject, an abjected outside, which is, after all, 'inside' the subject as its own founding repudiation" (*Bodies That Matter,* 3). As we will see, notions of the feminine and third-gender subjectivities are figured as "abjected" outsiders to performative masculine, idealized subjects of Spanish and, later, colonial discourse. These abjected outsiders, therefore, are left in the discourse as marginalized to dominant subjectivities, transformed from earlier performative identifications with different values and meanings.

In the Andes, the body of third-gender subjects signifies culturally meaningful relationships that are brought into discourse through ritual repetitions. What we know of third-gender subjects comes from the colonial record of their "performances" of ritual expressions of gender and sexuality. This brings us back to my earlier discussion of transculturation, for I am positing that we read third genders as performed subjectivities who have passed through processes of subjectivization in the highly contested contact zone. Third gender was acculturated and deculturated; the subjectivity acquires European notions of degeneracy associated with the sodomy trope while it loses part of its sacred, integrated identity associated with feminine and androgynous rituality. Out of this process emerge the neoculturations, performative iterations of the once-sacred subjectivity that continue to enact the *tinkuy* mediation in public ceremonies throughout the Andes.

DECOLONIZING QUEER TROPES
THROUGH *TINKUY* READINGS

The structure of this book reflects the spirit of the Andean concept of *tinkuy* in that the five chapters are arranged in complementary pairs mediated by an intervening chapter. I begin the study with an exploration of the performance of masculinity and its abject Other, femininity, in Spanish premodern culture, with the primary reading focused on *El poema del mio Cid* and the tropes of masculinity the text unleashes into early-modern Spanish literature and historiography. This chapter introduces the acculturating discourse that traveled to the Andes in the sixteenth century by tracing a "genealogy" of the relationship between the abjection of the feminine and the persecution of same-sex sexuality in the Iberian Peninsula.

Chapter 2 brings these Iberian tropes of masculinity into a *tinkuy* with the Andean sexual Other, represented in the writings produced in the third space of transculturation. Pedro de Cieza de León, one of the first chroniclers to write what I consider to be a protoethnography of the Andes, provides some of the earliest descriptions of Andean gender and sexuality, accounts that blend the Iberian tropes of sexuality with indigenous informants' and his own observations to produce queer texts that became enduring references in Andean historiography. This chapter reflects on colonial discourse and transculturation in the context of Conquest politics while adding to my characterization of third gender through critical readings of several other early colonial sources. The fragments, or neoculturations, that remained in colonial discourse as phantasms of previous, pre-Columbian performances of the ritual identity will be key sources for understanding third-gender subjectivity.

Chapter 3 constitutes the *chaupi* chapter of this study, as it reconstructs Andean notions of gender liminality from ladino scribes writing from the *chaupi* between the two cultures of the colonial contact zone. From their writings, I recover the importance of the feminine and the androgyne in Andean culture. My analysis of *The Huarochirí Manuscript* reveals a narrative strategy based on Andean notions of *yanantin* and *tinkuy,* which leads me to consider how pre-Hispanic mythology and colonial protoethnography express cultural values associated with bodily performances of the sacred androgyne. I will also introduce into the discussion late twentieth-century ethnographies that include reports of third-gender ritual activity in contemporary indigenous societies to aid us in understanding the continuity and change of Andean gender values through time.

Chapter 4 begins the second metaphoric *tinkuy* of the book by focusing on the transculturating discourse of Francisco de Toledo's viceroyalty and highlighting the role of indigenous informants in the Spanish collection of knowledge on third-gender subjects. To help us understand Andeans' agency in the process of transculturation, this chapter stresses how native Andeans contributed to the narrativization of their culture as informants and eventually as writers of their own histories. By analyzing colonial ordinances and other investigative questionnaires, I reconsider Michel Foucault's assertion that sex is a product of European, nineteenth-century discourse and rethink the colonial contact zone as one of the earliest spaces in which bodies were regulated and sexuality was registered as a potential threat to an imperial hegemony. This chapter, by studying the pedagogical ecclesiastical literature and exposing the gendered nature of the extirpation-of-idolatry campaigns, also explores the ways a transculturated version of Andean gender culture was turned back on native converts and penitents. The missionaries begin to occupy the *chaupi* of Andean culture, displacing the *amautas,* or knowledge keepers, of the pre-Hispanic Andes. This chapter continues the transatlantic reading I began in Chapter 1 by emphasizing the role of the Reconquest and evangelization of the Moors in Spain in the spiritual conquest of the Andes. I examine how Catholic notions of *luxuria* (lasciviousness) traveled to the Americas as tropes in the catechisms, confession manuals, and sermons and were deployed in the attack on indigenous religiosity, leading to the suppression, but not the erasure, of third-gender performance. I close this chapter with a reading of how the civil and religious discourses of the Toledo viceroyalty conflate in the queering of an Inca mother by examining Sarmiento de Gamboa's hyperbolic representation of the transgressive Mama Huaco, a pre-Hispanic, ambiguously gendered archetype.

Finally, I conclude this study with an example of how one Andean of mixed heritage, the Inca Garcilaso de la Vega, used the phantasms of colonial discourse in his representation of gender and sexuality. As Mary Louise

Pratt highlights in her definition of transculturation, "subjugated peoples cannot readily control what emanates from the dominant culture, they do determine to varying extents what they absorb into their own, and what they use it for" (*Imperial Eyes*, 6). In this final discussion of the effects of transculturation, we will explore how a transculturated "writing subject" sacrifices those queer subjectivities of his maternal culture that threatened his apology of the Incas. Inca Garcilaso steps into the "third space" of colonial hybridity armed with Westernized tropes of sexuality and displaces those who once mediated as the symbolic *chaupi* in his maternal gender culture. His foundational text is a *tinkuy*-like response to the Toledan discourse explored in the previous chapter and provides an opportunity for us to revise our understanding of subalternity and hybridity in the current scholarship on the colonial Andes by appreciating how processes of cultural hybridization, like those of Inca Garcilaso, obscured indigenous values of mediation. By ending this study with my analysis of Inca Garcilaso's *Los comentarios reales*, the most widely read colonial account of Andean culture and history, we cross back to Iberia to engage the mestizo writer's mediation between the conquered, colonized Andeans and the Renaissance Spaniards. The instability of the masculine Spanish subject, first encountered in Spanish medieval epic poetry, rears its head again, this time absorbed into a subaltern subject's portrayal of the Other that is partly himself. Inca Garcilaso's abjection of that part of himself that was the founding repudiation of the feminine in the Spanish literary tradition finds itself constituting the new mestizo subject as well.

In the Epilogue I reflect on implications and future avenues of this research by briefly considering how queer tropes of sexuality continue to be performed in the Andes, in both literature and ritual ceremonies. The endurance of difference in both hegemonic and subaltern cultural forms speaks to the dynamics of Andean *tinkuy* performances. Alterity is continually mediated and brought into complementary, sustainable relationships . . . despite the occasional *pachacuti*.

One   *BARBUDOS, AFEMINADOS,*
               AND SODOMITAS
               Performing Masculinity in Premodern Spain

I n this chapter I trace the performance of gender and sexuality in the Iberian Peninsula from medieval to early-modern times by reading primary texts from different genres and different historical moments. In addition to contextualizing these readings in a history of the treatment of non-normative sexuality, namely, sodomy, as it relates to the future colonizing power, premodern Spain, it is important to explore the constructs of masculinity and femininity as they appear in the proto-national Spanish discourse. While it is clear from the historiographic record that premodern authorities, both ecclesiastical and civil, proscribed sexual acts, this historiography does not always lend itself to understanding notions of gendered subjectivity. By reading foundational literary texts, however, we can further understand the prohibitions on bodily acts while also examining how we might perceive gender and sexuality as "performative" categories of subjectivity.

SODOMY: FROM MEDIEVAL ARTIFACT
TO EARLY-MODERN TROPE

As we will see throughout this study, gender transgression and sodomy became tropes in the rhetoric of conquest and colonization of the Andean region, in both civil and ecclesiastical discourse. These tropes have a particular history rooted in the Western tradition dating from Hellenist and Roman times and crystalizing in the medieval and early-modern periods, a history which is beyond the scope of this chapter. Here I wish simply to highlight a few characteristics of ancient and medieval sexuality so as to understand the ideas behind these tropes as they reappear in the early-modern period.[1] Early philosophers' concern with the ethics of personal pleasure constitute the roots of an attitude toward sexuality, a morality that will inform Christianity's influence in medieval and early modern writings.[2] This classical problemization of personal sexual conduct announces a tendency toward austerity that was intensified by the Romans and was an important antecedent to the tropes of masculinity performed in later times.[3]

The medical discourse of these times began to reflect a greater preoccupation with the body in general (Foucault, *Care of the Self,* 103) and with the dangers of sexuality in particular, dangers related to the violent tension and the physical exertion involved in the sexual act (ibid., 113). To restrain these dangers, philosophers began to rework the classical ideals of sexual austerity into a new emphasis on marriage in which "a stylistics of living as a couple emerges from the traditional precepts of matrimonial management: it can be observed rather clearly in an art of conjugal relationship, in a doctrine of sexual monopoly, and in an aesthetics of shared pleasures" (ibid., 149). This shift from a stylistics of the love of boys as the Platonic ideal to a new preoccupation with marital fidelity marginalizes the place of same-sex erotics, but does not yet consider them unnatural (ibid., 239). As a result, there is an overall distrust of the body and physical pleasure, experiences that must be confined to marriage in order to guard against the dangers to one's ethical self. Analogies to later Christian morality emerge, yet, as we will see below, what was but a suggested "style" of sexual conduct in the early centuries of our era became under Christian philosophy, in the words of Foucault, "other modalities of the relation with self: a characterization of the ethical substance based on finitude, the Fall, and evil; a mode of subjection in the form of obedience to a general law that is at the same time the will of a personal god; a type of work on oneself that implies a decipherment of the soul and a purificatory hermeneutics of the desires; and a mode of ethical fulfillment that tends toward self-renunciation" (ibid., 240).

State interpellation of the subject on matters of sexuality did not occur until the late Roman imperial and early medieval Christian institutions of authority began to codify appropriate behavior; until that time there were no laws of sexual behavior in the Greek and Roman cultures.[4] Boswell argues that it was not until the late empire, as the individual self-regulation described by Foucault gave way to increased "theocratic despotism," that Roman law began to address sexuality through legal codes (*Christianity, Social Tolerance, and Homosexuality,* 121–123). Here we begin to see the formation of a normative sexuality that drew on the evolution of ideas from the Greeks and early Romans, but whose rigid, proscriptive nature represented a fundamental change from the classical period and the first centuries of our era. In the Iberian Peninsula it is important to note the influence of the Visigoth invasions (AD 409), which displaced the Roman legal structure and established monarchies that converted to Christianity by AD 587. Visigoth laws were known to intercede increasingly in the private lives of the Hispano-Roman subjects of their kingdoms (ibid., 175). This new process of subjectivation took place throughout the old empire in the early Middle Ages, when the multiple discourses of power (fragmented by the dissolution of the Roman empire) unified under the agency of states as monarchies "that transcended all the heterogeneous claims (prior to unification), manifesting the triple distinction of forming a unitary regime, of intensifying its will with the law, and of acting through mechanisms of interdiction and sanction" (Foucault, *History of Sexuality,* 87). As the institution of marriage grew to normative status, those practices that transgressed the new standards of conjugal fidelity, namely, adultery and same-sex erotics, came under increased scrutiny and eventual interdiction.[5] In Iberia, the Visigoths are known to have passed a law against same-sex acts around AD 650, condemning offenders to castration (Boswell, *Christianity, Social Tolerance, and Homosexuality,* 174).[6] What was once an idealized form of love in the Greek and even Roman contexts took on a different character; a same-sex praxis, which before did not even have a name to signify its meaning, now emerged in medieval discourse as a problematized category of transgression that would become known as "sodomy."

Mark Jordan's commentary on the history of sodomy in Christian theology recognizes that "sodomy" can be identified as "a medieval artifact," given that *sodomy* as a term first gained currency in the eleventh century and acted both as a "category for classifying—for uniting and explaining—desires, dispositions, and acts that had earlier been classified differently and separately" and as a moral judgment.[7] This figuring of sodomy as medieval is pertinent to my study of the Catholic expansion into the Americas, for the religious institutions that were the vanguard of evangelization had their roots in the medieval period, both theologically and practically. Theologically, the doctrine that traveled to the Americas was fine-tuned in the medieval writings of the church fathers. In practice, the tactics employed in the Americas for the conversion of the indigenous populations were developed and perfected in Christendom's struggle against Islam and, in the specific case of Iberia, in the Reconquest of the peninsula that began in the eighth century, as I will explore more fully in Chapter 4.

Jordan's scholarship, one of most recent and relevant treatments of the Christian tradition's construction of the sin of same-sex erotics, explicates the confused and confusing term that *sodomy* has become and elucidates how the word came into the lexicon of medieval theology. Jordan reveals that the noun form, "sodomy" (*sodomia*), did not appear until the eleventh-century theologian Peter Damian coined it to be analogous to "blasphemy" (*blasphemia*). Thus, the term became an abstraction of what until then had been a proper name for the inhabitants of a biblical city, Sodom. Jordan insightfully asserts that this abstraction is an antihistorical essentializing of persons: those accused of "sodomy" (unnatural sexual intercourse) are linked to the "Sodomites," the inhabitants of the city destroyed by God's wrath. All other traits of personhood are erased; their essence is established without regard to historical and cultural evolution. The result has been damning: "As a recurring essence, it would seem to justify recourse to the same means of control in every case—to a punishment as near as one can get to the divine fires that poured down on Sodom" (*Invention of Sodomy*, 42). I argue throughout this book that "sodomy" became a performative term, a speech act that invoked an increasingly heightened notion of the abject and simultaneously condemned the referent to a marginal and subordinate state of being. In the act of pronouncing the word in reference to another person or class of persons, the speaker performatively positioned that objectified person or class in a subaltern status.

The instability of the term, what Foucault refers to as "that utterly confused category,"[8] originates from its unclear referent in the biblical story from whence the name comes. The complex Old Testament story, found in Genesis 19, is ambiguous about the exact nature of the moral transgression, though the textual innuendo implies that the Sodomites, that is, the residents of Sodom, threatened to sexually "know" the visiting angels. As Jordan, among other scholars,[9] has pointed out, the transgression at Sodom was not necessarily just of a sexual nature; God's wrath could also be considered a punishment for inhospitable behavior and arrogance (ibid., 30–37). Robert Alter ("Sodom as Nexus") reads the story as a "nexus" in the early biblical narratives that link the founding of the nation of Israel with procreation and posit Sodom as an example of an antination, a place whose inhabitants transgressed the socially constructed norms and were therefore punished for their nonprocreative behaviors. That the figure of the Sodomite became the figure for same-sex transgression and the object for divine punishment resulted from a process of theological simplification based on theologians' misreadings of the scriptures. Jordan traces sodomy's theological trail through many of the church fathers' writings, but I will refer only to his analysis of Thomas Aquinas, the medieval theologian of the Dominican order who most affected the doctrines of medieval and early-modern Spain that traveled to the Americas in the ecclesiastical literature. Thomas Aquinas's *Summa of Theology* was the preferred theological text in medieval universities and also informed the Council of Trent's doctrinal legislation (ibid., 136), which, as we will see in Chapter 4, became the guiding document in the late sixteenth-century evangelization of the Andes.

Thomas Aquinas's moral teachings address the issue of sodomy in his treatise's section on *luxuria,* which he understood as a "vice of excess in venereal pleasures" (ibid., 142). *Luxuria* is divided into six activities: simple fornication, adultery, incest, deflowering, abduction, and vice against nature (ibid., 144). And while Thomas Aquinas places little emphasis specifically on sodomy (vice against nature), he does remark: "Just as the order of right reason is from man, so the order of nature is from God himself. And so in sins against nature, in which the very order of nature is violated, an injury is done to God himself, the orderer of nature" (ibid., 146). With this statement he elevates the act of nonprocreative sex (sins against nature) from the marginal position of a vice to a much graver transgression against God's natural order. Jordan argues that this move is based on Thomas Aquinas's misreading of a passage in Augustine's *Confessions* regarding "disgraceful acts" and Aristotle's discussion of "unnatural desire" in *Ethics* (ibid., 149). Thomas Aquinas's version of Augustine places the onus on the misuse of created bodies rather than on Augustine's concern with the libido, and his glosses change Augustine's reference from the Sodomites' divine punishment to the nature of their purported crime. Thomas Aquinas's version of Aristotle's treatment of sodomy "collapses Aristotle's distinctions by connecting cannibalism, bestiality, and same-sex copulation under the notion of bestial desire" (ibid., 150). The power of this rhetorical move is its equation of same-sex desire with inhuman behavior. The Sodomites, then, are located outside the rationality of humankind, thus setting up their disciplinary treatment on par with that of other so-called inhuman acts, such as cannibalism.[10]

Finally, in Thomas Aquinas we find another feature of the discourse on sodomy that will inform the Andean evangelization: the prescribed silence on the whole issue of unnatural acts. His reticence in naming the vice, which is part of the theological tradition (ibid., 151), is most explicit in his *Scriptum super libros Sententiarum:* "The species of *luxuria* are divided first into lying together according to nature and against nature. But since *luxuria* against nature is unnameable, it will be set aside" (ibid., 150). The effect is an intensifying of the transgression by creating the taboo of its enunciation.

The subject is elevated to that place in discourse that merely to name it is to risk its transmission, for the theological tradition, based on Ephesians 5:3 and Aristotle's *Politics,* held that it was a practice of "epidemic" potential (ibid., 151). As I will argue in later chapters, the sodomy trope takes on this peculiar attribute, almost unique among speech acts: its performativity is taboo, even to the extent that it should not be uttered. It became the speech act that dare not speak its name; yet as we shall see, this nearly invisible, performative utterance did act out its ideological work and served to inform the representation of gender and sexuality in the early modern period and beyond.

While Jordan contends that in the "invention of sodomy" Thomas and other theologians considered the "unnatural" acts as vices and did not posit this behavior as related to gender constructions, I will argue there is a gender issue at the root of the Spanish preoccupation with sodomitic behavior. I base this contention, in part, on a theological premise mentioned in one of Jordan's footnotes that deserves further development (which I offer later in this chapter's explication of Spanish moral teachings of the early-modern period). Jordan argues that the sodomitic vice has nothing "specifically to do with gender inversions or exaggerations," that is, nothing to do with gender performance. However, in a footnote at this point in his essay (ibid., 155n52), he asserts that "Thomas does follow old traditions, both pagan and Judeo-Christian, in associating all *luxuria* with effeminacy." As we will see below, this gendering of *luxuria* is an important element in the construction of the "sodomite" and the assumptions that accompanied the use of the term. While I agree with Jordan's posture that in no way can we or should we equate *Thomas's* discussion of sodomy with any modern-day notion of homosexuality, it is important that we consider the issue of effeminacy as it was constructed in the early modern period and how it is implicitly related to the sodomy trope. In other words, we should take into consideration both the codified prohibitions of bodily acts of sexuality represented in the performative use of "sodomy" and the way in which notions of gender, as figured in the binary of effeminacy and masculinity, contribute to the construction of the abject status of the subaltern effeminate in relation to the masculine dominant. Before completing the picture of how the effeminate was often conflated with the discourse on sodomy, it is necessary to understand how some medieval Iberian texts represent gender constructs such as masculinity and effeminacy. As we will see, gender and sexual biases born in this period conflate and are reiterated in the colonial discourse that emerges from medieval and early modern Spain.

OF BOYS AND BEARDS: THE INSTABILITY
OF PREMODERN IBERIAN GENDER
AND SEXUALITY

Scholarship has begun to widen the lens of gender studies to include a closer examination of men, not just as the privileged gender of patriarchal, heterosexist cultures, but as gendered subjects as well. Feminist scholarship opened the field to and continues to inform a new understanding of gendered experience that includes this study of male subjectivities.[11] No longer are men left on a genderless pedestal, that safe place where they analyze the gendered Other, including women, effeminate men, and boys, but avoid turning their gaze back onto themselves. Medieval Iberia has been effectively "queered" in the groundbreaking collection *Queer Iberia* (Blackmore and Hutcheson).[12] Like the scholars represented in that study, I understand the peninsula to be a unique cultural space historically characterized as excessive, marginal, and dangerous to the rest of Europe. Its marginality, rather than breeding self-acceptance, tolerance, or even celebration of difference, became over time an abject sore on the social body of the protonation. This abjection became the motivation in the discourse itself to project out to the future empire's colonies and colonized Other a fictive purity of sexual morality, an ethics of sexuality that became the standard to which the peoples of the Americas would be judged. While the essays in *Queer Iberia* reveal the heterogeneous nature of the peninsula's gender and sexual culture, the discursive struggle between points of view on Iberian sexuality and the virtuosity of poetic voices that dared to speak the name of the unmentionable sin, I emphasize that which became the normative construction and performance of Spanish masculinity. Rather than leaving masculinity in a naturalized condition in this study of how hegemonic colonial discourse represents the gendered Other, I consider just how unstable the masculinist discourse was as it crossed the Atlantic to act out on new territories. In this sense, the "queer" voices in the literary and historiographic corpus of extant texts provide the context in which to understand what can be considered the "gender and sexual anxiety" that normative, masculinist discourse at once disavowed and was formed by. This task will begin with a look at two medieval texts related to the Christian Reconquest of the Iberian Peninsula and end with a reading of early modern texts.[13]

The "gender and sexual anxiety" in the period revolves around the contested nature of Iberian subjectivity in all its aspects. The peninsula, from its earliest "prehistoric" times, was a cultural crossroads, one in which processes of miscegenation and transculturation created a continuum of gender and sexual cultures ranging from those influenced by the Iberians, Celts, Phoenicians, Greeks, Romans, and Visigoths, to the Jews, Moors, and the heterogeneous mixtures of all who stepped foot on the peninsula. But it is the medieval "Christian mestizo" (principally a hybrid of the Visigoths, the Romans, and the Iberians) that began to forge the discourse that became the hegemonic culture in the peninsula. This discursive forging occurred in the intercultural flames stoked by the winds of the Reconquest, a struggle that was partially figured in literature and historiography through tropes of gender and sexuality.

The image of the effeminate, lascivious Moor, grounded in popular belief that Islamic people routinely and openly practiced sodomy or otherwise engaged in lascivious behavior,[14] informs a legend that took on mythic qualities around the well-known tenth-century Iberian Christian cult to Saint Pelagius (Santo Pelayo).[15] The narrative of his martyrdom depicts the performance of Christian masculinity at this moment of crisis in the context of the Reconquest. The first narrative of his martyrdom was written down before 967, by a priest known only as Raguel.[16] Although the narrative does not reflect codified attitudes toward same-sex sexuality, as discussed above, it does provide an intriguing look at the instability of male gender and sexuality in the period. By reading *La pasión de S. Pelayo* in comparison with another Christian text of a century later, *El poema del mio Cid,* believed to have begun its literary life as a *cantar* (ballad) sung by the *juglares* (traveling street performers and poets) in the early twelfth century, we can appreciate how this initial instability became transformed and how masculinity began to be inscribed in the Spanish literary tradition as early as the eleventh century. The two texts provide us with examples of medieval Iberian gender ideology taken from the popular oral tradition and later written down by religious scribes. Both works exalt Christian values at the expense of the Islamic enemy. Most relevant to our purposes, in both texts, gender and sexuality are figures that achieve these didactic objectives. By examining these tropes of gender and sexuality, we can begin to see how unstable notions of femininity and masculinity were "performed" in the protonational literature of what eventually became the Spanish empire.

In Raguel's *La pasión de Pelayo,* Pelagius, a ten-year-old Christian boy, becomes a captive of a Muslim caliph through an exchange for his imprisoned older cousin, the bishop Hermoygius, who fell into the hands of the victorious Muslims at Valdejunquera in AD 920 (37–39). Pelagius accepts his imprisonment as an opportunity to purify his sins (43) and dedicates himself to Christianity. In return for his piety and chastity over three and a half years of captivity (47–49), his body is transformed to meet the standards of his eventual union with Christ. His physical beauty begins to reflect his spiritual radiance:

> For he, Christ, who tutored him inwardly, was his exterior's beautifier, for the purpose of honoring his own Master with the physical beauty of him whom, without a doubt, he considered a worthy disciple; [Pelagius] also purified his body and prepared a dwelling in which, a short time later, he would enjoy as a spouse, and, in accordance with which, after being honored with his sacred blood, would be united with him, in his arms among the curia of the saints, as a servant of Christ worthy of glory; until that point in which, copiously enriched by the double crown, as much for his virginity as for his martyrdom, he would acquire a double triumph over the enemy, by refusing riches and by denying vices.

> En efecto, para el que interiormente permanecía como preceptor Cristo, para él era éste exteriormente su embellecedor, a fin de que honrase al propio Maestro solamente con su belleza física el que pensaba, sin duda, como digno discípulo suyo; el cual [Pelayo] también purificaba su cuerpo y preparaba una morada en la que, muy poco tiempo después, gozase como un esposo, y, conforme a la cual, una vez laureado con su sagrada sangre, estuviese unido a Él y a sus brazos entre las curias de los santos, como un servidor [de Cristo] digno de gloria; hasta el punto de que, enriquecido copiosamente por la doble corona, tanto por la de la virginidad, no menos que por la del martirio, consiguiese un doble triunfo sobre el enemigo, al rehusar las riquezas y no ceder a los vicios.

(51–53)

Here we note that the mystical union with God is figured as the culmination of a same-sex attraction between pious and pure Pelagius and his divine spouse, Christ. Divine marriage, as we will see below, was a common metaphor in the Spanish mystics' writings, especially those of the sixteenth century. While the Renaissance mystics figured the relationship in heterosexual terms, Raguel, at the end of the tenth century, inscribed the mystical union using homoerotic imagery, setting up a competitive and erotic triangle between Christ, Pelagius, and the caliph. Pelagius's corporeal beauty, however, was reserved for God; indeed, his ultimate reward would come only after he "triumphed" over the earthly threats of wealth and vice, dangers identified with the Muslim caliph. His purified body would become the "resting place" where he and Christ would be united in ecstasy and in the protective company of the saints. Ironically, this depiction recalls the imagery of an all-male harem, much like the caliph's more heterogeneous one described below. Pelagius, however, is promised this paradisiacal reward for his rejection of the *luxuria* associated with the Islamic enemy.

On hearing of Pelagius's physical splendor, that "the beauty of the saintly Pelagius's face was notably captivating" [la belleza del rostro del santísimo Pelayo era notablemente cautivadora] (55), the caliph has him brought to his banquet hall dressed in the finest robes. The Muslims' intentions are clear, as Raguel makes explicit: "to bury his corporeal beauty in the abysses of vice" [sepultar en los abismos de los vicios su hermosura corporal] (57). The Muslims threaten to violate Pelagius's union with God "by offering to a mortal king that which the soul of Christ had wedded in an inseparable fidelity" [con ofrecer a un rey mortal aquél cuya alma ya Cristo había desposado consigo en una fidelidad inseparable] (63). The caliph offers Pelagius all the niceties of court life (including the sexual companionship of the court's young men, *tironunculis*) in exchange for his renunciation of Christianity and his profession of Islam (65). These lascivious temptations correspond to the vices of *luxuria,* implicitly gendered effeminate, as we saw above. But the young Christian boy piously rejects his offer, declaring such enticements to be fleeting in the face of the permanent union he will enjoy with his divine Christian suitor (67).

Then the caliph reportedly reaches out to "touch him sexually."[17] Offended, Pelagius responds by lashing out at the Muslim, taunting him: "Step back, dog . . . Do you think I am like one of yours, an effeminate?" [Retírate, perro . . . ¿Es que piensas que soy como los tuyos, un afeminado?] (67–69).[18] Thus, Raguel establishes the opposition between Christian masculinity and Moorish effeminacy.[19] As if there could remain a doubt about the boy's virility, Pelagius strips off his robes and "posed like a strong athlete in the arena" [se hizo fuerte atleta en la palestra] (69). As his naked, athletic body stands mocking the caliph's desire, his sensual confidence is implicitly identified with the early Christian martyrs of Roman times. Pelagius's sexuality, rather than modestly contained, is employed in the moral battle against the infidels. One can only imagine the visual spectacle produced by the opposition of his masculine virility to that of the effeminate Moorish *tironunculis,* and the anger and desire his cocky display of manhood must have provoked in the caliph.

Patiently confident of his eventual victory over the boy, the caliph allows time to pass, hoping that the boy will give in to the earthly pleasures of the court (69). Finally, after being repudiated yet again, the caliph angrily orders that Pelagius be tortured until he renders unto Mohammad (71). Pelagius is steadfast in his devotion to Christ and is therefore dismembered by swords; his mutilated body parts are thrown into the river, later to be recovered by devout Christians and delivered to a tomb (73). The *pasión* ends with a plea for Pelagius to protect the church and Christian Spanish territories (81–83).

This account of the Spanish martyr is a significant moment in the constitution of an idealized prototype of Spanish gendered subjectivity. As we will see below, the text reflects an originary iteration of masculinity and sexual prudence that will become imbedded in medieval and, later, early-modern discourse. However, the rigid sexual austerity of subsequent Spanish heroes is still absent, for Pelagius is on the frontier between two cultures. Threatened by Moorish *luxuria,* his body becomes a weapon to be brandished in the moral battle against the Muslims and a means of entry into the kingdom of the Christian God. The pious boy's masculinity is figured as precariously trapped in the liminal space of Moorish captivity, a place where the Other's sexual culture tempts him into an "effeminate" lifestyle. This dramatic positioning of Pelagius's body heightens the effect of his rejection of Moorish ways. Here, Muslim lascivious culture is figured as the abject, the "outside," to Pelagius's formation of a "masculine" subjectivity.[20] The vile bodies of the effeminate Moorish *tironunculis,* metonymically representing the Christians' enemy, threaten the early Christians' processes of subjectivization. Pelagius's naked, virile, and defiant body signifies the subject's ideal form of masculinity, but the abject effeminacy he rejects remains "inside" subsequent representations of Spanish subjectivity while stoically controlled sexuality is performed as Christian, masculine, and anti-Muslim. The eroticized boy promised to God is subtly transformed into a fighting figure in the martyrdom narrative and in later manifestations is more overtly represented as a masculine soldier of Christ (Jordan, *Invention of Sodomy,* 26–27).

The homoerotic imagery common to the multicultural peninsular of medieval times will be gradually effaced, I argue, as the Christian Reconquest marches forward and as the larger processes of masculinization of the culture consolidate in the hegemonic discourse of early-modern Spain. The ephebe-like boy, whose physical beauty was too precarious a body on

which to build a national character at war with the infidel, would have to
be replaced in the popular imaginary by a man, a man whose body would
also be employed in the rhetorical battles but whose masculine qualities,
performed through tropes of sexuality, would leave no room for doubt and
no room for challenge.

As opposed to the story of Saint Pelagius, in which Christian masculinity is precariously threatened, the epic narrative of *El poema de mio Cid*
represents the Spanish masculine archetype, the Cid, as a performance of
an unchallenged ideal masculinity—the man, not the boy—that will become a model for the Christian Iberians to emulate. Whereas in the *Pasión
de S. Pelayo* Moorish *luxuria*—that "effeminate" lifestyle—is a tangible and
real hazard to be rejected by the young martyr for the love of Christ, in *El
poema de mio Cid* the Moor is all but displaced by the expansive presence of
the reconquering Christian hero. As Israel Burshatin has thoughtfully observed, the Moor in this epic poem "is reduced, metonymically, to an item
of value in the booty lists carefully drawn by the hero's *quiñoneros* ('officers in charge of counting and redistributing booty'), or he is the reassuring and Orientalized projection of the hero's sway over reconquered lands"
("The Docile Image," 100).[21] The "docility" of the Moor's image, though
this is not suggested by Burshatin, could be read as an effeminate figuring of the conquered enemy and newly established vassal, as Louise Mirrer
suggests in her study of how medieval Castilian epics and ballads represent
"Other" men, that is, non-Christians, as less than masculine (*Women, Jews,
and Muslims*).

Although Mirrer links the manliness of the Castilian Christian to his
military achievements (ibid., 171), she goes no further in an elaboration
of the Christian male's gender performance. Furthermore, she ignores the
gendering in the poem of other Christians as effeminate, a key rhetorical move that reenforces the Cid's masculinity. The very notion of vassalage has elements of the predominant gender ideology of the times, for as
women deferred to their male sponsors, be they father, husband, or brother
in secular life or male confessors and church superiors in the religious life,
so, too, did vassals participate in a stratified relationship with their lords.[22]
Indeed, one of the subplots of the narrative poem is the Cid's ridicule of
the dependent nobility, represented most obviously by the princes of Carrión. This landed nobility maintained its status not through active deeds of
heroism but through passive heredity.[23] Their well-being depended on the
protection afforded to them by the local lords, who, in turn, were vassals
of the king of the region. I will return to this aspect of the Cid's gender-

ing rhetoric below. First, let me reiterate why it is important to carefully examine the Cid's gender performance.

El poema de mio Cid represents the process by which normative gender categories were canonized in the Spanish literary tradition.[24] The Cid will become a phantasmagorical original in the discourse of later times, the personification of masculine values and attitudes that will become iterations in future literary texts. Here we have a most suitable example of how gender is not an essential characteristic of personhood, but how it must be iterated and reconstructed, imitated and reinvented in each specific cultural moment. The Cid steps into his cultural moment with a potency that reenforces the masculine gender ideal for an entire culture. This new identity is "performed" through explicit bodily gestures and through gendered acts. The body becomes a site on which these new values are inscribed, and the Cid's specific body becomes the dominant figure in a homosocial gender system whose influence will reach the Andean colonies hundreds of years later.[25]

My analysis will focus on two tropes that are prevalent in the poem: the knight's beard, and his sword, both corporeal, public symbols. The Cid's beard functions as a figure of masculinity and honor, a trope with a long tradition in Iberia's founding cultures. For the Greeks and for later Mediterranean cultures as well, the beard, and body hair in general, was a sign of masculinity, and its absence, as we saw above in the case of Pelagius, served as a marker of potential homoerotic objects of desire.[26] In fact, the first signs of an adolescent beard signified the end of the relationship between free men and their young male lovers.[27] Under Jewish law, shaving was prohibited along with other practices associated with ritual purity outlined in Leviticus.[28] The Old Testament story of Samson reminds us of the mythical source of his masculine strength, sapped from him by the Philistine Delilah's symbolic shearing–castration (Judg. 16:17). If we read this in relation to Pelagius's martyrdom narratives, we can begin to appreciate the importance that the popular imaginary invested in tropes of masculinity such as the beard. The ideal national hero has matured in the intervening two hundred years, and his beard performatively marks the transition toward a more stable masculine subject and celebrates his potency.

The first of nineteen references to the Cid's beard comes from his wife, Jimena, who kneels down in front of her husband to kiss his hand at the moment of his departure into exile and addresses him as "Grace, *Campeador*/of the excellent beard" (21) [mi Cid, que tenéis barbas crecidas (20, line 269)].[29] This reference to his virility in the context of the severance of his vassalage from King Alfonso is significant, for it underscores his wife's continued loyalty and admiration, figured as a gendered relationship between masculine dominant and feminine subordinate.[30] In addition, this scene sets up what I will argue is the dominant positioning of the poem's narrator and its other characters in relationship with the Cid; the Cid becomes the object of veneration by becoming the object of both the male and the female gaze. His body is on display throughout the poem, yet instead of resulting in an effemination of the object of the gaze, he becomes hypermasculinized through the use of language. The tropes of sexuality employed by the narrator construct a body that will become impenetrable by the enemy, be they Moorish infidels or rival Christians.

Paradoxically, the relationship between the Cid and his wife is best described as chaste; indeed, the Cid's sexuality is never explicitly represented. It is as austere as the epic tone of the poem, represented only through the evidence of his progeny, confirmation of the procreative use to which he engaged his wife, the mere vessel through which his daughters were born. And while exiled for long periods of time, with his wife waiting in the convent, the Cid not once strayed from marital fidelity. This sexual temperance in the text reminds us of Foucault's observation that, in classical philosophy, "moderation was a man's virtue" (*Use of Pleasure*, 83): a virile man exercised control not only over others, but over himself. The absence of temptation, such as that suffered by Pelagius in Moorish captivity, suggests that the Christian male subject is in a more stable position. Accordingly, the Cid's masculinity is not depicted through sexual acts, but through the repetition of other tropes, such as the leitmotif of the beard, which appears again a few lines later when the narrative voice, from the mouth of the *juglar*, repeats the symbol by referring to the Cid as "he of the splendid beard" (21) [el de la barba florida (20, line 274)]. The refrain serves to reinforce in the listener's mind the masculinity of the now-exiled knight, as if through repetition the hero's potentially damaged virility can be repaired or maintained.[31]

In his long journey to win back royal favor, the Cid displays spectacular bravery on the battlefields of the Reconquest, which is where we find the next reference to his facial hair. Again it comes from the narrator, whose hyperbolic exclamation interrupts a crescendoing description of victory:

> So many Moors lie dead   few are left living.
> Pursuing without pause   they struck them down.
> Already his men turn back   his who in good hour
>   was born.

He rode, my Cid	on his fine horse,
his skull-cap pushed back	*God, how splendid his beard!*
his mailed hood on his shoulders	his sword in his hand.
	(54, my emphasis)

Tantos moros yacen muertos	que pocos vivos dejaron,
pues al darles el alcance	a más iban golpeando.
Ya se vuelven del combate	los del aquel afortunado.
Cabalgaba nuestro Cid	montando su buen caballo.
Lleva una cofia fruncida.	*¡Oh Dios, cómo es bien barbado!*
La capucha, echada atrás;	la espada lleva en la mano.
	(785–789, my emphasis)

"God, how splendid his beard!" Here, strangely, the compliment is more eroticized than in the mouth of his wife. It is as if the *juglar,* caught up in the revelry of the moment, becomes overly excited with admiration at the sight of the Cid's beard. Here, the homosocial gaze is employed, though a homoerotic nuance charges the trope with an energy of poetic climax. The figure has now become a modifier that is understood in this chivalric discourse as one of the accouterments of masculine power, an emblem of virility on par with the wrinkled skullcap, the swept-back hood, the unsheathed sword, and the galloping horse. That the interjection comes at the end of a battle in which the Cid has acted valiantly is no coincidence, for its utterance invokes a reminder of the Cid's heroic actions and links them to the performance of his gender and sexuality. Both the beard and the "unsheathed sword" are phallic reminders of his increasing power.

The next reference to his beard in the first *cantar* comes after his lieutenant, Alvar Fáñez, has informed the king of the Cid's first victory, of his continued loyalty, and after contributing part of the booty to the church in order to support his wife and daughters. After this first victory the "*barba crecida*" has become the "*barba florida,*" a flourishing testament to the Cid's valor and accomplishment.[32] The last reference to his beard in the first *cantar* appears after the Cid's defeat of the Count of Barcelona: "Thus he won the battle/and honour to his beard" (70) [Allí venció la batalla,/por la que honra dio a su barba (1011)]. Here the beard functions metonymically as a synecdoche for the Cid himself. As a result of the knight's second great victory, the persona of the Cid, represented as a part of the whole, has become contiguously related to masculinity itself. As the Cid's gallantry and valor grow, so grows his beard, or his public persona.

With the great reconquest of Valencia, the Cid's reputation reaches its zenith, and the *juglar* again relates the hero's good fortune, bravery, and honor with the ever-growing beard:

> His beard grows on him   it grows longer upon him,
> these words my Cid   spoke of it with his mouth:
> "For love of King Alonso   who sent me into exile
> no scissors shall touch it   nor one hair be cut,
> and let Moors and Christians   all tell of this."
>
> (85)

> ¡Cómo crece al Cid la barba!   ¡Cómo mira su cuidado!
> Fue entonces cuando el Cid   ¡Y que lo dijo bien claro!:
>   dijo
> —Por amor del Rey Alfonso,   que de la tierra me ha
>   echado,
> no entrará en ella tijera   ni un pelo será cortado.
> Y que todos hablen de esto,   los moros y los cristianos.
>
> (1237–1241)

But this time the Cid himself addresses the topic of his beard, vowing in the name of his *señor*, King Alfonso, to maintain its integrity. As if the beard were as fragile as the hymen of a virgin, the hero pledges to keep away all threatening blades. This declaration also prefigures the beard's function in the last *cantar*, when the whiskers play a symbolic role in the king's court. Here, though, the beard becomes an emblem of the Cid's loyalty to his king, regardless of the *ira regia* that exiled him in the first place. It also becomes a propaganda tool for the knight's quest for royal pardon, for he asks that all speak of this commitment, Christians and Moors alike. From this verse on, the Cid will often take the beard in his hands as he speaks to his vassals, as if he were swearing on a sacred relic. Accordingly, the Cid calms his wife and daughters in the prelude to his defense of Valencia, in which the women tremble with fear at the sound of the Moorish war drums: "He stroked his beard/the good Cid Campeador:/'Have no fear, for all this/is to your favour'" (111) [Cogíase de la barba/el buen Cid Campeador:/—No tengáis miedo ninguno,/todo está a nuestro favor (1662–1663)]. In this way the Cid also gives thanks to God: "The Cid raised his hand/and grasped his beard:/'I give thanks to Christ/who is Lord of the world'" (164) [Entonces alzó la mano,/de la barba se cogió:/—Aquí doy gracias a Cristo,/que del mundo es el Señor (2476–2477)]. The Cid's masculinity is performed through the iteration of this gendered gesture, a phantasmagoric sign that recalls the biblical oaths sworn by the beard.[33] By invoking this scriptural image, the Cid's oaths take on greater importance, and his manliness is affirmed through this symbol of biblical masculinity.

Even though the Cid's beard grows in metaphoric correlation with his fame and honor—even King Alfonso, after pardoning the Cid, is transfixed by its length—the beard as a figure for manliness continues to be a fragile and precarious sign for the instability of medieval masculinity, one which is constantly threatened by the other male contenders in the poem. No longer is it the Moors who threaten the Cid's honor and position. As the Reconquest progresses, the Christians increasingly turn inward in their rivalries and purges of all that does not conform to Christian and masculine values. This struggle for power is prefigured in the poem through the familiar episodes involving the Cid's homosocial family building.

On learning of his sons-in-law's treason and their abuse of his daughters, the hero, as if reassuring himself that his honor and masculinity are intact, pronounces, beard in hand, that no one has dared pluck his beard: "I swear by this beard/which no one ever has torn" (185) [¡Lo digo por esta barba,/que a mí nadie me mesó (2832)]. The mere plucking of a hair from the beard represented an affront to one's honor and, I argue, to one's masculinity.[34] Beard plucking functions metonymically to represent the threat of castration, as noted in the Samson story, in which the cutting of the biblical hero's hair is carried out with Oedipal overtones: "And she made him sleep upon his knees" (Judg. 16:19). That the cropping occurs while Samson is in the lap of his motherlike lover emphasizes the vulnerable nature of his masculinity. We are also reminded of 2 Samuel 10:4, in which Hánun dishonors King David's ambassadors by shaving off half of their beards, precipitating a war between the children of Ammon and David.

Perhaps the symbolic beard was not enough for the Cid's honor and masculinity to remain intact, for its very fragility required its defense. The sword, phallic symbol par excellence, becomes like an appendage to the Cid's precarious body and is repeatedly invoked, along with the beard, as a sign of his power and prestige. We are often reminded that the sword was strapped to his waist in a knighting ceremony, as related in the refrain, "in a good hour/you first girded on sword!" (6) [en buen hora,/que habéis ceñido la espada (41)]. Reference to this public display of bodily transformation is repetitive throughout the poem, frequently invoked by the narrator or other characters as a sign of adoration and respect. The iteration of this trope has the effect of gender performance: the wearing of the sword is a visible sign of his phallic power, and therefore of his masculinity.

The fragility of this masculine subjectivity, as represented by the beard, is clearer in the Cid's preparations for the trial in Alfonso's court, at which the knight will appear to ask for justice and retribution. After dressing in the finest clothes, the Cid turns to his hair and beard, adorning and protecting both by donning a gold-lined skullcap and tying the beard with a cord:

> Over the furs he put   a hood of fine cloth,
> worked with gold   and set there
> so that none might tear the hair of my Cid the Campeador;
> his beard was long   and tied with a cord,
> for he wished to guard all his   against insult.
>   person
>
>   (201–202)

> de lino fino la cofia   que en el cabello llevó
> con oro trenzando el lino,   en sutil disposición,
> que no mesen los cabellos   del buen Cid Campeador;
> larga tenía la barba,   y atóla con un cordón.
> Para pedir lo que es suyo,   él hizo esta prevención.
>
>   (3094–3098)

His desire to protect his hair while flaunting it is explicit, as the last line emphasizes; however, there is also a fetishistic element to his beard's preparation, an excessive veneration of this metonymic part of the body. Indeed, as in the Bible, the beard of the powerful was to be cared for carefully, often to be anointed with oils, as in Psalms 133:2. Similarly, the Cid prepares his beard for his important entrance into Alfonso VI's court, where the people in attendance cannot keep their gaze off the long, tied-off beard: "All who are in the court/are watching my Cid,/and his long beard/tied with a cord; his appearance/was in every way manly" (203) [Del Cid no quitan los ojos/cuantos que están viéndolo./Era su barba muy larga,/y atada con el cordón. Tal como él se ha presentado,/muestra ser un gran varón (3123–3125)]. It is his presentation of the beard that distinguishes him, proving him to be a "great man."

This greatness, and his masculinity, are tied up not only in his beard but also in his vengeance against the princes of Carrión, which he calls for in three demands at the court, and in the name of his beard: "He raised his hand/and stroked his beard:/'By this beard/which none has ever torn,/thus proceeds the avenging/of Doña Elvira and Doña Sol'" (206–207) [Nuestro Cid alzó la mano,/y la barba se cogió:/—Por esta barba crecida,/que hasta hoy nadie mesó,/que irán quedando vengadas/doña Elvira y doña Sol (3185–3187)]. This quest for the reestablishment of his daughters' honor suggests yet another element of the symbolic nature of the Cid's beard. Not only does it figure his masculinity, honor, and loyalty, as we have seen, but it also functions as a sign for a homosocial system in which his daughters have been used as mediating terms in the negotiation of social bonds between the Cid, King Alfonso, and the princes of Carrión.[35] Each represents a different social rank and each uses the Cid's daughters to his advantage. The Cid offers them to the king for him to marry them to whomever he deems worthy, an act whose purpose seems to be yet another rendering of tribute to his *señor* (2068–2165). The princes of Carrión seek out the marriage in order to take advantage of the Cid's newfound wealth and prestige in the court (1879–1883). King Alfonso consents and arranges the wedding in order to repay the Cid for all the favors he performed for him in the Reconquest of the peninsula (1890–1891). The Cid accepts the marriage proposition, though he has premonitions, because he is thinking of the prestige that will accrue to him and his family on marrying into the nobility (1937–1942).

Implicit in the Cid's demands for retribution is a regendering of his sons-in-law. This is accomplished metaphorically by recurring to the other symbol of masculinity, the sword. The Cid takes back the swords he won in combat and gave to his sons-in-law as wedding gifts, thereby reminding the court of the virility related to the armaments:

gave them two swords	Colada and Tizón
—these I had taken	fighting like a man in the field—
that with them they might do themselves honour	and you service.
	(205)

Y les di las dos espadas,	a Colad y a Tisón,
que yo bien me las gané,	como lo hace un buen varón,
porque con ellas se honrasen,	y sirviesen bien a vos.
	(3153–3155)

The Cid had attempted to make men out of them by adding the phallic symbol to their symbolically incomplete male bodies, so that they, too, could serve the king with masculine valor, and thereby bring honor to the Cid's daughters and to their father-in-law. But now, while implicitly regarding the Carrión brothers as something less than "*buenos varones,*" for their cowardice on the battlefield and with the lion, the Cid strips them of the swords as if in an act of castration that leaves the Carrión princes effeminized and humiliated. Again, gender is figured as transmutable: the masculinity of the sons-in-law, in question from the second *cantar,* is now fully challenged, and the princes are left deprived of their manliness, status, wives, and fortune.

In a concluding passage that illuminates how gender, sexuality, and class ultimately intersect in the Cid's performance of subjectivity, we can appreciate more fully the contested nature of medieval masculinity. The lengthy exchange between the Cid and his archenemy, the most powerful of the Carrión clan, Count don García Ordóñez, begins as don García comes to the defense of his nephews:

"Grace, King the best in all Spain!
My Cid has rehearsed himself for this solemn court;
he has let his beard grow and wears it long;
he strikes fear into some and dread into others
The Heirs of Carrión are of such high birth,
they should not want his even as concubines,
   daughters
and who would command as their lawful wives?
   them to take them
They did what was just in leaving them.
All that the Cid says we value at nothing."
Then the Campeador laid his hand on his beard:
"Thanks be to God who rules heaven and earth,
my beard is long because it grew at its own
                              pleasure.

What have you, Count to throw in my beard?
It has grown at its own since it began;
   pleasure
no son of woman ever dared touch it,
no son of Moor or Christian ever has torn it,
as I tore yours, Count at the Castle of Cabra.
When I seized Cabra and you by your beard,

there was not a boy there who did not tear out his wisp;
that which I tore out has not yet grown again,
and I carry it here in this closed pouch."

(212–213)

—Favor hacedme, mi Rey, el mejor de toda España:
apercibido el Cid vino a las Cortes pregonadas.
La barba dejó crecer, y así la trae de larga.
Los unos le tienen miedo, y a los otros los espanta.
Los Infantes de Carrión son gente muy noble y alta.
Ni siquiera como amigas a sus hijas las tomaran.
¿Quién se las pudo haber dado por sus mujeres veladas?

En derecho, pues, obraron ellos a abandonarlas.
Todo lo que dice el Cid, no lo tenemos en nada.
El Campeador, entonces, echóse mano a la barba:
—¡Demos las gracias a Dios, que el cielo y la tierra manda!

Porque a su gusto creció, pues por eso ella es tan larga.
¿Qué es lo que vos tenéis, Conde, que reprocharle a mi barba?

Desde que apuntó, sabedlo, con regalo fue peinada.
Nadie me cogió por ella, hijo de criatura humana,
nadie de ella me mesó, hijo de mora o cristiana,
como yo, Conde, os lo hice en el castillo de Cabra.
Cuando yo a Cabra tomé, a vos tomé de la barba;
no hubo allí ningún rapaz, que la barba no os mesara.
El mechón que yo arranqué aún se os conoce en la cara,
que aquí lo traigo metido en mi bolsa, bien cerrada.

(3270–3290)

Count don García, whose own grudge against the Cid dates to the hero's first foray out of Burgos, insults the Cid where it hurts most: in the beard. He makes fun of its length and of the people's reaction to it and then justifies the princes of Carrión's actions by arguing that the Cid's daughters were of too humble origin for the nobility of his family. The insult is directed at the Cid's virility as well as his social ranking. The count's accusation that the Cid "let his beard grow" ("dejó crecer") insinuates the false masculinity of a braggart just as his daughters' marriages represent a spurious position in society in relation to the old nobility. At stake in the count's weak attack on the Cid's masculinity is his own social class's gendered status, for the princes of Carrión were effectively effeminized in light of the Cid's hypermasculinity, performed throughout the poem in valiant acts of courage. Indeed, the princes of Carrión metonymically represent the peninsula's old Christian nobility, whose "softness" effectively allowed a Moorish conquest of much of Christian territory. This epic poem is clearly articulated from the popular classes' opinions of this weakened nobility, through the voice of the *juglar;* the Cid, therefore, is emblematic of a new masculine ideal, one based on heroic actions, and not mere pretenses of greatness.

The Cid's response to the count's defense of his clan further establishes the Carrión men in effeminate positions. First, the Cid refutes the count's insult to his beard's growth by claiming divine interference in its prominence. This sanctifying of his beard is but the latest in a list of glorifications of his masculinity. What until now had been a profane symbol of his masculine prowess is now elevated to the sacred. The count's insult opens the door for the Cid's next rhetorical stab, for now the Cid can remind the count and all the court of the difference between his and the count's masculinity. While the Cid's manhood, that is, his beard, is intact, the count's is literally in the hero's pocket. Not only did the Cid shame the count by plucking his beard, but even the youngsters present got a piece of his manhood!

This effeminizing is carried on in the final verses of the court scenes, as the Cid's loyal vassals challenge the Carrións to duels. In the parlance that precedes the challenge, Pedro Bermúdez relates to the audience how Prince Fernando Carrión fled the battlefield in terror rather than face the attacking Moor, although he later took credit for the Moor's defeat. Accusing the humiliated prince of being a "tongue without hands" [lengua sin manos] (3328), the challenger continues the degradation, after reminding them both of their cowardice when faced with the escaped lion and by valuing them below the women they abused: "they are women/and you are men,/in every way/they are worth more than you" (217) [Siendo varones vosotros,/y ellas, que mujeres son,/aun de todas las maneras/más valen que no los dos (3348–3349)].

To be gendered below women was to be truly insulted. Viewed in the light of the Cid's masculinity and, by association, that of his vassals, the Carrión clan, and the nobility, by extension, is left completely dishonored. Into this void step the princes of Aragon and Navarra to ask for the Cid's daughters' hands in marriage; thus the disgrace is complete, transcending the class borders that were the Carrións' last defense. The Cid consents to arranged nuptials between his daughters and the future kings of Aragon and Navarra, which will bring even greater honor to his family (3392–3451).

With this noble union concerted and the duels of honor planned, the Cid takes leave of the court with one last flourishing display of his manhood: "Then the Cid Campeador/drew back his hood,/his coif of fine cloth/white as the sun,/and freed his beard/and undid the cord./All who are in the court/cannot keep from staring at him" (226) [Quitóse de la cabeza/nuestro Cid Campeador/su cofia trenzada de hilo,/que blanca era como el sol./Allí se soltó la barba,/y sacóla del cordón./No se cansan de mirarle/cuantos de la corte son (3491–3494)]. His honor restored and his masculinity unchallenged, the Cid releases his beard for all to see. The members of the court stare at it, entranced by its power and majesty, never tiring of gazing on its splendor. This homoerotic, homosocial moment is remarkable for its again blatant figuring of the Cid as erotic object, yet, paradoxically, the erotization of his phallic members, both the beard and the sword, serves to heighten his masculinity and does not effeminize him. The *juglar,* the court, and the *juglar's* audience, principally male, are positioned in the feminine stance, subordinate to the hypermasculine hero.

The hyperbole of these tropes of sexuality results in sustaining this mythic image of the Cid through thousands of oral performances and eventually in written text down through the centuries. As a metonym for the Spanish national character, this figure will take on a life of its own, both in the Reconquest of the peninsula and in the imperial projects of early modern Spain in the Americas. The hypermasculine Spanish conquistador finds his roots in the Cid and, as we will see in subsequent chapters, the tropes of his sexuality will travel and reassert themselves in myriad ways, but will continue to perform in the context of anxiety and contestation.

EARLY-MODERN SUPPRESSION OF THE FEMININE

Epic representations of chivalric masculinity continued throughout the medieval period. One only has to think of the fragments of the Spanish *epopeya* (epic poetry), the *romances* (ballads), to realize how this tradition that began with the Cid continues even today. And when the bards' lyrical-epic ballads began to tire their audiences, the early novelists took over, writing chivalric novels and courtly love stories, both genres that continued to exalt masculine heroes who protected and courted defenseless females. As Carmen Benito-Vessels observes, to find women in phallocentric Spanish canonical writings of the medieval period, one must look to the two poles of literature, the poetic and the juridical.[36] Benito-Vessels's study of the *Estoria de Espanna* demonstrates that the representation of women varied from the extremes of object of male violence, figured as the rape and eventual marriage between invading male and invaded female ("La mujer en *La estoria de Espanna,*" 49), to tentative representations of a powerful woman ruler of Alfonso X's lineage (58). Even this woman, doña Berenguela, who legitimated Alfonso X's claim to the throne, while important for the author's royal legitimacy, was depicted as an "anti-woman."[37]

As we will see in Chapters 2 and 3, a similar rhetorical strategy was employed against the powerful Andean women in the Spanish chronicles of conquest. Although a thorough treatment of these peninsular texts is beyond the scope of this study, we can see echoes of their influence by briefly observing how gender and sexuality began to be figured in the early-modern period.[38]

Ruth El Saffar discerningly links the formation of the eventual Spanish nation-state to cultural processes in the sixteenth century that weakened prior and competing loyalties—such as ethnicity, race, religion, and feudal organizations—to the formation of masculinized individuals who would become citizens under the monarch's control. "The crown's need to break down competing power agglomerates to create conditions appropriate to the formation of the new individual, also provided means by which men and boys were required to effect a severing from the feminizing forces in their lives" ("Evolution of Psyche," 166). What I identify in the medieval period as originary performances of a Spanish masculine ideal subjectivity will become the new protonation's choice for a model citizenry. The abject outsider against which this subjectivity is now performed is no longer the Moor, for the Reconquest has settled the seven centuries–old dispute; nor is it the old nobility we saw in the *Poema del mio Cid.* The outsider is now truly an "insider," for male subjectivity will reject the feminine from within its own culture as well as suspect, residual cultural influences from the "new Christians." The early-modern Spanish monarchy needed men to identify with the values the new society offered, values linked to the masculine: power, wealth, status, the city, literacy, and solitude. Feminine values, especially represented by the maternal figure, were associated with medieval Spain; the earth, the countryside, food, companionship, and orality were antagonistic to modernization.

One of the first and most popular literary texts of the sixteenth century, Fernando de Rojas's *La Celestina* (1499), establishes the confrontation between the premodern feminine represented by the female protagonist, witchlike go-between Celestina, and the newly emerging masculine subject, ironically personified by the only survivor of the tragic tale, Pleberio, Melibea's father and early modern businessman. Calisto, the young parodic figure of a courtly lover,[39] who finds himself torn between the two extremes, opts for the sensuous world of *voluptus,* the Senecan notion of erotic pleasure,[40] in which his longings for Melibea are satisfied through Celestina's magical intervention. Calisto's association with this maternal figure leads to his death, a fate shared by his male servants, who also become involved with Celestina. The old crone's chaotic, feminine space, in which the state's power is not yet absolute, devours the weak male figures, who rejected the modernizing influence of masculine values. The lesson is clear, as expressed in Pleberio's famous lament in the work's last lines: instead of modern order, the disheartened father sees only chaos, a disorder whose metaphors are all linked to the natural world, that feminine space.[41]

That Pleberio survives to lament the discordant condition of society while Celestina meets her destiny at the hands of her henchmen suggests that the momentum toward a separation from the maternal values she represents might continue. Indeed, fifty years later we find evidence of further suppression of the feminine in the anonymous *Lazarillo de Tormes* (1550). Lazarillo, prototypical Spanish *pícaro* (rogue), orphaned at a young age, leaves his mother to make his way in the world, searching for a place in the harsh circumstances of the Spanish lower classes. His "testimony" offers a critical perspective on Spain's incipient modernity, but does not turn back toward feminine values. Indeed, Lazarillo implicitly finds a "father figure" in the Arcipreste, who is responsible for Lazarillo's "prosperous" conditions, though the very same priest sleeps with Lazarillo's ill-reputed wife (Anonymous, *Lazarillo de Tormes,* 57).

We also find in the peninsular poetry of the epoch this suppression of maternal, feminine values. The mystical poetry of Saint John of the Cross, for example, casts the metaphorical representation of mystical union between man and God as a divine marriage, the metaphor we first observed in *La pasión de S. Pelayo.* But a closer reading of the poetry reveals the

transformation of gender ideology in this early-modern period. We recall that Raguel figured the divine marriage between Pelagius and Christ
in explicitly homoerotic imagery. Pelagius's beautiful male body became
the worthy vessel in which his divine "spouse" would take pleasure. In the
late sixteenth century, in his most widely read poem, "En una noche ob-
scura" [On a dark night], written between 1578 and 1591, Saint John of the
Cross uses the feminine voice to represent the soul that will unite with
God.[42]

From the first stanza of the poem the reader is aware that the narrative
voice is feminine, for the fourth verse ends with the feminine past parti-
ciple: "I went out unnoticed" (19) [salí sin ser notada (17)].[43] The poetic
voice, representing the soul that will eventually unite with God, is figured
as a woman in the precarious position of leaving her house at night, unde-
tected, drawn by inflamed passion toward her divine lover, "Amado" (Beloved) gendered male. Their encounter leaves her transformed by the lover:
"oh noche, que juntaste/Amado con amada,/amada en el Amado trans-
formada" (17) [night that drew together/the loved one and the lover,/each
transformed into the other (19–20)].[44]

By gendering the transformative agent male, Saint John of the Cross is
replicating the Aristotelian categories of gender dualism in which female
"matter" is the imperfection of male "form." The male force perfects the
incomplete female soul, reenforcing the hegemonic gender ideology of the
times. Caroline Bynum's study of gender and religion underscores how
the personification of the soul as feminine in masculine mystical literature
symbolizes renunciation and conversion, while women mystics' representation in masculine terms is considered a symbolic elevation (*Gender and
Religion*, 257–288). Both of these rhetorical moves positions the female as
implicitly inferior to the male. Daniel Dombrowski has shown how earlier
versions of Western religious traditions were matrifocal until the patriarchal Yaweh cult, mixed with Greek mythology, marginalized these feminine forces in a syncretic process that evolved into the Judeo-Christian
religion.[45] Saint John of the Cross's gendering of the soul privileges the
masculine God that emerged from the earlier, more diverse deities.

Humanist prose writings of the Spanish Renaissance reflect this gender
ideology, as well, but in more practical terms affecting the human existence of women and men in everyday life. Erasmus's *De matrimonio cristiano*,
which circulated in Spain between 1527 and 1535, though it argued for new
rights for women, concluded that the only appropriate spaces for legitimate women were the home or the convent. Even these thoughts were too
progressive for the post-Reformation church: the book was banned by the

Inquisition in 1551 (McKendrick, *Women and Society,* 8). Luis de León, another humanist of the times, also wrote of the proper place for women in society, as mandated by God, arguing that the perfect wife belonged in the home, because she lacked the natural intelligence and strength needed in public affairs (*La perfecta casada,* 16).[46]

Despite more "liberal" thought propagated by humanism, Aristotelian notions of the dichotomy separating man from woman continued to operate in the thinking of many sixteenth- and seventeenth-century scholars. The following passage from Juan de Dios Huarte Navarro's *Examen de los ingenios* (1604) reminds us of the deep-rooted belief in the essential differences between the two sexes. His comment not only exemplifies male resistance to females in pursuit of higher education, but also demonstrates Aristotle's continued presence and influence. This passage, an echo from the Greek philosopher's *Metaphysics,* in which the dualisms essential to women and men are outlined, is indicative of the growing displacement of the feminine in the early-modern period, a bias that will travel to the Americas and act out in myriad ways: "To think that a woman can be hot and drie, or endowed with wit and abilitie conformable to these two qualities, is a very great errour; because if the seed of which she was formed, had been hot and dry in their domination, she should have been born a man, and not a woman . . . she was by God created cold and moist, which temperature, is necessarie to make a woman fruitfull and apt for childbirth, but an enemy to knowledge" (Maus, "A Womb of His Own," 268).[47] Women were posited as reproducers of humankind but not as reproducers of knowledge, nor did they typically participate in other areas of the public sphere. As Ian Maclean discusses at length in *The Renaissance Notion of Woman,* "underlying this Aristotelian taxonomy of opposition are Pythagorean dualities, which link, without explanation, woman with imperfection, left, dark, and so on" (87–88). Women, therefore, were consigned to limited roles in society and, as even the more progressive humanists like Erasmus and León believed, if they were to be educated, it was with the goal of obtaining virtue in order to be better marriage partners or more devout servants of God.[48]

Mother is dead, father's authority is established, and God is the perfect male-gendered form whose subordinate followers are gendered female: thus a dominant gender ideology is established in Spain in which the feminine is suppressed, to be left as the abject in relation to the early modern, ideal Spanish subject. As Butler states in her clarification of gender performativity, "gender performance cannot be theorized apart from the forcible and reiterative practice of regulatory sexual regimes" (*Bodies That Matter,*

15). These regimes acquire power related to the performance of gendered subjectivity through repeated "citations" of norms. In the next section I discuss how the abject of the Spanish hegemonic masculine subjectivity, the effeminate male and the sodomite, is cited and subsequently regulated by powerful social institutions in premodern Spain.

INTO THE HEAT OF THE EARLY-MODERN PERIOD: THE INQUISITION AND EFFEMINATE TRANSGRESSORS

While the propagandistic *Poema del mio Cid* strived to set an example for masculine behavior by celebrating the austere values of moderation and fidelity, once established, Christian hegemony in the peninsula left nothing to chance in its approach to same-sex sexuality. Foucault has suggested that the relationship between power and sexuality emerged as the use of power evolved from authority over death to control over life, as the sovereigns in Western cultures began to relinquish their Roman *patria potestas* tradition, or right to kill those under their dominion. As the seventeenth century heralded the first signs of modernity, a new relationship between sovereign and subject unfolded in which the former began to exercise control over the latter by organizing life by means of disciplinary institutions such as schools, barracks, universities, and workshops and through regulatory controls Foucault refers to as the "bio-politics of the population." It was this "taking charge of life, more than the threat of death, that gave power its access even to the body" (*History of Sexuality*, 143). In protonational Spain, this access to the body was achieved largely through an intensification of the state and the church's interdiction in the lives of their converts and false converts, primarily through the emerging institution known as the Inquisition. Some objects of the nascent state's control were those bodies that did not conform to the patriarchal structures consolidating under the power of the church and the Crown: people who practiced same-sex erotics; nonconforming women; and effeminate men.

Rafael Carrasco has compiled an excellent collection of documents from the Inquisition related to the early modern persecution of "sodomites" in Valencia, Spain. His study, *Inquisición y represión sexual en Valencia (1565–1785)*, provides us with a history of the circumstances of those prosecuted as "sodomites" and how Spanish society reacted to same-sex behavior. Carrasco clearly demonstrates the power of the Inquisition in the regulation of morality and the control of society. The late fifteenth-century *Diccionario de los inquisidores,* composed by Valencia's Inquisition Tribunal, includes sodomy as one of the sins to be persecuted by the church. After invoking Saint Augustine's reminder of the divine punishment associated with Sodom, the authors characterize the offense as "a sin that is incomparably more serious than having sex with your own mother; sodomy violates the society in which we live, whose creator is he, who is soiled with the perversion of this desire" [un pecado incomparablemente más grave que acostarse con su propia madre, y que con la sodomía se viola la sociedad a la que pertenecemos, pero cuyo autor es Él, y se ensucia con la perversión del deseo] (Carrasco, *Inquisición y represión sexual,* 39). This passage clearly bespeaks the hyperbolic vehemence with which the Inquisitors approached the "crime against nature," considering it graver than maternal incest. The writers associate the sin with a "perversion of desire," linking it to the notion of *luxuria* mentioned above. Finally, punishments for sodomites are delineated: "By law, sodomites are decapitated. In canon law, the sodomite cleric is excluded from the clergy and is cloistered in a monastery for life so he can do penance; the layman is excommunicated and excluded from the community of the faithful" [En derecho, los sodomitas son decapitados. En derecho canónico, el clérigo sodomita es excluido del clericalato y encerrado toda la vida en un monasterio para que haga penitencia; el laico es excomulgado y excluido de la comunidad de los fieles] (ibid., 40). Below, I will discuss civil law, referred to here for its severe punishment of sodomy, but first we must consider the religious institution's application of these directives.

The hegemony of the Catholic institution was derived from a popular support rooted in the network of "*familiares,*" or informants, loyal to the higher strata of Inquisition officials and who had the power to arrest moral trespassers.[49] The trial records related to sodomites show the vehemence with which the *familiares* pursued and then testified against the accused. This apparently popular support of the Inquisition was directly related to the morality messages emitted from the pulpit and the confessionals.[50] In addition, the punishment of convicted sodomites was quite public, often attracting widespread attention in the media of the day: short printed narratives; announcements; handwritten flyers; and the chronicles of everyday life. The public sentencings and burnings at the stake (autos de fé) created great public spectacles (ibid., 17). Manipulation of fear was the explicit purpose of the public burnings of heretical sodomites and other offenders, as the sixteenth-century Inquisition manual *Directorium inquisitorum* makes explicit:

one must remember that the principal aim of the trial and the
death penalty is not to save the soul of the accused, but to
procure the public well-being and instill terror in the people.
Public well-being should be a higher goal than any charitable
concern about the well-being of the individual.

hay que recordar que la principal finalidad del proceso y de
la condena a muerte no es salvar el alma del acusado, sino
procurar el bien público e infundir terror al pueblo (ut alii
terreantur). Y el bien público debe ponerse mucho más alto
que cualquier consideración caritativa sobre el bien de un
individuo.

(Ibid., 20)

The frankness of this policy is testimony to the Inquisition's power
as a social institution engaged in the structuring of public morality. The
church's highest tribunal apparently enjoyed the support of the masses,
who at times even surpassed the inquisitorial fervor of the clerics. In 1519,
after an allegedly sodomitical baker was freed from the fires for lack of
evidence, an angry crowd assaulted the accused and, "carrying him [the
sodomite] violently and shirtless, in the formation of a cross, they walked
around the bonfire shouting for justice and they tried to burn him alive
upon arrival" [llevándole (al sodomitas) a empellones con una espada des-
nuda, en forma de cruz delante, caminaron la vuelta del quemador, apelli-
dando, viva la justicia, y quisieron quemarle vivo en llegando] (ibid., 27).
In effect, the baker was burned at the stake in a popular, not inquisitional,
auto de fé.[51]

This scene of a popular sodomite burning, inspired by the church's pastoral and inquisitorial zeal, suggests the hegemonic nature of the persecution of sodomy in the early-modern period. In Gramscian terms, the pursuit of the sodomites, which, as we will see below, was sanctioned by the
state, was not just an application of power from the higher echelons of the
social hierarchy, but also the result of a naturalized attitude that permeated society.[52] This hegemony legitimated the laws, both ecclesiastical and
civil, that were applied in the cases against sodomites. As we have seen in
this chapter, these attitudes accumulated over time, and the laws that went
with them began in the medieval period, along with the increased public
masculinization of the culture. Alfonso X's *Siete partidas* had addressed the
issue with the following law:

Sodomy is what they call the sin in which men lie with each other against nature and natural custom. And it is due to this sin that many evils on earth are born, and where committed, it is a thing that greatly grieves God. This sin creates a bad reputation, not just for the sinner, but, moreover, for the place where it is permitted to occur . . . for such errors our lord God sends to earth hunger and pestilence and torments, and many other horrible evils, which cannot be named . . . The people can accuse those men who lie with one another against nature, and this accusation can be made before the judge where the error was committed. If it is proven to be true, then the accused should die, along with he who consented.

Sodomítico dizen al pecado en que caen los omes yaziendo unos con otros contra natura e costumbre natural. E porque de tal pecado nacen muchos males en la tierra, do se faze, e es cosa q pesa mucho a Dios con el. E sale ende mala fama, non tan solamente a los fazedores: mas aun a la tierra, do es consentido . . . Ca por tales yerros embia nuestro Señor Dios sobre la tierra, donde lo faze fambre, e pestilencia, e tormentos, e otros males muchos, que non podria contar . . . Cada uno del pueblo puede acusar a los homes yaziendo unos con otros contra natura, e este acusamiento puede ser fecho delante del judgador do fiziessen tal yerro. E si le fuere prouado deue morir porende: tambien el que lo consiente.[53]

This law and, more important for my study, the language in which this law is written, became the legal and literary model on which tropes of sexuality that traveled to the Americas were based. As I will show throughout this book, the sodomy trope is performative as it is invoked as accusation against specific persons or whole peoples. Here we appreciate the originary legal language in the Spanish tradition that will slip into the ecclesiastical language of conversion and extirpation of indigenous religious practice in the Americas as well as into the rhetoric of the Inca Garcilaso de la Vega in his defense of the Incas. It is important to note both in the medieval version as well as the following, early-modern, version of this law that the accusation of sodomy justifies punishment of all implicated, whether direct participants or not. This element of the tradition will reappear in the Andes in myriad forms. The continuity and the differences in legal attitudes toward sodomy become apparent by comparing this medieval law with the early-modern version pronounced by the Catholic kings in 1497 in Medina del Campo:

> Among the other sins and crimes that offend our Lord God and defame our lands, the worst is the crime committed against the natural order; against which laws should be used to punish this nefarious crime, unworthy of naming, destroyer of the natural order, punished by divine justice; through which nobility is lost and the heart becomes cowardly. And it begets little firmness in the faith; and it is abhorrence in the eyes of God, who is so angered as to deliver unto humankind pestilence and other torments on earth; and from this sin is born shame and insult toward the people and lands that consent to it; and it is deserving of greater punishments that can be given . . . We establish and order that any person of any status, condition, as preeminent or dignified as he may be, who commits the nefarious crime against nature, and is convicted by evidence, that according to law it is sufficient to prove the crime of heresy or the crime of *laesae Majestatis,* that he be burned in the flames of fire on the spot . . . without any other evidence, along with his possessions and properties.

> Porque entre los otros pecados y delitos que ofenden á Dios nuestro Señor é infaman la tierra, especialmente es el crímen cometido contra órden natural; contra el qual las leyes y Derechos se deben armar para el castigo deste nefando delito, no digno de nombrar, destruidor de la orden natural, castigado por el juicio Divino; por el cual la nobleza se pierde, y el corazón se acobarda. Y se engendra poca firmeza en la Fe; y es aborrecimiento en el acatamiento de Dios, y se indigna á dar á hombre pestilencia y otros tormentos en la tierra; y nasce dél mucho oprobio y denuestro á las gentes y tierra donde se consiente; y es merescedor de mayores penas que por obra se pueden dar . . . Establecemos y mandamos, que cualquier persona, de cualquier estado, condición, preeminencia ó dignidad que sea, que comitiere el delito nefando contra naturam, seyendo en él convencido por aquella manera de prueba, que segun Derecho es bastante para probar el delito de heregía ó crímen *laesae Majestatis,* que sea quemado en llamas de fuego

en el lugar . . . y sin otra declaración alguna, todos sus bienes
así muebles como raíces.[54]

The sodomy explicitly expressed as male, same-sex erotic behavior in
the medieval law becomes more ambiguous at the end of the fifteenth century, as the old theological precept of not naming the crime returns. This
ambiguity lends the term more power, for as Jonathan Goldberg has observed, it is precisely the abstruseness of the term that makes it useful in
regulating bodies, especially in moments of social fluidity,[55] such as that
moment at the end of the fifteenth century when protonational Spanish
kingdoms are united through the sanctified heterosexual union of the king
of Aragon and the queen of Castile. Nonprocreative sexuality did not serve
the state's interests; since the Moors were defeated and eventually banished
from the territory, along with the Jews, and the state was on the eve of imperial expansion into the Americas, the Catholic monarchs needed to in-
crease the numbers of faithful, moral, and masculine citizens.

The parallels with the biblical story of Sodom in relation to Israel, as
read by Alter ("Sodom as Nexus"), is provocative; the "antination" in the
case of this early modern Spanish law is the sexual Other, who lived among
the population, committing sins that "shame[d] the lands." The infamy of
the antinationalist sexual acts is derived from biblical scorn of the Sodomites, who were understood in the popular imaginary as transgressors of the
natural order, as "destroyer of the natural order." Gender and sexuality conflate in this legal discourse in the law's expression of fear before the possible
effemination of the people: "through which nobility is lost and the heart
becomes cowardly." It is as if we had returned to that moment expressed
in the *Pasión de S. Pelayo* when again the fluidity of the social moment inspired fear of a loss of masculinity. This time, however, the state stepped
in to regulate sexuality and to specify the normative sexual behavior expected of its citizens. Otherwise, as Carrasco also observes, sodomy threatened to become "destroyer of lineages and ruiner of masculine virtues" [de-
structora de linajes y aniquiladora de las virtudes masculinas] (*Inquisición y
represión sexual,* 44). This threat to the established patriarchal order, as expressed in the Catholic kings' law, approached the level of heresy. While
sodomy never reached the formal status of heresy, this brief insinuation of
the heretical nature of the sin/crime further illustrates the ambiguity that
empowers the performative utterance.[56]

The sodomite as juridical subject in these laws evolved into the personification of something more ambiguous in the moralist discourse of
the times. The conflation of sexual deviant and gender transgressor, inti-

mated in the legal code analyzed above, appears as a third-gender category, neither male nor female, but a barbarous Other in the moralist writing I consider below. This manifestation of a liminal gender category for the sexual Other returns us to the issue of masculinity and the threat to its fragility as cultural construct, namely, effeminacy. Here again we have the abject outsider figured in relation to the hegemonic Spanish subject.

THE "TERROR" OF DIFFERENCE: EARLY-MODERN IBERIAN EFFEMINACY

If men in general seemed to enjoy the privilege of dominance over the female gender, we can imagine that some must also have felt pressure to conform to the normative gender categories to the extent of possibly feeling deprived of the freedom to realize their own identities, lest they be identified with the weaker sex. The harshness with which early-modern society dealt with sexual and gender difference can be appreciated by considering the bodily extreme of gender category confusion, the hermaphrodite. As Foucault points out, "hermaphrodites were criminals, or crime's offspring, since their anatomical disposition, their very being, confounded the law that distinguished the sexes and prescribed their union" (*History of Sexuality,* 38). These references suggest that early modern gender categories were not as stable as some might have liked. As Judith Butler comments in *Gender Trouble:* "Inasmuch as 'identity' is assured through the stabilizing concepts of sex, gender, and sexuality, the very notion of the 'person' is called into question by the cultural emergence of those 'incoherent' or 'discontinuous' gendered beings who appear to be persons but who fail to conform to the gendered norms of cultural intelligibility by which persons are defined" (17). There can be no doubt that such unintelligible beings populated the cultural landscape of early-modern Spain.[57] As we will see below, the personhood of the effeminate was called into question and denounced by the moralists of the day. Nearly five hundred years after Thomas Aquinas warned against effeminacy, we find similar precautions in Renaissance Spain.

An early-modern Spanish moralist, Sebastián de Covarrubias Orozco, expresses the dominant attitudes of his time in his encyclopedia of moral virtues known as *Emblemas morales* (1610). Covarrubias, best known for his dictionary, *Tesoro de la lengua castellana o española* (1611), was the quintessential Catholic lexicographer of his time. His work reflects a Tridentine lexicon of orthodox Catholic dogma, an ideology that is transformed into

pedagogy in the *Emblemas morales*.[58] The work combines allegorical etchings and their epigraphs with short explicative narratives that recount,
true to Renaissance tradition, classical myths tied to moral teachings. The
emblem functioned as a visual symbol of certain moral truths. Mercedes
López Baralt, in her study of emblematic literature in the Spanish Golden
Age, characterizes these icons as "techniques of persuasion" at the service
of the ethical and religious teachers of the period.[59] Calvo Pérez has noted
that Covarrubias's emblems reflect the author's baroque sensibilities in the
conflation of paganism and universalist Christianity, infused with a moralist spirit common to the reformist age (*Sebastián de Covarrubias,* 37). Included in Covarrubias's morality writings is an example of the extreme of
earthly creatures: the monstrous effeminates, represented symbolically by
the hermaphrodite:

> I am *hic,* and *hac,* and *hoc.* I confess
> I am a man, I am a woman, I am a third,
> Who is neither the one nor the other, and it is not clear
> Which of these things he is. I am a terror
> for those who believe me to be a horrendous and rare
>   monster.
> They take me to be sinister and a bad omen.
> Be advised each who has seen me
> That he is another like me, if he lives effeminately.
>
> Soy hic, y hac, y hoc. Yo me declaro,
> Soy varón, soy mujer, soy un tercero,
> Que no es uno ni otro, ni está claro
> Cual de estas cosas sea. Soy terrero
> De los q[*sic*] como monstro horrendo y raro.
> Me tienen por siniestro, y mal agüero
> Advierta cada cual que me ha mirado
> Que es otro yo, si vive afeminado.[60]

The etching that accompanies this epigraph (Figure 1) is of a bearded
person in a long dress, identified by the author as "the bearded one of Peñaranda" [la barbuda de Peñaranda] (Covarrubias Orozco, *Emblemas morales,*
165), and the narrative on the facing page recounts the myth of Hermaphroditus as told by Ovid in Book Two of *Metamorphoses*.[61] In the myth,
female Salmacis fixes her desirous gaze on male Hermaphroditus, embraces
his naked body, and prays never to be parted from him. Her wish is granted,

and Salmacis is forever effaced from earth and history, being subsequently represented only as the femininity of Hermaphroditus. The gendered binary oppositions are conflated onto one body, a body that privileges the masculine through the presence of the phallus, but that retains female features such as hair, breasts, and a "soft" shaping of arms, legs, and buttocks. There is no wholeness, no unity: oppositions are reenforced, the very oppositions originally represented by the pre-Salmacis Hermaphroditus, product of the mythical union of his parents, Hermes and Aphrodite.

The hermaphrodite, in the early modern cultural imaginary, was a classical trope of transgendering that appeared in art, sculpture, and literature. By bringing the hermaphrodite metaphor to bear on the early modern morality of Spain, Covarrubias further affronts the feminine qualities essentially assigned to women and that, through contamination, could be acquired by men. The warning is clear: to take on effeminate traits is to become a monster, a hermaphroditic creature that has no place as either gender.

After the myth's summary, the moralist adds his own interpretation:

> the fable has much of natural and moral history, because among other prodigious things of nature, we notice that She often makes a creature with both sexes, whom we call Androgyne, who is as much a man as a woman . . . I say along with Cicero . . . Néestturpius aut nequius efeminato viro. Which is the sentence that closes our octave.

> la fábula tiene mucho de historia natural y moral, porque entre otras cosas prodigiosas de la naturaleza notamos esta que suele hacer una criatura con ambos sexos a la qual llamamos Androgyno, que vale tanto como varón y mujer, . . . digo con Cicero i.3 de las Tusculanas: Néestturpius aut nequius efeminato viro. Que es la sentencia con que cerramos nuestra octava.

> (Covarrubias Orozco, *Emblemas morales*, 165)

This time, Covarrubias distorts a classical myth, that of the Androgyne from Plato's *Symposium*, in order to reinforce his admonition of the dangers of effeminacy. Whereas Plato imagined the Androgyne as an ideal state of unity and wholeness, Covarrubias marginalizes him/her as a freak of nature, a monster. Again, it is the effeminate qualities that he wishes to erase. Plato's Aristophanes explains in the *Symposium* dialogues that the origin of love and sexual difference came from the division of an androgynous pri-

CENTVRIA II.   164

UTRVM·Q. ·ET·VTRVM

EMBLEMA. 64

Soy *hic,& hac,& hoc. Yo me declaro,*
Soy *varon, soy muger, soy vn tercero,*
Que no es vno ni otro, ni està claro
Qual destas cosas sea. Soy terrero
De los q̃ como a mõstro horrẽdo y raro,
Me tienen por siniestro, y mal aguero,
Aduierta cada qual q̃ me ha mirad〉,
Que es otro yo, si viue afeminado.

Cu ჳ

FIGURE 1   *La barbuda de Peñaranda. From Covarrubias Orozco,* Emblemas morales.

mal being into two beings, man and woman, who are then destined to seek each other out because "human nature was originally one and we were a whole" (ibid., 147–148). Although Covarrubias does not mention the rest of the myth, Plato included two other androgynous primal beings who divided into a pair of males and a pair of females; these were then destined to seek a "homosexual" union as in the "heterosexual" one. Evidently, this apparent symbolic justification of same-sex coupling did not fit into the Renaissance writer's scheme of morality.

In any event, the important point here is that the effeminacy associated with androgynes and hermaphrodites becomes the object of the moralist's scorn. By incorporating and transforming classical versions of gender diversity as notions of "natural and moral history" into early-modern Spanish moralist discourse, Covarrubias acquired a broader base of authority. He appealed to tradition through use of myths and he invoked notions of natural law by contextualizing the appearance of the hermaphrodite/androgyne in "natural and moral history." His attitude toward the existence of these beings in nature is revealed in the comment that they are like "other prodigious things of nature"[otras cosas prodigiosas de naturaleza]; that is, they are extraordinary, things that exceed the normal limits of nature, further building the case for their monstrousness. Here the ideology of Thomas Aquinas is exposed: the unnatural, bestial nature of the effeminate is foregrounded. These "prodigious things" are culturally unintelligible; as a result, their "personhood" is questioned, and ultimately dehumanized.

By writing the emblem's octave in the first person, Covarrubias puts the misogynist warning in the mouth of the hermaphrodite/androgyne/effeminate. As a result, the narrator embodies in his/her declarations of selfhood the ambiguous identity of a third gender: "I am a man, I am a woman, I am a third." The binary is broken. The unknown "unnatural" steps into the liminal position between the two "natural" categories. The identity is confusion: "I am *hic,* and *hac,* and *hoc.*" Nonsense. This confusion leads to fear: "I am a terror for those who believe me to be a horrendous and rare monster." What is unknown or misunderstood becomes monstrous and rare. The third-gendered person is dehumanized; he/she becomes the bestial Other. The next step is to assign to the "third" a sense of threat to "natural" society: "They take me to be sinister and a bad omen." No longer just a rare monster, the "third" is now sinister and threatening, a bad omen for the society in which he/she lives. We remember the medieval theological warning of the "epidemic" potential sexual transgression represented; here, that threat is personified by the "third."

The final discursive move is to amplify the moral teaching to be applied to more than just the hermaphrodites. After all, just how many biologically hermaphroditic people were born into the world? But, "effeminate" men? There is the real object, I would argue, of the moralist's emblem. With the final verse, the equation is complete: "Be advised each who has seen me/That he is another like me, if he lives effeminately." The effeminate becomes the monster, the threat to patriarchal society. To take on characteristics of the essentialized and debased female is to transgress not only gender categories but also human qualities. Covarrubias's renaissance of classical ideals of masculinity reaches its logical conclusion. What Foucault observes in the Hellenist period is reborn here to justify the inquisitorial rage and the common prejudice of Spanish morality: the "definite aversion to anything that might denote a deliberate renunciation of the signs and privileges of the masculine role" was also anathema in the early modern Spanish imaginary (*Use of Pleasure,* 19). Once the effeminate man was dehumanized by rhetoric, the more easily could society's physical sanctions be imposed. As we have seen with the inquisitional evidence, transgressions of gender and sexual normativity were met with severe censure, a trend that would travel to the Americas.[62]

By observing how gender and sexuality are figured in premodern, protonational Spanish literature, I have laid the groundwork for the following chapters. It is my hypothesis that the tropes born in the medieval epic and sharpened in the early-modern morality literature traveled to the colonies in the sixteenth century. Spanish masculinity as a performative gender subjectivity was challenged again in the new cultural space of the Andes. The disdain for the abject, effeminate Other found in the peninsula was displaced onto the racial Other in the Andes. Spanish beards and swords came face to face not only with valiant Andean indigenous resistance, but also with indigenously valued subjects whose gender and sexuality were expressed in transgendered terms in complex ritual contexts. This violent encounter resulted in the transculturation of Andean subjectivities, a process that was narrated in chronicles, resisted in indigenous mythology, legislated in colonial regulations, reenforced in ecclesiastical literature, and, finally, rewritten by the mestizo foundational "father" of Peruvian literature.

Two

DECOLONIZING QUEER
TROPES OF SEXUALITY
Chronicles and Myths of Conquest

> *Heterotopias are disturbing, probably because they secretly*
> *undermine language, because they make it impossible to name*
> *this and that.*
>
> —MICHEL FOUCAULT, *The Order of Things*

Queer tropes of sexuality appear in the pages of Conquest narratives from the first expeditions to the Americas. The sodomitical tropes recorded in this colonial discourse are more than mere "medieval artifacts," as I understand Mark Jordan's use of the term in his theological history of sodomy.[1] To understand the full impact of the trope, Jordan's use of "artifact" needs to be complemented by the word's secondary meaning: "any object made by human work; esp. a simple or primitive tool, weapon, vessel, etc."[2] Rather than remaining static and relegated to medieval archives, the primitive sodomy trope reappeared at the dawn of the premodern period, paradoxically invoked to do the work of a tool or weapon in a medieval enterprise that belied the passage of time. Sodomy became one of the rhetorical armaments that the Spanish employed to justify the invasion and colonization of the Andes; it was a moral instrument wielded in the conversion of the indigenous colonial subjects. For the reader today, the sodomy trope is also a vessel that holds a history of marginalization and transculturation of gender and sexuality, for the history of sodomy, its theological "invention," was not confined to the scholastic seminaries or the inquisitional courts of Europe; this elusive trope crossed the ocean and was employed in the pacification and evangelization of the indigenous peoples of the Americas. These tropes characterized as queer figures those Andeans who threatened the moral order of the Old World and embodied the anxiety related to the inherent instability of hegemonic Iberian masculinity discussed in the last chapter. To glean meaning from these textual artifacts we must decolonize the tropes through deconstruction and reinterpretation from a more Andean perspective of indigenous culture and society.

The textual fragments I consider in this chapter are vestiges of a process that brought together these medieval European values and indigenous Andean cultures, whose language, ritual practices, and myths represented different sexual moralities. Because of the power imbalance implicit in colonial discourse, what we can know of Andean same-sex practices in this historical and spatial context is limited. The colonial representation of indigenous gender and sexuality was a process of literary transculturation that left behind textual artifacts neither wholly European and medieval nor exclusively indigenous and pre-Hispanic. Also of interest here, beyond the reconstruction of a transculturated subjectivity, is how the writers of the times, both Spanish and native, portrayed gender culture and sexuality in this conflictive colonial context. We will see, on the one hand, a Christian soldier-chronicler, Pedro Cieza de León, come to terms with an American "heterotopia," that "disturbing" place of the Other that Foucault has contrasted to the comforting utopias of one's fantasy. Confronted with the real differences of Andean culture, Cieza de León's challenge was to narrate with a language limited by its origins and ideologies. To obtain the information he recorded, he had to engage with native informants, Andeans with their own political and social agendas, that is, agents in the process of transculturation. Indeed, what he saw and heard in the Andes undermined the language of conquest and challenged the writer to find a "third space" from which to narrate his chronicle. His struggle to find commonality in order to communicate these differences was reiterated some fifty years later by native ladino writers whose narratives reflect nearly a century of transculturation (the subject of Chapter 3). In all of these texts, the authors grapple with different cultural codes in their reinterpretation of Andean culture. The writers left us fragments of third-gender subjectivity, pieces of a heterotopic gender culture distorted by prejudice and fear.[3]

GENDER AND SEXUALITY IN
SPANISH CONQUEST POLITICS

In one of the first reports from Pizarro's early expedition along the Ecuadorian coast, Juan Ruiz de Arce describes his shock and disgust at an apparently different gender/sexual culture. Featured prominently in his account is a disdain for those elements of the culture consid-

ered feminine in the Spanish mentality. His descriptions reveal a conquistador who was, as James Lockhart has commented, "given to moralizing,
and convinced of the superiority of Hispanic values—a fanatic" (*Men of
Cajamarca*, 346). Ruiz de Arce informs us that the ruler of the people on the
Ecuadorian coast was a woman and insinuates that the men were immoral
and less than masculine: "es gente muy bellaca son todos sométicos no ay
principal que no trayga quatro o cinco pajes muy galanes[.] Estos tiene
por mancebos" (*Relación de servicios en Indias*, 32) [these ruinous people are
all sodomites. There is not a chief among them who does not carry with
him four or five gallant pages. He keeps these as concubines]. His narrative, therefore, links the feminine power of the leader to sodomy among
the men. By reporting the sodomitical practices of the local males, Ruiz de
Arce played to the European imagination and subtly set the stage for future
justifications of conquest. In addition, he symbolically positioned the Andeans in a subordinate role in relation to the masculinized conquistadores.

Ruiz de Arce's attitude was not uncommon in the early years of the
colonization of the Americas. Christopher Columbus's physician during
his second voyage to the Indies, Diego Álvarez Chanca, wrote the first
extant description of indigenous sexuality in 1494, in which he conflates
the castration and sexual use of boys with cannibalism, claiming that the
Caribs practiced sodomy and ate the flesh of the castrated men (Guerra, *Pre-
columbian Mind*, 45). Rolena Adorno and Patrick Charles Pautz's discussion
of Indian slavery in New Spain and the Caribbean islands explains what
was at stake in these depictions of cannibalism and non-normative sexuality (*Álvar Núñez Cabeza de Vaca*, 334–335). In the shifting laws concerning
Indian slavery of the first forty years of the sixteenth century, royal decrees
were issued "permitting the capture and enslavement of Indians reported
to be cannibals" (ibid., 335) in the Caribbean. Proof of these indigenous
transgressions, therefore, became important in the early colonial economy.
Adorno and Pautz point out that the proscribed practices justifying enslavement expanded to include sodomy:

> Since the alleged cannibalism of the Caribbean Indians was
> questioned by antislavery critics, an inquiry was authorized on
> 18 June 1519 to call witnesses for the purpose of citing direct or
> hearsay evidence about the practice. Unlike the rulings cited
> above, this hastily executed investigation broadened the range
> of legitimate offenses for which Indians could be enslaved
> beyond anthropophagy to include "infidelity," idolatry, and the
> "abominable sin against nature," that is, sodomy. The resultant

"cannibal questionnaire," transcribed by Hanke ("Studies" 388–
93) and discussed in context and fully identified as "A.G.I.,
Justicia, 47, fols. 69–72" by Castañeda Delgado (84), was used
to solicit testimony from Castilian ship captains and officers.

(Ibid., 335)

This cannibal questionnaire is an early iteration of the interrogation of
indigenous practices Peruvian viceroy Francisco de Toledo undertook in
his *visita* investigations in the 1570's, which I analyze in Chapter 4. The
questionnaire in this Caribbean case was directed to Spaniards and not to
indigenous informants, as were the Toledo reports. Its author, Alonso de
Zuazo, chief justice of the island of Hispaniola, conflated idolatry, cannibalism, and sodomy to justify slavery: "Likewise, if they know that the
Carib Indians who live in these parts and on the coast are infidels and
idolaters and eat human flesh and commit the nefarious sin against nature"
[Yten sy saben q los dhos yndios caribes q abitan en las dhas partes e costa
son ynfieles e ydolatros e comen carne umana e ussan del pecado nefando
contra natura] (Hanke, "Studies," 388). The testimony was taken on June 19,
1519, and the judge ruled the following day to allow the Spaniards to en-
slave the Caribbean Indians (Castañeda Delgado, "La política española con
los caribes," 81, cited in ibid., 335). In the Andes some fifty years later, this
investigative technique would be employed to justify the conquest of the
Incas.[4]

Another of the earliest and most violent of these descriptions records
cross-dressing sodomites and the Spaniards' unrestrained reaction to them.
Vasco Núñez de Balboa, en route to discover the Pacific Ocean in 1513,
came upon a village and defeated and killed approximately six hundred
Quarequa Indians. Subsequently, he fed forty "sodomites" to his dogs. Peter
Martyr recorded the spectacle in *Decades* (1516): "[Balboa] founde the house
of this kynge infected with most abhominable and unnaturall lechery. For
he found the kynges brother and many other younge men in womens
apparell, smooth & effeminately decked, which by the report of such as
dwelte abowte hym, he abused with preposterous venus. Of these abowte
the number of fortie, he commanded bee gyven for a pray to his dogges"
(quoted in Goldberg, "Sodomy in the New World," 47).[5] Here the conflation of transvested males and sodomy led to Balboa's visceral reaction. The
narrator highlights the effeminacy as well as the king's sexual "abuse" of
the young men. The event was sensational enough to become the subject
of an engraving by T. de Bry that accompanied the account (Figure 2).

FIGURE 2   *Balboa's dogs devouring sodomites. From Peter Martyr,* Decades, *engraving
by T. de Bry.*

As Goldberg comments, this excessive act of violence following the defeat of the Quarequa village serves to lend moral purpose to Balboa's actions, after the fact. Martyr goes on to report that the sodomitical transgendering was practiced among the elite and that the common people
were offended by the effeminate behavior of their rulers. Balboa not only
frees them of sexual depravity but also liberates the commoners from their
supposed oppressors (ibid., 48); thus, Martyr begins what will become
the standard discourse on Amerindian sexuality, a differentiation between the "noble savage," clean of what Europeans considered to be vices,
and the barbaric Indians, immoral usurpers of authority.[6] The trope not
only achieves a justification of conquest and a differentiation of the vanquished, but any notion of indigenous meaning of what might have been
a sacred cultural practice is obscured. Martyr records that Balboa understood the commoners' disgust with the transgendered sodomites because
"the people lyftinge up thyr handes and eyes toward heaven, gave token
that god was grevously offended with such vyle deeds" (ibid., 48). Considering that their entire village had just been decimated, it may be dis-

ingenuous to interpret these gestures as expressions of disgust with their own rulers rather than displays of sorrow and disbelief at their plight at the hands of the conquistadores.

Balboa's men, as visually depicted by de Bry, provide a stark contrast to the sodomites. The engraving is structured on two planes, with the Spaniards boastfully positioned on top, seemingly delighted by the spectacle of the naked Indians writhing in agony as the muscular mastiffs devour them in the foreground. Metonymically representative of the colonial gaze and its relationship with the Amerindians in general, these conquistadores control the viewer's focus of interest by staring at the sodomites and thus exerting power over them. Their scrutiny of the scene delimits and defines the Quarequas as weak and helpless, unarmed and thus unmanly, while the Spaniards pose fully dressed, displaying in a leisurely manner the armaments that won them the control they now exert over the natives. Any explicit markers of the Quarequas' "sin" is absent in this visual rendering of the episode; the only reference to effeminacy is achieved through contrast. It is the nakedness and the relative passivity with which the sodomites struggle with the mastiffs that echoes the narrative account. But the power of the image is in its ambiguity, for depiction of Spaniards on top of defeated men metonymically expands the meaning to represent the expansion of Spanish power to yet another ocean, the Pacific. Only one conquistador averts his eyes, reminding us of the instability of the male subject we discussed in Chapter 1, for he seems repulsed by either the massacre or the sodomites themselves, as if he recognizes the abjection within himself that is being acted out in the scene below him.

The model for later conquests, Hernán Cortés and his subordinates mobilize the sodomy trope, as well. Inscribed in one of the first reports from Veracruz in 1519 is the barbarity of Cortés's adversaries in Mexico, who, in addition to performing human sacrifices, "we have learnt and been informed for sure that they are all sodomites and use that abominable sin" (quoted in Guerra, *Precolumbian Mind*, 52). Cortés's soldier-chronicler, Bernal Díaz del Castillo, also reported that, in addition to cannibals and sorcerers, "all the rest were sodomites, especially those who lived on the coasts and in warm lands; so much so that young men paraded around dressed in women's clothes in order to work in the diabolical and abominable role" (Díaz del Castillo, *Historia verdadera*, 579) [eran todos los demás de ellos sométicos, en especial los que vivían en las costas y tierra caliente; en tanta manera, que andaban vestidos en hábito de mujeres muchachos a ganar en aquel diabólico y abominable oficio]. Here, again, the trope invokes the

abjection of "effeminate," reminiscent of the "*tercero*" from the Spanish emblem analyzed in the last chapter; the cross-dressing sodomites, a product
of climate, mimicked that early-modern fear.

But it is Gonzalo Fernández de Oviedo who raised the accusations of
sodomy to their most exaggerated level of hyperbole, claiming that the
practice was universal among the Amerindians. An example of his descriptions taken from *Natural Historia de las Indias* (1526), which was published
throughout Europe in the early sixteenth century, reveals how he, like his
predecessors, continued to establish a link between aberrant sexuality and
transvested Indians:

> In many parts of Tierra Firme the Indians are sodomites. Very
> common among the Indians in many parts is the nefarious sin
> against nature; even in public the Indians who are headmen or
> principals who sin in this way have youths with whom they
> use this accursed sin, and those consenting youths as soon as
> they fall into this guilt wear naguas [skirts] like women, which
> are certain short cotton clothes with which the Indian women
> cover themselves from their waist to the knees and they wear
> strings of beads and bracelets and the other things used by
> women as adornment; and they do not exercise in the use of
> weapons, nor do anything proper to men, but they occupy
> themselves in the usual chores of the house such as to sweep
> and wash and other things customary for women.
>
> (Quoted in Guerra, *Precolumbian Mind,* 55)

While his admonishment of the sexual practices is written in the standard,
dogmatic language of the church, Oviedo seems most intrigued by the
gender-crossing and clearly expresses how these "sodomites" transgressed
the dominant European gender roles of his day by abdicating masculine
privileges "proper to men" such as military pursuits. His description represents the indigenous sodomites as young victims of powerful rulers who
objectify and abuse them until they finally choose to live as women.[7] These
queer tropes of sexuality, based on the Spaniard's superficial understanding of Amerindian gender culture, began to circulate and influence how
others would represent the Amerindian, as we shall see below.[8]

Oviedo's correlation between indigenous sodomites and barbarity set
the stage for the infamous Las Casas–Sepúlveda debates in the court of
Carlos V. These debates centered around the moral question of whether

the Spanish could justly wage war on and claim rights to the American territories. There is ample scholarship available on the details of this intellectual exchange in the middle of the sixteenth century;[9] therefore, I will limit my comments to how the discourse on just war and the Amerindian's humanity involved sodomy. The issue of indigenous sexuality is not tangential to the debate, but in fact is related to the issue of the Amerindian's humanity and relationship to natural law, first raised by Antonio de Montesinos and later addressed by Francisco de Vitoria.[10] Finally, in 1550, Carlos V convened a council in Valladolid, Spain, where Juan Ginés de Sepúlveda presented his *Democrates secundus,* in which he argues that the Amerindians lacked rationality and, therefore, in agreement with Aristotle's doctrine of "natural slavery," should be governed by the Europeans. Sepúlveda had already published his text, also known as the *Tratado sobre las justas causas de la guerra contra los indios,* in 1547. His definition of "natural law" rested on the classical philosophical notion of the essential inferiority of some people in relation to others, the idea that "perfection should prevail and dominate over imperfection, excellence over its opposite" [lo perfecto debe imperar y dominar sobre lo imperfecto, lo excelente sobre su contrario] (*Tratado,* 83).

The gendered nature of this principle is revealed in Sepúlveda's illustration of natural law, wherein "the father controls his children . . . the husband, his wife" [manda el padre á sus hijos . . . el marido á su mujer] (ibid., 83). Echoing the teachings of Aristotle, in the medieval attitudes toward *luxuria* and sodomy and the early-modern postures toward women, Sepúlveda imbeds in his just causes of war on the Amerindians the gendered superiority of men, implicitly basing that superiority on his observation that "it is natural and just that the soul dominate the body, that reason preside over appetite" [lo natural y justo es que el alma domine el cuerpo, que la razón presida al apetito] (ibid., 85). As we saw in Chapter 1, this Aristotelian notion of form over substance held that men represented form and women, substance, so that in Sepúlveda, "the man prevails over the woman, the male adult over the child, the father over his children, that is, the most powerful and most perfect over the weakest and the imperfect" [el varón impera sobre la mujer, el hombre adulto sobre el niño, el padre sobre sus hijos, es decir, los más poderosos y más perfectos sobre los más débiles é imperfectos] (ibid., 85). Taking this moral paradigm into account reveals how ideologically charged the first descriptions of the coastal peoples of Tawantinsuyu were. A woman ruler and sodomites, considered deviant and monstrous, transgressed natural law and justified the severe actions the Spaniards would undertake in the course of the Conquest.

While this classical and Renaissance gender ideology informs the jurist's second cause of just war,[11] Sepúlveda resorts to biblical discourse to specify that sins against God are grounds for an armed crusade: "the second cause that justifies the war against the barbarians is that their sins, impieties, and obscenities are so nefarious and so abhorred by God, that being offended principally by them, he destroyed with the universal flood all mortals except Noah and a few innocents" [La segunda causa que justifica la guerra contra los bárbaros es que sus pecados, impiedades y torpezas son tan nefandos y tan aborrecidos por Dios, que ofendido principalmente con ellos, destruyó con el diluvio universal á todos los mortales exceptuando á Noé y á unos pocos inocentes] (ibid., 113). The implication that sodomy is one of the "*torpezas,*" or lascivious behaviors, becomes clearer a few lines later when he recalls that because of "the sin of nefarious obscenity, fire and sulfur fell from the heavens and destroyed Sodom and Gomorrah" [el pecado de torpeza nefanda cayó del cielo fuego y azufre y destruyó á Sodoma y á Gomorra] (ibid., 113). Here again we find medieval theological ambiguity informing proscriptions of sodomy; indeed, Saint Thomas Aquinas's writings on just-war theory were important sources for Sepúlveda and other early-modern jurists (Hanke, *La lucha,* 260). The abstruseness of the particularities of natural law becomes clarified in Sepúlveda's subsequent explanation that such divine punishment is not inflicted in the case of individual offenses, but is the result of a whole people's transgressions; this echoes the medieval and early modern laws that mandated the destruction of whole peoples involved in sodomy:

> if there were a people so barbarous and inhuman that they did not consider some of these crimes I have listed as obscene and if they did not punish them . . . of this people it would be justly and properly said that they do not observe natural law, and the Christians would be within their rights . . . to destroy them for their nefarious crimes and barbarity and inhumanity.

> si hubiese una gente tan bárbara é inhumana que no contase entre las cosas torpes todos o algunos de los crímenes que he enumerado y no los castigase . . . de esa nación se diría con toda justicia y propiedad que no se observa la ley natural, y podrían con pleno derecho los cristianos . . . destruirla por sus nefandos delitos y barbarie é inhumanidad.

> (Ibid., 125)

This issue becomes crucial in Bartolomé de Las Casas's response to Sepúlveda, his defense of the Amerindians based on his *Apologética historia
sumaria* of 1559, in which he sets out to prove their rationality by drawing
on both the religious and the political discourse employed by Sepúlveda,
by equating the Amerindians with the pagans of European antiquity, and
by illustrating their humanity through a monumental summary of ethnographic information collected during his travels and through his extensive
epistolary relations. Central to his discursive strategy was refuting Sepúlveda's second just cause by claiming that Sepúlveda misunderstood Aristotle (Hanke, *La lucha,* 357). For Las Casas, the Amerindians were rational
in the three fundamental ways Aristotle had theorized human behavior:
monastically (personal behavior), economically, and politically (ibid., 361).
While there was no official outcome of the debate, in effect, Las Casas's
position was vindicated through his subsequent freedom to publish his encyclopedic writings, while Sepúlveda was censured by the court, and his
works did not reach the printer until the late nineteenth century (ibid.,
374–375). The debate frames the context in which the early chroniclers recorded their observations of the native gender culture; some adopted a Lascasian perspective while others subscribed to Sepúlveda's arguments.

Las Casas's representation of indigenous sexuality, in particular, his
treatment of sodomy, inspired as a response to Oviedo's perceived exag-
geration and distortion of same-sex practices in the Americas, contributed
to what José Rabasa has called Las Casas's invention of "a form of utopian discourse" in which the indigenous are figured as "noble savages" in
a "natural garden" (*Inventing America,* 164–179). Rabasa's treatment of the
tropes of cannibalism and human sacrifice is useful for our understanding
of Las Casas's rhetorical use of sodomy: "Las Casas does not refute the 'facts'
about cannibalism and human sacrifice that one could find in Oviedo, the
Franciscan ethnographers, and other encyclopedic texts on the New World;
rather, he produces a fiction that not only provides an alternative interpretation but also dismantles the criteria upon which one could articulate a
colonialist discourse" (ibid., 179).

In regards to the third-most-infamous trope of barbarity, Las Casas selectively denies or refigures his predecessor's accusations of sodomy. In his
Brevísima relación de la destrucción de las Indias (1552), Las Casas vehemently
denies the existence of sodomy in the Americas. This text is his most sche-
matic writing, one characterized by some as propagandistic and simplistic
and with greater emphasis on denouncing the Spaniards than on representing indigenous practices. His refutation is informed by the same gender

anxiety that mobilized the charge of sodomy by his contemporaries, as we can appreciate in his defense of the Amerindian's manhood; here again we see how discourses on sexuality and gender conflate and how the notion of effeminacy is attached to that of same-sex sexuality. His unequivocal rejection of the accusation of sodomy served his need to refute the likes of Oviedo and Sepúlveda in the minds of European readers.

Las Casas's representation of sodomy is more complicated, however, in the nuanced and more ethnographically rich accounts of his "encyclopedic" works, *Historia de las Indias* (1547) and *Apologética Historia Sumaria,* published posthumously. In these texts, he "dismantles the criteria" (Rabasa, *Inventing America*) of his adversaries in the polemic over the Amerindian's sexuality by subtly introducing the cultural context in which sodomy was practiced. By expanding the reader's knowledge of the cultural background and history of indigenous same-sex practices, Las Casas refigures the sodomy trope and leaves in his texts fragments that serve us in a reconsideration of indigenous gender and sexuality. I will consider one example from each of his major works.

In the chapters dedicated to Guatemala in *Apologética,* Las Casas addresses the accusations of the "nefarious sin" in the context of his detailed account of indigenous conceptions and punishments of "sins" as they related to the Catholic commandments. In the section on the sixth commandment he reports:

> Regarding the nefarious sin, what must be truthfully told is that it was never seen among those people, and they held it to be a great and abominable sin until a demon disguised as an Indian named Cu, and in another language named Chin and in others Cavil and Maran, appeared to them and induced them to commit the sin, just as he committed it with another demon, and from there it happened that not all of them held it to be a sin, saying that the god or the devil did it and persuaded them that it should not be considered a sin.

> Cerca del pecado nefando, lo que hay que con verdad decir es que nunca se vido entre aquellas gentes, antes se tuvo por grande y abominable pecado, hasta que les apareció un demonio en figura de indio, llamado Cu, y en otra lengua Chin, y en otras Cavil y Maran, que los indujo a que lo cometiesen, como él lo cometió con otro demonio, y de aquí vino a que no lo tuvieron algunos dellos por pecado, diciendo que pues

aquel dios o diablo lo cometía y lo persuadió, que no debía ser
pecado.

(Chap. 239, 358)

Here, Las Casas casts his apology in terms of a pre-Hispanic corruption
of the noble savage, blaming the "abominable sin" on the personified "de-
mons" who committed the act and later persuaded some of its accept-
ability. Subsequently, Las Casas slips in the idea that the perpetrator may
have been a deity ("dios o diablo"), thus providing the reader with a cultural analogy that he would later draw in comparison with the French,
the Greeks, the Romans, and the Philosophers (ibid., 358). That is, the
reader and the authorities should not judge the Amerindian without recalling their own ancestral experience with same-sex erotics. For these
Maya peoples, according to Las Casas, their deity's use of sodomy led to
the practice of fathers giving their adolescent sons young boys "to be used
as women" (ibid.), though a few lines later he adds that this custom was
frowned on by some and regulated by the community rules that controlled
female prostitution (ibid.). We begin to appreciate the double discourse
Las Casas employs: on the one hand, he provides cultural explanations of
these practices and connects them to European antiquity; on the other, he
condemns them as sinful.

   In a chapter on Cuba in the *Historia de las Indias,* Las Casas explicitly rejects Oviedo's assertions of pandemic sodomitical behavior in the Caribbean.[12] He goes on to say that he had never heard any reports of sodomy
from any of his contemporaries, including his father, and emphasized the
Amerindians' "natural goodness and lack of vices" [bondad natural que
tenían y carecían de vicios] (*Historia de las Indias,* 231).

   Las Casas's return to the "noble savage" rhetoric again opens his narrative to more ethnographic interpretations and analogies with Old World
traditions. In the subsequent paragraph he tells of finding one transvested
Indian on the island of Cuba, which raised suspicions regarding the sexuality of this one man, who "wore a skirt, which is female clothing" [traía
unas naguas, que es vestidura de mujer] (ibid., 231). Instead of confirming
that he was a "sodomite," Las Casas digresses by comparing this transvested
islander and the ancient European Scythians in order to defend him.[13] Las
Casas carefully undermines the dominant sodomy trope of his predecessors
by again establishing the correspondence between Old World sexuality and
the transvested Amerindians. This time he gives a "medical" explanation,
from classical sources, as to why the Scythians transvested and even trans-

gendered; that is, they not only dressed as women but also assumed the social roles of women. Thus, he denies sodomy while accepting cultural and
ritual explanations for the transvested Amerindians.

These transgendered subjects of Las Casas's "natural garden" will appear
again in writings by his followers. As I will argue below, Las Casas's discursive strategy informs the most extensive early writings on the Andes,
the subject of the rest of this chapter. The double discourse, highlighted
in Las Casas's writings, can be detected in his followers' attempts to write
protoethnographies in the Andes and affords us an opening to decolonize
the queer tropes of sexuality to reveal the deeper significance of the maligned transgendered subjects of coloniality.

TOWARD THE THIRD SPACE: CIEZA DE LEÓN AS PROTOETHNOGRAPHER

One of the most important fragments informing our knowledge of third-gender subjectivity in the Andes comes from the exhaus-
tive work by Pedro de Cieza de León (1518–1560), author of *La crónica del
Perú,* whose three volumes were first published between 1553 and Cieza's
death. Considered among the *"cronistas libres"* (free chroniclers) by Peruvian literary scholar Luis Alberto Sánchez,[14] Cieza has been regarded as
one of the few colonial scribes relatively independent from colonial authorities such as the church or the viceroyalty. While Sánchez characterizes
Cieza as a chronicler who "writes episodic history, without examining motives, without 'moralizing'" (*Literatura peruana,* 75), Sabine MacCormack
observes that Cieza's "was the first account to combine observation with
sustained reflection and analysis" (*Religion in the Andes,* 80).

This supposed "objectivity" with which Cieza describes Andean cultures will serve as a good starting point for our examination of the post-
Conquest representation of gender and sexuality. Although the new
generation of chroniclers, represented by Cieza, was much more ethnographically sophisticated than their predecessors, their texts do not necessarily prove to be "transparent" representations of indigenous practices. As
MacCormack has pointed out, "in the very process of translating and writing down what they were told, Spaniards inevitably introduced notions
of their own that had, strictly speaking, no Andean counterparts" (ibid.,
83). For Cieza, like other chroniclers, worked within the sixteenth-century
paradigm in which, in the words of Foucault, "to search for a meaning is
to bring to light a resemblance" (*Order of Things,* 29).

I sense in Cieza's writing, however, a certain recognition of difference that he cannot quite express in intelligible terms for his European reader(s). Cieza's writing seems to struggle for objectivity on topics that were ideologically charged in the cultural imaginary in which he wrote. He compels a subtle reading, for the complexity of the representation of gender and sexuality in his writings at times transcends the limits placed on him by the Las Casas–Sepúlveda debates, yet often the weight of that discourse seemingly pressures his sensibilities into moralistic rhetoric, despite Sánchez's claim to the contrary. I will highlight these tensions in the selections that discuss gender and sexuality.

In the first chapter of the first part of his chronicle, Cieza orients his reader to the ideology that will inform his entire narrative; conscious of his audience's prejudices, that is, that he is writing for the Spanish court, Cieza immediately differentiates between good and bad government.[15] Following the attitudes and writings of Las Casas, who had recently denounced the encomienda system and related abuses of the Amerindians, Cieza plainly states his position as loyal to the Crown's attempt to control the runaway power plays of the colonial encomenderos and governors. By aligning himself with the recently installed government of La Gasca, Cieza, once an encomendero himself, distances himself and the Crown from the abuses Las Casas outlines in *Brevísima relación* (1552) and earlier writings.[16] He applauds the Spanish Crown for the "gran cuydado se tuuiesse de la conuersión de las gentes de todas aquellas pouincias y reynos" [the great care with which they converted the people from all those provinces and kingdoms] while he scolds the encomenderos and governors for "causing the Indians many hardships and evil" [haziendo de los Indios muchas vexaciones y males] (25). Cieza alludes to the success of the "new laws of the Indies" put into place in November of 1542 to establish the Viceroyalty of Peru (25–26).

Although we know from recent scholarship that the abuses of Indians did not cease and that indigenous resistance to colonial aggression began to manifest itself in myriad ways, it is important to observe the rhetorical strategies employed by Cieza to present his history of the Andes to the ultimate colonial authorities.[17] A short, inconspicuous sentence in the first chapter sets the tone for the rest of the narrative. Having just described the results of the new "good" colonial government, Cieza adds, in good apologist form, that the Incas were good rulers, too (26), a discursive move equating the legendary Andean leader and empire-builder, Topa Inga Yupanque, with the Spanish emperor, Charles V. From the outset the reader is encouraged to encounter the Other, the Incas, as near equals. However, as

we will see, non-Inca indigenous groups are represented as less "civilized,"
as members of *behetrías* (free towns), without the advanced social and political structure he attributes to the Incas.[18]

While Cieza cannot be equated with the *chaupi*-like narrators of later
writings I discuss in this book, he does move toward a "third space" of
transculturation through this self-reflective positioning of his narratives in
the turbulent early years after the Conquest. His apologist style distances
him from the earlier and later chroniclers, who employed the tropes of
sexuality from the decidedly Spanish perspective discussed in Chapter 1.
Cieza's writings, along with those of the other apologists, provoked a reaction that motivated other historians and chroniclers to focus on the dele-
gitimation of the Incas as a justification for the Conquest and colonization
of the Andeans, a theme I explore in Chapters 4 and 5. Cieza fits in between these two extremes, and his rhetoric borrows from both discourses.

He further creates this "third" position in relation to the other chroniclers and historians by adding a new twist to his account. While his rhetorical strategy follows the traditional model of chronicling, protoethnographic tendencies slowly slip into his narrative, much as they did in Las
Casas's writings. Perhaps due to more contact with native informants,
greater fluency in native languages, and a more open mind-set, Cieza becomes one of the early transculturators, though the influence of the subjugated is still tempered by his European heritage.[19] Cieza creates an "alternative fiction," in the Lascasian tradition.

His protoethnographic tendencies begin to emerge from traditional
colonial discursive practices in chapters 2 through 5 of the first part, which
report on the navigation and exploration of the western South American
coast, paying particular attention to ports and navigable rivers. Even in this
standard chronicle fare, however, there are short passages that foreshadow
Cieza's ethnographic interests, fragments of cultural information that catch
the reader's attention, encouraging him or her to continue through the
detailed narrative. Here, Cieza uses tropes of gender and sexuality to en-
tice the reader, perhaps to awaken latent desire, just as his brief mentions
of buried gold and silver stimulate greed and ambition.[20] Observe his description of an island near Túmbez (near present-day Guayaquil, Ecuador):

> It is well known that since ancient times there are great sums
> of gold and silver buried in their temples. The Indians alive
> today say that the inhabitants of this island had grand religions
> and they were accustomed to telling the future and other

abuses: they were very prone to vices, and even though many of them practiced the abominable sin of sodomy, they also slept with their sisters and committed other great sins.

Ay fama que de antiguamente está enterrado en ella gran summa de oro y plata en sus adoratorios. Cuentan los Indios que oy son biuos, que usa-/uan los moradores de esta ysla grandes religiones, y eran dados a mirar agueros y en otros abusos: y que eran muy viciosos, y aunque sobre todo muchos dellos usauan el pecado abominable de sodomía dormían con sus hermanas carnales y hazían otros grandes pecados.

(34)

A few lines later Cieza implicitly contrasts these non-Inca peoples with the Incas, whom he describes as "the royal Incas of Cuzco and lords of all Peru" [los Yngas reyes del Cuzco y señores de todo el Perú]. By equating their customs with the ancient Romans, he elevates their status in the eyes of his European reader: "And there were sun temples, and a house for the Mamacones: which means important virgin women dedicated to the service of the temple. Almost like the custom that they had in Rome, where the vestal virgins lived and stayed" [Y auía templos del sol, y casa de Mamaconas: que quiere dezir mugeres principales vírgines, dedicadas al servicio del templo. Las cuales casi al uso de la costumbre que tenían en Roma las vírgines Vestales biuían y estauan] (35). Sodomites and virgins, two colonial tropes laden with significance, mark the two extremes of Andean societies that Cieza will travel in his chronicle. Sodomy and incest suggest depraved humanity of the *behetrías,* while the organization of virgins in the worship of the Sun echoed the Spaniards' own heritage. Thus the apology begins.

This rhetorical strategy of differentiation, which the Inca Garcilaso de la Vega will adopt in his famous *Comentarios reales* (analyzed in Chapter 5 here), begins in earnest with Cieza's chapter 6, when he begins tracing his route from the coast of Nueva Granada to Cuzco, Peru. The most remarkable characteristic of this description is his focus on cannibalism, which he claims the peoples of this area practiced with impunity. Álvaro Félix Bolaños has examined this other prevalent trope of colonial discourse in the writings of a later chronicler of Nueva Granada, observing that anthropophagy was a common feature of all late fifteenth-century representations of exotic lands and peoples (*Barbarie y canibalismo,* 152). It is no surprise, then, that cannibalism would form part of the colonial discourse of the Andes. Indeed, as I observed above, Christopher Columbus's first writings, accusing the indigenous Other of eating human flesh, were employed in the rhetorical battle for the Americas.[21] As Bolaños remarks, "The other, barbarous, savage, ferocious, and cannibal is, then, an extreme and intolerable challenge to Hispanic culture that demands a Spanish delimitation of their own nature in contrast to the bestiality of the indigenous American, on the one hand, and a 'just' eradication of the Indian, on the other" (*Barbarie y canibalismo*, 151). Bolaños follows Peter Hulme's understanding of these tropes as ways "to mark the boundary between one community and its others" (Hulme, *Colonial Encounters*, 86). In Cieza, we can appreciate similar discursive maneuvers.

What was implied before becomes explicit in chapter 13, in which Cieza compares Popayán, which was to the north of Quito, to the Incas' Perú: "all of the Indians subject to the government of Popayán have always been and are behetrías. There was not one lord among them who could subjugate them. They are indolent, lazy: and above all they hate to serve and to be subjugated" [todos los Indios subjetos a la gouernación de Popayán, han sido siempre y lo son behetrías. No vuo entre ellos señores que se hiziessen temer. Son floxos, perezosos: y sobre todo aborrecen el seruir y estar subjetos] (58). The Popayán people's laziness somehow turned into an intransigence that halted the Incas' northward expansion and troubled the Spanish colonization of the area, as Cieza notes. In contrast, the indigenous people of Peru (the southern Andes) were perfect colonial subjects, both for the Incas and for the Spaniards:

> Those of Peru serve well and are controllable: because they have more use of reason than these: and because all were subjugated by the lord Incas: to whom they paid tribute, always serving them; And in that condition they were born, and if they did not want to do it, necessity forced them to: because the land of Peru is unpopulated, full of mountains and snow-covered fields.

> Los del Perú siruen bien y son domables: porque tienen más razón que éstos: y porque todos fueron subjetados por los reyes Ingas: a los cuales dieron tributo, siruiéndolos siempre; Y en aquella condición nascían, y si no lo querían hazer, la necesidad les constreñía a ello: porque la tierra del Perú toda es despoblada, llena de montañas y campos nevados.

(58–59)

Cieza's is not a simple discourse of demonization of the indigenous non-Inca peoples. Indeed, his narrative construction of the Popayán Other is predicated on climate and geography; environmental determinism explains why the northern, more temperate climates spawned less sedentary and thus less easily dominated people. While the Popayán region had "fertile and cultivable land ready to produce . . . and they never lacked for food" [tierra fértil y aparejada y dispuesta para darles fruto . . . y nunca les falta de comer] (58), the harsh environment of the Peruvian Andean highlands required more discipline to produce sustenance. In these many chapters devoted to Popayán and its surrounding populations, Cieza offers an abundance of ethnographic detail. The thoroughness of his descriptions of customs and beliefs belies his more explicit rhetoric of differentiation. While Cieza differentiates the social and political structure of the two regions, cannibalism is the primary vice or sin that he accuses the non-Incas of practicing. There is no mention of sodomy and only marginal comments on incest. The lack of accusations of sodomy, which we will find in later chapters, encourages us to take those later discussions more seriously. In other words, Cieza does not merely employ the sodomy trope as a means of justifying the Conquest, without actually observing the practice or without having reliable witnesses to its existence; his narration is linked to his careful observation of Andean culture and to his translation of the culture into the European episteme. By providing ethnographic details, Cieza undermines the typical deployment of queer tropes of sexuality in Spanish colonial discourse.

In Quito, for example, Cieza encounters gender roles that are reversed from his European standard. Still, he judges the people to be hardworking, though different from others,

> it is the women who till the fields and care for the plantings and the harvests, and the husbands spin and weave and occupy themselves in making clothes and other women's work, which they must have learned from the Incas. For I have seen among the Indians of the time of the Incas in the villages near Cuzco that while the women were plowing, the men were weaving and preparing their arms and clothing and doing things more appropriate to women than to men.
>
> (*Discovery and Conquest,* 44–45)

porque las mugeres son las que labran los campos y benefician las tierras y miese: y los maridos hilan y texen, y se ocupan en hazer ropa, y se dan a otros oficios feminiles que deuieron aprender de los Ingas. Porque yo he visto en los pueblos de Indios comarcanos al Cuzco de la generación de los Ingas, mientras las mugeres están arando, estar ellos hilando, y aderezando sus armas y su vestido: y hazen cosas más pertenecientes para el uso de las mujeres, que no para el ejercicio de los hombres.

(131)

That gendered work roles were different in the Andes came as a surprise to Cieza, but not as something he should suppress, as would be the case with the Inca Garcilaso, as we will see in Chapter 5. These work roles, transgendered from the Spanish perspective, seemed to be common throughout Tawantinsuyu, even in Cuzco, he reports, where men would do yarn spinning and weaving while women would work in the fields. He even speculates that these customs were learned from the Incas.

Once in the Cañaris' territory, farther to the southeast of Quito, Cieza dedicates a chapter to the description of the Tomebamba lodgings, an Inca complex of palaces and temples favored by Inca Yupanque and his son, Topaynga (148). While Cieza's principal objective was to give an example of the Inca's system of empire building through establishing reciprocal relationships between conquered peoples, such as the Cañari and the Cuzco Incas, he also underscores how the female virgins served the Sun temple (145) and mentions male sentries who also served the temple:

> They and the priests were well supplied by those in charge of the maintenance of the temple, at whose gate there were gate-keepers (some of whom were said to be eunuchs), whose duty it was to watch over the *mamaconas,* as the virgins living in the temple were called.
>
> (70)

> Y ellas y los sacerdotes eran bien proueydos por los que tenían cargo del servicio del templo: a las puertas del qual auía porteros, de los quales se afirma que algunos eran castrados, que tenían cargo de mirar por las mamaconas: que así auían por nombre las que residían en los templos.
>
> (145–146)

Some of these guards were castrated and their role was to watch over the virgin *mamaconas*.[22] What was earlier the equivalent of a rhetorical flourish to get the reader's attention has become a richer and more detailed account of cultural difference.

While this brief mention reminds us of the Eastern tradition of eunuchs, which were familiar to the Spaniards through commercial and other cultural contacts with the East, we must ask ourselves if their roles were limited to being protectors of these women. Whether or not these castrated men are related to the third-gender subjectivity of other temples discussed below remains unclear. However, taking "third" in its metonymic capacity to represent "more than two," we might consider the possibility of multiple third-gender subjectivities in the Andes. Kathryn M. Ringrose has studied eunuchs in Byzantium and suggests that they be considered third-gender subjects due to their unique gender status: they were nonprocreative, of an altered physiology, assigned social roles inappropriate to other genders ("Living in the Shadows," 94), and occupied a liminal, sacred space (97). Although we have far less information from which to draw conclusions, Cieza's temple-dwelling, castrated virgin-watchers appear to have characteristics similar to those of the Byzantine eunuchs, which suggests the fluidity of Andean gender constructions. As his protoethnography continues, the reader begins to realize how complex the indigenous gender and sexual culture was, and how the chronicler framed cultural differences within Spanish morality, often vacillating between outright condemnation of what he witnessed to simply recording what he observed. His discourse is ambiguous, as if his curiosity battled with the moralist impulse of his Catholic background.

As Cieza turns his attention again to the Cañari women, their lecherous sexuality is linked to industrious productivity: "Some of the women are beautiful, and not a little lascivious, and fond of the Spaniards. They are hard workers, for it is the women who till and plant the fields and harvest the crops" [Las mugeres son algunas hermosas, y no poco ardientes en luxuria: amigas de Españoles. Son estas mugeres para mucho trabajo: porque ellas son las que cauan las tierras, y siembran los campos, y cogen las sementeras] (71). Is this an invitation or a condemnation? With a new twist on the "natural garden" figure, in which the Amerindian is represented in paradisiacal terms, as either a utopian or a critical trope,[23] Cieza presents the reader with an image of Cañari women as hardworking, sensual "friends" of the Spanish invaders. Their sexuality is judged within the Christian framework of *luxuria*, yet their nonprocreative sexual activity does not hinder them from producing agricultural harvests, which are generated because of their systematic perseverance, for the Andes is not the place of easily exploited abundance depicted in other, more temperate regions of the Americas. By inscribing the Cañari women's supposedly excessive sexuality in the Christian terms of *luxuria,* Cieza forgoes any other explanation of their "friendliness," such as the possible political agency of sexual acts I underscore in my reading of the gendered myths in the Huarochirí manuscript (Chapter 3). Could the Cañari women's sexual proclivities toward the Spanish have been their way of reestablishing social order through pairing with the conquering invaders? Or was Cieza's comment meant to discursively create a sense of Spanish magnanimity, as if the women's supposed "friendliness" could signify their acceptance of the Spanish colonization of the region? Indeed, the following sentence suggests that the women's new friends had displaced their own culture's men, for the Cañari men, instead of working in the fields, occupied themselves with "effeminate" tasks: "While their husbands for the most part stay indoors spinning and weaving and preparing their arms and clothing and caring for their faces, and other feminine occupations" (71–72) [Y muchos de sus maridos están en sus casas texendo, y hilando, y aderezando sus armas, y ropa, y curando sus rostros: y haciendo otros oficios afeminados (146)]. Meanwhile, when Spanish armies pass by and need porters for their gear, the local men send women to do the duty (146), which Cieza explains as being the result of the overabundance of women, who reportedly outnumbered the men twenty to one (147).

This noting of the "effeminate" roles Cañari men played in the post-Conquest society does not pertain only to the discourse of feminization other scholars have identified in colonial discourse. This shortage of men is blamed on Atahualpa's cruel massacre of the Cañari people to avenge his brother Antoco's murder (147). Here Cieza perhaps records the voice of the defeated Cañari; the voice of doubly subaltern people (the twice-conquered Cañari) finds its way into Cieza's writings, contributing to the process of transculturation. Is Cieza reporting what he observes or is he being fed information based on local ideologies and the agency of his informants? His next comment goes as far as to insist that while there were some oracles and "warlocks," "they do not indulge in the abominable sin and other idolatries" (72) [no se usan el pecado nefando, ni otras idolatrías (147)], thus recording these peoples as nonsodomites. Idolatrous practices that did exist were done in secret, while most lived as "Christians" (147). In contrast to these peoples, Cieza digresses to discuss an example of

Andeans who were considered more "barbarous" and lascivious than the Cañari.

The peoples of Puerto Viejo, because of their vicinity to the equinoctial line, were believed to be "not too healthy" [no muy sanos]. Cieza situates his ethnography in the classical debates of the uninhabitability of the torrid zone, to which he contributes his observations of the inhabitants, their customs, and the region's ecology. He informs us that it was reported by some that these Amerindians were never subjugated by the Incas, while others insisted that they were Inca subjects, conquered by Guaynacapac himself (155). Here the chronicler makes an aside that advances our understanding of transculturation in colonial contexts and that should caution all colonial scholars reading the chronicles and *relaciones* of the Americas, a bit of advice that will become even more relevant in Chapter 4 here. The following passage reveals how the local informant adds to the process of transculturation; that is, as an agent of the culture being deculturated he contributes to the dominant discourse by way of his so-called *fábulas y novelas:*

> since all things about these people are confused versions and they never tell the absolute truth, it does not surprise me that they say this, since in greater matters they dissimulate without thinking, which later remains a part of the people's understanding, and should not serve sane people except as fables and novels. . . . most of the things the common people tell of events that have occurred in Peru are versions such as these.
>
> como todas las cosas del pueblo sea una confusión de variedad, y jamás saben dar en el blanco de la verdad: no me espanto que me digan esto, pues en otras cosas mayores fingen disuaríos no pensados: que después quedan en el sentido de las gentes: y no ha de servir para entre los cuerdos: sino de fábulas y nouelas. . . . en las más de las cosas que el vulgo quenta de los acontecimientos que han passado en Perú, son variaciones como arriba digo.
>
> (155)

The lack of confidence Cieza has in his sources reflects the precarious nature of all the colonial "fictions" that constitute Andean historiography; however, the fact that Cieza broaches the subject at this point in the text merits our attention. He is intimating the conflicted nature of the history of this region, a region that ferociously resisted the expansion of the Inca empire. He reports that the first Inca incursions into the area left some governors from Cuzco to "civilize" the inhabitants (156). It would seem that Cieza's informants, partial to the Inca perspective, serve to propagate the notion of the Incas' civilizing mission, a project that was rejected by the peoples of Puerto Viejo. After telling of the Incas' difficulty in conquering these people, Cieza reveals the "real" reason the Incas did not reside in the area: there were no opulent lodges like those of the Cañari, because of the poor state of the land and the few people who inhabited it.

There are slippages, however, in this rhetoric of civilization, for Cieza informs us that the inhabitants of Puerto Viejo made use of "great religions," organized by a group of priests and carried out in temples, where they conducted elaborate ceremonies and sacrifices (157). Of course, these devotions are attributed to the powers of the devil, who spoke to the people through the oracles (158). In contrast to the virgin *mamaconas* exalted in the Inca-occupied territories, here the women were married only after having been "corrupted" by other men in the community (159–160). While the implication is that the civilized culture kept its women virgin and the barbarians violated their young girls, Cieza is actually comparing the supposedly "sacred" use of virgins with the profane custom of "marriage." The effect is to discredit the people of Puerto Viejo, to represent them as barbarians in comparison with the civilizing Incas.

Corrupt female sexuality was not the only "vice" reported by Cieza, who after digressing a few lines about their delicious cornbread and making a brief insinuation of cannibalism, declares that the inhabitants of Puerto Viejo practice sodomy:

> Since these people were evil and full of vices, despite there being many women among them, and a few beautiful ones, most of the men practiced (which they attested to me) publicly and shamelessly the nefarious sin of sodomy, which they say they enjoyed too much.

> Pues como estos fuessen malos y viciosos, no embargante que entre ellos auía mugeres muchas: y algunas hermosas, lo más dellos usauan (a lo que a mí me certificaron) pública y descubiertamente el pecado nefando de la sodomía: en lo qual dizen que se gloriauan demasiadamente.

(160)

Cieza seems surprised that, even though there were ample attractive women, the men still openly partook of same-sex sodomy. By using the imperfect verb tense Cieza implies that they used to commit this sin in the indeterminate past, an accusation that was somehow "attested" to him, presumably by indigenous informants. The chronicler is quick to add that two Spanish captains, Pacheco and Olmos, punished the sodomites and so shamed them that they stopped their practices, including other religious customs (160).

From this information we learn of the Spanish disciplinary actions carried out against those accused of sodomy, a practice documented in chronicles and *relaciones* from other parts of the Americas and the Andes, such as the Balboa massacre discussed above.[24] Here Cieza records the first moments in the Andes of the violent process that will lead to the transculturation of indigenous sexuality, a process whose effect reportedly took hold first among the youths: "It is true that the faith is better imprinted on the young than on the elderly" [Verdad es que la fe imprime mejor en los mozos que no en muchos viejos] (160). The older Andeans, on the other hand, continued to practice their customs in secret, despite the punishment administered by the Spanish authorities. This linking of sodomy with other religious practices deemed to be idolatrous foreshadows what Cieza will report later in his chronicle. In fact, as we will see below, the sexual practices that went from public to clandestine may have been used in sacred ways. But first, Cieza tells a fabled story.

THE UNINTELLIGIBLE MYTH OF SODOMITICAL GIANTS

At this point in his chronicle, Cieza interrupts the observation of the environment, peoples, and customs to relate a story told to him about a group of giants who came to the area near Puerto Viejo. The rendering of this story takes on characteristics of a didactic, moralizing text populated by superhuman characters whose flaws or sins are punished through divine intervention. I read this story as one of the richest of the early textual evidences of transculturation of same-sex sexuality in the Andes, a point that can be understood only by taking into consideration the information that Cieza has already offered us about the people of Puerto Viejo. The critics I discuss below lift this myth out of the context of Cieza's narrative, primarily because they take it from Inca Garcilaso's quote of Cieza, and not directly from Cieza's chronicle.

This story, which will be retold by several other chroniclers and historians, is about a group of giant, sodomy-practicing men who arrived from the sea by boat to Santa Elena, a point near Puerto Viejo. The hyperbolic description of their bodies creates an image of fearsome monsters; their body parts exceed the indigenous people's notions of normalcy: "greatly deformed bodies," "it is a monstrous thing to see their heads," "eyes as big as plates" [cuerpos tan difformes, cosa monstrosa ver las cabeças, ojos . . . como pequeños platos] (166). To nourish their excessive bodies, the giants consumed fifty times the normal portion of food, which soon depleted the locals' food supply. But it was their sexuality that marked them for divine destruction.

Because the giants arrived without their own women, they were said to have tried sex with the local women: "They were greatly hated by the locals because, when they used their women, they killed them, and with the local men they also practiced their lasciviousness" [Biuieron en grande aborrecimiento de los naturales: porque por usar de sus mugeres las matauan, y con ellos también vsauan sus luxurias] (167). Because of their (implied) abnormal size, they killed the local women, which left them no other choice but to pursue sexual pleasure with the local men, and as the following passage reveals, among themselves, as well:

> since they had no women of their own and the local women were too small for their great size or because it was probably a vice used among them because of the inducement and advice of the devil, they practiced among themselves the nefarious sin of sodomy, so serious and horrendous. Which they did publicly and openly, without fear of God and little shame of themselves.

> como les faltassen mugeres: y las naturales no les quadrassen por su grandeza, o porque sería vicio vsado entre ellos por consejo y induzimiento del maldito demonio, vsauan unos con otros el pecado nefando de la sodomía, tan gravíssimo y horrendo. El qual vsauan y cometían pública y descubiertamente, sin temor de Dios, y poca vergüença de sí mismos.

(167)

Cieza blames their use of the "nefarious sin," if not on the limits of the native women's physical ability to satisfy them, then on the devil, who "advised and induced" them into their public display of male-male sexual licentiousness. Cieza retells this story within a Christian frame of reference, as if the informants understood the giants in terms of Christian good and evil. The audacity of the giants is that they acted "without fear of God," conforming instead to the will of the devil. Cieza goes as far as to place the Christian moral message in the mouths of the terrorized locals:

> And all the locals affirm that since our lord God could not dissuade them from committing the sin, he sent them a punishment equal to the ugliness of the sin. And they say that when they [the giants] were all together partaking of their evil sodomy, a terrifying and fearsome fire fell loudly down from the heavens: and from out of this fire emerged a resplendent angel with a sharp and shining sword with which he killed them all with one swing of the blade and the fire consumed them; only a few bones and skulls remained from the fire, as a reminder of God's punishment. This is what they say of the giants, which we believe happened because in this area they have found and still find gigantic bones.

> Y afirman todos los naturales, que Dios nuestro señor no siendo seruido de dissimular peccado tan malo, le embió el castigo conforme a la fealdad del peccado. Y assí dizen, que estando todos juntos embueltos en su maldita sodomía, vino fuego del cielo temerosos y muy espantable, haziendo gran ruydo: del medio del qual salió vn ángel resplandesciente con vna espada tajante y muy refulgente, con la qual de vn golpe los mató a todos, y el fuego los consumió: que no quedó sino algunos huessos y calaueras, que para memoria del castigo quiso Dios que quedassen sin ser consumida del fuego. Esto dizzen de los gigantes: lo que creemos que passó: porque en esta parte que dizense han hallado y se hallan huessos grandíssimos.

(167–168)

The obvious intertextual relationship between this description of the divine punishment of the sodomitical giants of Puerto Viejo and the biblical passage regarding Sodom and Gomorrah has been observed by several critics. Efraín Kristal has observed the classical antecedents of this story in the presence of havoc-wreaking giants in Genesis 6:4, who are destroyed in the universal Flood, which may have inspired Ovid's myth of Jupiter destroying with lightning the bad giants in the first book of Metamorphosis ("Fábulas clásicas y neoplatónicas," 58). Richard Trexler reads the story as a Pan-American fable of the dangers of sexual infection (*Sex and Conquest,* 143–145). Jonathan Goldberg offers the most nuanced reading of the story, investigating the possibilities with a series of questions:

> Is this story about native tradition one that the natives tell about the Spaniards, whose concepts have forever altered the native understanding of their own myths and practices? Or is it a story that the Spaniards tell as if it were a native account, in order to produce "good" Indians who "properly" abominate sodomy? Or is it a story that the natives tell to the Spaniards as if it were traditional, accommodating their beliefs to Spanish ones, but keeping in reserve their own story under the cover of this acceptable one? By the time this story is told, can one separate native and Christian beliefs?
>
> ("Sodomy in the New World," 50)

Goldberg insightfully concludes that the story, no matter its cultures of origin and precisely because of its ambiguity, reflects the instability of sodomy as a trope employed in either or both traditions.

I argue that it is impossible to separate out the different cultural strands of discourse that create this hybrid myth. As we will see, each teller of the tale has his objectives and adds his own (or his informants') twist to the story in accordance with his needs and desires. Indeed, Cieza's account embellishes the story with the discourse of "divine punishment" while his contemporary, Agustín Zárate, in *Historia del descubrimiento y conquista del Perú* (1555), tells the story in order to explain the mystery of oversized bones found by the Spanish explorer Juan de Olmos, the same Spaniard who reportedly disciplined the average-sized sodomites he found in Puerto Viejo. The inclusion of an avenging angel, the archangel Michael, perhaps adds to the transculturation of the story, creating a hybrid text with both Spanish and Andean signs and referents. An engraving of the destruction of the giants, complete with flying angel pouring fire down upon them, accompanied Cieza's chronicle, suggesting that this episode caught the imagination of his readers, or at least of the printer of his manuscript (Figure 3).

Can we get beyond this ambiguity to understand what the myth might have signified for the locals of Puerto Viejo? That is, can we answer the

FIGURE 3   *Sodomitical giants of Santa Elena. From Cieza,* La crónica del Perú.

questions posed and left unanswered by Goldberg? It seems unlikely that
a native version of this myth is a metaphorical explanation of the Spanish invasion, except insofar as the biblical punishment for sodomy, already
mentioned by Cieza, might have been incorporated as an appeasing and
assimilating gesture, that is, as a gesture of cultural resistance that covers
the story's original meaning. To approach the "original meaning" is to risk
an assertion of a native myth that may never have existed. Could the giant
story be purely an imaginative fable that Cieza inscribed on the already
established "immoral" Puerto Viejo peoples? Three elements of the story
encourage us to risk an indigenous version, despite this possibility: first,
that giants seem to be, as Trexler points out, a Pan-American mythic trope,
although not all are depicted as sodomites (*Sex and Conquest,* 145); second

are the metanarrative comments Cieza offers as prelude to the myth; and third is the mention of the deep wells constructed in the area.

The statement that the giants came from the sea to the Andes could be a reference to giants from other parts of the Americas, perhaps the natives' strategy to displace on outsiders rather than on their own culture what, with the arrival of the Spaniards, had become a dangerous sexual practice due to the public punishments inflicted on the practitioners. Indeed, as we saw above, Cieza mentions the Spaniards' severe punishment of sodomy in the area. This element of the story assumes that the native version includes the divine-retribution aspects of the account; that is, it assumes that the natives considered sodomy immoral. If the natives did tell a story of invading giants, their principal grievance was more likely the intruders' consumption of resources than their sexual behavior, for Cieza has already told us that the Puerto Viejo peoples practiced, unashamedly, same-sex erotics. In this light, we see how Cieza's rendering of the myth slips when read in the context of his complete ethnography. Why would a people who earlier were reported as unabashed sodomites fabricate a story that delegitimizes their own cultural practices? The only answer lies in a broader strategy of cultural survival that depended on interlacing resistant silences with fictitious confessions conforming to Spanish morality. Here we see the workings of transculturation, for the natives' transformation of their local myths, as a strategy of survival, ends up influencing the discourse that will represent them to the world. The myth is left in the colonial discourse as a neoculturation, a phantasm of originary performances of gender and sexual subjectivities.

Before Cieza even tells the story, however, he warns us of the unreliability of the informants; in fact, he purports to ignore the commoners' opinions and recounts what he has understood from local stories passed down from generation to generation:

> I thought it would be good to report what they said of these [giants], according to how I understood it, without considering the opinions of the common people and their diverse tales, since they always exaggerate things more than they were. The natives repeat stories they heard from their parents, which they had heard very long ago, that they [giants] came from over the sea.

> me paresció dar noticia de lo que ay dellos según que yo lo entendí, sin mirar las opiniones de el vulgo y sus dichos varios,

que siempre agrandece las cosas más de lo que fueron. Cuentan
los naturales por relación que oyeron de sus padres, la qual
ellos tuvieron y tenían de muy atrás que vinieron por la mar.

(166)

This ambiguity of the chronicler's sources might lead one to discount
the entire myth as his own or another outsider's fabrication; at the very
least we should inquire about who the *"naturales"* [natives] who tell the
stories are. Why does he establish the opposition between the *"vulgo"* [com-
mon people] and the "natives?" Do both refer to the Puerto Viejo people,
or could "natives" refer to Inca-identified informants from Cuzco or Lima,
two places from which Cieza wrote and polished his account?[25] If the "natives" were indeed Inca-identified informants, then the entire myth could
be read as a text of interethnic rivalry in which the Incas, all too familiar with Spanish colonial rhetoric, demonize the Puerto Viejo peoples in a
narrative that then suggests the giants to have been figured as indomitable,
for this was a region that successfully resisted the Inca expansion. The accusation of sodomy would then function to explain in Christian terms the
cultural difference that in indigenous terms was figured as bodily excess.
This rhetorical strategy would at once excuse the Incas' weakness vis-à-vis
the enemy and establish the Other as monstrous.

If, however, the informants were locals from Puerto Viejo, then the
giants might take on another significance, one related to the topography
of the region, and serve specifically as a mythological explanation of deep
wells constructed there: "to make up for the lack of water they made some
extremely deep wells, a task certainly worthy of memory, achieved by such
strong men, as one would presume them to have been, given their large
stature" [para remediar la falta que della [agua] sentían hizieron unos pozos
hondíssimos: obra por cierto digna de memoria, hecha por tan fortíssimos
hombres, como se presume que serían aquellos: pues era tanta su grandeza]
(167). The awe-inspired tone of this passage, along with later remarks about
the freshness of the water and the timeless quality of the construction of the
wells suggest that the locals were proud of these industrious accomplishments.[26] One might assume that the locals would assign positive values to
those responsible for constructing such a beneficial structure in the area.
But, just after this affirmation, Cieza relates how the giants ate the locals
out of their food supply, even depleting the ocean of its fish (167).

If this story is an Andean myth of Conquest politics, like the ones I analyze in the Huarochirí manuscript in the next chapter, then we can under-

stand the connection between outside invader and aquatic technology in much the same way as we understand the invading Yauyo water *huacas* (deities) and the water-needy, conquered Yunga peoples of the lowlands.[27] Just as indigenous sexuality played a role in the retelling of the post-Conquest relationships between *huacas,* here in Puerto Viejo there might have been similar meanings of the sexuality between invading "giants" and the aboriginal peoples. How these relationships became figured in Cieza's version as same-sex sodomy remains a mystery. Reinscribing this myth in a Christian discourse, however, clearly served the chronicler's purpose of transmitting unintelligible cultural concepts, such as water-deity, Conquest politics, to a European reader while at the same time distinguishing the barbarian Puerto Viejo peoples from the more "civilized" Incas, the true object of Cieza's Lascasian apologetic tendencies.

The mythic giants took on a literary life of their own, appearing in many subsequent chronicles and histories. Pedro Gutiérrez de Santa Clara (1522–1603), the son of a *converso* (converted Jew) from Salamanca and an indigenous mother from New Spain, joined Gonzalo Pizarro's group of soldiers around 1542 and participated in the Conquest and later civil wars in Peru. His chronicle, *Quinquenarios o Historia de las guerras civiles del Perú* (1580), includes a chapter on the giants and provides additional details for an understanding of this transculturated myth. His accounting of the giants follows his brief and celebratory survey of the Inca empire, a digression from his primary objective: to narrate the tumultuous intrigues of the civil wars in post-Conquest Peru.

After apologizing for having bothered his "pious reader" with his circumlocutions through the glories of the Incas, Gutiérrez cannot resist one more "*cuento,*" a story he is compelled to relate before returning to the Spaniards' political complicities. His version contextualizes in the dynamics of the governance of Tawantinsuyu the same basic tale that Cieza tells. Whether Gutiérrez found in this myth an analogy to the Pizarro rebellion is an intriguing possibility worth considering, though I will concentrate on the connections between his version and Cieza's. Here again we can appreciate how the queer tropes of sexuality are activated for the chronicler's ideological purposes, this time in a transculturated fable of insurrection and restoration of central authority. The link between the locals of Puerto Viejo sending for help to imperial Cuzco finds its parallel in Gutiérrez's subsequent chapter, in which he narrates how Spanish loyalists embark to Spain to ask for help from Prince Phillip (bk. 4, chap. 1). We begin to appreciate the historicity of myths, the idea that myths are related to a locus of enunciation, just like any literary or historical text. In Gutiérrez's version, the presence of the Incas is a new addition. Did Cieza keep the Incas out of the story for some reason? Perhaps they did not play neatly into his narrative strategy of differentiation. Or maybe his informants simply did not include the Incas in the story.

According to Gutiérrez, Topa Inga Yupanque was the reigning Inca at the time the giants are said to have appeared in Puerto Viejo, arriving in reed boats from southern islands and disturbing the peace of the land (*Quinquenarios,* 257). The giants began to displace the locals and the Inca forces in the area, until Topa Inga Yupanque sent two great *curacas* (chiefs), one from Chimo and one from Piura, to pacify them. Gutiérrez gradually builds the hyperbole in his use of epithets to describe the giants, beginning with "luciferous monsters" [luciferinos monstruos] and "demonic and ferocious" [endiablados y feroces] until reaching "very ferocious and gigantic disturbers of the peace" [ferosísimos gigantes perturbadores de la paz] in the moments leading up to the Incas' rescue of their local "vassals" (ibid., 257). The Incas pacify the region and assign the surviving giants, at the behest of the locals, to a plot of barren land in the peninsula of Tangarara, named Santa Elena by the Spaniards (ibid., 258). To survive the infertile environment that was their prison, the giants dug the deep wells Cieza mentions, which produce fresh water, and they began to build houses.

The bachelor giants eventually try to mate with the local women, but their size, as in Cieza's version, ends up killing their lovers and provoking another reproach by the Inca protectors of the locals. The giants, fearing more reprisals from the Incas, promise to leave the women alone. This abstinence leads to frustration and sin:

> These wicked ones, who found themselves so long without women, and the devil, who had tricked them and blinded them and distracted them from natural reason, had a huge drunken party in which they began to use the nefarious sin; and they were in this state of diabolical vice for so many years that they no longer were ashamed of it and they practiced it publicly. The natives, when they learned that these luciferous Indians used this evil sin, said that they were dogs and brutish animals or that they were demons who had come to this world in the figure of men.

> Viéndose éstos endemoniados tanto tiempo sin mujeres, y el demonio que los traía engañados y ciegos y distraídos de la razón natural, hicieron una gran borrachera, en donde co-

menzaron a usar el pecado nefando, y así estuvieron en este
diabólico vicio muchos años, que ya no tenían verguenza ni
se les daba nada usarlo públicamente. Los naturales, cuando
supieron que estos indios luciferinos usaban este tan maldito
pecado, decían que aquellos eran perros y brutos animales,
o que eran demonios que habían salido del infierno a este
mundo en figura de hombre.

(Ibid., 258–259)

The locals are said to have reproached the giants for their use of sodomy,
seemingly distancing themselves from cultural practices that were so obviously anathema to the Spanish, as they learned when the local encomendero began to burn the sodomites. The latter, in Gutiérrez's opinion, had
learned the behavior from the "diabolical giants":

> For my part, I believe that the Indians of Manta whom we
> see today learned this diabolic and horrendous vice from their
> ancestors and from the older of these giants, because to this
> day they use it in their rituals and ceremonies and in their
> drunken parties. Juan de Olmos, a citizen and the highest
> judicial official of the village of Puerto Viejo, burned a great
> many of these perverse and diabolic Indians, even though the
> town was part of his encomienda, so that they would stop
> practicing this pestilent and luciferous vice.

> Para mi tengo creído que los indios de Manta que vimos
> en nuestros días, deprendieron de sus antepasados y de los
> mayores destos gigantes este diabólico y horrendo vicio, por-
> que el día de hoy lo usan ellos en sus ritos y ceremonias y en
> sus borracheras. Juan de Olmos, vecino de la villa de Puerto
> Viejo, quemó gran cantidad destos perversos y diabólicos
> indios, como justicia mayor que era allí entonces, aunque el
> pueblo estaba en su encomienda, para que se apartaran deste
> tan pestífero y luciferino vicio.

(Ibid., 259)

Gutiérrez records that Juan de Olmos, being the good encomendero
that he was reported to be, burned a great number of sodomites to punish
them for their sins. It is important to note that, in this version, the prac-

tice of sodomy is reported to be linked to religious practices, to rituals and ceremonies, an issue I take up in the next section of this chapter. The locals, or the chronicler, as in Cieza's version, however, seem to have conflated this act of violence with the catechism lessons and sermons that I study in Chapter 4, for the fires of destruction, according to the locals, came from a resplendent, "beautiful youth" flying from the sky:

> The natives say that one day, while the giants were performing certain terrible sacrifices and using the nefarious sin, a very beautiful young boy came flying down from the sky, with great splendor, and that he rained down so much fire over them that he burned them all alive, but a few escaped because they were down under the earth.

> Dicen más los naturales, que estando un día estos gigantes en ciertos sacrificios pésimos y usando el pecado nephando, vino un mancebo muy hermoso, volando del cielo, con gran resplandor, y que derramó tanto fuego sobre ellos que los quemó a todos vivos, y que escaparon algunos dellos porque estaba dentro en la tierra.

> (Ibid., 259)

The beauty of the angelic boy fighting the *luxuria* of the giants recalls Saint Pelagius and his stand against the sodomitical Moors. The heavenly fires hark back to the destruction of Sodom and Gomorrah. This representation of sodomites breaks with the trope of effeminacy we saw with the Moors and even the third-gendered Barbuda de Peñaranda discussed in Chapter 1; the giants are figured as ferocious, demonic warriors, while the "beautiful" boy, in contrast, signals chaste purity. What remains, though, is a sense of the monstrous, of the excessive and transgressive bodies that threatened patriarchal order. As if the angel's appearance could be too fantastic for his readers, Gutiérrez finishes his story by offering material proof that the giants did indeed exist: the presence of the inexplicable deep wells and the giant bones that even Francisco Pizarro was known to have seen (ibid., 259).

QUEER BODIES IN SACRED SPACES

As we have seen thus far, Cieza seems to struggle with the ethnographic material, wrestling with his Christian conscience while trying to represent the Incas as proto-Christians. His most difficult test might have been whether to include what perhaps is the most transgressive of protoethnographies in his entire chronicle. This passage is written in the double discourse of other Lascasian writings; on the one hand, the indigenous practices are condemned through a rhetoric that became standard in the extirpation-of-idolatry campaigns; on the other, the text reveals an understanding of cultural practices that undermine colonial discourse's criteria of queer tropes of sexuality. The dilemma presents itself as Cieza turns his attention to the Yungas, the people who lived in the *llanos,* or plains, that are located in the valleys along the northern Peruvian coast. Cieza provides detailed information based on his observations and on reports given to him by Domingo de Santo Tomás, a Dominican friar who spent long periods of time in the region (191) and is known for his Quechua grammar and lexicon, as well as a Quechua-language sermon.[28] After dedicating two chapters to the burial customs of the Yungas, Cieza transmits a text that the Dominican friar gave him concerning same-sex temple sodomy and cross-dressing temple attendants. While several critics have referenced this scandalous passage, none has remarked on Cieza's caution in presenting it to his reader(s) or given it the in-depth critical attention it deserves.[29] By placing this text in the center of my reconstruction of third-gender subjectivity, I move toward a decolonization of the queer tropes of sexuality discussed above and in later chapters. This account of temple sodomy performed by transgendered subjects not only provides the reader abundant ethnographic details, but also suggests the need for rereading many other reports of sodomy and cross-dressing in the Andes. Furthermore, the evidently sacred context of the sexual act poses the question of how the body and sexuality, including same-sex sexuality, played culturally procreative roles in Andean society. Perhaps it is this public use of the body, a corporeal semiotics of cultural reproduction, that most disturbed the missionaries and chroniclers and made the inclusion of this report a dangerous act.

Cieza writes an extended preamble to the Santo Tomás text, justifying the addition of the text to his chronicle: "For it is just that those of us who are Christians be curious: for knowing and understanding the evil customs of these allows us to separate them from them and make them understand the path of truth, so that they be saved" [porque es justo, que

los que somos Christianos tengamos alguna curiosidad: para que sabiendo
y enteniendo las malas costumbres destos, apartarlos de ellas, y hazerles entender el camino de verdad, para que se salven] (199). Here, curiosity is a
Christian virtue, for only through the power of knowing the Other could
the Spanish hope to convert them. Taking into consideration the censor-
ship of the Inquisition and the Consejo de Indias, this prelude might have
been necessary, for as Lydia Fossa has pointed out, only Cieza's first volume
was allowed to be published; the rest of his chronicles languished in the archives until the twentieth century.[30] Fossa has gone as far as to suggest that
the ideology informing Cieza's chronicle can be stripped away in order to
obtain a more indigenous reading of his observations, a strategy she employs in her reading of the Capac Hucha Inca ritual and that informs my
own interpretation of the passage in question. Cieza insists in these pre-
paratory remarks that he has witnessed sodomy only in the areas around
Puerto Viejo and the island of Puna and claims that the Incas were "clean"
of this sinful vice (199).

Cieza's denial of sodomites among the Incas is an echo from Las Casas's
invention of an American "natural garden" free of same-sex sexuality.
Cieza extends his disavowal of Inca sodomites in the second part of his
chronicle, in which he dedicates a whole chapter to this theme: "de cómo
los Yngas fueron limpios del pecado nefando y de otras fealdades que se
an visto en otros príncipes en el mundo" (chap. 25) [Of how the Incas
were clean of the nefarious sin and other ugliness that has been seen in
other princes of the world]. This second installment in his Andean trilogy,
also known as the *Señorío de los Incas,* was written in Cuzco between the
years 1548 and 1550 ("Introducción," *Segunda parte,* xxix). Unlike the sources
in the *Primera parte,* Cieza's sources for this account of the Inca ascendancy and rule in the Andes were mostly the official historians of Cuzco's
Inca elite (xxxi). This chapter refuting the practice of sodomy among the
Incas, therefore, comes as no surprise. By the 1550's the rhetorical battles
had begun over whether the Incas were "natural lords" of their region or
"tyrannical usurpers" and colonizers of the Andean people, a debate that
would reach its climax with the arrival of the reformist viceroy, Francisco
de Toledo, twenty years later (to be discussed in Chapter 4). The official
Inca historians and their apologist interpreters would increasingly position
the Incas as preparing the way for Christian evangelization. Cieza's literary mission, as the official chronicler of Gasca and in good Lascasian form,
was clear: to continue the distinction between civilizing Incas and barbaric non-Incas. Sodomites in Cuzco were untenable. As we will see below,

however, this queer-free Cuzco was yet another colonial fiction, one that falls apart as Cieza's ethnographic impulse undermines the ideology of his overall project.

Given Cieza's preamble to this text, we can begin to appreciate its potentially transgressive appeal: a queer passage that both expresses and interrupts the hegemonic ideology carried in the tropes of sexuality that the Lascasian-identified writer, Domingo de Santo Tomás, and compiler, Cieza, wished to undermine, yet also employ, in their differentiation between Incas and non-Incas:

> It is true that as a general thing among the mountaineers and the Yungas the devil has introduced this vice under a kind of cloak of sanctity, and in each important temple or house of worship they have a man or two, or more, depending on the idol, who go dressed in women's attire from the time they are children, and speak like them, and in manner, dress, and everything else imitate women. With these, almost like a religious rite or ceremony, on feast [days] and holidays, they have carnal, foul intercourse, especially the chiefs and headmen. I know this because I have punished two, one of them of the Indians of the highlands, who was in a temple which they call *huaca,* for this purpose, in the province of the Conchucos, near the city of Huánuco, the other in the province of Chincha, where the Indians are subjects of His Majesty. And when I spoke to them of the evil they were doing, and upbraided them for the repulsiveness of the sin, they answered me that it was not their fault because from childhood they had been put there by the caciques to serve them in this cursed and abominable vice, and to act as priests and guard the temples of their idols. So what I deduced from this was that the devil held such sway in this land that, not satisfied in making them fall into so great sin, he made them believe that this vice was a kind of holiness and religion, to hold more power over them.

(314)

> Verdad es, que generalmente entre los serranos et Yungas ha el demonio introduzido este vicio debaxo de specie de sanctidad. Y es, que cada templo o adoratorio principal tiene vn hombre o dos, o más: según es el ydolo. Los cuales andan vestidos como

mugeres dende [*sic*] el tiempo que eran niños, y hablauan como
tales: y en su manera, trage, y todo lo demás remedauan a las
mugeres. Con estos casi como por via de sanctidad y religión
tienen las fiestas y días principales su ayuntamiento carnal y
torpe: especialmente los señores y principales. Esto sé porque
he castigado a dos: el vno de los indios de la sierra, que estaua
para este efecto en un templo que ellos llaman Guaca de la
prouincia de los Conchucos, término de la ciudad de Guánuco:
el otro era en la prouincia de Chincha indios de su magestad.
A los quales hablándoles yo de esta maldad que cometían, y
agrauándoles la fealdad del pecado me respondieron: que ellos
no tenían culpa, porque desde el tiempo de su niñez los auían
puesto allí sus Caciques, para vsar con ellos este maldito y
nefando vicio, y para ser sacerdotes y guarda de los templos
de sus Indios. De manera que lo que les saqué de aquí es, que
estaua el demonio tan señoreado en esta tierra: que no se con-
tentando con los hazer caer en pecado tan innorme: les hazía
entender, que tal vicio era especie de sanctidad y religión, para
tenerlos más subjetos.

(199–200)

This detailed account of what I characterize as third-gender ritual subjectivity merits an extended analysis and requires an understanding of a
number of Andean cultural concepts. It is the richness of detail that ultimately subverts Cieza's claims of the Incas' sodomitical impunity. My interpretation of this excerpt will lead us to reconsider fundamental concepts
of Andean gender culture and cultural reproduction in general, the subject
of Chapter 3.

First, it is important to understand that Domingo de Santo Tomás contradicts Cieza's assertion that sodomy was not to be found among the Incas,
for we learn that two of the third-gender subjects the Dominican disciplined lived in Inca-controlled areas, Huánuco in the northern Peruvian
Andes, and Chincha to the south of Lima. Domingo de Santo Tomás claims
that it was the devil who inspired this practice. Luis Millones has pointed
out how the figure of the devil operates in Cieza's chronicle as a way of
incorporating the Andeans into the Christian world view and into universal history (183). We have already seen how Las Casas uses the "devil" as a
synonym for indigenous deities in the double discourse of his apology. In
Chapter 3 I will return to this issue of causes or mythical origin of same-

sex sacred praxis and discuss more fully the Andean paradigm in which the "devil" as instigator of cultural practice can be understood.

We have other evidence that disproves the notion that third gender was limited to the coastal areas. Ludovico Bertonio, a Jesuit linguist who arrived in Peru in 1578 to work in the missions, began compiling a dictionary of Aymara terms in 1595, which was published seven years later. Bertonio was known for his careful gathering of linguistic material, which he accomplished through working with native informants in Juli, a Jesuit mission in the southern Andes near Lake Titicaca.[31] Among the various entries related to third-gender subjectivities we find this definition: "*Huaussa, Keussa, Ipa:* One (a male) who lives, dresses, speaks, and works as a woman, and is the passive participant in the nefarious sin, just as in olden times there used to be many in this land" [Uno que vive, viste, habla, y trabaja como muger, y es paciente en el pecado nefando, al modo que antiguamente solía aver muchos en esta tierra" (ibid., 154)]. Here Bertonio has left us a concise image of third-gender subjects as reported to him by native informants and has suggested that the practice was more widespread than Cieza had earlier reported. Furthermore, Cieza contradicts himself much later in his chronicle when discussing the peoples of Lake Titicaca, who also practiced temple sodomy: "Of these it is understood that they detest the nefarious sin: given that they say that some of the rural countrymen that shepherded livestock practiced it secretly: and those that they put in the temples induced by the devil: as I have already told" (278) [Destos se tiene, que aborrescían el peccado nefando: puesto que dizen que algunos de los rústicos que andaban guardando ganado los vsauan secretamente: y los que ponían en los templos por induzimiento del demonio: como ya tengo contado (Cieza de León, *Crónica del Perú,* 278)].[32]

The similarity between these descriptions, taken from distinct geographical areas by missionaries from different religious orders, suggests that there was, before the Spanish arrived, a pan-Andean tradition of third-gender subjectivity. That is not to say that all manifestations of what I characterize as third gender were the same. We must take into account the pre-Hispanic cultural diversity of the Andes, the fragmentary sources, and colonial transculturation. It is impossible to contain our understanding of the fluidity and multiplicity of these subject positions in one discrete definition or description. Over the course of this study, the fragments of the multiple positions signified by third space–occupying Andeans will come together to suggest, at times, temporal, and, at others, more permanent, subjectivities. I do not conflate the evidence, however, into the narrower characterization of some of these subjects that Trexler names "berdache";

on the contrary, I am more interested in the symbolic and ritual meanings of mediation.[33] This remarkable text, couched in idolatry discourse by
Domingo de Santo Tomás and included by Cieza in his chronicle, creates
an opening for us to understand these subjectivities that were represented
in the ambiguous language of the queer tropes of sexuality found in earlier
colonial discourse.

What distinguishes Domingo de Santo Tomás's text from Cieza's other
accounts of sodomy in the Andes is the former's emphasis on the religious use of male same-sex sexuality. The ritual specialization described
here provides us with the cultural meaning of their social relationships.
Although the missionary envelops the description of temple sodomy in a
discourse of idolatry, the repetition of the sacred nature of the sexual act
intimates a desire to communicate the indigenous cultural values informing same-sex praxis.[34] He describes the sodomitical act as being carried out
in a sacred space, the "temple or place of worship," *huacas* dedicated to certain ritual activities. The sexual rites were performed on special days of the
ritual calendar. The act was performed by transgendered specialists, and the
number varied according to the "idol" involved. As we will see in the next
chapter, these special attendants are described as much like the figures observed in pre-Inca, Moche iconography. Here the details are explicit: they
dressed like women from childhood; they talked like women; and their
mannerisms and dress were imitations of women's. As we have seen, Bertonio's definition also includes "works as a woman" along with the other
gender markers mentioned in Domingo de Santo Tomás's text. In this iteration, the subject seems permanently identified with a third-gender subject position.

Domingo de Santo Tomás provides information on how these specialists were reared in a transvested state; evidently, certain male children were
chosen for this ritual role at a young age and trained to fulfill their responsibilities. Trexler reads the reported comments from the third-gender
temple of attendants being punished as evidence that they were forced into
their roles as debased sex objects (*Sex and Conquest*, 107). I believe, however, that we must consider the colonial context in which the Dominican
friar was receiving the information from the two third-gender attendants
and we must consider the broader cultural context in which young Andeans entered into ritual life.

First, Domingo de Santo Tomás, no doubt referring to the Sodom and
Gomorrah lesson that was standard evangelical material, admonishes the
attendants for the sinfulness of their acts.[35] Second, his report implicitly
had as an objective the glorifying of the missionary project; his two pun-

ished, and perhaps repentant, subjects naturally would blame their "errors" on others, as the Christians and, later, ladinos, blamed the idolatries of the indigenous Andeans on the devil. Following this logic, what does it mean to say that the youths truly considered themselves "forced" into their sacred roles or that they felt ashamed of their positions? This interpretation would have to be predicated on a sense of shame associated with occupying a gender-liminal or feminine status, which, as we will more fully appreciate in Chapter 3, was not demeaned in the way it was in European culture. Therefore, we should use caution in interpreting the assumption of the passive role and cross-dressing as necessarily inferior activities. Trexler's reading of the temple sodomites as "debased sexual subordinates" (ibid., 117) is based on a notion of power in which the female gender and same-sex behavior were devalued in European culture, a conceptualization that informs the Spanish colonial sources from which he constructs his understanding of berdache. As I will demonstrate below, and as Silverblatt, Isbell, and Harrison have likewise argued, the feminine was not devalued in the Andes; indeed, it was a vital force to be ritually and politically negotiated. Furthermore, as we will see below, the feminine sphere of culture and same-sex praxis were mythologically sanctioned in Andean religious beliefs.

The practice of young children taking on responsibility, both mundane and sacred, was (and still is) the norm in Andean society. At times this includes practices that shock and even disgust outsiders.[36] The practice of child sacrifice is an obvious example.[37] I do not argue that the temple attendants described by Domingo de Santo Tomás freely chose their role in the temple, just as sacrificial victims surely did not elect to be offered to their deities. Guaman Poma de Ayala, writing in the beginning of the seventeenth century, records the routine and sacred duties of children. Both boys and girls aged five to nine years worked around their homes (*Primer nueva corónica*, f209:lines 157 and f230:171). Boys and girls aged nine to twelve began to serve their communities, at times even working for the deities by killing birds for feathers and gathering flowers for offerings (ibid., f205–207:lines 154–157 and f228:171). Perhaps exaggerating the youths' enthusiasm for work, Guaman Poma exudes the boys' commitment to their superiors: "All of these activities were done for the love of the Republic and to magnify the Inca's majesty" [Todas estas diligencias se hacían por amor de la república y aumento de la grandeza de la magestad del Inga (*Primer nueva corónica*, f205:line 154)]. The ladino historian continues by discussing the Andean concept of reciprocity, *sapsi*, which was the work all members of an *ayllu* contributed to the community. The ethics of reciprocity in Andean communities motivated service, values that the youths learned from an early age.

Ultimately, we have too little evidence with which to form a solid hypothesis regarding the temple attendants' feelings about their role. Silverblatt's discussion of a young female sacrifice in the annual Inca Capacocha ritual might offer further insights into the participants' feelings in Andean sacred ritual (*Moon, Sun, and Witches,* 96–98). Silverblatt comments on an extensive description of the ritual by the chronicler: "Overwhelmed, ecstatic, exhilarated by her experience in the imperial capital, Tanta Carhua must have partaken of the divinity that was bestowed upon her by the son of the Sun" (ibid., 98). Of course, the girl's comments ("Finish now with me, for the celebrations which were made in my honor in Cuzco were more than enough") were reported to the chronicler by the elders of her community and therefore reflect the ideology behind the imperial ceremony, but Silverblatt's characterization of her "divine" state of mind is an attempt to make intelligible for outsiders what is difficult to fathom without understanding the cultural context of the practice. Furthermore, we cannot ignore pre-Hispanic and contemporary evidence of shamanic induction into ritual practice as a possible motivating factor for third-gender subjects.[38]

Other than the comments offered in Domingo de Santo Tomás's text, we have only one mention of how young men in the Andes might have felt about adopting these temple roles, be they those of an *orua,* a eunuch, or a temporarily cross-dressed man. Mestizo Jesuit missionary Blas Valera's description of the indigenous "priests" suggests that they "offered themselves" to serve their deities, even going so far as to castrate themselves or be castrated: "Many of these offered themselves from childhood and lasted, not only in continence until old age, but in virginity . . . Many of these or others were eunuchs, what they called *corasca,* and either they castrated themselves, in reverence to their gods, or others castrated them when they were children, so that they served in this way of life" [se ofrecían desde mochachos y duraban, no sólo en continencia hasta la vejez, pero en virginidad . . . Muchos destos o los más eran eunuchos, que ellos dicen corasca que, o ellos mismos se castraban, en reverencia de sus dioses, o los castraban otros cuando eran mochachos, para que sirviesen en esta manera de vivir] (*De las costumbres antiguas,* 83).[39] In my comments on the castrated guardians of the *acllawasi* mentioned above, I list the characteristics of eunuchs from Byzantium that Ringrose uses to justify her designation of these subjects as third gender. We see the same characteristics here. Blas Valera is careful to use terms that the European reader could understand; his entire description of Andean religion is one of correspondences between familiar Catholic religious institutions and Andean practices. His choice of "eunuch" as the name for the castrated temple attendants should not surprise us. Indeed, his more ethnographic description of the Andean "eunuchs" encourages us to reconsider Cieza's earlier descriptions of the castrated attendants in the *acllawasi,* where the virgin women worked and lived. Did they, too, serve in ritually significant roles?

Valera comments that the people considered the castrated priests sacrosanct: "When they went out into the streets and squares, all the people followed behind, since they regarded them as sacred" [Cuando salían por las calles y las plazas, llevaban tras sí toda la gente, que los tenían por sanctos] (*De las costumbres antiguas,* 83). That the people of Cuzco, the Inca imperial capital, held these priests in high esteem is further evidence that the gender-liminal or even effeminized position in ritual contexts was a venerable one. Indeed, Valera continues his description by explaining how the priests "prayed publicly for the Inca and the people" [Oraban publicamente por el inga y por el pueblo] (ibid., 83), thereby demonstrating their public religious role and their relationship with the Incas. These comments suggest that the third-gender priests occupying liminal positions, corporeally marked through castration or transvesting, participated in religious institutions of the power structure of Tawantinsuyu and enjoyed a certain status in society.[40] This position may have been temporal, given that Valera goes on to relate how these priests often ended their lives in isolation in the mountains (*De las costumbres antiguas,* 84). This passage from one of the most quoted of early Andean historians, cited extensively though selectively by Inca Garcilaso, for example, provides us with an alternative portrait of third-gender ritualists, one that challenges Cieza's assertions that sodomy and transgendering were anathema to Inca culture.

The presence of femininity in the description of third-gender temple attendants also relates to their speech. Both Domingo de Santo Tomás's and Bertonio's observations that third-gender subjects speak like women could refer to the grammar constructions and idioms they used or could refer to the pitch of their voices.[41] Both meanings are possible and find support in Andean historiography, but because there are no extant texts in which third-gender subjects' speech is represented, neither in Spanish nor in an indigenous language, we will never know for certain. The Quechua (and Aymara) language marks the gender of the speaker, so that an interlocutor would understand the speaker's gender not only by cultural markers like clothing and hair, but also by the way he or she formed words and sentences. For example, a woman refers to her brother as "*tura*" while a man refers to his brother as "*wawqi.*" A man addresses his sister as "*pana*" and a woman speaks to her sister as "*naña.*"⁴² Therefore, a third gender speaking as a woman might choose "*naña*" to address her sister and "*tura*" to address her brother. This "cross-speaking" would further mark the third gender's identity in ritual, and perhaps even profane, contexts.

There is further evidence, based on kinship relations, that a third gender might indeed abide by the linguistic rules of a woman. Tom Zuidema's study of the Inca *ayllus* and kinship relations explains the way the term *ipa,* the Aymara name of the third gender and passive participant in same-sex sodomy, is also the name given to a "father's sister" in Quechua and Aymara (*Inca Civilization in Cuzco,* 29). Zuidema relates this signifying of a male in a "female sexual position" as symbolically enabling the male to take a female position in the kinship system; specifically, younger brothers are often gendered female, symbolically as a "sister" of the older brother (ibid., 29–30).

Zuidema offers three examples of how this gendering may be related to same-sex ritual sexuality. First, he cites Cieza's description of temple sodomy, which I am analyzing here. Second, he mentions Jesuit Pablo José Arriaga's 1621 manual, *La extirpación de la idolatría del Perú,* which, in the context of the extirpation of idolatry that he and others undertook in the first years of the seventeenth century, mentions agricultural rituals in which men spoke in a female voice (ibid., 31; Arriaga, *Extirpación,* chap. 3: 207). The "ministers" who performed these rites, named *parianas* by Arriaga, were chosen each year from the community and prepared themselves up to two months in advance by fasting and avoiding contact with their wives (ibid.). Third, a 1621 account relates how younger brothers of a sacrificed older sister "officiated as their sister's priests in time of sowing and harvesting. They exercised these religious functions for their entire lives and transmitted them to their descendants. During the ritual celebrations, these priests spoke in a woman's voice" (Zuidema, *Inca Civilization in Cuzco,* 32).⁴³

While Zuidema and Silverblatt emphasize the pitch or tone of the voice, thus characterizing it as female, the positioning of ritual priests in "female" positions within the kinship system might also imply the use of the gendered semantics mentioned above. Bertonio's dictionary offers us further evidence of this vocal transgendering: "*cutita chacha:* hombre que habla con voz mugeril" [a man speaking with a woman's voice] (*Vocabulario,* 61), which suggests a change in the pitch or tone of the voice. González Holguín's Quechua dictionary does not record a word for the voice change, but there is an enigmatic entry, "*Pau Ola:* de hombre a mujer" (*Vocabulario,* 281) [from man to woman], which might signify transgendering, though we do not know specifically in what context the words would have been used.

Again, these fragments add to the evidence that feminine or gender-liminal characteristics were elicited in ritual performance during the pre-Hispanic and colonial periods and were similar to features shared by the third-gender temple attendants recorded by Domingo de Santo Tomás. Were the transgendered subjects considered debased for participating in such activities? Should we read them as metaphors of dependency? Or, on the contrary, can we interpret these ritual attendants as liminal subjects invoked in the re-creation of Andean culture? Their gender is performative in the sense that Butler calls the "effect of a regulatory regime of gender differences in which genders are divided and hierarchized under constraint. Social constraints, taboos, prohibitions, and threats of punishment operate in a ritualized repetition of norms, and this repetition constitutes the temporalized scene of gender construction and destabilization" ("Critically Queer," 16). Here, the repetition is literally "ritualized" in that the invocation of the feminine or androgynous occurs in a ceremonial context. Ritual norms required the presence of a man who spoke in a feminine voice, perhaps like the *chacrayupay* and *mujonomiento* ceremonies (considered in the next chapter), and required the cross-dressing of a male. We are left with a "temporalized scene" of a gender subjectivity neither male nor female, but third. To understand why the society called for third-gender presence in important community ceremonies, we must consider possible mythological sanctions that Andeans felt compelled to follow in mediating between their world, *kaypacha,* and the worlds of their deities and between the complementary genders, the *qhari* (man) and the *warmi* (woman). We must comprehend the value of the feminine and androgyne in Andean culture, given the masculine bias that clouds the colonial record. To understand more fully how this third-gender figure, what the Spanish narrators considered "temple sodomites," fit into Andean gender culture and into the reproduction of culture in general, we must turn to the ladinos who wrote from the *chaupi* between two cultures in the late sixteenth century, the subject of the next chapter.

In this transition to ladino sources, I will refer back to the queer tropes of sexuality found in Cieza and his contemporaries, which continue to appear in the ongoing transculturation of Andean gender and sexuality. The polyphony of voices inscribed in his chronicle from the oral tradition and his observations created a complex narrative woven from competing strands of discourse of the multicultural Andes. Cieza moved us toward the third space of transculturation; the ladino writers discussed in the next chapter will fully occupy that space, revealing subaltern *conocimiento* of the Andes, specifically, how the Andeans used the body and sexuality as culturally, and not just biologically, procreative.

Three

FROM *SUPAY HUACA*
TO QUEER MOTHER
Revaluing the Andean Feminine and Androgyne

One of the more enigmatic pre-Columbian sculptured vessels recovered from the Andean region is a Moche *guaco* of a seated figure whose braided hair and headdress signal that she is a woman.[1] A closer look reveals, however, that the molded figure is apparently a hermaphrodite, depicted with both a vagina and a penis, in the process of guiding a sharp instrument toward the ambiguous site of his/her genitals. Holding the penis with one hand, he/she directs a blade to its base in an apparent gesture of castration (Figure 4).

This figure offers us an interesting puzzle: Why is the hermaphrodite severing his/her penis? Does this symbolically represent something about Moche gender ideology? Is this *guaco* a representation of routine ritual practice in the Moche culture? Does he/she choose to be castrated or is he/she forced into castration by ritual obligation or other ideological pressures? Does this represent a step in the process toward symbolic gender liminality — toward assuming a third-gender subjectivity? While these questions will most likely go unanswered, raising them invites a deeper reflection on the role of the feminine, the androgyne, and the "in between" in the cultures of the Andes.

I begin the chapter with this enigma as a way to invoke a material cultural reference, from Andean antiquity, to a state of gender liminality in the Andes that informs several aspects of transculturation in the colonial period. As opposed to the abjection of the feminine in Spanish discourse, as discussed in Chapters 1 and 2, the value of the feminine and the androgyne in the Andes led to a necessary ritual negotiation between the masculine and the feminine cultural spheres that can be appreciated in indigenous ladino narratives from the colonial period. While we may never know the precise symbolic meaning of the hermaphroditic *guaco,* we can reach a deeper understanding of how third-gendered ritual subjects, what the Spanish often deemed to be lascivious sodomites, played vital roles as

FIGURE 4   *Moche hermaphrodite. Courtesy Museo Larco, Lima.*

cultural mediators in Andean society. In addition, I will show how colonial writing subjects in the Andes assumed similar metaphorical positions of liminality, writing from the *chaupi,* to express themselves and reveal or obscure knowledge and traditions, including values related to their gender culture. As we have seen, the early reaction to Andean gender and sexuality began a discursive tradition that objectified the Andean body and used it in myriad ways in representing Europe's Other. At stake in my study of this tradition is how we read for the feminine and the androgynous in the culture of Europe's Other and how we appreciate the role queer bodies played in Andean rituality.

    Literary critics of the colonial era have emphasized the discursive tropes that effeminized the Amerindian,[2] an abjection of the feminine, as we

saw in Chapter 1, with deep roots in the Spanish peninsula. These readings of the effeminizing colonial discourse lucidly explicate the conquistador mentality present in the historiography of the Americas. I ask, on
the other hand, how has this discourse obscured our understanding of
pre-Columbian gender culture? By marking the defeated Amerindians as
effeminate, equating them with weakness and debased humanity, have
Hispanic sources on pre-Columbian cultures obfuscated a deeper com-
prehension of gender and sexuality in the Americas? Did the effects of
transculturation lead ladino and mestizo writers to conflate European and
Andean gender values to such an extent as to render an intelligible, pre-
Hispanic gender culture unrecoverable? What reading strategies might en-
able us to revalue the role of the feminine and the androgyne in Andean
culture? The hermaphroditic *guaco,* depicted as castrating the phallus to
choose the female, or perhaps even a third, gender suggests that we reconsider our understanding of these topics, including a deeper understanding
of third-gender ritualists as signs of gender liminality (which I began to
explicate in Chapter 2).[3]

An appreciation of how the feminine and the androgynous fit into pre-
Hispanic Andean culture requires a revision of the material record that
has survived hundreds of years in stone and clay. One of the most important ancient Andean civilizations, the Moche culture, flourished between AD 100 and AD 750 on the north coast of present-day Peru, between
the Piura valley in the north and the Huarmey valley in the south (Bawden, *The Moche,* 8).[4] As these valley centers expanded into larger, more
powerful complexes, the Moche began to trade with more distant neighbors, with the pre-Hispanic "Ecuadorians" of the north and the offshore
Pacific islands (ibid., 50–51). Also integrated into Moche society were important contacts with the Yunga, the highlands, and Amazonia. Not only
did these three eastern regions provide commercial and ritual products to
the Moche, they also figured prominently in Moche cultural production
through their iconography and art, which reflect the integral relationship
the Moche had with the natural environment.[5]

This artistic language is a considerable symbolic record of this early culture, and our understanding of Moche culture depends on the recognition
of patterns that Moche artists followed in representing characters, ceremonies, and events. Christopher Donnan, in his presentation and analysis of Moche art and iconography, was one of the first to propose that we
can read the Moche legacy as "a symbolic system that follows consistent
rules of expression" (*Moche Art and Iconography,* 5). Donnan and his associ-
ates accumulated more than seven thousand samples of iconographic rep-

resentations and concluded at the time of his research that the archive was nearly complete, accurately representing all known Moche iconography (ibid., 13). As specialists worked with the patterns, they began to discern discursive regularity in the iconography that allowed for interpretation of cultural values.

There has been some disagreement among Moche iconographers as to whether the figures represented in the ceramic etchings are historical persons acting out in rituals or representations of Moche myths and deities. Jürgen Golte, who has reconstructed a narrative sequence from some of the iconography, points out that traditional Moche iconology has maintained a difference between a descriptive or realist and an imaginative or mythic representation of events (*Iconos y narraciones,* 19). The discovery of the material remains from the burial of the principal officiant of the well-known Sacrifice Ceremony depicted in much Moche iconography is providing scholars with unprecedented information about Moche gender culture. The remains of the figure known as the Lord of Sipán, for example, dated at around AD 200 or 300, reveal that the figure, iconographically depicted as male, was the central character in the ritual (Bawden, *The Moche,* 114). The coincidences between the accouterments found in the Moche burial sites and the elaborate costumes on the iconographic characters suggest that the iconography represents actual human participants in ritual activity, at times in interaction with deities.[6]

Moche gender culture, as represented in the ideologically charged iconography, made a space for the feminine as well as the masculine. Joan Gero has contributed to our understanding of this space by considering the role women played in the early intermediate period in the Callejón de Huaylas, the area in which the Moche had great cultural influence.[7] It is in this time period, as Donnan and Castillo note, that the area underwent a consolidation of power among a dense population, which led to a greater stratification of the society. Some lineages began to exempt themselves from reciprocal relationships, which led to changes in kinship groups and hierarchies. Archeologists have found ceramics that represent ritualized feasting most likely associated with these newly privileged lineages with access to agricultural surpluses.

Gero has explored the ritual complexes and found copper brooches known as *tupus* as well as spindle whorls, indicating the presence of high-status women in the sacred spaces. In addition, there is evidence that high-status women were present at ritual feasts, where they prepared *chicha* (maize beer) and ritual foods. Most suggestively, her analysis of the area's ceramic iconography reveals that women's power was not derived from coupling with powerful males; they were autonomous. While traditional anthropological records categorize these women as attendants, Gero asserts that we should read them as ritually important coproducers of culture. Just as men were represented with llama herds as markers of their prestige, women were typically associated with rooftops and entrances to buildings, symbolizing an ideology in which women were affiliated with divine oversight and human procreation. By recognizing the linkage between *chicha* and food production and the ritual reproduction of culture, Gero moves toward feminist scholars' call to measure gender-informed power in new ways, beyond the traditional, male-defined parameters of power relations (Conkey and Gero, "Programme to Practice").

In the important ceremonial center of San José de Moro, Jequetepeque, archeologists have recovered the remains of a female officiant also depicted in the iconographic representations of the Lord of Sipán. Donnan and Castillo describe the excavation: "Of the three excavated chamber tombs, the most complex corresponded to an adult woman of high status. This is the wealthiest woman scientifically excavated to date and clearly demonstrates that, at least in the later period of this society, wealth and power were not the exclusive patrimony of men" ("Excavaciones de tumbas," 417). This priestess of San José de Moro corresponds to the iconography's "Figure C," first identified by Donnan in 1975, later classified as female by Hocquenghem, and now definitively related to the remains found in the tomb (ibid., 419). The coincidences between the burial tomb and the iconographic representations of Figure C suggest convincingly that the priestess officiated in the sacred Sacrifice Ceremony, a ceremony that spanned hundreds of years and covered large portions of the Moche empire. Any doubt as to whether Figure C was a continuing presence in Moche culture was resolved when Donnan and Castillo found yet another tomb with an almost identically buried priestess (ibid., 421).

The female officiant's iconographic prominence and now the discoveries of her material existence suggest that the feminine played an important role in the ritual reproduction of Moche ideology. The priestess's participation in the Sacrifice Ceremony, her link with the highest levels of power, suggests a deep-rooted tradition of respect for the feminine sphere of culture in the late Moche period, as Donnan and Castillo conclude (ibid., 424). Her adornment with silver, rather than gold, and her role as porter of blood further establishes her connection with the liquid elements of Andean culture, with blood and water, to that which is related to the moon, to the cycles of life. Her possible link to the sea is an important element of feminine power that reappears in later cultures' mythology, as we will see below.

Alana Cordy-Collins has discovered a connection between the sacred Spondylus shell and the Moche priestess, concluding that she used the shell to catch blood in bloodletting rituals in the cult of the Moon.[8] In addition, she notes a transformation in the priestess's iconographic representation as the Moche began to transition to the Lambayeque tradition: her image becomes "hybridized," taking on iconic markers of masculinity ("Blood and the Moon Priestesses," 46–47). In effect, it seems that the Lambayeque men co-opted the cult and began to cross-dress to represent the Moon priestess.[9] Although more research is needed, this phenomenon may provide an explanation of the origin of some third-gender performances in the Andes and further substantiate the connection between the spheres of the feminine, the Moon, and the sea. In addition, the link to the Santa Elena area, where much of the Spondylus was harvested and third-gender subjects were reported, should be explored.

THE PERFORMANCE OF THIRD GENDER IN MOCHE ICONOGRAPHY

Moche iconography represents same-sex sexuality and transgendering in ritual contexts.[10] Manuel Arboleda was the first Andean scholar to seriously treat the theme of what he calls "homosexuality" in the erotic ceramics of the Moche. While others had mentioned it in passing or denied that there was such evidence, the most prominent attention devoted to the topic before Arboleda's research explained the scenes in terms of Moche morality.[11] Rafael Larco Hoyle, one of Peru's pioneering archeologists and preservationists of material culture, was captive to the homophobia of his time when it came to reading the Moche depictions of same-sex sexuality. Both the Larco Hoyle museum and his book dedicated to the subject of pre-Hispanic erotic art, *Checan,* project colonial and twentieth-century morality onto the Moche ceramic narratives.

Arboleda undertook a more precise study of the material culture related to erotic Moche art, analyzing seven hundred erotic and noneritic pieces. He paid close attention to details other than the sexual positions; he observed the vestments and other articles present in the scenes and *guacos* in order to establish the gender of the characters represented in the art. He established that one of the *guacos* described by Larco Hoyle as a moraliz-

ing depiction of sexual excess that may or may not be of same-sex partners is of two male subjects. The skeletal figure's male genitals are show-
ing, and the "sleeping" human figure is dressed in typical masculine attire,
including a male headdress and tunic (Arboleda, "Representaciones artísticas," 103). Another *guaco* from his sample, which is also housed at the Larco
Hoyle museum, is a pair of skeletal figures whose genitals are not shown,
but whose vestments indicate male gender. This pair is not involved in anal
sex, but the reclining figures are kissing and embracing each other (ibid.).

Arboleda's survey of Moche erotic art also includes analysis of what he
names "mythic-religious" figures and focuses on the iconography represented in the "Tema de la preparación." This scene suggests that the same-
sex sodomy represented by the Moche may have had religious significance,
for the sexual act at the center of the series of iconographic scenes is highly
ritualized. The series begins with a group of three male anthropomorphic
figures preparing a liquid substance, which in the following scene is poured
over the genital area of two copulating figures. Arboleda speculates that
the substance was a hallucinogen and adds that John Rowe has suggested
that it might have been injected into the anus of the passive figure through
an enema, which would have been an efficient and quick entry of the drug
into the bloodstream (ibid., 102). The scene represented to the right of
the copulation scene is of an iguana-faced anthropomorphic figure that
mirrors a doglike figure to his left in a prayerlike position. Jürgen Golte
reads these postures in Moche iconography as gestures of respect (*Iconos y
narraciones,* 40). In the sequences that Golte has analyzed, the iguana-faced
figure, which he calls "Figure J," is associated with different ritual contexts, including sacrifices and divinations (ibid., 58–59). To Figure J's right
there is also a winged figure, possibly symbolizing shamanic dream flight.
Farther toward the right of the copulation scene is a pair of female figures
less elaborately dressed than the central figures.

The copulation scene takes place in a structure whose architecture is
common in Moche iconography, often represented on top of platforms and
pyramids, and whose material remains have been excavated by archeologists (Donnan, *Moche Art and Iconography,* 72–75). Actions taking place in
these covered venues generally denote important activities, such as presentation of prisoners, sacrifice ceremonies, and, in this case, ritual copulation.
In this sequence, the kneeling figure's genitals are not visible in the copulation scene; however, Arboleda notes that the headdress and breechcloth
worn by the figure, as well as the *rodilleras* (kneepads), are usually seen on
male figures in Moche art. He also notes their association with supernatural beings. The reclining, face-up figure has no supernatural characteristics;

however, the figure is wearing *trenzas* (braids) and a breechcloth, that is, both feminine and masculine markers of gender. Arboleda points out the rarity of finding a mixture of gender markers in the same figure in Moche iconography and suggests that "perhaps the presence of these characteristics in one single individual represents an ancient tradition of representing 'berdache,' that is, male individuals who assume and perform the role of the opposite gender."

This reading of the iconography as a representation of a third gender (what Arboleda calls "berdache") is a great advancement in the treatment of the sodomy motif in Moche art. Trexler agrees that these scenes depict same-sex acts and relates these images to colonial reports on the Pachacamac prayer postures (*Sex and Conquest,* 109–110). He proposes that the sexual act is carried out between male rulers and berdache, concluding that these ceramics represent hierarchical sexual posturing that expresses "dominion of Moche rulers over their male subjects" (ibid., 114).

The Cordy-Collins research on the Moon priestess's transformation in early Lambayeque culture encourages us to consider other possibilities. Due to the shamanic icons included in the scene, a magic-religious rite is more likely the theme of this depiction. As I continue to develop my reading of these rituals below, I propose that we move toward an interpretation that reflects the meaning of the cumulative performances of third-gender ritual sexuality that I piece together in this book.

Indeed, the context in which these figures appear suggests that they played a ritual role in Moche society. The temple architecture, the ritual attendants (the Iguana-faced figure, the winged figure, and the praying dog), and the libations poured on the genital area all indicate the sacred nature of the sexual act being represented. While Arboleda affirms that the ritual most likely was not associated with fertility rites, due to the nonprocreative nature of the sexual acts represented, he goes no further in speculating on a possible meaning of same-sex copulation in Moche culture and makes no attempt to place the scenes described above in relation to other iconographic representations in Moche art.

Anne Marie Hocquenghem, in her thorough study of Moche iconography, has gone a step further in offering an explanation for some sodomy rituals. She has established a relationship between the representations of nonprocreative sexuality, such as heterosexual sodomy and masturbation, and rituals associated with death. Theorizing death as an inversion of life, she posits that sodomy and masturbation reflect inverted sexual practices that may have been employed to affect the transition from this world to the "other world" after death, which might explain the presence of skeletal figures in the copulation scenes. Hocquenghem's principal argument is based on her reading of death and mourning rituals described in Guaman Poma's *Primer nueva corónica y buen gobierno* of 1615. Guaman Poma discusses three periods of death rituals: the funeral, the mourning, and the reorganization and replacement of the dead in the community (Hocquenghem, *Iconografía mochica,* 137). As part of the mourning process, women cut their hair short and spun thread in the opposite direction from the normal one. Hocquenghem considers these two practices symbolic of the inversion of daily reality; that is, women inverted the normal order of things. Although her analysis brings us closer to an understanding of the iconography as representation of liminal moments in the Moche ritual calendar and her interpretation might explain heterosexual sodomy and masturbation, her approach does not explicate third-gender presence in the ritual sex acts depicted in Moche iconography.

The theoretical puzzle inherent in Hocquenghem's interpretation centers on how we identify the genders of the participants in the ritual represented in the Moche iconography. If we agree that the reclining figure is a third gender, that is, a transvested male living as a woman but whose status and roles are different from those of women and men, then to speak of sodomy as an inversion is problematic. Same-sex sodomy as an inversion would depend on a binary gender system in which opposite-sex practices were the norm. Two gendered males copulating would then be the inverse of a heterosexual act, and vice versa. In a gender culture in which there exists a third gender, what does same-sex sodomy between a male and a third gender signify? Although any absolute explication is risky, perhaps a jump forward in time can help us answer the question.

The recuperation of the roles of women and transvested ritual attendants in the Moche culture sets the stage for us to understand various cultural values related to the feminine in the Andes. Some scholars have ignored the importance of these values for centuries, thereby obscuring a more holistic view of Andean gender culture. As a result, our interpretations of even more marginal forms of gender and sexuality have been either nonexistent or severely flawed. Recognizing the power of the female in the pre-Columbian Andes, accessed through new anthropological and archeological findings, will help us interpret a colonial literary source on pre-Hispanic gender culture. Once we do that, we can propose a reading strategy that more creatively explicates Andean modes of narrativization and reveals subaltern Andean *conocimiento.* That strategy can deepen our understanding of the cultural context in which third gender was performed.

The hermaphroditic Moche *guaco*, therefore, becomes more suggestive, perhaps as a "phantasmagoric original," of the subsequent iterations of Andean third-gender subjectivity that appear in the colonial period and beyond. This Butlerian notion of performative subjectivity is useful, as I outline in the Introduction, because it provides for the inherent fluidity of gender and sexuality and for the transformations of gender and sexual subjectivities over time. Material artefacts such as the Moche *guaco* can be interpreted as signs of gender diversity in a genealogy of subject positions in Andean culture; investing them with alternative meanings opens our interpretations of other material artefacts as well as literary, queer tropes of sexuality found in Spanish colonial discourse.

WRITING FROM THE *CHAUPI* IN HUAROCHIRÍ

I would like to return to my theory, advanced in the Introduction, of the *chaupi* as an in-between space in order to frame my rereading of one of the most valuable colonial sources on pre-Hispanic culture, *The Huarochirí Manuscript*. In my theorization of the inherent queerness of transculturation, I will continue to highlight how the third space of the *chaupi* in the Andes affords a place for alternative histories that give voice to the culturally and sexually queer. This section of the chapter explores a "third space" in Andean colonial literature and proposes that we listen carefully to the *chaupi* voice(s) that communicate across the centuries and provide us with an alternative vision of the indigenous gender culture of the region.

The Huarochirí Manuscript is a unique early seventeenth-century narrative written in Quechua by an anonymous ladino scribe who transcribed from native oral testimony a series of myths and descriptions of rituals.[12] Although the text owes its existence to Father Francisco de Ávila's zealous campaign to extirpate indigenous idolatry in the region, perhaps as revenge for the locals' attempted prosecution of his abuse of the natives,[13] the myths and rituals express Andean cosmogony and the religious and social history of the Huarochirí region in terms relatively unmitigated by Spanish influence. Frank Salomon, in his authoritative introduction to his and George L. Urioste's English translation of the Quechua manuscript, appreciates the "freshness and unfamiliarity" of the text as the result of the "provincials' lack [of] the know-how to package and process their culture in terms familiar to Spanish speakers, [therefore] the myth tellers in the Huarochirí manuscript created an image still largely framed by conceptual categories proper to local thought" (28). One cannot overstate the manuscript's value as a source of local knowledge, given that these myths from Huarochirí offer one of the only and the most complete Andean cosmogonies and mythohistories, different from the more abundant Inca versions found in the Spanish chronicles.

We know nothing of the manuscript scribe's identity, except that his name was Tomás; he may have been an *escribano de naturales* (a bilingual scribe), a village scribe, or a native functionary of the colonial regime (24).[14] His prose reveals use of what is known as Quechua II, or the general-purpose Quechua that had been propagated by the Incas throughout their empire and was adopted by Spanish colonial authorities as the lingua franca in both civil and evangelical enterprises after the Conquest (30). However, scholars question whether Quechua would have been the original language in which the testimony was given and whether the religious practices described in the narrative would have been expressed in Quechua or a local language (30). The Huarochirí scribe's writing is also peppered with loan words from Spanish, both words without Quechua equivalents (e.g., *horse, church*) and words with different semantic fields. Nor do we know who narrates the different transcribed passages of the text. At times, the narrator is identified in the passage, but most myths and descriptions of rituals are transcribed by Tomás, the scribe, from anonymous oral informants.

The text is marked by the in-between positions of the scribe and the narrator-informants. The scribe was writing from the *chaupi* and was a ladino (acculturated, literate Indian) whose bilingualism and knowledge of writing positioned him in the third space of transculturation.[15] The informants most likely varied between monolingual locals with minimal contact with the colonizers to other ladinos like the scribe. The decontextualization of the retelling of the myths and rituals, no matter what the informants' level of acculturation, placed them in the in-between position of the *chaupi*, as well. The scribe self-consciously corrects his use of language and adds remarks that reflect his concern for the watchful eye of Father Ávila. While it is unknown whether the native scribes and informants were aware of the final use of the manuscript they helped to compile, that is, the looting and destruction of the indigenous sacred spaces in Ávila's extirpation-of-idolatry campaigns, the textual clues of self-conscious narration suggest that they were cognizant of the necessary cultural negotiations between their native traditions and the hegemonic colonial society in which they lived. This *chaupi* positioning is first evident in the self-conscious preface the narrator-scribe includes in the manuscript:

> If the ancestors of the people called Indians had known writing
> in earlier times, then the lives they lived would not have faded
> from view until now. As the mighty past of the Spanish *Vira*
> *Cochas* is visible until now, so, too, would theirs be. But since
> things are as they are, and since nothing has been written until
> now, I set forth here the lives of the ancestors of the *Huaro*
> *Cheri* people, who all descend from one forefather: What faith
> they held, how they lived up until now, those things and
> more; Village by village it will be written down: how they
> lived from their dawning age onward.
>
> (41–42)

Analysis of the original Quechua reveals a subtlety that Salomon and Urioste gloss "the people called Indians" (runa yndio ñiscap), a phrase that the
narrator seems to have purposefully employed to distance himself from the
Spanish nomenclature that referred to the diverse ethnicities of his people
as "Indians."[16] The narrator removes himself from that colonial categorization of his people, the Indians, identifying instead with the indigenous
runa (Quechua word signifying "people"). Lamenting their lack of writing and the resulting loss of cultural memory, he assumes the pen for his
people and steps into that third space of transculturation. He appropriates
the tools of the Spaniards and becomes a writing subject, a culturally queer
position in relation to his ancestors and most of his contemporaries.

As Cora Lagos has argued in the case of Nahua scribes ("Confrontando
imaginarios"), the physical and psychic transformation of the ladino who
adopted European writing technologies cannot be underestimated in its
alienating effects. Rolena Adorno has shown how ladinos were often perceived in the colonial Andes as "big talker[s] and charlatan[s]" and as "zealous converts and busybodies" ("The Indigenous Ethnographer," 381). These
contemporary attitudes toward the ladino reveal how he was no longer an
unmarked insider of his native culture, yet, despite his peers' opinions of
him, we can appreciate the Huarochirí narrator's posture in the text as one
of resistance to the oblivion to which his people's history was doomed had
he not taken on this heroic mission to "set forth the lives of the ancestors of
the Huaro Cheri people." His audacity is palpable, for he is confident that
his narration will be equal to the power of Spanish writing, and he dis-
misses the colonial Spanish versions that preceded his, saying that he must
write his people's history, "since nothing has been written until now."

His resistance, however, is not a monocultural strategy of using only his ancestral ways of preserving and recounting history, nor does he wholly adopt European discursive practices. But, as I will argue below, he uses and preserves a rhetorical artifice that reflects an Andean mode of storytelling in the new medium of the alphabet, one preserved in the process of transculturation and through the unlikely and sorrowful operations of the extermination of indigenous religious practices.

This theorization of the narrator-informants' subjectivities highlights the value of their manuscript as an alternative source of knowledge in the colonial Andes and opens the text to readings on myriad topics; however, I will focus this study on recovering knowledge of feminine autonomy and echoes of an androgynous creative force in both the symbolic and the material levels of Andean culture. One of the great frustrations for those interested in the pre-Hispanic gender culture of the Andes is the paucity of texts that give voice to the feminine sphere of society. While much anthropological, archeological, and historical work has been done to recover Andean pre-Columbian and colonial women's versions of history and culture, in nearly all cases related to colonial historiography, it is a matter of reading between the lines of texts written or transcribed by men, whether they be indigenous, mestizo, or European. As far as we know, nearly all of the chroniclers' informants were male, and the *quipucamayocs,* reportedly the "official" Inca historians, were also male.[17] The cultural memory of the feminine sphere is particularly difficult to recover, given that much of the knowledge related to and communicated through ritual practices was interpreted by the Spanish as idolatrous and therefore as dangerous continuities of Andean religion. For example, the preservation and veneration of the *mallquis,* or mummified ancestors, represented the feminine side of the Andean elite's deceased spirit. Symbolically embodying the seed of future generations, the *mallqui* was an important link between the past and the future (Isbell, "De inmaduro a duro," 256). These cultural icons were destroyed by the Spanish, severing the intergenerational memory as well as contributing to the near-effacement of one of the public roles of the feminine in the culture.

In what follows, the Andean body, transcribed and frozen in letters rather than in burial shrouds, will play an important role in how I explore ways to appreciate the subaltern feminine voice found in the myths and descriptions of rituals from *The Huarochirí Manuscript.* The violent colonial campaign to extirpate idolatry from the indigenous Andeans resulted in the conservation in the manuscript of at least some cultural knowledge related to the feminine sphere of Andean society. This knowledge can be recovered by turning to the body as a subaltern sign. Much of the feminine is recorded in tropes of sexuality found in the descriptions of agricultural rituals, textual representations of moments of ceremonial liminality in which the body signified power and autonomy. The inclusion of these descriptions is remarkable, given early-modern Spanish attitudes toward the public use of the body. As the individual reemerged in Renaissance Europe, there was a privatization of the body, a divorce from the collectivist, medieval institutions that left the body as a symbol in the arts and as a privatized entity to be dressed, domesticated, and regulated.[18] While on the one hand, the Spanish persecuted indigenous rituals or encouraged a resemanticization of rituals to express Catholic dogma and faith, on the other, Ávila and fellow missionaries recognized the ritual importance of corporeal expression as indicators of idolatrous practices, and therefore encouraged the narrators and scribes to record them in the manuscript to aid in their extirpation. The textual third space of the manuscript, one that is of neither the colonizer nor the colonized, reveals knowledge that would have otherwise been lost or so severely acculturated as to be nearly unrecognizable in today's indigenous rituals. If this *conocimiento* is overlooked or ignored, because the privileging of Western rational, lettered discourse over that which is expressed through the transcribed, idolatrous body, then we receive only half of the story of pre-Hispanic and colonial Andean gender culture.

GENDERED MYTHS OF *SUPAY HUACAS*

The Huarochirí Manuscript comprises several cycles of myths that repeat similar structural relationships of Andean culture expressed through metaphors of gender and sexuality. These metaphors serve the purpose of telling the story of gender pairings between insider and outsider *huacas. Huaca*, according to the seventeenth-century authority on Inca religion, Father Bernabé Cobo, was a term used "for all of the sacred places designated for prayers and sacrifices, as well as for all of the gods and idols that were worshiped in these places" (*Inca Religion and Customs,* 47). In the Huarochirí text, *huacas* are represented in a variety of ways: from personified deities to sacred topography. They function as the mythic actors in the region's history, as oracles, as recipients of sacrifice and as petrified markers of history. The first cycle of myths (chaps. 1–4) tells of the region's early mythohistory, the male "Trickster" *huaca* Cuni Raya, and the eventual *pachacuti* (cataclysmic change) that represents the end of the cycle. This first mythic cycle is predicated on a gender symmetry dysfunction: the failure of the invading Trickster *huaca* to pair up with a local female counterpart. The two female *huacas* of the myth resist Cuni Raya's advances and refuse to settle into a reciprocal relationship. As Isbell has observed, the resistant female huaca, Cauri Llaca, controls sexual desire in this myth and returns to the female-gendered sea, to what Isbell calls the "unmarked feminine whole" ("De inmaduro a duro," 254). Symbolically, this is important, for it suggests that male *huacas* did not have a priori rights over female *huacas*. The pairing of deities in pursuit of balance and complementarity is revealed to be a process that respected the status of both the masculine and the feminine forces. If we understand Cuni Raya to be the representation of an outsider who attempted to establish local ties to the region, then we see that the female *huacas* enjoyed prerogatives in the process of negotiation of interethnic relations.[19] The feminine is represented as being as autonomous and powerful as the masculine.

In the second cycle, the gender metaphor enters the mythic discourse when the male mountain *huaca* Paria Caca seeks to partner with the female valley *huaca,* Chaupi Ñamca. Salomon has characterized this sequence of myths as an allegory for the ethnic group Yauyos' expansion toward the Pacific Ocean, a mythology that "construes a folk memory of conquest as an ideology of affinal interdependence" (8). The new relationship established between invader highlanders (the Yauyos) and aboriginal lowlanders (the Yuncas) is symbolically based on a marriage alliance that responds to the Yauyos' need for cultivable land and the Yuncas' need for water resources. As Salomon clarifies, the "union between invaders and aborigines is ideologized in terms of a fraternal tie between the highest male deity of the invaders and the highest female deity of the aborigines" (9). Paria Caca "was born in the form of five eggs on Condor Coto mountain" (54), which in later chapters is transformed into five falcons and eventually into five men, while Chaupi Ñamca is represented as a fivefold sisterhood, whose *huaca* was "a stone with five arms" (77).

The myth that relates this union of the two *huacas* (chap. 5), which I will refer to as the primary narrative, is told in a story in which Chaupi Ñamca's ailing father, Tamta Ñamca, is saved by Huatya Curi, a son or incarnation of Paria Caca. Huatya Curi is represented as a poor but wise "Baked Potato Gleaner" (55) who outsmarts all the shamans and wealthy wise men of the region by discovering the cause of Tamta Ñamca's malady: his wife's "adultery."[20] Tamta Ñamca's wife eventually confesses her transgression and Huatya Curi cures him by dismantling his house and in return receives Chaupi Ñamca as his wife. Symbolically, this episode represents the dis-

placement of the local chief's house and rule by that of an outsider, pre-
cipitated by the sexual disequilibrium metaphorically represented by the
local chief's wife's adultery. This imbalance in local gender relations was
replaced by the complementary relationship between the highlander Paria
Caca and the lowlander Chaupi Ñamca: "the man who had recovered his
health gave him his unmarried daughter" (57). The tension underlying this
newly established relationship is demonstrated by the protests by Chaupi
Ñamca's brother-in-law, who challenges Huatya Curi to a series of contests: dancing, drinking, puma-skin dressing, and house building. Huatya
Curi prevails in all the contests and drives off the brother-in-law and his
wife. In this primary narrative, Chaupi Ñamca is passive and objectified.
She is represented without agency, as a mere reward or gift for the invading
entity.

Salomon insightfully emphasizes the complementary relationship between the fraternal pair, Paria Caca and Chaupi Ñamca, and reads the gender metaphor as a "conflict model of society" in which "every complementarity, whether marital, ritual, ecological, or political, [is] shadowed by
submerged conflicts that had to be repressed in order to institute it" (10).
I propose that we read for the subaltern voice of the Andean feminine by
highlighting Chaupi Ñamca's preunion autonomy and by emphasizing the
power of the feminine in this Andean mythohistory. While I agree that
the narrator recorded how the social tensions between the invading highland Yauyos and the aboriginal valley Yuncas were mitigated through the
fraternal union of the two huacas, Chaupi Ñamca's powerful preunion autonomy signals a need to reconsider the narrative structure of the myths in
order to better understand both the status of the feminine in pre-Hispanic
Andean culture and the way this knowledge was communicated and preserved in the colonial text.

Within the collection of myths there is a counter- or supplementary
narrative that suggests more female autonomy than is usually perceived or
related in the primary narrative of patriarchal supremacy. This counternarrative is fragmented and incomplete, but suggests an underlying feminine
power autonomous from masculine power. A reading of this counternarrative requires a reconsideration of the notion of "wife exchange," a cultural practice that Claude Lévi-Strauss characterizes as fundamental to the
very foundations of culture in that "the emergence of symbolic thought
must have required that women, like words, should be things that were
exchanged" (*Elementary Structures,* 73). The notion of wife exchange as a
strategy for achieving social harmony between opposing ethnic groups implies that the father or other male figure in the wife's family has power over

the female in that he can give her to the opposing side in an act of reconciliation. Irene Silverblatt has described this exchange in terms of a process that established "prestige hierarchies" at local levels in the pre-Incan
Andean societies (Silverblatt, *Moon, Sun, and Witches,* 68). This homosocial,
patriarchal structure evident in the primary narrative, however, is challenged by the counternarrative I have identified in the myths.[21]

Vestiges of this counternarrative give voice to the female *huaca* Chaupi
Ñamca's power and autonomy and illustrate the deeper incongruity between the sexes in Andean culture that requires the elaborate ideological
process of yanantin. Yanantin is a Quechua concept theorized by Tristan
Platt in his study of Andean symbols, "Mirrors and Maize." The etymology
of the word yanantin reveals the complementary relationship of the male
and female couple, figured as an expression of pairs united in symmetrical harmony.[22] A common use of the word is to describe the union of man
and woman, the *qhariwarmi,* the male-female couple, a union sanctioned
through elaborate rituals, since each member of the pair enjoys preunion
autonomy and unequal terms of power. Therefore, the pairing of man
and woman in the Andes is problematic, since, "although the perfect pair
must be composed of congruent individuals, man-and-woman in fact lacks
this congruence. Their union must be forged, their disparities countered"
(Platt, "Mirrors and Maize," 252). This tension, I argue, implies female resistance, not just male privilege; this resistance is a display of agency rooted
in her traditional autonomy. The "forged union" between the sexes in the
conjugal pair occurs over time, by way of rituals and their everyday interdependence as helpmates. To understand this tension between men and
women, which Platt has identified in Andean culture, we must listen to
another version of the feminine in the Huarochirí tradition: a subaltern
feminine voice.

The fragments of this discourse on gender complementarity reveal a
feminine power that belies the wife-exchange narrative discussed above
and foregrounds Chaupi Ñamca's agency, which is conveyed through
powerful sexual imagery, which is a hallmark of Andean gender constructions. The power and autonomy of the feminine is manifest in the myth
told immediately after the Huatya Curi episode, in which Paria Caca,
transformed from egg into a falcon and then into a man, encounters the
beautiful Chuqui Suso. Chuqui Suso is the counternarrative's incarnation
of, or at least counterpart to, Chaupi Ñamca, one of the five mythic manifestations of the feminine sphere of the *huacas.* This relationship between
Chaupi Ñamca and Chuqui Suso is based on two fundamental coincidences

that structurally link the two characters: both are related to valley agriculture, and both manifest sensual ritual practices. In both, the body is figured prominently in their respective cult's ritual observances.

Paria Caca meets Chuqui Suso as "this woman was weeping while she irrigated her maize plants because they were drying out so badly" (62). Paria Caca offers to irrigate her land if she will have sex with him first (62). Chuqui Suso agrees only if Paria Caca waters her field. Having fulfilled his promise, Paria Caca asks for his recompense, but again Chuqui Suso asserts her sovereignty and negotiates another irrigation canal for a different field. In response, Paria Caca widens a ravine called Coco Challa, and "pumas, foxes, snakes and all kinds of birds cleaned and fixed that canal" (62). Having completed this task, Paria Caca again asks to have sex with her. This time, Chuqui Suso consents, but entices him to a high ledge, where they finally do have sex. In a final act of self-determination, Chuqui Suso goes to the head of the Coco Challa canal and metamorphoses into a stone *huaca* that was known to the narrator by her name (63). In this myth, Chuqui Suso, as the metaphor for the female cultural sphere, is represented with agency and negotiates the terms of the union between her and the invading male *huaca*.[23]

In the following chapter, the narrator explains the importance of the Chuqui Suso *huaca* to the region, where she was the *huaca* of canal cleaning, an important agricultural task in the Andes that takes place in September.[24] The narrator explains that the local people would go to the *huaca* of Chuqui Suso and offer "maize beer, *ticti* [sacrificial maize], guinea pigs, and llamas to worship that demon woman" (64). The reference to "demon woman," Salomon and Urioste's translation of the Quechua "supay huarmicta," suggests that, indeed, Chuqui Suso was known as a powerful force in pre-Hispanic Andean culture. The earliest Quechua-Spanish dictionary, compiled by Father Domingo Santo de Tomás in 1560, records the translation for the word *supay* as "ángel, bueno, o malo, demonio"[angel, good, or bad, demon], reflecting the colonial ambiguity of the term.[25] Billie Jean Isbell recognizes, following Duviols, that this ambiguity is gendered in a dualistic fashion: the ancient meaning of the term can be glossed as "shadow or light, the volatile part of a living being" ("De inmaduro a duro," 271, my translation). This duality that Isbell characterizes as androgynous corresponds to the male-female counterparts represented by the *mallqui* and the *huaca* (ibid.). Isbell, again working from Duviols's notion of the androgynous double nature of dead Andean elites, who at death transformed into the two parts, the feminine *mallqui* and the masculine *huaca*, argues that the feminine was valued in the pre-Columbian Andes and that this duality present in *supay* evidences the power women had to control excessive masculine sexuality (ibid.).

Regina Harrison's work on Ecuadorian Quichua women's songs recorded in the 1970's demonstrates that, while the notion of *supay* in contemporary oral tradition, just as in the colonial period, can have a positive or negative connotation, depending on the context, there is a special meaning for the word in women's spheres of work and ritual. "When women use *supay* often their first name is attached to the phrase, or that of their *ayllu,* which designates a personal female strength handed down for generations" (*Signs, Songs and Memory,* 137). This notion of strength, as expressed in the song translated and analyzed by Harrison, is related to agricultural skill: "*chakra warmi supayga*" (spirit force in the *chakra,* or field) is the designation given to those women who are especially successful with their crops (ibid.). The full text of Harrison's translation follows:

> A woman who goes to the fields
> lacking strength,
> what strength will be lacking?
> Andi women's strength.
> I am, perhaps, man-woman.
> I will do all kinds of work.
> I'll only lie down to die.
> Now, for sure, I'm on my feet.
> Spirit force in the chakra.
> [Nothing] will be lacking [in me].
> Nobody will equal [me].
> Whatever anybody wants,
> my desire is to keep on standing up
> in every type of work.
> A woman [who] stands up,
> a worthless woman.
> No matter how diminished, I'll stand,
> half man,
> half woman.
> Like that for sure I'll stand up.
> In what way will I be lacking?
> Men won't be lacking for sure!
> Whatever they desire sexually
> I have sexually desired, for sure.

Me, for sure, whatever
work they want me to do,
I'm [there for] that, for sure,
all kinds of work.
Never diminishing, standing up woman,
Andi woman spirit strength.

(Ibid., 139–140)

This power is also related to the woman's sexuality, as seen near the end of the song (ibid., 139). The spiritual strength that is *supay* in this woman's song is able to satisfy sexual desires, hers and her partner's. Furthermore, the gendered subjectivity of the *supay* woman is one that suggests androgynous power: she is "half man, half woman." Her special strength allows her to do "all kinds of work," both male and female tasks. Rachel Corr has highlighted the gendered duality present in the contemporary Festival of Caporales in Salasaca, Ecuador. In addition to the presence of transvesting (the young men or boys who dress and dance as *doñas* [ladies] with the male *caporales*), the centerpiece of the ceremony is the bread baby funeral, in which a symbolic loaf of bread in the shape of a baby is mourned and buried. The "baby" is actually two-headed, one of a male child and the other of a female child ("Reciprocity, Communion, and Sacrifice," 15). Corr concludes that this ceremony reflects gender parallelism in the Andes and echoes the abundant Andean myths with motifs of gender duality, twins, and fertility (ibid., 17).

Here again, as Isbell suggests, *supay* conjures the androgyne. Is the connection between agricultural productivity and female sexuality in this Quichua song an echo from the same oral tradition as the myths of Huarochirí? Can we read this as a trope that encourages us to appreciate the cultural significance and resilience of female power, androgyny, and autonomy in the Andes?

Indeed, the Huarochirí narrator of chapter 7 recorded this connection between bodily sensuality and agriculture in his description of Chuqui Suso's day of veneration. Whereas the ritualistic activities associated with the post–canal cleaning festivities did not have any reported sexual activity, such as that in Chaupi Ñamca's story, described below, attention to sensual pleasure abounded: "On that occasion they say people celebrated a major festival, dancing and drinking all night long" (65). The *ayllu* group and any others who helped clean the canals would build a "*quishuar* enclosure," [26] in which all would remain for five days (64). One woman from the group would emerge as an embodiment of Chuqui Suso, serving maize beer to all attending. The *huaca* would come alive through the body of this female participant, known as a *huacsa*.[27] Thus, the reciprocal connection between female *supay* power, so necessary for the hard work of canal cleaning, and the Andeans' bodies, represented by the sensuous acts of dancing and drinking, was established. The canal cleaners gave Chuqui Suso ritual offerings, and, in return, she gave them the power of her *supay* through the maize beer and other foodstuffs. I will return to the figure of the huacsa below as I consider other gendered performances of rituality in the Andes.

This public performance of gendered power reflects a reiteration of a "phantasmagoric original" in the Andes, a manifestation of female, and perhaps androgynous, vitality needed in the agricultural cycle. As Judith Butler has posited, gender subjectivity is "performed" through the re-iteration of phantasmagoric notions, that is, previously performed, culturally constructed notions of a gendered subjectivity. These performances are often contained in ritual exhibitions of the original understanding of the subjectivity (*Bodies That Matter,* 95). The narrator ends his description of this festival by asserting that, despite the colonial influence of Spanish Catholicism, the people still practiced this ritual homage to Chuqui Suso in the early seventeenth century. But, as if he realized he should be more cautious with his remarks, especially in light of Father Ávila's active role in the manuscript's compilation, he adds: "True, some don't do it anymore because they have a good *padre*" (65). The Spanish extirpation of idolatry had begun to inhibit the gendered performances recorded in the colonial texts.

Here again we appreciate the narrator's *chaupi* position. As he recounts the *conocimiento* of his people to please his patron, he consciously, though feebly, distances his contemporaries from the idolatrous practices under attack. The corporeal, sexualized ritual recorded in this counternarrative provides us with two important pieces of subaltern cultural knowledge. On the one hand, we see the continuity from and connections to Moche iconography in which sexual rituality was tied to the feminine; and, on the other, we appreciate the autonomous power of the feminine *supay* that must be negotiated through *yanantin* processes. In addition, as I will discuss below, this testimony provides a cultural context for understanding ritual same-sex sexuality and transgendering reported in other sources.

Chaupi Ñamca's own counternarrative begins in chapter 10, as a description of her "cult" that comes after the longer description of Paria Caca's cult in chapter 9. Here the narrator foregrounds the agency of Chaupi Ñamca, who reportedly "went around saying *runacunacta camac cani,*" which Salomon and Urioste's translation glosses as, "I am a maker of people" (77).[28] The *huacas* are the *camacs* to the people; that is, they provide the life-force needed to live or exercise certain functions. Therefore, Chaupi Ñamca (and the narrator and oral tradition) sees herself as a powerful *huaca,* a life-giving *camac.* And, as the narrator continues, the people also understood her in relation to the male *huaca* Paria Caca: "Some people say about Chaupi Ñamca, 'She was Paria Caca's brother'" (77). This sibling relationship is a common leitmotif in the founding dynasties of Andean civilizations and suggests the parallel power enjoyed by the two gendered spheres, metaphorically represented through this kinship structure. Chaupi Ñamca's importance to the local Andeans was such that her lithified representation, the stone with five arms, was hidden during the Spanish invasion, "underground in Mama, near the Catholic priest's stable" (77). This area is called "Mama" because, according to the narrator, "all the people called Chaupi Ñamca 'Mother' when they spoke to her" (77), a memory that further evidences the complementary power relations between the male "father" figure and Chaupi Ñamca's "mother" figure.

The ritual adulation of Chaupi Ñamca was overtly sensual and establishes a clear relationship with the agricultural cycle. Here, the relationship between the divine and the body is explicit: the *huaca*'s power manifested itself through tropes of human sexuality. Of the several dances that were performed in honor of Chaupi Ñamca during her paschal festival, coinciding with the Christian Corpus Christi, the *casa yaco* was said to be her favorite: "They say that when they danced the *casa yaco,* Chaupi Ñamca rejoiced immensely, because in their dancing, they performed naked, some wearing only their jewelry, hiding their private parts with just a cotton breechcloth. 'Chaupi Ñamca enjoys it to no end when she sees our ⟨crossed out⟩ [cocks] private parts!' they said as they danced naked" (78).

In an interesting reversal of Western representation of the female body as desirable object, in this case, it is the female *huaca* who objectifies the male body, controlling the voyeuristic gaze. Chaupi Ñamca's sexuality and her sensual objectification of the male body metaphorically represent her autonomy in relation to the male *huacas.* "In the old days this woman used to travel around in human form and used to sin with the other *huacas.* But she never used to praise any male by saying 'He's good'" (78). As Salomon points out, the word *sin* used by the narrator is "a Christian-style euphemism" (78n290) that does not correspond to Andean sexual morality, which, as we have seen, celebrated female and male sexuality. The fact that Chaupi Ñamca "never used to praise" males suggests that she enjoyed independence and power vis-à-vis the male *huacas,* just as Chuqui Suso displayed her own prerogatives in her relationship with Paria Caca.

Chaupi Ñamca's eventual lithification in Mama further evidences her importance and sovereignty in the Andean cultural imaginary. As the story goes, her powerful feminine sexuality finally finds its reciprocal match in the male mountain *huaca* Rucana Coto, whose name translates as "finger-shaped mountain" (78n291). Rucana Coto seems to have been a phallic force specializing in penis enlargement: "Men who had small cocks would implore Rucana Coto, thinking to themselves, 'It'll get big'" (78). Only he could satisfy Chaupi Ñamca's voracious sexual desire: "One time he and his big cock satisfied Chaupi Ñamca deliciously" (78). Exercising her prerogative, Chaupi Ñamca reportedly said, before turning to stone: "Only this man, alone among all the other *huacas,* is a real man. I'll stay with this one forever" (78).

This version of Chaupi Ñamca's reciprocal pairing is very different from the primary narrative's version. This supplemental narrative emphasizes her prerogative, her ability and propensity to choose her partner based on her needs and desire. Symbolically, this partnering between Chaupi Ñamca and Rucana Coto functions in the same way as did the partnership, predicated on Paria Caca's demands, between her and Paria Caca. Her version is still a partnering of a mountain water deity with a valley agricultural one, and this narrative's explanation of the newly established relationship between the highlanders and the lowlanders is different only in that the narrator chose to emphasize Chaupi Ñamca's agency in the forming of the complementary relationship. The sexual imagery serves the purpose of highlighting her *supay* power and pre-*yanantin* autonomy, thereby providing the reader with an alternative to the primary narrative, which emphasizes the authority of the male invading force.

We might read this counternarrative as a resistant text, one that voices the local people's pride in their culture and in the power of their *huacas* at a time of colonial violence toward those traditions, an ancient echo from times in which matriarchal lineages enjoyed more power in the area, when the feminine sphere was more overtly celebrated in the valleys. This complementary text represents a more balanced version of Conquest politics in the pre-Hispanic Andes. This counterdiscourse suggests that the negotiation between the invaders and the invaded was not a simple wife-exchange process in which the female had no voice in the partnering. These myths and rituals indicate that the female *huaca* actively participated in the building of the new relationship, actively sought out the most powerful mountain deity, the biggest penis, the strongest portal for the aquatic semen that her valley so desperately needed. From the invaders' viewpoint, this voracious *supay* sexuality, symbolic of the valley's verdant fertility, functioned as a positive ego-building symbol: only the most potent could handle the insatiable thirst for semen (water). Perhaps this is why this version of Chaupi Ñamca's story survived to be retold by the Huarochirí narrator, for, ultimately, this version reestablishes the Andean ideal of gender complementarity that is absent in the dominant narrative.

This reading suggests that the Andean concept of *yanantin* was a highly contested process in which women and men negotiated the establishment of the conjugal bond. Could this bond reflect the value of the androgyne, of the joining of the masculine and the feminine to represent the primordial creative force?[29]

Isbell, in her reading of the Huarochirí text and analysis of Andean ethnographies, argues that feminine desire (personified in the *huacas*) controls masculine sexual energy, metaphorically represented by surging river water. By highlighting feminine agency in the cyclical movements of time and reproduction ("De inmaduro a duro," 289), Isbell adds to our understanding of the value of the complementary narrative discussed above. Moreover, she recognizes the androgyne as the original, powerful energy in the re-creation and reproduction of the world (ibid., 253). Andean androgyny functions as a synecdoche in which the androgynous whole is greater than the sum of its feminine and masculine parts (ibid., 259). Both parts, for example, the androgynous double *mallqui-huacas,* are represented as energizing forces (*camay*) capable of reproducing new *pachas* (ibid., 296). Isbell concludes that the pre-Hispanic "Symbolic," in Lacanian terms, is androgynous and not patriarchal, an idea she corroborates with ethnographic studies of Andean communities in the 1970's. Her work on Andeans' gendered conceptions of the life cycle, fertility rites, and adolescent courtship reveals the enduring importance of the androgyne, though the forces of transculturation, beginning with the Conquest and colonization, have tended to "masculinize" Andean cultural topography and obscure the earlier meanings (ibid., 297).[30] I return to this theme of the androgyne later in this chapter.

TINKUY READINGS

In reading these myths and descriptions of rituals, the reader must fit the fragments together in order to get the whole story. The tensions between the dominant and the subaltern must be negotiated in a reading style that we might characterize as *tinkuy,* the Quechua concept for the bringing together of two opposites into harmony through ritual-

ized confrontations.[31] *Tinkuy,* as I briefly explained in the Introduction, is
an Andean practice that affirms social relations and was (and is) expressed
ritually and symbolically in both the Quechua and the Aymara cultures.
Platt explains how the ritual "battles" are performed within the context
of a four-part symmetrical division of the cultural space. In this division,
ecology plays an important structural role, as do kinship relations. Eco-
logically, the space is divided between the *puna* and the valley, with the dividing line being a liminal space known as *chawparani.* Each of these divisions is subdivided between two principal *ayllus* known as *hanan* and *hurin.*
Hanan is symbolically gendered masculine while *hurin* is symbolically gendered feminine (Platt, "Mirrors and Maize," 232). The members of the immediate family and of the patrilocal group maintain exogamous relations,
while the ideal is to form matrimonial relations exogamously between the
hanan and the *hurin ayllus* and between the *puna* and valley divisions (ibid.,
235). This structure forms part of what John Murra has called the ecological verticality that creates regional economic interdependence in the
Andes (*Formaciones económicas*). For our purposes, it is important to understand that *tinkuy* occurs between the two halves, *hanan* and *hurin,* in a ritual
in which the men from the *hanan ayllu* oppose the men from the *hurin ayllu*
and the women from *hanan* oppose the women from *hurin* (Platt, "Mirrors
and Maize," 239–240). This symmetrical pairing of men and women is also
repeated in other ritual contexts, such as "ritual plowing" (ibid., 240–241)
and "house building" (ibid., 238–239).

The narrator-scribes of Huarochirí cryptically inscribed the *tinkuy* formula in the narrative structure of the manuscript, a composition that gives
voice to the two versions, one from the male, invader, point of view, and
the other from the perspective of the invaded, of the female. Understanding the narrator-scribes' subjectivity in terms of Anzaldúa's *nepantlismo,* and
in Andean terms as occupying the *chaupi,* in-between, space, helps us appreciate their unique privileged position as transmitters of *conocimiento,* or
sacred knowledge. Identifying the two complementary discourses in the
manuscript highlights the liminal position of the narrator-scribe, his in-
between balancing act not only vis-à-vis his native culture and the Spanish colonial institutions of alphabetic writing, Catholic dogma, geographic
displacement, and so on, but also in comparison with the *chaupi* maneuvers
he carried out in representing the two spheres of Andean gender culture.
By reading the two versions of the myths in a reciprocal way, the tensions in the narrative become resolved, just as in Andean society the opposing forces, be they invader/invaded, male/female, night/day, wet/dry,
high/low, come into balance through ritual practice. These tensions of dif-

ference, however, are not erased. This is the distinction I draw between *tinkuy* and transculturation: in *tinkuy*, difference remains a presence. In terms of gender, the female and the male spheres are iterated in an ongoing negotiation in which there may be temporal inequities and *pachacutis* but in which the ideal of balance and complementarity is continually restored, at least in ritual moments of liminality.

Perhaps we should approach the transcribed oral narratives "ritualistically." Reading, therefore, becomes a ritual in which we readers become mediators, the *chaupi,* charged with bringing into balance the different versions of mythohistory. This perspective on our role as reader in approaching Andean narratives is a step toward restoring some of what is lost in the decontextualized narratives that originally would have been recounted in the *chakras, huacas,* and *quishuars* of the pre-Columbian Andean highlands, spaces with multiple narrators adding their (whether male or female) version to the oral renderings of the myths.

A LADINO'S QUEER STORIES: FROM MYTHIC ANDROGYNY TO FOUNDATIONAL SAME-SEX RITUALITY

A *tinkuy* reading strategy also informs my interpretation of one of the most provocative works by an Andean ladino and leads to the formulation of my theory about the place ritual same-sex sexuality and third-gender subjects occupy in Andean culture. To explore the nexus between mythology and third-gender subjectivities I will analyze pivotal figures in myths recorded by native Andean Juan de Santa Cruz Pachacuti Yamqui Salcamaygua's (Santa Cruz Pachacuti Yamqui) *Relación de antigüedades deste reyno del Perú* (1613).[32] The indigenous descendent of *curacas* (chiefs) from the area of Canas and Canchis, Santacruz Pachacuti offers us a unique perspective on Andean history, beliefs, and cultural practices. Only recently have scholars recognized the exceptional view of the early colonial period that he offers us. Regina Harrison ("Modes of Discourse," 67) was one of the first to recognize the quality of the text, not for Santacruz Pachacuti's ability to conform to Renaissance Spanish rhetoric and stylistics, which had been attacked by traditional historians, nor for the much-cited cosmological drawing I analyze below, but for the manipulation of linguistic codes that achieves the communication of "the essence of Andean cognition in the language and liturgy of the Spanish lords" (ibid., 68). For Santacruz Pachacuti was, as Rolena Adorno has emphasized, a ladino, that is, a native Andean "competent (speaking, and possibly reading and writing) in the language of the colonial overlords" ("Images of *Indios Ladinos*," 235). This linguistic ability, as both Harrison and Adorno point out, positioned him to relate pre-Hispanic Andean culture to Christian history. Verónica Salles-Reese has proposed that Santacruz Pachacuti's motivation for writing the *Relación* came from the extirpation-of-idolatries campaigns in which he may have played a role as translator. Reading the text as a *probanza,* a legal petition commonly used by ladinos to establish their rights under Spanish law as well as to respond to accusations of idolatry, Salles-Reese suggests that Santacruz Pachacuti may have feared that his status as a Christian was in jeopardy. Therefore, at the insistence of the fearsome extirpator, Francisco de Ávila, the same priest who oversaw the writing of *The Huarochirí Manuscript,* he wrote the *Relación* to defend himself ("Yo Don Joan de Santacruz Pachacuti" [1995], 112), and, implicitly, responded as the voice of his people to the overall Christian attack on Andean culture.[33] Duviols and Itier's introductory study to their edition stresses the didactic nature of the text, suggesting that it may have been destined for the recently established Colegio de Caciques, a Jesuit school founded for the indoctrination of the children of the Andean elite (Santa Cruz Pachacuti, *Relación* [1993], 94).

We can imagine that the structure of the narrative would have made for a nice history primer, for Santacruz Pachacuti organized his story into three distinct epochs: *purun pacha,* in which the Andean people are depicted as still barbarous; the age of Tunapa, in which the apostle Saint Thomas is said to have preached the Gospel, being accepted by only Manco Capac's father; and finally, the age of the Incas, who, under Manco Capac, are chosen by God to prepare the way for the Spaniards' Christian message.

Like the narrator-scribes of *The Huarochirí Manuscript,* Santacruz Pachacuti writes from the *chaupi* between two cultures. He occupies the "third space" of transculturation, a space discursively marked by his writing style, use of language, and, most provocatively, unique interpretation of Inca history. His singular narrative is barely intelligible to an uninitiated reader of Andean colonial writings by newly converted indigenous historians, whose language, style, and world view could be characterized as queer, that is, as eccentric to the Spanish metropolis's official histories and suspicious of even his indigenous contemporaries' versions of history. His text is queer in another sense of the word, that is, as it applies to what I consider to be the "subaltern knowledge" cryptically transmitted by the author in this text, knowledge that challenges his contemporaries' versions of Inca history, mythology, and, especially, Andean gender and sexual culture.[34] Like the subaltern *conocimiento* of feminine autonomy in pre-Columbian culture derived from the *tinkuy* reading of the Huarochirí myths, Santacruz Pacha- cuti's stories I read below center around the body and ritual, performative iterations of androgyny. His version of the foundational story of the Incas establishes the basis for a ritual relationship between an Andean moun- tain deity and an Inca priest, a relationship figured and expressed through same-sex sexuality. This mythic story also sanctions third-gender ritual subjectivity and enhances our understanding of the *yanantin* negotiation, which must take place in the dimorphic gender culture based on the reci- procity between the male and the female. Santacruz Pachacuti reveals that the founding dynasty of the Incas, mythically expressed in the relationship between the male progenitor Manco Capac and the female sibling-spouse Mama Ocllo may have relied on a same-sex ritual before consummating their relationship, and later Incas called on the third-gender priests during liminal moments during their reigns.

Santacruz Pachacuti's history of the Incas begins with a journey: the foundational family of the Incas travels from Lake Titicaca, where Manco Capac had received the *tupayauri,* a magical staff given to his father by Tu- napa, or Saint Thomas, from his father and mother, Apo Tampo and ⟨Pacha⟩ Mama Achi (f6:line 193). From the outset of the narrative we can appreciate the unique constitution of his story, one that conflates Andean mythology and Christian evangelical teachings. Straddling two cultures, Santacruz Pa- chacuti creates a new story, one that it is neither of his originary culture nor of the newly hegemonic one. He brings the two threads of his new reality, the indigenous and the Spanish, together as in a symbolic *tinkuy.* His creation is a narrative of difference produced from the union of oppo- sites, a culturally queer neoculturation that preserves the tension of its composition.

As in any epic narrative, Manco Capac and his siblings meet different challenges and suffer certain setbacks during their journey toward Cuzco. The first occurs as they approach Sañuc, a village near Cuzco, where the youngest brother spots a sitting figure: "And arriving they say that he saw him seated like a fierce and cruel Indian, with reddened eyes, then one of the brothers arrived (the youngest one, the one that looked like a person); [the Indian] called him to his side and then as he neared closer he touched them on the head, saying: very good that you have come looking for me, finally you have found me, I was also looking for you, finally you are in my hands" (Y llegado dizen que le bio sentado como a un yndio más fiero y cruel, los ojos colorados, luego como llegó uno de los ermanos ⟨que fue el menor, el dicho que parecía persona⟩ le llamó junto a sí, y luego como lo llegó los tentó de la cabeza diziendo: muy bien abéis benido en mi busca, al fin me hallasteis, que yo también os andava en busca buestro, al fin estáis ya en mi mano) (f7:line 195). The figure, here described as a fierce and cruel-looking "Indian," seems to have inexplicably drawn Manco Capac's youngest brother to him. Mysteriously, the Indian speaks of the encounter as an inevitable certainty as if each searched for the other. The Indian's control over the youngest brother keeps him there until, finally, Manco Capac sends a sibling to look for him; that sibling stays with the Indian and the younger brother: "and they both remained there, *ojeado* by that *huaca* Sañuc" [Y se quedó el uno y el otro, ojeado de quel uaca de Sañuc] (f7:line 195).[35] Thus, we learn that the Indian is actually a *huaca,* with whom the two siblings have become "*ojeado,*" or entrapped through enchantment.[36] Manco Capac finds them "half dead," and they signal to him that "the idol and the *huaca* had done him that evil" [Aquel ydolo y guaca lo avían hecho aquel mal] (f7:line 195).

At this point exactly what the *huaca* has done to them is ambiguous, but then Manco Capac becomes angry and starts pounding the *huaca* on the head with the *tupayauri* given to him by the apostle at Lake Titicaca. The *huaca* then threatens Manco Capac, telling him that, if it were not for the *tupayauri,* the *huaca* would have "also done him." The mysterious act perpetrated on the siblings is clarified when the *huaca* says: "Go away now that you have achieved great fortune, I want to enjoy your brother and sister because they have seriously sinned ⟨carnal sin⟩, and it is fitting that he be in the place where I am, which will be named Pituciray, Sauasiray" [Andad que abéis alcansado gran fortuna, que a este su ermano y ermana lo quiero gozar porque pecaron gravemente ⟨pecado carnal⟩, y así combiene que esté en el lugar donde estubiere yo, el cual se llamará Pituciray, Sauasiray] (f7:line 196).[37]

The two siblings who originally became entangled with the *huaca,* brother and sister, are said to be converted into two tall peaks in the region. The original manuscript carries an annotation in the margin, believed to be written by Ávila, that explains the meaning of the two peaks' names: "They are probably together, one stuck to the other," a likeness that reiterates the sexual imagery suggested in the narrative [Que quiere dezir estarán juntos apegados uno sobre otro] (f7v:line 196).

While Duviols, in the introductory study to his edition of the *Relación,* interprets this story as an "*exemplum cristiano*" (87) that warns against incest, I would like to look through the evangelical veil that shrouds the myth and consider the encounter between the siblings and the *huaca* in terms of an indigenous echo of ritual sexuality and as a possible figuring of *yanan-*

tin.[38] Perhaps what is most interesting about this possibility is the rhetorical maneuvers employed by Santacruz Pachacuti in presenting this myth in a form recognizable to Christian moralists. As an Andean ladino, one whose purpose for writing might have been to teach the new generations of Andeans their history or to prove his true conversion to Christianity, Santacruz Pachacuti may have obscured the full original meaning of a local myth. Duviols notes Santacruz Pachacuti's refashioning of Spanish chronicler Pedro Sarmiento de Gamboa's version of the Ayar myth, arguing that he substituted the two peaks for Guanacauri because the mountains represented a local myth related to incestuous erotics and therefore would have been meaningful to local natives (*Relación,* 86).[39] While I agree that Santacruz Pachacuti rewrote a myth in Christian terms and related it to local traditions, I propose that the original story did not only refer to incest, but also established the basis for a ritual relationship between mountain deity and Inca priest, one figured in part through same-sex sexuality and one that may have mythically sanctioned third-gender ritual practices in the negotiation of *yanantin,* in this case, the pairing of two foundational Inca siblings.

First, it is significant, given what we learned from Zuidema, that the first brother who is drawn to the *huaca* is the youngest. We recall from Chapter 2 that a younger brother in Andean kinship could be symbolically considered a third gender, an *ipa,* and he reportedly played priestly roles in ritual contexts. In Sarmiento's version of this myth, the only brother involved with the *huaca* is named Ayar Ucho, the Ayar sibling who served a religious function among the founding Incas (*Historia índica,* 216). In that version, after the *huaca* seduces him, Ayar Ucho is transformed into Guanacauri, an important ritual site for the Incas, where adolescent boys underwent ceremonial initiation. Second, the fact that he does not return to his family indicates that he remained alone with the *huaca,* unable to escape his "enchantment." That the youngest brother was physically attached to the *huaca* is metaphorically suggestive, as well, of a sexual liaison, especially in light of the fact that Ayar Ucho was left, "as if dead" but still enchanted, after the encounter. Third, the *huaca's* comment about how he is going to "enjoy" the siblings who remained behind is enigmatic. Duviols, understanding the encounter as incest between brother and sister, has interpreted it in terms of the devil's enjoying a lost soul in hell. He believes that Santacruz Pachacuti is implying that the *huaca* is a demon (*Relación,* 84). This explanation, however, ignores the initial sexual imagery between the *huaca* and the younger brother before the arrival of the sister (and Sarmiento's account in which the encounter is limited to the *huaca* and Ayar Ucho). I interpret the incestuous imagery between the male and female siblings, after the initial homoerotic encounter between the religious Ayar brother and the *huaca,* as the logical result of the ritual pairing of one of the foundational Inca couples. Santacruz Pachacuti relates the Ayar story to local topography, the two peaks, which is common Andean narrative practice: remembering and explaining abstract and historical relationships through reference to physical geography familiar to the speaker (see Howard-Malverde, *The Speaking of History*). Guaman Poma de Ayala records the two peaks in one of his drawings depicting the *huacas* of Andesuyo, narrating in the accompanying text that the people made sacrifices to these "idols" (Figure 5). In the same drawing he includes an *otorongo,* to whom a man and a woman make offerings (f268:line 198).[40]

If we read this hybrid myth, this product of Santacruz Pachacuti's *chaupi* position, in light of our earlier analysis of third-gender ritual sexuality, then the episode can be understood as the vestige of an origin myth that explains and sanctions same-sex ritual sexuality with the *huacas.* The homoerotic encounter between the *huaca* and the Ayar brother, in which the powerful deity seduces and sexually exhausts the priest, serves as a mythical phantasmagorical original for the performance of third-gender ritual sexual praxis. In the continuation of Santacruz Pachacuti's foundational narrative, Manco Capac proceeds to Cuzco, where he establishes the Inca lineage. The narrative immediately following the encounter between the Ayar brother and the *huaca* is marked by the spatial division of the Cuzco valley, in which the dual sectors of *hanan* and *hurin* are established. Following this symmetrical figuring of the sacred space, Manco Capac marries his sister, Mama Ocllo. The foundational pairing alluded to in the first fraternal pair is repeated.

Was the encounter between the younger brother and the *huaca* a necessary prelude to the union of the Inca foundational couple, one which provided the symmetrical reflections needed to achieve the *yanantin* that ultimately united Manco Capac and Mama Ocllo? And what role did the remaining sister, Ipa Mama Huaco, play?

TOWARD AN ANDEAN THEORY
OF RITUAL SAME-SEX SEXUALITY
AND THIRD-GENDER SUBJECTIVITY

To understand the conceptual place a third gender might have inhabited in the highly symmetrical cosmology of the Andeans, I re-

FIGURE 5   *Sauasiray and Pituciray. From Guaman Poma,* Nueva corónica y buen gobierno.

turn to Tristan Platt's explanation of *yanantin*. This discussion will further our understanding of the complex system of gender complementarity referenced above by underscoring the performative nature of gender relations in the Andes. This dualistic symmetry is achieved through complex ritual performances such as *tinkuy*, an Andean practice, as we have seen, that affirmed social relations by bringing opposites into harmony. We recall from above that *tinkuy* occurs between the two gendered halves, *hanan* and *hurin*, in a ritual in which the men from the *hanan ayllu* oppose the men from the *hurin ayllu* and the women from *hanan* oppose the women from *hurin* (Platt, "Mirrors and Maize," 239–240).

This opposition between same-sex groups in the *tinkuy* ritual battles presents an interesting question for Platt in his study of *yanantin*: "Why do men battle with men and women with women during the *tinkuy*, if I am right in seeing the encounter as in part a ritual copulation between male and female moieties?" (ibid., 246). Platt offers an explanation of the sexual nature of *tinkuy* by noting the relationship between food and copulation and between fighting and copulation. Catherine Allen also notes the sexual nature of the *tinkuy* during contemporary *puqllay*, or carnival, in the Peruvian highland *ayllu* of Sonqo (*The Hold Life Has*, 183–185). I find a passage in the indigenous chronicle of Felipe Guaman Poma de Ayala that confirms that, in his time, the late sixteenth century, *tinkuy*, or *tinquichi*,[41] did indeed implicate sexuality as the metaphor for conflict resolution between the sexes. Guaman Poma's reference to *tinquichi* is found in his description of *hechiceros* (shamans): "The Indian shamans used to perform *tinquichi*: they join man to woman so that they fall in love and make the men wear out" (Los indios hechiceros hacían tinquichi: ajuntan al hombre con la mujer para que se enamoren y haga gastar al hombre) (f276:line 203). This passage is very suggestive of the inherently conflictive nature of Andean opposite-sex relations, for the joining of the man and the woman, as we saw in the Ayar myth and according to Guaman Poma, leads to the potential consumption, or "wearing out," of the man, that is, until the negotiation between the masculine and the feminine is consummated. In this case, the *hechicero* becomes the mediator in the ritual pairing of the *qhariwarmi* (man-woman pair), a potentially dangerous relationship for the man. Union required a ritual or magical impulse so that the opposites could form a complementary relationship. If the heterosexual relationship implies conflict of opposites, how does same-sex sexuality fit into the Andean cosmology?

Platt provides a partial answer to this question by positing a symbolic structure from which I will more directly address same-sex sexuality in the pre-Hispanic Andes. For Platt, the key to understanding Andean gender relations and sexuality is the mirror. It is a potent symbolic tool for the Machas. It is used, for example, in the two most important liminal contexts: during the marriage ceremony; and at death ("Mirrors and Maize," 232). Platt observes the symmetry that results from a reflected image in a mirror. For example, a right hand reflects back a left hand, which would represent perfectly the concept of *yanantin,* the expression for perfect dualistic, gendered symmetry. What, then, happens when human bodies are reflected in the mirror? The human body represents perfect symmetry of the left and right sides, yet the reflection of a man in the mirror is not that of a woman but of another man; a woman's reflection is that of another woman. Remembering that the goal of *yanantin* in this context is to unite the man and the woman for social and human reproduction, we can understand the importance of the predicament.[42] To understand how the union is symbolically achieved, we must take a closer look at the mirror effect.

If we consider all four possible pairings of man and woman, and their respective reflections within the *yanantin* model, we have, in Platt's words, "male men, male women, female men, and female women" (ibid., 247–248). This four-part construction of relationships corresponds to the four-part construction of the Andean cosmos and the four-part division of the Inca empire, Tawantinsuyu, which in colonial Quechua meant "All of Peru, or the four parts, which are Antesuyu, Collasuyu, Contisuyu, Chinchaysuyu" (González Holguín, *Vocabulario,* 336). The first two pairings of same-sex couples reflect the gendered groupings involved in the *tinkuy* ritual battles, the house-building and ritual-plowing ceremonies. The pairing of the groups from *hanan* with the groups from *hurin* is achieved through the symbolic reflection of perfect symmetry represented in the same-sex pairing. The man from *hanan* is reflected back to the man from *hurin.* The woman from the *puna* is reflected back to the woman from the valley. Platt concludes that the two figures of the same-sex pairings create a certain ambiguity that leads to the union of the gender opposites: "The very ambiguity of the middle two elements allows them to be presented, not illogically, by men and women respectively. And we can now understand the ideality of such an arrangement: Two actors of the same sex can affirm the relationship of mirrored symmetry that *should* pertain, in real life, to the conjugal pair" ("Mirrors and Maize," 248). Platt clarifies and confirms this hypothesis by comparing an analysis of the Quechua word *yana's* semantic field with that of related root words, namely, *pampa* (a flat place, a thing in common, a common and universal thing); *cuzca* and *pacta* (synonyms: to join two unequal things); and *chulla* (antonym: a thing without a mate, unequal images) (ibid., 249–252). After considering these terms and concepts within the context of his previous discussion, Platt concludes that the commonality of the terms is found in the pairing of opposites, just as we have seen *yanantin* function in the context of gender relations. Bringing these opposites together, in each of the concepts discussed, implies the elimination of inconsistencies and disproportionate halves. In the *tinkuy* ritual the goal was to reaffirm borders between *ayllus,* so that each side symmetrically reflected the other. In the marriage of man and woman, the ritual aimed at uniting two opposite genders so that each complemented the other in daily interdependence. For this symmetrical pairing to occur, the things to be paired must share limits or borders. Before proposing what this symbolic border was, we must gain a better understanding of the negotiation process ritually represented in Andean matrimony.

Inge Bolin, in her ethnography on contemporary family and community rituals in the Quechua community of Chillihuani, in the high Peruvian Andes, has observed the ritual negotiation of gender in the *casarakuy,* or Andean marriage ceremony. Her rich description exhibits the attention to gendered symmetry that Platt found in the Macha culture and reveals the continuity of *yanantin* from past to present: "These rituals coherently and spectacularly illuminate ancient ideological concepts rooted in duality and are expressive of the constant struggle of opposing yet complementary forces. These forces achieve equilibrium as they unite and transform" (*Rituals of Respect,* 124). Symbolic configurations of *yanantin* abound; Bolin stresses the relativity of gender categories in the ceremony represented by the presence of the *hatun padrino* (vertical godfather) and the *ara padrino* (horizontal godfather), who stand on the right side of the couple, and the *hatun madrina* (vertical godmother) and *ara madrina* (horizontal godmother), who stand on the left side (ibid., 131). That is, both the vertical (masculine) and the horizontal (feminine) are represented in the patrons' presence at the side of the groom and the bride. The two axes are united symbolically in the sign of the cross, "the union of husband and wife, which is crosscut by the *hatun* (erect) *padrino/madrina* and *ara* (flat) *padrino/madrina.* The fluidity between male and female, vertical and horizontal, and upper and lower, is ever present" (ibid., 132). This concept is an important one, especially as it applies to symbolic gendering in different spheres of Andean culture. The ritual performance of in-between gender states, as we have seen in several examples, is a recurring motif that represents an iteration of androgyny as a vital force in the culture. In this case, it is a protective energy represented by the duality of the godparents.

The "androgynous" godparents accompany the bride and groom with great seriousness on their way to the Andean ceremony. The other primary actor in the wedding party is the *runa pusaq,* a respected elder elected guide, who "opens the path" for the wedding party as they advance by playing his *antara* (panpipes) (ibid., 128, 131). The group is joined by ten young men, *yana uyakuna,* or black-faced dancers, who protect the bride and groom as they pass through this precarious time before their final union. Five of the *yana uyakuna* are cross-dressed as "traditional" women and five as "modern" men. They dance around the wedding party, making jokes in high falsetto voices and acting out in parodic gestures, including simulating sexual intercourse (ibid., 137–140). Bolin reports that the color black protects from the evil spirits and that the *yana uyakuna* communicate with Pachamama, the *apus,* and Qhaqya, the god of thunder, through their high-pitched voices (*Rituals of Respect,* 139). She insightfully explains the duality present in the pilgrimage as the expression of opposites: "civilized," serious wedding party, and the disorderly and, at times, grotesque antics of the *yana uyakuna* parallel the gendered duality of the wedding party and the *yana uyakuna* (ibid., 140). It is clear that uniting the *qariwarmi* is no simple task; the couple depends on ritual mediation of third parties, be they the symbolically androgynous godparents, the cross-dressed *yana uyakuna,* or the music-playing guide.

Having fleshed out an example of the dualistic complexity of *yanantin* in Andean marriage ceremonies, I return to the exegesis of a Quechua synonym for *yanantin, pactachani,* which will help us understand the full meaning of the ritual union of opposites and its corresponding geometrical symbolism. Santo Tomás translates the term as "to pair up unequal things" (cited in Platt, "Mirrors and Maize," 249). One of its other synonyms, *cuzcachani,* has as its root *cuzca,* or "something flat," leading Platt to conclude that this concept of uniting unequal things has a geometrical attribute, a symbolic character that signified for the Andean a commonality between the notion of flatness and equality (ibid., 250–251). "The elements to be paired must first be 'pared' to achieve the 'perfect fit.' Here, the crucial notion is that of the sharing of boundaries in order to create a harmonious coexistence" (ibid., 251). Again we recall the importance of duality and borders in Andean cultural production. The *chawparani* divides the ecological zones; the *kaypacha* separates the cosmological worlds, *hanaqpacha* and *ukhupacha;* and in the *tinkuy* ritual, competing *ayllus* share borders marked by stones. What was the *qhariwarmi*'s border?

We have already noted that *yanantin* signifies giving assistance to others and the symmetrical pairing of things. But, the colonial dictionaries offer other meanings that help explain what might be considered a "border" in the symmetrical *qhariwarmi* pair. Domingo de Santo Tomás's 1560 *Lexi-*

con o vocabulario de la lengua general del Perú records the word *yanachani* and its meaning, "One woman embraces another naked" [Abrazarse dos mujeres desnudas (cited and translated by Platt, "Mirrors and Maize," 252)]. González Holguín's 1608 *Vocabulario* includes the word *yanachacuni* and its definition: "One man to make use of another, or the devil, or the sin of man" [Servirse un hombre de otro, o el demonio, o el pecado del hombre" (ibid.)]. These entries reflect what I argue in more detail in Chapters 4 and 5: that same-sex sexuality would undergo a process of transculturation as the colonial discourse matured.[43] Ideology aside, the entries imply that, symbolically, same-sex praxis was related to the *yanantin* concept. To clarify, Platt returns to the mirror images and reminds us that the ideal partner, in order to create the symmetrical reflection, is the same-sex partner (ibid.).

And the border? The liminal space between the ideal, same-sex pair seems to be symbolically represented by the sexual act, the moment the two bodies come together physically, thus reflecting the perfect symmetry of same-sex bodies. Through this symbolic union, the opposite genders, each with its own autonomous power, can hope to achieve *yanantin,* symmetrical harmony, that is, to live together as helpmates and reproduce both Andean people and culture. The transgendered male performs, based on a third-gender phantasmagoric original, a liminal subjectivity that mediated between absolute gender opposites. By transforming the body toward the feminine, yet still retaining the sex of a male, he might be seen as that which a mirror's reflection could not achieve. He is the manifestation of the symmetrical opposites doubled over on the other. He is the *qhariwarmi* embodied.

This conceptualization suggests that Andeans conceived of nonprocreative sexuality, at least symbolically, as culture building at the thresholds of time and space in community rituals. However, does this conceptualization provide for a temporal or even an ongoing subject position in the culture? Thinking from an Andean paradigm in which both male and female genders struggle for harmonious union, achieved through symbolic ritual same-sex pairing, leads us to explore third-gender subjectivity in the pre-Hispanic and colonial record from a perspective that considers the performance of feminine or androgynous characteristics and passive same-sex sexuality in culture-producing terms.[44] I propose, then, that ethnographic reports of cross-dressing during festivals represent vestiges of third-gender ritual participation, iterations of subjectivities that might have also performed sexual acts, such as the one depicted in Domingo de Santo Tomás's description of temple sodomy, in the foundational story of the Incas, and in the Moche iconography, as part of their *"cargos,"* or ritual responsibilities. The cross-dressing is the performance of an original sacred subject that once mediated between the male and the female genders and between the kaypacha and beyond. They also acted as corporeal signs of mythical stories and represented symbolic moments in the ritual calendar and agricultural cycle, the topic of the rest of this chapter.

IPA MAMA HUACO: A QUEER MOTHER OR A THIRD GENDER?

When we left the Inca foundational couple toward the end of their journey, Manco Capac and Mama Ocllo, according to Santacruz Pachacuti's version, had married and started a family. I asked, What happened to Manco Capac's other sister-wife, Ipa Mama Huaco, as Santacruz Pachacuti refers to her? It seems she was relegated to be the keeper of the corn, as I will discuss below, and her presence may still be invoked in today's agricultural rituals, as a memory of a queer Inca mother. Mama Huaco is presented in myriad ways throughout the colonial record, but those who wrote from the *chaupi,* like Santacruz Pachacuti and Guaman Poma de Ayala, remembered her as an important female and, perhaps, third-gendered archetype. Can we detect markers of gender liminality surrounding the performance of her subjectivity in the colonial record and in contemporary ethnography? Mama Huaco, as I argue in the conclusions of Chapter 4, is an ambiguous figure in colonial representation of the mythohistory of the Andes, and became for the Spaniards a perfect symbol to represent the Incas as tyrannical conquerors. For now, I will discuss what may have been her pre-Hispanic significance and her connection to third-gender subjectivity.

Guaman Poma de Ayala records two versions of Mama Huaco in *Nueva corónica y buen gobierno.* Rolena Adorno characterizes the double representation of Andean figures in the text as the author's strategy to create credibility with his readers, thus representing Mama Huaco from both the native Andean and the Christian perspectives (*Guaman Poma,* 131). For his Christian reader, ideally, the king of Spain, to whom his letter-chronicle is addressed, the narrator distances himself from the indigenous culture, representing Mama Huaco as an idolatrous witch, a warrior woman, and a trickster. This last trope, that of "deceiver" (engañadora), relates her to the Christian tradition's female traitor, Eve. In his "native" version, however, which is the text that accompanies Mama Huaco's portrait drawing

(Figure 6), Guaman Poma treats her as an idol, naming her "the daughter of the Sun and the Moon" [la hija del Sol y la Luna]. She is said to have married Manco Capac, with the Sun's permission, and to have had two sons who became Inca rulers. She is described as beautiful and benevolent toward the poor. In short, this version of Mama Huaco portrays her as an Andean saintlike figure, a positive image of the female gender and her complementary power. She is even the mother of the Inca dynastic lineage.[45]

There is little doubt that Guaman Poma synthesized elements from both the indigenous and the Spanish cultures in his representation of Mama Huaco, reflecting how forces of transculturation affected the ladino's cultural memory and how he, as an agent writing from the *chaupi* in the transformative process, created a hybrid figure, a queer subject, eccentric to both cultures. Something of that queer eccentricity, however, seems to have been autochthonous to her archetypal role in pre-Hispanic times.

Rodrigo Hernández Príncipe, a priest charged with extirpating idolatry in the early seventeenth century, reported that Mama Huaco had her own cult, "because she sowed the first corn there was" (in Silverblatt, *Moon, Sun, and Witches,* 40). Pierre Duviols has examined several early colonial sources that report Inca myths confirming Mama Huaco as the sister who planted the first corn in the *chakra* of Sausero in Cuzco. Cristóbal de Molina, for example, recorded in 1574 that the body of Mama Huaco was venerated and *chicha* was made in her honor (in Duviols, "De la Tarasca a Mama Huaco," 337). There is a clear symbolic correspondence between the mythic representation of the conquest of the Cuzco valley and the corn-planting rituals that later legitimized Inca sovereignty in the region through annual, public reenactments that highlighted the role Mama Huaco played as a mythic actor in the conquest of the valleys, as I will discuss below and in the next chapter.[46]

Consistent in the mythological record is the idea that Mama Huaco disemboweled a local Hualla, a pre-Inca inhabitant of the valley, which created her image as a warrior woman, a *warmi auca*. This warrior-woman figure, suggestive of women's agriculture-related *supay* power, is reflected in the opening of the earth in the corn-planting ritual, an echo of the foundational act perpetrated by Mama Huaco, metonymically, on the body of the Hualla. The corn-planting ceremony ended with representations of war and hunting (Duviols, "De la Tarasca a Mama Huaco," 340), again invoking the original scene of Inca expansion and domestication of the Cuzco valley.

Guaman Poma visually represents this ceremonial tradition in his Edenic depiction of the first generation of Andeans after the epoch of the

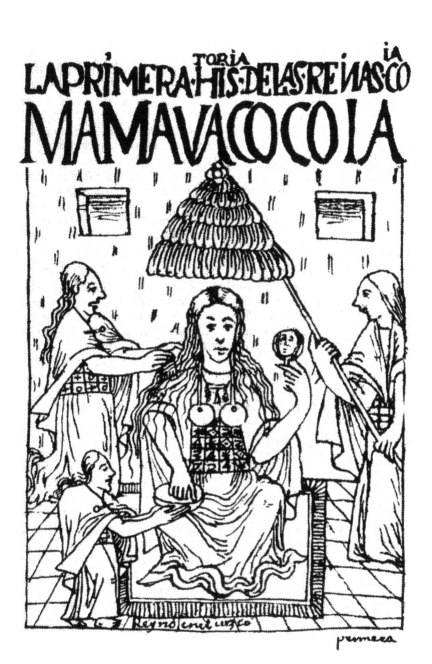

FIGURE 6   *Ipa Mama Huaco. From Guaman Poma,* Nueva corónica y buen gobierno.

creator deity, Viracocha (f48:line 43), and in his representation of *chacra-yupay,* the annual ceremony commemorating the first corn planting (Figure 7) (f250:line 185). As Guaman Poma informs us in the accompanying text, August is the time of sacrifices, celebration, dance, and song (f251:line 186). His drawing clearly delineates the gendered space of the ritual. The men open the ground with their phalliclike *lampa* (Andean hoes), while women place the seeds in the earth. The gender symmetry is highlighted by the presence of the sun and the moon. The only element in the drawing that does not have a counterpart is the figure approaching the planting scene, carrying two tumblers, perhaps *queros* (ceremonial vessels) with *chicha* or another ritual libation, or perhaps corn seeds. As we will see below, the *llijlla* shawl that the figure is wearing signifies a ceremonial *cargo* and may be a marker of third-gender subjectivity in this context. The enigmatic figure recorded by Guaman Poma seems to perform a binary mediating role. Could it be a representation of Mama Huaco? In the ceremony, could the figure be a *huacsa,* that is, a ritual impersonator like the ones who embodied Chuqui Suso and Chaupi Ñamca in the Huarochirí rituals? If so, does a third-gender figure represent her, and not a woman, as in the case of the *huacsas* from Huarochirí? Remarkably, there is ethnographic evidence that cross-dressed males performed in the ritual at least until the late twentieth century.

Billie Jean Isbell, in her ethnography of a small south-central Andean village, based on fieldwork from the late 1960's and the early 1970's, discusses the August corn-planting ritual, *chacrayupay,* in which "a man dresses as a woman, blackens his face, and 'plants' the plaza with the remains left in the bottoms of the brewing pots used to prepare corn beer. This is a reverse portrayal of actual planting. The plaza is planted instead of fields; a transvestite with a reverse-colored face performs the task using 'that which is thrown away' as seed" (*To Defend Ourselves,* 206). Isbell offers a provocative interpretation of this ritual, one that further substantiates the symbolic connection between agriculture and the power of the female gender (discussed above), which helps us understand third gender's ritual participation in Andean culture. She explains that it was the woman's role to place corn seeds in the ground while men covered them with earth using the native *lampa* hoe (ibid., 57), as we see depicted in Guaman Poma's drawing.

Of the transgendering involved in the ritual she observed, Isbell proposes that "men are balancing the scale of procreative power between males and females" (ibid., 206). In order to maintain social and cosmological equilibrium, the men reverse the order of the planting tradition, thus allaying fears that women's procreative power could create an imbalance. Based

FIGURE 7   Chacrayupay. *From Guaman Poma*, Nueva corónica y buen gobierno.

on my interpretation of third gender, however, I would modify Isbell's reading of the reversal. The symbolic reversal was not conducted by a man, which would have been the opposite gender of the female protagonist of ritual corn planting, but a cross-dressed man. Instead of invoking the masculine to restore the balance, the Andeans chose to invoke an in-between gender, a third gender. This intervention of a third gender as a mediation between the two opposing genders, between the feminine and the masculine, suggests that the ritual's meaning, which Isbell insightfully explicates, might be the same, only our understanding of the participating subjects changes. The third gender is the embodiment of the liminal space between the two sides. What does the feminine attire of the third gender signify in the performance? Could it be a symbolic border between the ideal reflection that Platt posits as the key to *yanantin*?

Yet another ethnographic report advances my argument and confirms the importance of ritual dress in Andean symbolic acts while providing yet another example of third-gender ritual performance that had survived into the late twentieth century. Anne Paul's study of Paracas textiles includes an insightful introduction to the symbolic importance of textiles in the Andes from pre-Hispanic to contemporary times. Ethnic dress communicates everyday distinctions of social status as well as messages unique to ritual contexts: "Embedded in items of apparel are visible indicators of such things as ethnic group, *ayllu* affiliation, cosmology, economic status, gender, age, family ties, marital status, and offices held within the community" (*Paracas Ritual Attire,* 17). One such garment invested with ritual symbolism in the Chinchero region (near Cuzco) of the southern Andean highlands is the *llijlla,* or shawl, commonly worn by women. The *llijlla* marks a woman's *ayllu* affiliation while portraying the wearer's identity, since each shawl is produced by the wearer. But the *llijlla* is also used as a symbol of transgendering. Paul records ethnographers Ed and Christine Franquemont's observations that "during the running of their *ayllu* boundaries, a land-based ritual called *mujonomiento,*" a man known as a *waylaka* cross-dresses by wearing a *llijlla:*

> The *ayllu*'s officers bring with them their staffs of office and
> plant them in the ground, indicating a formal government
> occasion. The most important officer, the *alcalde,* wears a
> special red poncho that is different from the standard walnut-
> dyed brown sheep's wool poncho worn by the other men.
> A central participant in the celebration is the *waylaka,* a man
> who recites humorous poems and orations about the history

of the stone markers that border the *ayllu,* and dances with a
white flag. The *waylaka* dresses as a transvestite, with clothing
like that worn by Chinchero women. He wears two *llijllas:*
one is held shut with a *tupu* (pin) made of a silver spoon, and
the other is draped over one shoulder and under the opposite
arm, tied in front. The outer *llijlla* symbolizes a ritual burden,
indicating that the wearer has a *cargo* (special responsibility or
obligation) for the fiesta.

(Ibid., 19–20)

This rich ethnographic account, while not addressing the meaning of the
cross-dressing, provides us with more clues about the ritual context in
which such practices occur in the late twentieth century.

We can note the differentiation of three distinct gender categories: man,
woman, and the transvested *waylaka.* This categorization is marked by both
the subjects' vestments and their roles in the ceremony. The *waylaka,* performing as a third gender, is invested with the special responsibility of recalling the history of the *ayllus'* borders. The fact that the men and women
are separated in distinct groups and the transvested *waylaka* performs a
ritual to mark borders confirms the relationship suggested above between
tinkuy and *yanantin.* Here, the cross-dressed *waylaka's* body is employed in
the determination of a community's borders, through dance and song. His
feminine attire evokes a memory that stretches back to pre-Hispanic times
and may be similar to the figure recorded in Guaman Poma's drawing,
who is dressed in a *llijlla*-like shawl with *tupu,* strikingly similar to that of
the *waylaka* in the Chinchero ceremony. Duviols remarks that the *tupu* is
included in the portrait drawings of only two *coyas* (Inca queens), Mama
Huaco and Mama Anahuarque, both related to the agricultural calendar.
He then notes that the figure in the *chacrayupay* drawing also wears a *tupu*
("De la Tarasca a Mama Huaco," 350n11).

The question remains as to why Mama Huaco would be associated with
gender liminality. Her name is suggestive of connections to the fragments
of third gender discussed in this chapter. Santacruz Pachacuti calls Mama
Huaco "Ipamamauaco" (f7:line 196), as does Guaman Poma, who refers to
her as "Ipa Uaco" (Duviols, "De la Tarasca a Mama Huaco," 347). As I note
in Chapter 2, Zuidema has shown that "*ipa*" in Quechua and Aymara could
refer to a "father's sister" (*Inca Civilization,* 29) or be a signifier of a male in
a "female sexual position," symbolically enabling the male to take a female
position in the kinship system; specifically, younger brothers can be gen-

dered female to symbolize a "sister" of an older brother (ibid., 29–30). In most accounts, Mama Huaco is the "sister" to Manco Capac, the mythic father of all Incas. The colonial dictionaries, as we saw in Chapter 2, record *ipa* as signifying a man living as a woman, as well. Duviols analyzes the second element of her name, *huaco,* relating it to the Quechua word *huacon* (mask) and the word *huaco* (eyetooth or fang). He uses this connection in his argument that Guaman Poma associated her with the Corpus Christi processional figure, the Tarasca. He notes that there is a dance of the "*huacon*" in which fanged masks are worn by dancers who act out like ogres and hypothesizes that Mama Huaco must have invoked this image in Guaman Poma's imagination because of her mythical history as a fierce warrior woman and her association with infertility. I would add that this may explain the use of a third-gender *huacsa,* if Mama Huaco was indeed perceived to be "ugly" or "manly," as Guaman Poma describes her in one of his two descriptive portraits. Henrique Urbano, however, suggests tracing the etymology of her name, *huaco,* to the Aymara word "*huaccu,*" which reveals "mujer estéril" (sterile woman) and "mujer varonil" (manly woman) (*Wiracocha y Ayar,* xliv) as the original meaning. Both etymologies suggest gender liminality and reference her aesthetic representation as in between a man and a woman. I will return to the issue of sterility below.

The question becomes, then, why would there be an association between Mama Huaco and the epithet "*ipa*"? Further, why would a liminally gendered subject be involved in one of the most important rituals in the Inca calendar? Duviols provides more clues that may help us decipher this enigma. First, through a study of the sacred spaces and *ceques* (sacred lines) involved in the myths and terrain around Cuzco, Duviols ("De la Tarasca a Mama Huaco," 339, 357–358) suggests that we relate Mama Huaco with the household *huacas* known as *mamasaras,* the "mother corn" that was guarded each year to be used in subsequent planting seasons (ibid., 357), the corn that is brought out in the *chacrayupay* ceremony. Silverblatt explains that the Pachamama, the "goddess of fertility" and "embodiment of the earth's regenerative powers" (*Moon, Sun, and Witches,* 24), had "daughters" who were symbolic of highland agricultural production, such as maize, represented by Saramama (ibid., 25). Silverblatt's archival research uncovered several examples of cults and ritual practices related to Saramama, and she notes that, "although celebrations of Saramama accentuated female powers, the interdependent dualities of the Andean cosmos, metaphorized as male and female forces, were expressed and realized in carrying out this ritual of fertility" (ibid., 26–27). This included rites celebrating the Mamayutas, another designation for Corn Mothers, who, Silverblatt explains, "had a masculine aspect as well as a feminine one, but clearly the latter predominated" (ibid., 35). The duality of the *mamasara* is the key to understanding why Mama Huaco may be represented in a masculinized way, that is, as in between the male and the female and represented by third-gender markers.[47]

Duviols's research suggests that Mama Huaco "represented both the sterility of the dry season and the capacity to store the fertility and the hope to regain that fertility after the sterile season is over" ("De la Tarasca a Mama Huaco," 340). Duviols concludes that Mama Huaco was not the mother who gave birth to corn—the Pachamama—but the mother who kept it safe, the symbolic "granary" (ibid., 357) during the dry season. Thus, it was she who carried the corn out to be planted on the first day after the end of the dry, sterile time of year.

Who better to guard the seed of future generations than an in-between, nonprocreative subject, analogous perhaps to the "eunuchs" who guarded the fertile, yet virgin, *acllas*? The ambiguous figures in the *chacrayupay* ceremonies recorded nearly four hundred years apart seem to be related to Ipa Mama Huaco. They cross-dress to invoke gender liminality; they bring out the seeds for the first planting. In Guaman Poma's drawing the third gender figure is a *huacsa,* the impersonator of Ipa Mama Huaco, bringing forth the seed she kept safe during the sterile season. The women prepare the earth, representing the fertility of the female, while the men break the earth open so the seeds can be planted. Neither male nor female guards the ceremonial seed during the lead-up to the planting; a third-gender *huacsa* performs the role Ipa Mama Huaco would have represented, thereby commemorating the primordial scene reenacted in *chacrayupay.* In the ethnographic report, we appreciate how that role began to be performed by cross-dressed performers taking on the special *cargo* as a ritual duty to invoke that long-ago foundational moment.

One last fragment from Guaman Poma helps us understand that in the colonial period there were men cross-dressing in ritual dances to represent liminal gender subjects. He records that the Andesuyos held a celebration in which one of the dances involved cross-dressing. He presents it along with fiestas from other regions, assuring the reader that the ceremonies had nothing to do with witchcraft, idolatry, or enchantments, but were purely for enjoyment, though in reality he is explaining how local Andeans worshiped *huacas* (f315:line 239). As they danced in a circle holding hands, participants sang "in their language," which the author records as *"cayaya caya, cayaya caya,"* an unidentified language of the area (Figure 8). They also sang, however, in Quechua, which Guaman Poma includes in his description:

FIESTAS DELOS ANDISVIOS
CAIACAIAVARMIAVCA

curipata anti   fiesta   fiesta

FIGURE 8   Huarmi auca *Andesuyu dance. From Guaman Poma,* Nueva corónica y buen gobierno.

"And to the sound of a flute they celebrate, walking in a circle hand-in-hand, they enjoy themselves and celebrate and they dance the *huarmi auca,* all the men dressed as women with their arrows; the one who plays the drum: warmi auca chiauan uaylla uruchapa panascatana anti auca chiuan uaylla" [Y al son de ello (una flauta) hacen fiesta, andan al ruedo asidos las manos unos con otros, se huelgan y hacen fiesta y bailan huarmi auca todos los hombres vestidos como mujer con sus flechas dice así el que tañe tambor: uarmi auca chiauan uaylla uruchapa panascatana anti auca chiuan uaylla] (f323:242).

Cross-dressing for ritual dance seems to have been a public and perhaps common practice, at least common enough to justify a specialized vocabulary. Bertonio includes a word in his Aymara dictionary for a man dressed in women's clothes during dances or "when using masks."[48] The Quechua *huarmi auca* means "warrior woman," which leads Duviols to conclude that the dance may have been in honor of another warrior woman, Manco Capac's sister, who married the chief of the Chancas ethnic group, Anca Uallo.[49] They both are said to have fled to the mountains, where she became a *huarmi auca* (Duviols, "De la Tarasca a Mama Huaco," 367). The fact that both Mama Huaco and Tupa Huaco share the second name is suggestive, again, of a connection between both mythical figures and the image of warrior-like strength, *supay* power, perhaps, and gender ambiguity.[50]

ANDROGYNY, THE *CHUQUI CHINCHAY,*
AND THIRD GENDER

I opened the introduction to this book with the story of the *chuqui chinchay,* the mountain deity of "Indians of two genders." Santacruz Pachacuti is the only colonial scribe to record this ambiguous figure, which appears in both his text and his well-known cosmological drawing, analyzed below. Harrison glosses this image as "a fierce puma constellation with brilliant eyes" (*Signs, Songs, and Memory,* 68), a gloss confirmed by Urton's study of southern Andean astronomy (*At the Crossroads of the Earth and the Sky*). Duviols refers to an Amazonian stellar cult with this figure ("De la Tarasca a Mama Huaco," 35). For our purposes it is important to relate the figure in the drawing with Santacruz Pachacuti's comments about the animal, which he made after recounting Pachacuti Inga Yupangui's expansion of the Inca empire (f19–f21:lines 219–224). Upon returning to Cuzco and finding his father old and ill, the Inca celebrates several rituals, including Capac Raymi and rites associated with the birth of his son (f21:line 224). After expelling all the "wild animals" from Cuzco, "the chieftains (from Carabaya) bring a *Chuqui Chinchay,* an animal that is painted in all the colors. They say that it was the *apo* [deity] of the jaguars, in whose protection were the hermaphrodites or Indians of two genders" [Los curacas y mitmais ⟨de Carabaya⟩ trae a chuqui chinchay, animal muy pintado de todos los colores. Dizen que era apo de los otorongos, en cuya guarda da a los ermofraditas yndios de dos naturas] (f21–f22:lines 224–225). The *chuqui chinchay* seems to have been the protector of the third-gender subjects; whether they were actual hermaphrodites or transgendered is not clear, but their ritual significance is. While we do not know precisely why the *apo* was called to Cuzco at this time, it is suggestive that its presence played a ritual role in Andean society during a liminal moment, the near-death of an Inca and the birth of a new generation. The connection to the jungle star cult and its clear association with the moon, and therefore the feminine sphere of Santacruz Pachacuti's drawing, is further substantiation of the relationship between gender liminality, Andesuyo, and the supernatural, mentioned above.

Perhaps the most widely remarked aspect of Santacruz Pachacuti's *Relación* is his cosmological drawing of the Andean creator god, an image that supposedly adorned the wall of Coricancha, Cuzco's temple of the Sun (Figure 9). Isbell, expanding on Zuidema's unpublished interpretation of the drawing, proposes that the sketch represents the complementary nature of gender in the Andean world view and compares this colonial drawing with Andean children's drawing from the early 1970's to demonstrate the continuity of these conceptions. As we have seen, Duviols's introductory study to the *Relación* privileges the European influence in Santacruz Pachacuti's writing; in a similar fashion, his analysis of the cosmological drawing centers on how it reflects Western paradigms rather than Andean ones (Santa Cruz Pachacuti, *Relación,* 30–64). Harrison, on the other hand, highlights the importance of the visual code in Andean cognition ("Modes of Discourse," 74–75; *Signs, Songs, and Memory,* 57–71) and argues that Santacruz Pachacuti's drawing is just one instance of his dependence on the visual to express Andean cultural concepts. She also finds the same code in his discussion of Inca social ranking (*Signs, Songs, and Memory,* 58), the *tocapu* sign system and *pacarina* ordering of ethnic housing (ibid., 60), and in Andean divination practices (ibid., 62). Harrison contextualizes Santacruz Pachacuti's drawing in the more general discursive strategy that included resorting to visual as well as verbal representation; her reading encourages us to search for the autochthonous meanings of Santacruz

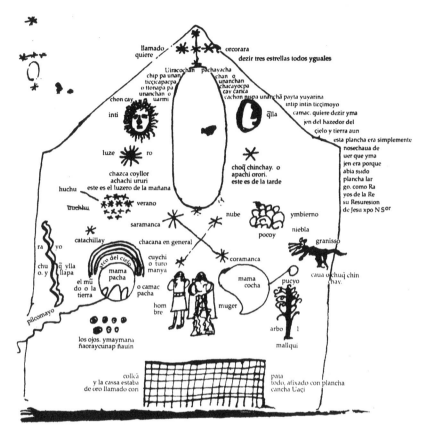

FIGURE 9   *Primordial androgyny and complementarity. From Santacruz Pachacuti,*
            Relación de antigüedades deste reyno del Perú

Pachacuti's *Relación* in the drawing as we did in the text. I continue to read him as a ladino writing from the *chaupi* between two cultures.

Instead of repeating a thorough analysis of this drawing, for which I direct the reader to Duviols, Harrison, Silverblatt, and Isbell, I will simply pull out three elements that relate to third-gender subjectivity. First, the overall structure of the drawing, agreed on by all of the scholars mentioned above, reflects the complementary relationship between genders in the Andes, given the symmetrical presentation of a male-identified left side and a female-identified right side. On the male side we find, from the top, etchings of the sun, the morning star, summer stars, a rainbow, a lightning bolt, *camac pacha* (male earth), a male human figure, and some eyes. On the female side, more or less parallel to the male elements are the moon, the evening star, winter clouds, the *chuqui chinchay* (a feline figure), Mama Cocha (female lake), a female figure, and a *mallqui* (a tree that represents Andean ancestors) (208). These correspondences remind us of the symmetry discussed above, where I hypothesize that third gender performed as a symbolic, liminal subjectivity mediating for the *qhariwarmi* in the context of *yanantin*.

Here, in Santacruz Pachacuti's drawing, the only element that transcends and connects the parallel gender divisions is the oval-shaped figure identified by the author as Viracocha Pacha Yachachic, the creator god of the Andes; this shape was said to have adorned the Sun temple. Harrison (*Signs, Songs and Memory,* 70) and Isbell ("La otra mitad esencial," 38) have recognized the androgynous nature of this representation of the progenitor of the gendered vertical lines of descent listed above. If we think of the oval in terms of an egglike figure, which has correspondence in Andean myths, as identified by Lehmann Nitsche and as seen in the Huarochirí myths, then the notion of an androgynous source of life seems reasonable.[51] The notion of androgyny is confirmed by recalling the ambiguous gender qualities of heroes in the Viracocha cycle of Andean myths.[52] In addition, Silverblatt's observation that the pre-Inca, Huari creator-god's gender was ambiguous, reportedly either "hermaphroditic" or female (*Moon, Sun, and Witches,* 70), adds more evidence to a pan-Andean tendency to represent the creator deity as androgynous.

As John McDowell has stressed, more study is needed in exploring the connection between the Andean highlands and the Amazon lowland jungles, where "vibrant peripheries such as the Sibundoy Valley, areas that never came under the influence of Incaic empire-building, hold their own clues to the enigmatic quality of 'Andeanness'" ("Exemplary Ancestors," 112). In McDowell's ethnographic work on the northern Amazonian, Quechua-speaking jungle culture of the Sibundoy, we find a myth with strong transgender content. In the myth, the hostile Sun god's daughter, the Moon, transforms herself into human form and promises to marry a human miner. She gives the man a wad of cotton after rubbing it on her body, which he then stores away in his gear (ibid., 103). The man's younger brother discovers the cotton and rubs it all over his body, including his crotch area, causing him to transgender into a woman (ibid., 104). The older brother takes him/her to the river and allows animals to lick his/her vagina, but he/she ends up being devoured by the animals. Only his/her head remains, which the older brother sends down the river in a drum, to be found by washerwomen who, on opening the drum, find an infant in place of the head. The infant is said to be Wangetsmuna, who is figured as a Viracocha-like civilizing hero in Sibundoy mythic tradition (ibid.). In fact, McDowell identifies Wangetsmuna as "probably cognate with Viracocha of the central and southern Andes" (ibid., 112).

Again we are confronted with a younger brother who becomes gendered female, reminiscent of Ayar Ucho, Manco Capac's younger brother, who was enchanted and implicitly "sodomized" by the *huaca,* and of the *ipa* in Andean kinship relations. That the civilizing demigod of the Sibundoy is produced from such a magical, and sexualized, encounter with the Moon suggests a parallel between Santacruz Pachacuti's androgynous Viracocha and the tacit transgendered androgyny of Wangetsmuna. These myths, involving younger brothers and deities, together with the supernatural figure *chuqui chinchay,* indicate the complexity of the third-gender subjectivity and its role in Andean ritual practices. Through both visual and written codes, Santacruz Pachacuti recorded mythological sanctions for the performance of third-gender subjectivity in ritual contexts.

The abundance of fragments from multiple sources suggests that we understand the existence of third-gender ritual subjectivity as a symbolic position in culture-producing rituals. Summarizing, we find the performance of this subjectivity in the context of a gender culture in which the feminine enjoyed autonomy, power, and respect. The feminine and the masculine were to be negotiated and mediated through signs of androgyny reminiscent of an originary, androgynous creator. The evocation of gender liminality is consistent with a step in the process of *yanantin,* in the uniting of opposite forces. While the corporeal manifestation of this in-between, *chaupi* position varied in the different textual fragments of colonial discourse, the Andean third-gender subjectivity was often performed as a biologically sexed male, socially recognizable through castration, cross-dressing, or both. These males reportedly were sexually passive on ritual and perhaps profane occasions. Evidence suggests that they fit into the Andean kinship system as *ipas* and often spoke "like women," either in falsetto voice or through conforming to gendered linguistic rules. Their ritual roles were related to agriculture and perhaps to the channeling of ancestors' voices in ceremonial contexts. In one example, they seem to embody a mythic founding mother of the Inca dynasty. They enjoyed supernatural sanction through myths and supernatural protection from a stellar cult figure, the *Chuqui Chinchay.* In their contemporary iterations, they are respected and integrated members of the community who perform the role in ceremonial occasions.

We cannot think of gender and sexuality in the Andes in absolute terms. This is an important lesson for those who read Andean Conquest politics in strictly gendered terms, in which the masculine is understood as dominating the feminine. A sustained position of masculine dominance would have been anathema to the balance and complementarity expressed throughout Andean philosophy. Even when such imbalances occur, Andean cultural practices ideally bring the spheres back into balance. In culture-producing rituals, neither masculine nor feminine forces prevail; the two are mediated by androgynous signs of originary wholeness. The ideal of complementarity is repeatedly restored.

Now that I have posited a subjectivity whose very reconstruction depended on "reading from the *chaupi*" of colonial discourse, in the following chapters I will discuss the process through which the representation of Andean gender culture, same-sex sexuality, and third-gender subjects became transformed under colonial regimes. As we will see, the marginalization of third gender was part of a more extensive transculturation of indigenous gender and sexuality carried out in civil and ecclesiastical discourses of the Toledo viceroyalty and, finally, in the foundational history of Peru, Inca Garcilaso's *Comentarios reales.*

Four   **CHURCH AND STATE**
Inventing Queer Penitents and Tyrannical Others

> *It is one thing to be erased from discourse, and yet another to be*
> *present within discourse as an abiding falsehood.*
> —JUDITH BUTLER, *Bodies That Matter*

Andean notions of the feminine and the androgyne, ritually represented by third-gender subjects and analyzed and characterized in Chapters 2 and 3, experienced a transformation in the waning years of the sixteenth century. Rather than being erased by the more stringent civil and ecclesiastical texts, indigenous gender culture was transculturated and left in colonial discourse as "an abiding falsehood." Indeed, as we have seen, one cannot speak of "sodomites" or "third genders" without recognizing these figures as discursive constructs, tropes with a history, or performative subjects of ritual liminality. The textual descriptions offered in the preceding pages, drawn from chronicles, *relaciones,* histories, dictionaries, and pre-Hispanic ceramic iconography were the phantasmagorical originals of what I shall suggest became a new, regulated subject of coloniality. As Butler has theorized, gender is constructed, negotiated, and contested in a long stream of iterations, or imitations of phantasms of "original" gender constructs.[1] In this chapter, I continue to trace this stream of iterations in order to explicate the mechanics of transculturation of the phantasmagorical originals in a new colonial context, that of the Toledo viceroyalty.

Viceroy Francisco de Toledo, who governed Peru from 1569 to 1581, initiated an effort to regulate the colonized indigenous Andeans in part by controlling their bodies; that effort is represented in two powerful discourses: the civil *ordenanzas* and *visita* reports, and the ecclesiastical *Doctrina christiana.* My reading of these documents suggests that Michel Foucault's genealogy of the relationship between power and sexuality can be traced back farther than the eighteenth and nineteenth centuries. As Ann Laura Stoler has suggested, Europe's discourses on sexuality cannot be examined on that continent alone: "In short-circuiting empire, Foucault's history of European sexuality misses key sites in the production of that discourse, discounts the practices that racialized bodies, and thus elides a field of knowledge that provided the contrast for what a 'healthy, vigorous bourgeois body' was all about" (*Race and the Education of Desire,* 7). Indeed, I hypothesize that it was the colonial discourse of Spanish empire, a full two centuries prior to the period Foucault studies, that created "sodomites" from third-gender subjects, much in the same way Foucault proposed that the "homosexual" as a recognizable and regulatable identity was born out of the discourses of modernity. While Rudi C. Bleys's provocative *Geography of Perversion* has pushed back Europe's "new cognitive definition and classification of sexual desire" (2) to the Enlightenment, I will highlight rhetorical moments in which this cognition occurs even earlier. Bleys recognizes this early discourse on same-sex behavior and cross-gender identities reported in colonial chronicles and other travel narratives outside the West as a "pre-Enlightenment legacy" that informed a cognitive shift in European thought as it related to same-sex sexuality. He studies how the European "ethnographic imagination," beginning in 1750, initiated a linking of male-to-male sexual practices to cross-gender identity that ultimately led to the European construction of the effeminate homosexual as a distinct identity (ibid., 44). In this chapter, I explicate the colonial practices that formed the context of these later writings, of this knowledge that traveled back to the "Old World," historicized and naturalized in Enlightenment narratives. Moreover, the legacy effect was actually more immediate, as I explore in Chapter 5; we will see how transculturation of indigenous gender and sexual norms finds its way into the foundational historical text of Peru as early as 1609, in Inca Garcilaso's *Comentarios reales.*

By critically reading the Toledo-era *ordenanzas* and *visita* reports and the viceroy's official history and by analyzing the Spanish catechists' resemanticization of indigenous language words (in Quechua and Aymara), I demonstrate how power asserted in the political and religious discourses initiated in Toledo's administration cites and then reconstructs same-sex sexuality and third-gender subjectivity in the Andes. Again, as in the previous chapters, I focus on third gender in the larger context of colonial discourse's transculturation of indigenous gender culture. I posit the feminine as "abject outsider" to Toledo's colonial discourse's construction of a masculine reordering of Andean space. The queer tropes of sexuality from earlier descriptions of indigenous culture are mobilized in the discourses of power that begin to regulate the conquered subjects of the Spanish empire.

As Viceroy Toledo consolidated imperial power in the Andes, the native Andeans began to receive, through a pedagogical discourse, an adulterated version of their culture based on the systematic gathering of cultural information then filtered through European conceptions and prejudices. Homi Bhabha has used the term "pedagogical discourse" to describe the nationalist narratives that interpellate individuals in the process of nation building. The citizens are objects of these pedagogical narratives: they receive a homogeneous image of the nation, or protonation, an image whose authority rests in its accumulative tradition, rooted in the past (*Location of Culture,* 145). Although they were not citizens of a nation, the late sixteenth- and early seventeenth-century Andeans underwent similar processes, what we might consider protonational processes of transculturation, that ultimately led to the true nation building that began to take place in the nineteenth century. Both the official history of the Toledo period—Pedro Sarmiento de Gamboa's *Historia índica*—and the *Doctrina christiana*—the body of official ecclesiastical texts used in the evangelization of the Andes beginning in the late seventeenth century—attempted to totalize the moral universe of the indigenous past and re-present it as error and sin in the colonial present. The authority for this discourse is found in the accumulated traditions of the Europeans, specifically, in the Judeo-Christian and classical philosophical and historiographic traditions. We will see how the heritage of conversion, especially within the context of the Spanish Reconquest of Christian territory in Iberia, informs the *Doctrina christiana* as it creates what we might call a Toledan pedagogical discourse, one with ecclesiastical and secular components. Sarmiento, for example, employs the queer tropes of sexuality I examine in Chapter 2, in justification of the conquest of Tawantinsuyu in what we can consider the first official historicization of the Toledo era.

It is important, however, to take into account the native Andeans' participation in the narrativization of their culture and history. Bhabha's theorizing of nation includes a second strand of narrative that he characterizes as "performative," in which the people act as subjects of and in the narrative (*Location of Culture,* 145). This contestatory voice is intertwined with the hegemonic, pedagogical narrative to form what he calls "DissemiNation," a liminal, temporal space between the past (represented by the dominant discourse) and the future (represented by the performative discourse) (ibid., 148). In other words, to theorize the writing of nations or, in this case, that of a colonized people, one must take into account both the hegemonic and the contestatory, subaltern voices.

I read the Toledo-era writings as texts produced in this liminal tem-

poral space of the imperial colony, as hybrid texts that both express fragments of Andean indigenous culture and distort the cultural knowledge
contained in those fragments. They are texts that reflect Bhabha's "double-
time" of the protonation, that moment when two or more cultures are
struggling for survival, when the subaltern voices of the present battle the
hegemonic discourse of the authoritative past. In this confrontation of two
world views, in which the invading culture is privileged over the invaded,
we can explore how the native's silencing of ritual sexuality, for example, is
reflected back to the colonial subjects through official history, catechisms,
sermons, and confession manuals. The Toledo *visita* reports, based on interviews with native informants, informed how Sarmiento wrote his history
of the Incas. The church's teachings and confession manuals (analyzed below) were shaped in part by the chronicles and reports that the catechists
and civil officials, with the purpose of converting the native population,
wrote from information gathered from indigenous informants. What I
posit as resistant silence or strategic and ethnically informed misinforma-
tion found its way into this hybrid text, thus contributing to the transculturating narratives of conversion. As we will see in the precursor ecclesiastical literature, the pedagogical discourse itself had a tendency toward
suppressing discussion of same-sex sexuality. As the two discourses conflate
to form an Andean version of evangelical tools, native notions of ritual
sexuality are all but effaced.

I am particularly interested in how sexuality became a focal point in
the evangelical mission, at least, rhetorically. More than just an issue of
religious conversion, the censure and eventual near-erasure of indigenous
erotic ritual practices is a violent act of transculturation that had profound
effects as it established colonial control of the indigenous community by
divorcing sexuality from its Andean ritual, communal context and by individualizing once-sacred acts in terms of personal sin. I focus on the linguistic battles that ensued to eradicate same-sex sexuality, though the campaigns targeted other forms of sexuality as well.

In addition to advancing my argument that indigenous notions of gender and sexuality were transculturated by this colonial discourse, I answer
some of the questions that other scholars have raised concerning the third
gender's status in pre-Columbian society, thereby adding to our understanding of third-gender subjectivity (discussed in Chapters 2 and 3). Were
same-sex practices a "sin" under the Incas? Were the subjects in question
ridiculed and debased in indigenous society? Due to the scarce sources on
this topic, and to the nature of the written sources available, that is, biased
by European ideologies, it is imperative that these questions be addressed

in the context of a detailed analysis of the colonial discourse that produced the knowledge. Only then can we hope to understand how these identities were constructed and how they related to larger Andean society. To separate Spanish attitudes and political purposes from a historical reconstruction of these identities is a spurious methodology. The language that is left for us to use to read about these subjects, the language that produced what we think we know about them, is the very language that worked to destroy them or to obscure them as a resistant mode of preservation. This paradox must continue to be prominently focused in all discussions of pre-Hispanic subjectivity.

TOLEDO'S CONSOLIDATION OF COLONIAL POWER

Francisco de Toledo served King Philip II as viceroy of Peru from 1569 to 1581, having been sent to the Andes to reorganize after the conquistadors' civil wars left the colony in administrative disarray and to squelch an indigenous rebellion. His viceroyalty marks a shift in the colonial discourse's predominant ideology, from that of the apologists I discuss in Chapter 2, best represented by Cieza de León and Bartolomé de Las Casas, to one of justification of the Spanish Conquest in response to the Lascasian critique. Juan de Matienzo, a jurist who first proposed reforms to the colonial system in 1567, was one of the first historians to write the history of the Conquest as a vindication of the Spanish, arguing that the conquistadors liberated the inferior Indians from the Incas.[2] This was the beginning of the proliferation of two distinct discourses, one civil and the other ecclesiastical, that converged to reshape the colonial life of the indigenous Andean peoples in response to the crisis that struck the Andean colony in the 1560's. The change in ideology was signaled by Toledo's prohibition of Las Casas's writings in Peru.[3]

As Steve Stern has illustrated with his thorough history of the Huamanga region, early Andean colonial society consisted of alliances between the local Indians, represented by their *curacas,* and the Spanish encomenderos.[4] Structurally, the systems of tribute collection echoed pre-Hispanic relations the local ethnic groups had with the Incas; therefore, a semblance of stability was achieved in which the Andeans worked in the encomiendas and added the Christian God and saints to their pantheon of native deities, while continuing to respect their traditional allegiances to *ayllu* and regional *huacas.*[5]

This adjustment to the new central authorities seems to have reflected an Andean tradition of adapting to changing power structures, the most recent of which, before the Spanish invasion, was the expansion of the Inca empire. Under the Spanish encomenderos the local Andeans' economy continued much as it had before the European conquest, and the local *curacas* took advantage of the Spaniards' need for intermediaries between themselves and the native laborers. This structure became increasingly problematic for the Spaniards in the 1550's, when the combination of increased demand for labor in the newly flourishing mines and the concomitant decimation of the native population from disease, geographic relocation, and abuse led to initial breaches in the Spanish-Andean alliances.[6] The Andeans began to question these relationships, especially in light of the demographic change their communities were suffering, and the colonizers began to debate publicly the effectiveness of the encomienda system (Stern, *Peru's Indian Peoples,* 43–50). Meanwhile, the rebellious neo-Inca leader, Titu Cusi Yupanqui, had consolidated an armed resistance in the southern jungle of Vilcabamba.

In the context of this initial unrest was born a more radical crisis, which spread throughout the Andean highlands. By the mid-1560's a native religious movement known as Taqui Onqoy had extended from Huamanga north toward Jauja and Lima and east toward Cuzco and Charcas (ibid., 51; Millones, "Nuevos aspectos del Taqui Onqoy," 97). Taqui Onqoy, which can be translated as the "dancing sickness," was the result of a propagation of the belief that the *huacas* were finally rebelling against the foreign Christian deity by seizing and possessing the Andeans' bodies, which then went into trembling convulsions. Using millenarian language, native religious leaders predicted a *pachakuti,* or radical change, in the lives of their people, a change led by a united force of indigenous deities that would resist the Christians and reconquer the Andean territory. This proposed reconquest was to unite the *huacas* from Titicaca to Pachacamac, that is, from the extreme southern end of Tawantinsuyu to Lima (Millones, "Nuevos aspectos del Taqui Onqoy," 97). Together with a man named Chocne, two women formed the leadership of the movement and took two of the most revered names in Christendom, María and María Magdalena (ibid., 98).

The Spaniards responded to this threat by beginning what would become an obsession for many of the colonizers, especially the ecclesiastical leaders: the extirpation of idolatries. These campaigns would become for the Andes and for the indigenous peoples what the Inquisition was for the contemporary Spaniards in the metropolis and the colony.[7] Cristóbal de

Albornoz led the repression of Taqui Onqoy by investigating the movement and holding trials for those accused of being "*taqiongos.*" It is this repression which interests me most for the study of the transculturation of native gender culture, especially as it relates to public performances rooted in bodily expression, for this reaction to indigenous religious practices frames the new colonial relationships that were ushered in with the Toledo viceroyalty.

Pierre Duviols, one of the earliest researchers to concentrate on the extirpation campaigns, emphasizes the repressive nature of the visitations and trials, tracing their beginnings back to 1541, when church authorities in Cuzco first cited the need to repress the Inca cults.[8] Archbishop Loayza issued an *Instrucción* (1545–1549) that elaborated on how the *doctrineros,* the priests in charge of the colonial communities organized for the indoctrination of the Andeans, were to conduct these early extirpations. This repression soon became institutionalized by the first, second, and third Councils of Lima, held in 1551, 1567, and 1583, respectively. The *Sumarios* of these councils describe offenses and prescribe punishments for those found guilty of idolatry.[9] Griffiths's study of the extirpations describes the campaign as "an instrument of repression . . . characterized by denunciations, accusations, investigations, interrogations, judgements, sentences, and punishments" (*Cross and the Serpent,* 29) and succinctly summarizes its nature: "It was juridical rather than pastoral, condemnatory rather than forgiving, destructive rather than constructive. It smashed representations of sacred entities and rent asunder the reputations of native religious specialists and the timeless hallowed bond between the human inhabitants of this world and their supernatural tutelary deities" (29). A study by Kenneth Mills also illustrates the brutal nature of the extirpation campaigns: "A whole range of public acts of punishment (usually floggings of persons who had been shorn, tied and stripped), penance, and 'processions of shame' (in which the guilty were often dressed in the conspicuous pointed headgear known as *corozas,* made to carry crosses in their hands, and attended by criers to broadcast the religious crimes) were administered to those with the heaviest sentences" (*Idolatry and Its Enemies,* 267).

While the Taqui Onqoy movement was brought under control for the complex reasons outlined by Stern, its companion political and military rebellion, led by Inca Titu Cusi Yupanqui from his stronghold in Vilcabamba, continued to destabilize the Andean highlands until the execution of Tupac Amaru in 1572. Toledo's primary objective during his first years in the viceroyalty was to put an end to the native rebellions, a mission which included the persecution of Andean religious specialists (Duviols, "La destrucción de las religiones andinas," xxix). In Cuzco, Toledo called for an assembly to create guidelines for the punishment of Andean religious specialists. Duviols summarizes these disciplinary measures, which ranged from incarceration and forced labor to the death penalty for those Andeans accused of being "warlocks," "apostates," or "dogmatizers" (ibid., xxix–xxx). It is clear from these instructions and the Lima Councils' *Sumarios* that the civil and ecclesiastical authorities were working together to eradicate Andean religious practices, and their targets were the Andean ritualists.

THE GENDERED HISTORY OF
VISITATIONS AND EXTIRPATIONS

Although it was not made explicit in these punishment guidelines, the extirpation of idolatry had a definite concern with issues of gender and sexuality. Irene Silverblatt's archival research has resulted in a groundbreaking study of the effects of Spanish colonization on Andean gender relations. She specifically focuses on the erosion of status and privilege women suffered at the hands of both Spaniards and Andean males. Andean women, from both the elite and the peasantry, lost inheritance rights, relinquished traditional political participation, suffered from double tribute collection, and were subjected to physical and sexual abuse by Spaniards and corrupt *curacas* (*Moon, Sun, and Witches,* chaps. 6–8). Silverblatt concludes that Andean women, by escaping to the Puna and avoiding the *reducciones* (forced resettlement communities), became protectors of pre-Columbian religious practices and guardians of the *huacas* and ancestral burial sites. Silverblatt recounts several trials for idolatry, in which women were accused of witchcraft and duly punished for their heresy and idolatry, as evidence of women's resistance to colonial evangelization. While Spanish authorities attempted to characterize these women as devil worshipers comparable to European witches, who were often social outcasts in Iberia, Andean women, considered "*comadres*" (godmothers) actually reflected pre-Columbian Andean values and participated fully in the community (ibid., 195).

One example of this commitment to traditional values is Juana, a *curandera* (traditional healer) tried for heresy in a seventeenth-century trial for idolatry. Silverblatt concludes that the accusations against her reveal "that her malevolence was usually directed against people who had transgressed community norms: the mayors and headmen who, taking advantage of their position in the political structures imposed by the colonial regime, defied traditional Andean expectations regarding the behavior of community authorities" (ibid., 187). Implicit in her conclusions is a tension between Andean males, who often either were forced or opted to relinquish ties to their native religious cults, and the "priestesses of idolatry." In some extreme cases, women re-created pre-Hispanic matrilineal culture in the Puna by resorting to male infanticide in rejection of the new patriarchal colonial order. The Puna came to be regarded as a female space and, concurrently, the sacred space of the *apus* and Andean ancestors (ibid., 198–210). Silverblatt offers an important insight into the reading of chroniclers' accounts of purportedly negative male reaction to Andean "witches" by suggesting that such reactions, if not outright falsehoods created by the Spanish, could be read as professions of fear by Andean men, fear inspired by their own abandonment of traditional religion (ibid., 195).

As women were increasingly marginalized by the colonial patriarchy and as *curacas* and other elite Andean men began to deny their cultural heritage through political accommodation to the new hegemony, the colonial apparatus also targeted same-sex praxis and transgendered subjects. The place of third gender in this new reality was precarious, for as the "feminine sphere" of Andean culture became increasingly devalued, any manifestation of gender crossing or androgyny was considered not only a transgression of acceptable gender norms but also a threat to the patriarchal, heteronormative colonial state.[10]

To understand the official reaction to gender diversity, it is useful to analyze the documents of the viceroy's greatest enterprise, the General Visitation, or *Visita*.[11] As Rolena Adorno has suggested, literary critics have much to learn from the juxtapositions of juridical narrative forms and what has more traditionally been categorized as literary accounts.[12] While Adorno considers this juxtaposition to be a way of unraveling the multiple threads that are woven together in the formation of an author's subjectivity, I suggest that this strategy can also lead to a better understanding of the author's referents. Toledo's *visita* reports are official documents that illustrate how colonial subjectivities were discursively conceived and constructed through the interpellation of the nascent state apparatus. The questionnaire considered below is the textual embodiment of the colonial gaze, which looks on the Other with interest for purposes of control. This scrutiny delimits and defines the Other, privileging the Western culture of the colonizer while incorporating local knowledge of the colonized to support new hegemonic ideologies. The questionnaire follows the tradition initiated early in the colonial period by Carlos V to compile "scientifically" gathered information on the territories of the Spanish kingdom, a tradition that led to the *Relaciones geográficas de Indias* and to the *visita* reports conducted by colonial authorities.[13] The reader will recall my discussion of the "cannibal questionnaire" in Chapter 2; the same ideology behind that early "investigation" informed Toledo's *visita* survey. Unlike that document, however, the Toledo *visita* report records answers from the indigenous interviewees.

The following preface to the *visita*'s questionnaire explicitly identifies the colonial project's dependency on the formula "knowledge is power." Indeed, the questions are posed in order to gain the knowledge necessary to govern the colonized Andeans and to find their sites of resistance and cultural nostalgia:

> It is important to know and to discover the order and customs the Incas and chiefs and other wealthy Indians had in the time of their gentility and idolatry; the burials and the riches they carried with them to their graves . . . which gods and idols they worshiped and what offerings they gave to them and to the dead Incas, and how they preserved them and what things they dedicated to them. What customs did the natives of this kingdom have before the arrival of the Spanish and what forms of government did they have so that the people worked hard rather than be lazy? To this end I order that Secretary Álvaro Ruiz de Navamuel of the governing and general visitation of these kingdoms, along with interpreter, Gonzalo Gómez Jiménez, question the Indians, the older ones and the elderly, and anyone from whom the truth can be acquired, using the following questionnaire.

> combiene saver y averiguar la horden y costumbres que los Ingas y Curacas y otros indios ricos tenian en tiempo de su gentilidad y idolatrias, de enterrarse y que riquezas llevaban consigo á sus sepolturas . . . , é á que Dioses y Ydolos adoraban, y que las ofrecían á ellos y á los Yngas muertos, y que orden y recaudo se tenia en la guarda de esto, y que cosas tenian dedicadas para ello; y ansi mismo, las costumbres que los naturales de estos Reynos tenian antes que los españoles

entrasen en ellos, y que modo tenian los Yngas para los gober-
nar, aplicandolos al trabajo porque no se hiciesen ociosos; por
ende que mandaba y mando á Alvaro Ruiz de Navamuel su
Secretario y de la Gobernacion y Visita general destos Reynos
que con indios y viejos y ancianos, y de quien se pueda saber y
entender la verdad, haga la dicha informacion é averiguacion,
tomando por interprete á Gonzalo Gomez Jimenez Lengua, y
examinando los testigos por el Ynterrogatorio siguiente.

(Toledo, "Informaciones," 131–132)[14]

The objects of inquiry make clear the Spaniards' priorities: social order;
native customs; indigenous burial rites; Andean treatment of idols; and
valuables associated with burials. The colonizers' search for these "secrets"
would aid them in colonial governance, religious conversion, and personal
enrichment. In the explanatory prose that follows this preface, one learns
that, indeed, it is the burial treasure that most interests the questioners
(ibid., 132). The issue of idols was second on the list of questions, for the
continued worship of *huacas* was a principal failure of evangelization efforts, especially in light of the Taqui Onqoy movement. Finally came a section on customs and practices, which is where we find the questions pertaining to third gender, cross-dressing, and sodomy. All of the questions
were answered by groups of Indians gathered according to a clearly defined methodology outlined in the same document (ibid., 135–136).

It is clear that the informants were providing testimony at the insistence of the colonizers and in the context of the extirpation of idolatries,
the redistribution of the native population in *reducciones,* and the reorganization of the work force into *mitas* (compulsory labor). All the informants' answers must be read in light of what must have been a stressful and
potentially dangerous procedure. Yet, as Foucault reminds us, power relations require the participation of the masses, which, ultimately, are controlled by the institutions installed.[15] I wish to pay particular attention,
therefore, to the indigenous interests that may have been served in the answers given by the Andean informants. Recognizing the agency of the indigenous people in the process of change representing third-gender subjectivity is imperative, for, as we have already seen in Stern's work on the
post-Incaic alliances, the Andeans were not passive in the face of the discourses of power that swept their lands. Silverblatt's lesson in native gender relations and colonial power also reminds us to read with caution all
sources of Andean testimony. To take at face value testimonies given under

duress and, in particular, native political context, is to risk misinterpretation. Silverblatt's study of Andean "witches" highlights the tension between genders in the colonial context, and we should be just as mindful of similar tensions between male, female, and "third" genders in these testimonies.

Another useful model of interpretation, which I apply to these *testimonios,* is Gary Urton's astute study of the construction of Andean myth-history, *History of a Myth.* Urton's archival research illustrates the intersections between local, indigenous interests and the Spaniards' writing of official Andean history. By comparing Sarmiento de Gamboa's official history of the Incas with a local *curaca*'s legal proceeding, Urton explicates the workings of indigenous agency in colonial transactions while shedding light on the interaction between indigenous informants and their colonial investigators. He guides us in the study of pre-Hispanic and colonial Andean ethnohistory by insisting that "the highly interpretive and hierarchical nature of Inca mythohistory provides the rationale for going beyond the apparent content and structure of the myths that were told about the Incas by their postconquest descendents to a consideration of some of the local political, social, and even geographical features that are 'embedded' within those myths" (12). It is with this caution and diligence that we must read the reported testimonies on third gender that can be gleaned from the Toledo *visita* reports. I will focus on the biographical information given in their statements in order to suggest a possible interpretation of the information provided. Of course, they are not recounting myths, per se, yet their motivations for constructing the narratives they provide to the *visita* interrogators were also informed by "local political, social, and even geographical features." In this way we can better appreciate how the indigenous informants participated in the reshaping of the Andean cultural space, specifically, how their contributions entered into the colonial discourse on same-sex practices and cross-dressing.

The document contains interviews with six groups from different residential areas around Cuzco, though the informants were not all natives of the Cuzco region. Each group was interviewed between June 2 and September 5, 1571. I have analyzed each group's response to the "sodomy question," for although they all confirm for their questioners the existence of the practices in question, each provides a different perspective. Because the *visita* report provides only one answer for each group, it is impossible to know if that answer truly represents the opinion or knowledge of each individual in the group, as is purported by the leading statement "each one spoke for himself and later all together" [dijeron cada uno por sí, y después todos juntos] or if the dynamics of the interview were such that one speaker's opinion or knowledge was confirmed by the rest (Toledo, "Informaciones," 148). All nuances of oral interaction, discussion, debate, and so on were lost in the formalistic approach taken by the *visita* questionnaires. One is left wondering about the effects of hierarchies of power within the witness groups, for the Spaniards' short biographical sketches of each witness include social rank in some cases. All the witnesses are said to be eighty years old or older and are characterized as professing their Christianity: "they professed to be Christians and they swore to God, making the sign of the cross with their right hands" [dixeron ser cristianos é juraron por Dios Nuestro Señor y por la señal de la Cruz, que hizieron con sus manos derecha] (ibid., 136). These answers were reported speech, not direct quotations; therefore, they were filtered by the interpreter Gonzalo Gómez Jiménez, and *visita* secretary, Álvaro Ruiz de Navamuel.

The first group, the smallest of the six, was interviewed on June 2, 1571, in the Yncay valley and consisted of only four witnesses. As we will see, these witnesses provided the most detailed information on third-gender subjectivity, even providing the name by which the pre-Hispanic identity was known in one region. According to their biographical information, all four were in subordinate capacities linked to the Inca dynasties: don Pedro Cayocuxi was an "Inca contractor," don Diego Ytopongo was one of "Guaynacapal Ynga's soldiers," Juanapicardo's "father was a servant to Guaynacapal," and Alonso de Cauparpullo was "*curaca*" of an encomienda near Cuzco. While all four lived in the Cuzco area, Juanapicardo claimed to be originally from Chachapoyas (ibid., 137).

Following seventeen questions on how the Incas controlled their subjects' work habits, on the use of coca, the system of *curacas,* the life span of several Inca rulers, and cannibalism, the *visita* questionnaire asks the following:

Do you know if they [Incas] used the nefarious sin of sodomy and in which province and if they punished them or not? Do you know if all over Collado there were men dressed like women, who used makeup on their faces in order to commit this sin against nature?

Si saben que usaban el pecado nefando de sodomia y en qué provincia y si los castigaban ó no. Si saben que andaban todo

el Collado hombres bestidos como mugeres y afeitados los
rostros para usar este pecado de contra natura.

(Ibid., 135)

Before considering the answer given by the informants, we should note
how the question is phrased. First, the language used by the interrogator is standard for the Spanish inquisitorial rhetoric on sodomy, as we saw
in the preceding chapters. Sodomy is named a "nefarious sin," presuppos-
ing the proscriptive nature of the sexual act. We might ask how the interpreter translated this legalistic and moralistic term from the Spanish to
the Quechua. As we will see below, my analysis of the *Doctrina christiana*
reveals that contemporary translations of the term "sodomy" employed a
transculturated notion of sexual transgression in the Amerindian language.
This built-in attitudinal prejudice must be taken into account when we
consider the answers. The other remarkable element of the question is the
interrogator's interest in one particular region, Collado, that is, the Lake
Titicaca region, or the Inca empire's Collasuyu. Why is this region in particular isolated from the rest of the Andes? Below is the informants' testimony in its entirety regarding question number eighteen:

> before the arrival of the Spaniards in these lands, in the prov-
> ince of Collado and in other parts, the Indians practiced the
> nefarious sin against nature, though they [these interview-
> ees] did not see it, but they had notice of it because it was
> talked about and discussed since they [those from Collado]
> committed the nefarious sin and among themselves they were
> known as *orua;* and the Indians suspected of this were laughed
> at and called *orua,* which means a man who acts like a woman,
> and they were not punished, just laughed at, as was said; and
> these were called *orua* and went around dressed in women's
> clothes with painted faces in order to commit this sin; and this
> is what they know of this question.

> antes que los españoles entrasen en esta tierra, que en la provin-
> cia de Collado y en otras partes se usaba entre los yndios el
> pecado nefando contra natura, que ellos no lo vieron, mas de
> que tubieron noticia dello porque se decia y se trataba y co-
> metian el dicho pecado nefando, y entre ellos se dice orua; y de
> los indios de quien se tenian sospechas se reian y los llamaban

Oruas, que quiere decir hombre que hace de muger, y que no los castigaban mas que reirse dellos como dicho tiene, y que estos tales se les llamaban orua y andaban vestidos en hábitos de muger y afeitados los rostros para usar de este pecado; y que esto saben de esta pregunta.

(Ibid., 148)

The reported responses of the four witnesses account for the existence of third gender in Collasuyu and "other areas." The terms used in this testimony reflect European terminology: "pecado nefando contra natura" (nefarious sin against nature), "pecado nefando" (nefarious sin), "pecado" (sin). However, the informants also include the word *orua* as the indigenous name for the third-gender identity in Collasuyu. For the informants, *orua* signified more than just the sexual act of sodomy; it also referred to a man living as a woman, cross-dressing, and using facial makeup. However, this information was not firsthand, as reported by the informants: "though they did not see it, but they had notice of it." Although we do not have the original Quechua-language answers, from the wording by the translator and scribe, we can appreciate what appear to be Andean epistemological categories for narrating testimony.

Rosaleen Howard-Malverde's work on Andean oral narratives in the 1980's shed light on how Quechua speakers today tell stories and recount myths and legends. Her work dovetails nicely with Urton's analysis (considered earlier) by tracing the grammatical elements of Quechua that mark the telling of history to further substantiate the theory of indigenous agency in narrative strategies: "The nature of oral history as a report of past events uttered by a speaker in the present, leads to a staking out of an opposition between three sets of coordinates: spatial—'there' vs. 'here;' temporal—'then' vs. 'now;' and personal—'he/she/they' vs. 'I/you/we.' It becomes of particular interest to note the way these distinctions collapse at certain moments in the process of utterance. The speaking of history is found to be an activity that breaks down the barriers between an objectual past and a present praxis" (*The Speaking of History*, 81). In other words, the "grammar of testimony," as Howard-Malverde calls it, structures testimonies in such a way as to express an intimate relationship between the speaker, his or her spatial place, and time. The speaker's involvement in the testimony is expressed through the very grammar used to structure his or her thoughts. Regina Harrison has detected these kinds of Quechua grammatical residues in the colonial Spanish of Santacruz Pachacuti, whose narrative I analyze in Chapter 3, and points out that "the reportative past tense (*sqa*) . . . is used to narrate an event where there is no direct participation by the speaker, such as mythic discourse, dreams or situations where the speaker is unconscious" (*Signs, Songs, and Memory*, 73).[16]

In the translated and paraphrased testimony under consideration, the three elements of the Quechua "grammar of testimony" may have been present in the original Quechua. The time is said to be "before the arrival of the Spaniards in these lands," which alludes to a remote past most likely not experienced by the speaker. Quechua language employs verb suffixes that "can be classified according to two semantic categories, one temporal and one modal (of epistemic modality): concluded pastness vs. non-pastness and personal knowledge vs. non-personal knowledge, respectively" (Howard-Malverde, *The Speaking of History*, 75). I propose that the temporal phrasing quoted above and the phrase "though they did not see it" suggest an original Quechua testimony expressed with a grammar that included the *sqa/si* suffixes, which necessarily distanced the speaker from personal experience with the "*orua.*" Temporally, the occurrence of sodomitical activity is located in the remote past, and relates to the speaker in a nonpersonal mode. Spatially, the *orua* are confirmed to be in Collasuyu and other unspecified places.

Our question then becomes, Why did the informants choose this tense and mode of telling of the third-gender Andeans? Can we detect a narrative strategy in this passage? The informants achieve two things with the grammatically marked testimony I have hypothesized. First, they distance themselves temporally and geographically from the *orua*, which in the context of the *visita* interviews could be read as a strategy of self-protection, one that focused the inquiry on another cultural area of the Andean region. By following what Urton has uncovered in his research on the testimonial strategies of other Cuzco informants, we might also speculate that the Collasuyu region is identified or confirmed by the informants as the place in which third-gender activity took place in order to contribute to the Cuzco-centered discourse of the period, a discourse that was just beginning to construct a cultural identity privileging the Cuzco version of the Inca origin myth and Cuzco as the legitimate center of the Inca empire. We remember that this effort by the Cuzco region's indigenous elite contradicted the Toledo regime's official rhetoric, which sought to prove the Inca's illegitimacy. By distancing Cuzco from what the Spaniards had been insisting was errant and immoral behavior, the informants may have wished to counter the obvious bias in the interrogators' questions. Here we see the workings of the performative strand of colonial discourse, the agency of the indigenous informants, and how silence and resistance enter the historiographic record.

The second element of the grammatical construction is that it allowed for authentic indigenous cultural knowledge to be communicated to the Spaniards while the informants protected themselves. By removing themselves and the Inca dynastic culture from suspicion, the informants were able to provide ethnographic information about the *orua*. We learn their names, that they cross-dressed, that they had sexual relations with men, that they painted their faces, and that they were not punished by the Incas, merely "laughed at" by their own people. Each of these points merits critical attention.

The question as to whether at least some third-gender subjects lived permanently transgendered seems to be further affirmed with this testimony, at least as it applies to this manifestation of the subjectivity. It is reported that an *orua* was a "man who acts like a woman" and that they "dress in women's clothes." Another new piece of information given here is that they applied makeup to their faces in order to "commit this sin," that is, the "sin" of sodomy. This might imply an erotic appeal to *orua*'s would-be sexual partners; that is, the *orua* was purposely shaping his features to appeal to the sexual desire of his partner.[17]

Finally, the issue of punishment or ridicule requires further discussion. This admission that the Incas did not punish the *orua,* which is consistent with and may have informed Polo de Ondegardo's report on the Inca morality laws, discussed below, substantiates my argument in Chapters 2 and 3 that third-gender subjectivity was an integral part of at least some Andean cultures. The informants' comments that the *orua* were laughed at should not necessarily be interpreted as indigenous scorn toward these people, as Trexler argues (*Sex and Conquest,* 166). Indeed, scholarship on indigenous peoples' relationships and humor suggests a different way of interpreting these comments. Walter Williams has pointed out that in several North American Indian tribes, joking is the normal, expected behavior among kinsmen, and the joking often takes on a sexual connotation (*Spirit and the Flesh,* 39–41). David Greenberg addresses the same issue but related specifically to the berdache. He notes that so-called ridicule may have related more to the third gender's prestigious status in his community, to his kinship ties, and to indigenous kinship joking relationships than to his sexuality.[18] Jesuit Blas Valera's account of the Incas' reverence of the "castrated priests," discussed in Chapter 2, adds credence to a more tolerant interpretation of the "laughing at" of the third-gender *orua.*[19] Contemporary ethnographies, such as Bolin's experience with the *yana uyakuna,* who cross-dressed with the purpose of creating laughter as supernatural protection in the ceremonial context, guide us to be cautious in our assumptions regarding the meaning of the laughter in this report (*Rituals of Respect*). Fritz Villasante's research on humor and sexuality in contemporary Andean ritual dances emphasizes the playful nature in which transvested dancers interact with their partners and the public, including the use of verbal jokes and sexual puns ("De fiestas y rituales," 1–5).

The issue of the Andeans' acceptance of third gender becomes an ambiguous question for the colonial interrogator, for the informants in other groups give different and conflicting answers to the question concerning Inca punishment. Three of the other groups, those who testified on July 17, 18, and 28, 1571, stated that they knew nothing of Inca punishments, or their answers are so ambiguous as to be of little use except as further evidence of the elusiveness of the colonized informants, perhaps as a strategy of resistance. Two groups, however, did describe punishments that the Incas reportedly applied to third-gender subjects.

A group of twelve informants interrogated on June 19, 1571, consisting of a variety of individuals from the lower strata of Inca society, many of whom had been relocated to Cuzco by the Incas, reported that they "[had] heard talk of the very public and notorious" [han oido decir por cosa muy publica y notoria] existence of acts of sodomy, cross-dressing, and face painting in Collasuyu (Toledo, "Informaciones," 160). This group testified that the Incas punished such behaviors, "putting them together in the torrents of a river, covered in salt and tied to a dog, and they made them cross it downriver and they drowned" [poniendolos juntos a un raudal de un rio, con mucha sal y atados á un perro y que los hacia cruzar por rio abajo y se ahogaban] (ibid., 160).

The other group that reported Inca punishment of same-sex behavior was interrogated on September 5, 1571. It consisted of six informants who all claimed to be Inca descendants. They reportedly had "heard" that in pre-Hispanic times sodomy and face painting were practiced in Collasuyu, but they added that "they heard that some Indians and Incas from the plains used it, and that in this land they considered it a very ugly thing, and that when they knew of it or found out about it, the Incas punished them by hanging them or leaving them where they would never reappear" [oyeron decir que lo usaban algunos yndios y Yngas de los Llanos, y que en esta tierra lo tenian por cosa muy fea, y que cuando se sabia y averiguaba, los Yngas, los hazian castigar ahorcandolos y dejandolos donde nunca pareciesen] (ibid., 213). This testimony presents us with a curious contradiction with the testimony of other informants who maintained that same-sex practices were confined to the Collasuyu region and non-Inca Andeans. The Inca descendants admitted that some Incas also were involved in such behavior, even though it was taken to be an "ugly" behavior and was punished. Again, this group contradicts the earlier groups, which reported no Inca punishment of the *orua*. Could their Inca-identified positions inform their report of punishments? Such testimony does not show up anywhere else in the historical record on Inca punishments and prohibitions, except in Cieza's Lascasian apology, as we saw in Chapter 2, which is then echoed in Inca Garcilaso's *Comentarios reales*. Could this testimony be read as a strategy to distance the Incas from what the new converts understood to be a Spanish and Christian sin?

As we saw in Chapters 2 and 3, cross-dressing and same-sex practice had ritual meaning, at least in some Andean cultural contexts; however, in this testimony from the *visita* reports, there is no mention of such an association. This silence on ritual aspects of sodomy raises other questions. How do we read this silence? Were the informants ignorant of the ritual use of sodomy? Or is their silence a strategy of cultural protection? This issue is crucial to the construction of third-gender identities in later texts, for we are left with silence on the topic of ritual sodomy in Polo de Ondegardo's report on indigenous religious practices and in the colonial dictionaries, silence, as we shall see below, that was reinforced by the teachings of the *Doctrina christiana* and that informed the discourse on sodomy in virtually all of colonial and later literature.

Do we ignore the silence, assuming that the informants' reticence on the issue is merely lack of knowledge or even proof that there was no connection between third gender, sodomy, and ritual space? The ethnographic record, discussed in Chapter 3, suggests that the performance of gender liminality and the simulation of sodomy in rituals continues to this day in some parts of the Andes, indicating that these ritual practices were transformed over time. Therefore, I propose a different reading of this silence, one that considers the informants' agency in the interaction between colonizer and colonized by characterizing the informants' contribution to the discourse on sodomy that finds its way to the *Doctrina christiana* as part of the "performative," resistant strand of colonial discourse. In order to interpret oral "performances" such as these testimonies, the reader must take into account not only the global context, which we analyzed above, that is, the colonial context, but also the interpersonal activity between the speaker and his interlocutors.[20]

The informants' interlocutors in this case were colonial civil authorities who were operating in the global context of the extirpation of idolatries and the "*reducción*" of Andean communities. This suggests that the colonized informants may have chosen not to divulge their words for these practices or descriptions of them, which might have been sacred knowledge, in order to protect themselves, especially in light of missionaries' severe censure of same-sex practice, which began in the first days of the Conquest, as we saw in previous chapters. We have evidence of third-gender resistance in other parts of the Andes and the Americas.[21] For example, the Andean Araucanian culture protected third-gender shamans by transferring their public ritual duties to women, and third genders went underground after colonization (Williams, *Spirit and the Flesh,* 141; Murray, *Male Homosexuality,* 161–163). As we have seen, in colonial Tawantinsuyu during the years preceding the Toledo viceroyalty there was the perception that the indigenous peoples were reviving their religious practices through the Taqui Onqoy movement. As a result, punishments for native religious practitioners increased, and Toledo's visitation augmented the scope and severity of the colonial crackdown on indigenous religious practices. In this context, Andean sacred knowledge became dangerous to the well-being of those who professed it.

A 1586 text reveals that indigenous Andeans had quickly learned what information to keep secret from colonial interrogators. Andean shamans warned their followers not to mention the *huacas* or the ritual practices associated with them: "that when they [the Indians] went to confess during Lent to the priests, did not let them reveal or confess acts of idol worship because they [the Catholic priests] did not know about the idols and once they found out they would persecute them" [que cuando se fuesen a comfesar por tiempo de cuaresma con sus curas no descubriesen ni comfesasen estas ydolatrias porque no se supiesen y descubiertas las afrentasen] (Duviols, *La destrucción de las religiones andinas,* 152). Guaman Poma also recorded this warning in one of his drawings depicting priests confessing the newly converted, captioned with the plea of an Andean penitent: "Have me confess all my sins, Father, but do not ask me about the *huacas* and the idols" (Guaman Poma de Ayala, *Primer nueva corónica,* f635:line 515).[22] These two testimonials reveal the indigenous people's resistance to extirpation and their attempts to guard secrets from the Spanish.

We have evidence that civil authorities had already begun to regulate gender through *ordenanzas* initiated in the years preceding Toledo's administration.[23] Gregorio Gonzales de Cuenca carried out a *visita* for the Real Audiencia in the northern provinces of Trujillo, Huánuco, and Chachapoyas in 1566, dictating the *ordenanzas* late in that year.[24] María Rostworowski recognizes these laws, at least the spirit of order that they sought to impose, as the precursors of the more elaborate Toledo *ordenanzas* that would follow in the early 1570's. These regulations, in addition to myriad laws concerning other aspects of Andean culture, demonstrate a colonial impetus to control the indigenous construction of gender. There are two *ordenanzas* in particular that are worth examining. First, there is concern for the length of the hair of the male and the female Indians:

> Because male Indians wear their hair as long as the females, which is a cause of their being unclean and having diseased heads; and so that there be differences between men and women; and because of other inconveniences, it is ordered that the men cut their hair above the forehead and on the sides under their ears.

> Yten que de traer los yndios cauellos largos como las yndias es causa que no anden limpios y tengan enfermedades de cabeça y porque aya diferencia de los varones a las mugeres y por otros ynconvinientes que dello se sigue se manda que los yndios traigan cortados los cabellos por cima de la frente y por los lados debaxo de las orejas.

> (Rostworowski, "Algunos comentarios," 150)

While this regulation is not necessarily directed to the cross-dressing third-gender subjects, it does illustrate to what extent the Spaniards were concerned with gender distinctions among their colonial subjects.

Although indigenous hygiene is ostensibly one concern, the other justification for the *ordenanza*, while vague, seems closer to the true colonial motive: "that there be differences between men and women" and "other inconveniences," which speak to Spaniards' discomfort with the ambiguity of indigenous gender constructions. This discomfort was such that the authorities were instructed to punish transgressors of this regulation: "if they continue to wear their hair long, they will be publicly sheared" [que si los traxeron largos como hasta aqui sean tresquilados publicamente] (ibid., 150).

Inca Garcilaso comments on the importance hair played in the Inca semiotics of identity, especially as a practice of ethnic differentiation and as a privilege that allowed newly incorporated allies to wear their hair in the same style as the Incas (*Comentarios reales*, bk. 1, chap. 22, 50). Father Bernabé Cobo also discusses the care with which the Incas arranged their hair, explaining that the "Indians identify their honor with their hair to such an extent that the worst disgrace that one can inflict on them is to cut their hair, and for that reason, the judicial authorities are accustomed to pass this sentence on those who commit grave and infamous crimes" (ibid., bk. 2, chap. 2, 185). These two testimonials to the significance of hair, an uncanny cross-cultural echo from my discussion of the Cid's own obsession with his beard, remind us how invasive and demeaning these colonial *ordenanzas* were to the indigenous Andeans.

The second gender-related *ordenanza* specifically addresses the issue of cross-dressing and most likely refers to third-gender subjects:

> Moreover, if a male Indian dresses in women's clothes or if a female Indian dresses in male clothes, then the authorities should seize them and give them one hundred lashes for the first offense and should shear their hair off publicly; and for a second offense they should be tied to a post for six hours in a public place for all to see; and for a third offense they are to be remitted to the magistrate of the valley or to the mayors of the village of Santiago of Miraflores in order that they be brought to justice.

> Yten si algun yndio condujere en [h]abito de yndia o yndia en [h]abito de yndio los dichos alcaldes los prendan y por la primera vez le den çient açotes y los tresquilen publicam[en]te y por segunda sean atados seis [h]oras a un palo en el tianguez a vista de todos y por la terçera vez con la ynformaçion preso lo remitan al corregidor del ualle o a los alcaldes hordinarios de la Villa de Santiago de Miraflores para que hagan justiçia dellos conforme a derecho.

> (Rostworowski, "Algunos comentarios," 131)

For the transgression of cross-dressing, the indigenous were submitted to harsher punishments, including public whippings and being tied to a post for six hours. The public display of these punishments, as in the case of other colonial infractions, was intended to modify indigenous behavior by teaching the subjugated the consequences of their actions. The progressive nature of the punishment suggests a possible resistance on the part of the Andeans; perhaps one incident of punishment was not enough to dissuade them from cross-dressing. These attitudes toward gender ambiguity and cross-dressing surely encouraged the Andeans to reconsider the safety of their third-gender religious specialists and may have led to the silence on ritual same-sex praxis in testimonies on sodomy.[25]

As Doris Sommer has pointed out, "signs of resistance lack a recognizable pattern for readers, they remain obscure and unexpected" ("Resisting the Heat," 410). One resistant strategy that she has identified in the writings of Inca Garcilaso, Rigoberta Menchú, and others is the survival tactic that distances the reader from the narrator's cultural knowledge. Could the Andeans' silence on third-gender ritual sodomy be an example of these distancing tactics? We recall how the informants disclosed little cultural knowledge to the interrogators, answering their questions as mimics, basically telling the examiners what they wanted to hear. The only exception was the revelation of the name "*orua,*" and the information on the cross-dressing and use of makeup. Indeed, the characterization of third genders' ritual roles that I propose in Chapter 3 is based on protoethnographic observances of outsiders and on the writings of Guaman Poma—an indigenous perspective believed to be freely given, not forced by interrogators—and on other uncoerced sources. Santacruz Pachacuti embedded the ritual nature of gender liminality in transculturated myths and obscure visual and verbal references to the *chuqui chinchay.* Therefore, the mimicry of the informants can be characterized as a distancing strategy that protected any ritual connection that may have existed between the third genders and same-sex praxis. By choosing not to disclose indigenous knowledge of sodomy rituals, the informants contributed to the narrative fabric that became the *Doctrina christiana* and Toledo's official history.

Reading the text in this manner redirects our attention to the workings of transculturation as a process that necessarily requires the participation of that culture which undergoes the transformation. The informant's agency in protecting his or her cultural knowledge ultimately leads to a representation of the culture that belies the original meaning. In this case, third-gender ritual subjectivity is displaced by sodomite; collective identity is replaced by individualized identity. In turn, this identity is more easily regulated by the hegemonic colonial discourse, relegating the original subjectivity to a subaltern status. This marginalized position in historical discourse and colonial society resulted in a transformation, not a total erasure, of third-gender subjectivity, a deculturation of third gender from its pre-Columbian ritual connection to the indigenous community. The following section traces how the silences, both pedagogical and performative, found their way into evangelical discourse of the Toledan colony, the *Doctrina christiana.*

TRANSCULTURATION OF GENDER
AND SEXUALITY IN THE ANDEAN
DOCTRINA CHRISTIANA

The colonial reorganization of the Andes and the initial steps in the extirpation campaigns, initiated under Toledo, also included a concern about the textual representation of the catechistic discourse to be introduced to Andeans. Toledo was anxious about the lack of progress in the evangelization of the Andeans. Above all, he lamented the lack of communication between the missionaries and the indigenous converts: "Who would not lament the fact that confessions are often carried out without the Indian understanding the priest or the priest understanding what the Indian tells him?" [¿Quién no llorará que las confesiones se hagan muchas veces de manera que ni el indio entiende al sacerdote, ni el sacerdote lo que le dice el indio?] (Durán, *El catequismo,* 191). Toledo blamed these failures on what he perceived to be the nomadic living conditions of the indigenous people, thus justifying his policy of *reducciones,* which would force the Andeans to live in Spanish *doctrinas,* or communities, rather than in their traditional ways (ibid., 193). Thus it was on two impediments to successful evangelization that the lack of progress was blamed: language and social organization.[26] Both these causes, according to authorities, led to a superficial understanding of Christian doctrine and were responsible for the Indians' continuing idolatries and sinful behavior.

These deficiencies had plagued earlier Spanish colonial authorities' efforts at conversion, as well. According to church historian Rubén Vargas Ugarte, there was a relative scarcity of priests and friars in the early days of colonization (*Historia de la iglesia,* vol. 1, 112). This shortage of manpower led to diminished conversion and evangelization. The *cartilla,* an abbreviated catechism, is one example of how the early missionaries summarized and presented Christian teachings to their new subjects. The use of *cartillas* for the translation of the Christian doctrine and for indigenous peoples' confessions dates from the first years of colonial occupation. Domínguez Faura has suggested that chronicler Juan de Betanzos was responsible for the early Quechua translations used in the evangelization process ("Juan de Betanzos," 67). His research suggests that by 1542 the Dominicans had a first draft of the *Doctrina christiana,* which included a confession manual. No copies of these documents remain, although one might speculate as to whether Domingo de Santo Tomás's extant sermon was part of them.[27]

The shortage of clerics also resulted in two other strategies that would have long-term effects in the Christianization process. The first archbishop of Peru, Fray Jerónimo de Loayza, prioritized the evangelical practices of his clergy in his *Instrucción*. First, the decision was made to concentrate on teaching indigenous children (Vargas Ugarte, *Historia de la iglesia*, vol. 2, 112). The Franciscan missionaries, as they passed from town to town, are known to have taught indigenous children songs that summarized the Christian catechism (Estenssoro Fuchs, "Descubriendo los poderes de la palabra," 78). Second, in order to reach more of the population, the encomenderos were charged with the responsibility, by the same authority that granted their encomiendas, of indoctrinating the Indians.[28]

The use of *cartillas* and other materials not approved by the councils was prohibited. Instead, clerics were to use Loayza's *Instrucción* and an official *cartilla* and *catecismo menor* (Durán, *El catequismo*, 187). The first Lima Council, a meeting of ecclesiastical authorities charged with strategizing the evangelical project in Peru, postponed the writing of a *catecismo mayor* until they received instructions from the Council of Trent. It was not until the third Council of Lima met that the ambitious project, boosted by Toledo's new authority, got under way. On the eve of the third Council of Lima, the mission for the composition of the new catechistic materials was clear: a multilingual and uniform presentation of Christian teachings.

The third Council of Lima was held in 1583. This council was the culmination of a series of meetings held in the wake of the Council of Trent (1545–1566). Felipe II issued an order on July 12, 1564, addressed to officials of both church and Crown, to implement the reforms dictated at Trent throughout the Spanish empire's territories. The reform consisted of two parts: the effective and correct evangelization of his subjects; and the reform of corrupt practices within the church itself (Villegas, *Applicación del Concilio de Trento*, 281). Several scholars have treated the internal reform aspects of the Council of Lima (e.g., García [*Ofensas a Dios*] and Acosta ["Los clérigos doctineros"]). I am more interested in the first part of the mandate, specifically, how this mandate was carried out in the redaction of new evangelical didactic materials. The most important documents to emerge from the three consecutive church councils and the first works printed in Lima were the *Doctrina christiana y catecismo para instrucción de indios* (1584), *Confesionario para los curas de indios* (1585), and *Tercero catecismo y exposición de la doctrina cristiana por sermones* (1585). The third Council of Lima (1583), called by the archbishop of Lima, Toribio Alfonso de Mogrovejo, formed a committee to standardize several documents that had been used for years in the colony.[29] The committee, led by José de Acosta, recognized the need to standardize the catechism, the confession manual, and a series of sermons in the three most diffused colonial languages: Spanish, Quechua, and Aymara.[30]

The missionaries worked in teams, first writing the catechism in Spanish and then translating the text into Aymara or Quechua. The text was to be inspired by the Tridentine catechism, taking the form of questions and answers, so that the Indians could better understand and remember the lessons (Durán, *El catequismo,* 201). The writers were instructed to choose models from the many already printed catechisms (ibid., 212). One such model was the early catechism written in Quechua by a Mercedarian friar, Melchor Hernández (ibid., 214). In a letter to Commander General Claudio Aquaviva dated November 1, 1576, Jesuit José de Acosta comments that he has been working on the *Doctrina christiana* and its supplements and reports that the texts are being redacted "in the three languages and adapted to the indigenous intellect" [todo en tres lenguas, y muy acomodado al ingenio de los Indios] (ibid., 240). This letter points to the fact that Acosta and his team of writers, translators, and printers consciously wrote the documents to be intelligible to the Indians.[31]

In other words, as I will show below, the Andean *Doctrina christiana* is a hybrid text, one that draws on the pedagogical and the performative strands of colonial discourse. Understanding the role sexuality plays in these texts requires us to return to the Iberian Peninsula to examine the origins of their pedagogical components, especially the queer tropes of sexuality mobilized to convert the indigenous Andeans, tropes previously used in the evangelization of the Moor and the representation of Moorish sexuality.

RECONQUEST AND CARIBBEAN ANTECEDENTS TO THE ANDEAN *DOCTRINA CHRISTIANA*

Transatlantic iterations of the Moor expressed European epistemologies and colonial ideologies in several ways. For the chroniclers and historians writing for a European audience, references to the Moors served as an intelligible correspondence or analogy between Old and New world imaginaries. Moreover, writing the medieval "infidel" into the early chronicles promoted and justified the colonial project in providential and Christian terms, associating the recent victory over Islam with a sense of divine right for the expansion of empire to the Indies.

Christopher Columbus began this intertextual posturing in his famous journal, the first literary and historical text of Hispanic America. Taking an image of the final capitulation of the Moors in Granada, an image repeated in the peninsular chronicles and *romances* of the Reconquest, Columbus places the defeated Moor at the threshold of a new heroic enterprise: the Conquest of the Americas:

> Most Christian and most exalted and most excellent and most mighty princes, king and queen of the Spains and of the islands of the sea, our sovereigns: Forasmuch as, in this present year of 1492, after that your highness had made an end of the war with the Moors who reigned in Europe, and had brought that war to a conclusion in the very great city of Granada, where, in this same year, on the second day of the month of January, I saw the royal banners of your highness placed by force of arms on the towers of the Alhambra, which is the citadel of the said city, and I saw the Moorish king come out of the gates of the city and kiss the royal hands of your highness and of the prince, my lord.

> (*The Voyages of Christopher Columbus,* 135)

> Porque, cristianíssimos y muy altos y muy excelentes y muy poderosos Príncipes, Rey y Reina de las Españas y de las islas de la mar, Nuestros Señores, este presente año de 1492, después de Vuestras Altezas aver dado fin a la guerra de los moros, que reinavan en Europa, y aver acabado la guerra en la muy grande ciudad de Granada, adonde este presente año, a dos días del mes de Enero, por fuerza de armas vide poner las vanderas reales de Vuestras Altezas en las torres de la Alfambra, que es la fortaleza de dicha ciudad, y vide salir al rey moro a las puertas de la ciudad, y besar las reales manos de Vuestras Altezas y del Príncipe mi Señor.

> ("Diario del primer viaje," 95)

This textual reenactment of the victory at Granada was repeated in various forms throughout the early years of the colonization of America, as we shall see below in an example from Peru. This image of Moorish submission reverberated across the ocean from its original locus of enunciation because writers understood that as a trope of conquest the Moor could be mobilized in the rhetoric of triumph over the indigenous Americans.

Columbus, as a writing subject in need of self-legitimation and royal patronage, positioned himself at the site of two momentous events in Iberian
and world history: as a witness at the Moors' surrender at Granada, and,
later, as an intermediary arguing for the Catholic kings to undertake a
similar mission of conquest and conversion in what Columbus thought was
the East Indies:

> and afterwards, in that same month, on the grounds of infor-
> mation which I had given your highness and the prince, my
> lord, concerning the lands of India, and concerning a prince
> who is called "Gran Khan," which is to say in our Romance
> tongue, "King of Kings," how many times he and his ancestors
> had sent to Rome to beg for the men learned in our holy
> faith, in order that they might instruct him therein, and how
> the Holy Father had never made provision in this matter, and
> how so many nations had been lost, falling into idolatries
> and taking to themselves doctrines of perdition, and your
> highness, as Catholic Christians and as princes devoted to the
> holy Christian faith and propagators thereof, and as enemies
> of the sect of Mahomet and of all idolatries and heresies, too
> thought to send me, Christopher Columbus, to the said parts
> of India, to see the said princes and peoples and lands and the
> character of them and of all else, and the manner which should
> be used to bring about their conversion to our holy faith.

> (*The Voyages of Christopher Columbus,* 135)

> y luego en aquel presente mes, por la información que yo
> había dado a Vuestras Altezas de las tierras de India y de un
> Príncipe que es llamado el Gran Can (que quiere dezir en
> nuestro romance Rey de los Reyes), como muchas veces él y sus
> antecessores avían enbiado a Roma a pedir doctores en nuestra
> sancta fe porque le enseñasen en ella, y que nunca el Sancto
> Padre le avía proveído y se perdían tantos pueblos, cayendo en
> idolatrías e rescibiendo en sí sectas de perdición; y Vuestras
> Altezas, como católicos cristianos y príncipes amadores de
> la sancta fe cristiana y acrecentadores d'ella y enemigos de la
> secta de Mahoma y de todas idolatrías y heregías, pensaron en
> enviarme a mí, Cristóval Colón, a las dichas partidas de India
> para ver los dichos príncipes (el Gran Can) y los pueblos y las

tierras y la disposición d'ellas y de todo, y la manera que se
pudiera tener para la conversión d'ellas a nuestra sancta fe.

("Diario del primer viaje," 95–96)

Here we have the second image of the Moors I examine below: an analogy
between heretic and idolatrous Moors and the peoples of the Indies, mis-
takenly believed by Columbus to be the subjects of the Great Khan of the
Mongols. Columbus represents himself as fulfilling the request that supposedly had been issued to the pope years before by Marco Polo on behalf
of the Great Khan: to send missionaries to convert those who had fallen
into "sects of perdition," that is, to save their souls from damnation. Thus,
the stage is set on the very first page of Latin American literature: the
Moor will serve both civil and ecclesiastical discourse in the Conquest of
America as a model for conquest rhetoric. This model will influence both
public performances and the more private domain of the confessional.

In her study of Corpus Christi in colonial Cuzco, Carolyn Dean discusses how a reenactment of the triumph of Christ over heresy was performed in the streets of early modern Spain. The processions often associated the abstract notion of Christ's victory over evil or death with
Christian political victories over the Muslim "infidels" (*Inca Bodies*, 12–13).
This model was applied with great success in the Andes; the Moors were
replaced by Incas as the vanquished in Corpus Christi processions. The
Spaniards included indigenous Andeans in their Corpus Christi celebrations in order to signify their triumph over the heretical native. As Dean
points out, "In performing alterity—usually through Andean costume,
song, and dance—they [the natives] provided the necessary festive oppo-
nent whose presence affirmed the triumph" (ibid., 15). Following a policy
of substitution in which Christian symbols and rituals were introduced
to replace or be laid over autochthonous religious practices, the Spaniards
would eventually lose control of their signs, as the Inca elite began to assert their political agency and use public performances to signal their own
precarious status in the colonial power structure.[32]

For the missionaries charged with the conversion of the indigenous
peoples of the Americas, the Moor was a sign that signified the successful
implementation of strategies used in the Iberian Reconquest ecclesiastical
literature. My examination of both peninsular and American catechisms,
confession manuals, and sermons reveals how the Christian reinterpretation of Moorish beliefs reduced Islam to the level of a lascivious sect;
sexual connotations were used to defame the Other's beliefs, setting up

a model for the characterization and eventual conversion of the indigenous peoples of the Americas. The catechists and missionaries were adept
at adapting their materials to the cultural reality in which they operated.
This attention to the local culture is integral to the transculturation process, for the subaltern participates in the creation of the neoculturations
being produced in the new contexts of post-Conquest America. This participation is often limited to the role of informant or interpreter of the
cultural difference that the hegemonic discourse brings into the "war machine" of transculturation, the process that attempts to erase differences
and homogenize culture. The evangelization of the Moors in Spain and
Spanish territories provided antecedents to the conversion process that
took place in the Andes. The literary instruments used in the missionary
efforts were transformed by the missionaries' protoethnographic incorporation of local, subaltern knowledge into their understanding of the Other,
which, in turn, found its way into the pedagogical discourse of conversion
texts such as sermons, catechisms, and confession manuals.

I take as an example of this heritage of conversion Martín de Ayala's
Catecismo para instrucción de los nuevamente convertidos de moros. Ayala, who
lived between 1504 and 1566, developed his missionary career in Valencia
and Guadix. After attending the Council of Trent, he was named bishop
of Seville. He wrote the catechism before the Council of Trent, when he
lived in Guadix, where he learned Arabic and was a missionary to the recently converted Muslims.[33] The prologue, written by don Juan de Ribera,
suggests the utility of the catechism in the Christianization of converted
Moors and also illuminates just how the local culture was represented to
the converted: "Because it not only shows through natural and moral reason and utility the purity and beauty of our Holy Faith, but it also demonstrates the obscenities and absurdities of Mohammad's sect" [Porque no
solo muestra con razones y conveniencias naturales y morales la pureza y
hermosura de nuestra Santa Fe; pero haze demonstraciones de la torpeza, y
desatinos que hay en la secta de Mahoma] (Ayala, *Catecismo,* 3). As we shall
see, this Christian rendering of Islam reduces the religion to the level of
abjection; from the beginning, sexual connotations are used to defame the
Other's beliefs.

Ayala employed a structure that would be used in the American colonial catechisms, as well, and his catechism begins with a series of dialogues between a Christian cleric and a Moor who has traveled to Andalu-
sia from the coast of Africa to receive the word of the Christian God and
to convert to Christianity. The narrative depicts the conversion process as
one in which the Moor sought out conversion, of his own free will, and

ignored the violent repression and inquisitorial process behind the Christianization of Jewish and Moorish peoples on the Iberian Peninsula. In
the first dialogue, several salient issues of premodern Spain's evangelical
project surface, issues that are quite similar to concerns that the ecclesiastical authorities in the Americas would face, as well. For example, the
cleric states that language is an impediment to the Moor's potential conversion, for "many of these newly converted do not understand the Castilian language" [muchos de estos nuevamente convertidos no entienden
bien la lengua vulgar Castellana] (ibid., 6). In the Andes, the need for communication became a pressing issue for both the Crown and the church, as
we have seen.[34] Pope Pius V went as far as to grant indulgences to Catholic
missionaries who could preach in an Amerindian language, and the monarchs established chairs in Quechua language in Lima (1580) and Quito
(1581) and issued decrees urging missionaries to learn the languages of their
parishioners (Harrison, "Language and Rhetoric of Conversion," 4–5). The
priest in the Ayala dialogue has spent five years in Africa and speaks Arabic; he therefore offers to interpret the Christian doctrine for the Moor.
In the subsequent dialogues, the cleric begins to discuss Christian teachings while either invoking Muslim religious authority or demonizing the
Moor's native beliefs.

Part of Ayala's discursive strategy was to invoke *Mohammad* to bolster
Christian teachings, as in the example found in the cleric's explanation of
original sin, in "Dialog IX" of the catechism: "And thus even Mohammad
in one place explains that we are born with a stain, or poison in the heart,
which he calls the devil's portion, understanding this portion as corruption and a bad inclination toward sin" [Y asi el mesmo Mahoma en un lugar
da a entender, que nacemos con una mancha, o ponçoña en el corazon,
que el llama porcion del diablo; entendiendo por esta porcion, la corrup-
cion y mala inclinacion del pecado] (Ayala, *Catecismo*, 52). We will see this
strategy employed in the Andes, when the Inca is called on to transmit certain Christian concepts.

Of course, the Other's authority cannot be left as a lingering option
for the recently converted, so the subsequent dialogues, the first of which
is entitled "In which it is shown that there is no more than one path to
God; and therefore there cannot be many religions" [En que se muestra,
que no hay mas de un camino para ir a Dios en substancia; y asi que no
puede haber muchas religiones] (ibid., 54), develop arguments against the
Moors, Jews, and "Philosophers," or Greek pagans, and proclaim Christianity above all others as the true religion. But since the principal focus
of the catechism is to convert Moors, there are seven dialogues devoted

to discrediting the teachings of the Koran. While the peninsular Christians battled an equally literate religious tradition, where Moorish beliefs were codified by alphabetic writing, in the Andes the evangelical project was carried out against a primarily oral tradition in which collective memory was maintained through ritual re-creations of history, social alliances, and metaphysical relationships.[35] Rather than focusing principally on the extirpation-of-idolatry rituals, as they would do in the Andes, the Spanish battled the Muslims' written theology. The use of the dialogue, with its classical roots in Western theology and philosophy, enabled the Christian clerics to employ reason to discredit their theological adversaries.

Sexuality became an object of the Christians' condemnation and grounds for the undermining of the Koran's teachings, as in "Diálogo XV," "En el cual se ponen los errores, y mentiras, y fabulas que Mahoma puso en el Alcoran" [In which the errors, and lies, and fables that Mohammad put in the Koran are considered]. After a litany of differences between Mohammad and the Christian God, the bishop begins his discussion of the Moors' errant sexuality, which centers around the Moorish practice of bigamy. The Moor points out that, in the Old Testament, there are examples of church patriarchs with multiple wives, which the Christian cleric explains away while insisting that the Moors' practice of bigamy is illicit in the Christian church. He warns that such licentious behavior "opens the door to sodomy, the brutish sin against nature" [abre la puerta al pecado brutal, y contra natura de la sodomia] (ibid., 119). Whether the bishop is alluding to same-sex sodomy is unclear, but the passage suggests that Ayala is referring at least to *luxuria,* which, as we discussed in Chapter 1, included same-sex sodomy. Given the Christian belief of the time that the Moors lasciviously indulged in such "effeminate" practices, it is not surprising to find this reference in the catechism.

"Diálogo VII" of the second book of the catechism lists the four sins that require God's vengeance, including "the sin against nature" (ibid., 365). The bishop goes on to mention the Sodom and Gomorrah story, which exemplifies the wrath of God and connects the punishment to the sin of sodomy (ibid.).

Finally, in his explanation of the Ten Commandments, the bishop clarifies the sixth as follows:

> D. The sixth, thou shall not fornicate. M. Which is to say, do not have carnal access, except with your own wife or the woman with her husband; nor do things antecedent to nor consequential of nor close to the filthiness of the sin of lascivi-

ousness; moreover, each should try to maintain the chastity of his status.

D. El sexto, no fornicaras. M. Es a saber, no tener accesso carnal, mas que con la propia muger, o la muger con su marido; ni hazer las cosas antecedentes, o consequentes, o annexas a la suciedad del pecado de luxuria; mas antes que cada uno procure de guardar la castidad de su estado.

(Ibid., 354–355)

Here, the connection between carnal excess and *luxuria* is inscribed into the commandment and, when read with the preceding lessons, suggests a clear condemnation of all nonnormative sexuality. Bigamy, *luxuria,* and sodomy are isolated as the three Moorish cultural practices most in need of elimination. In the Andes, as we will see below, Christian evangelization was concerned with these and other issues of indigenous sexuality.

In other Spanish confession manuals, ones aimed at "old Christians," the elaboration of the sexual sins is different, placing emphasis on aspects more germane to the hegemonic Christian culture of the times. For example, Martín de Azpilcueta Navarro wrote a guide for confessors, *Manual de confesores y penitentes,* in 1554, a few years after Ayala's catechism. In his extensive explanation of the sixth commandment (110–125), he concentrates on issues such as adultery, sex with virgins, and sodomy, but there is no mention of bigamy. He defines "sin against nature" [pecado contra natura] by referring to the teachings of Saint Thomas and clarifies that it is "as when a man sins with a man, a woman with a woman, or a man with a woman outside of the natural vessel" [como cuando pecca varón con varón, hembra con hembra, o hombre con mujer, fuera del vaso natural] (111). He goes on to explain the danger of discussing this sin openly with the penitents, a warning we recall from the discussion in Chapter 1 of sodomy as the unmentionable vice. The confessor should censure himself when approaching this topic, for it is "a great and abominable sin, and unworthy of being named, even if it is between a husband and wife, or with a brutish animal, which is the sin of bestiality, and the greatest of all the sins against nature, according to Saint Thomas" [peccado grandísimo, y abominable, e indigno de ser nombrado: aunque sea entre marido y muger: o con bruto animal, que es peccado de bestialidad, y el mayor de todos los que son contra natura, según S. Thomás] (ibid., 111).

Although abstruse in this first lesson, a few paragraphs later he clarifies that "sodomitic copulation" [copula sodomético] is "sodomy, if it is of the same sex" [sodomia, si era del mismo sexo] (ibid., 112). This admonishment to keep silent on "aberrant" sexuality will appear in the American versions of the ecclesiastical literature and will lead to the ambiguous treatment of sodomy in the Andean *Doctrina christiana.*

Foucault has suggested that the proliferation of discourses on sexuality in the seventeenth century was accompanied by a "policing of statements" (*History of Sexuality,* 18) that found its way into contemporary pastoral instructions such as the confession manual (ibid., 19). Prudence in confessors' questions, which during the medieval church were much more detail-oriented, was now a Counter-Reformation trend (ibid.).[36]

In the shorter version of the manual for confessors, the sins related to the sixth commandment are even more obscured. The confessors are instructed that "penitents should explain the ways in which they are guilty of *luxuria,* of sinning against the commandment, without naming nor explaining with whom they have sinned" [explicar deue aqui el penitente los modos, en que acerca del peccado de la luxuria contra este mandamiento se viere culpado: sin nombrar, ni explicar en singular las personas con quien ha peccado] (Azpilcueta Navarro, *Manual de confesores,* 54). Remarkably, however, when the writer goes on to name the six sins of *luxuria,* sodomy is not mentioned. Here the "unmentionable vice" has been completely suppressed.

Although the topic is not mentioned in the standard manual used for Christians, in the manuals used for the recently converted, such as Bishop Ayala's manual, used explicitly for converting the Moors, we find that it is broached more openly. This explicitness reflects a deep-rooted practice of adapting the conversion materials to the Other's cultural practices and to foregoing the precaution proscribed in the post-Tridentine atmosphere described above. This strategy required the bishop to research and learn the Moorish religion and cultural practices and then to communicate to the recently converted the error of their ways; this method is analogous to missionary work in the Andes, where the *Doctrina christiana,* to be an effective tool of evangelization, had to include an analysis of Inca customs and beliefs in order to discredit them.

There is evidence that this strategy had already been employed in the earlier evangelization of the Caribbean and New Spain. Friar Pedro de Córdoba's *Doctrina christiana,* used in Santo Domingo since 1510, included an extended treatment of sodomy in its explanation of the sixth commandment. This reappearance of the topic, and the detailed explanation of the divine punishment related to sodomy, may have been in response to the Caribbean chroniclers' reports of same-sex sexuality in the islands.[37] In addition, as we saw in the discussion of the "cannibal questionnaire," the practice of sodomy, like cannibalism, was used to justify the enslavement of the Caribs.

While Córdoba makes no specific reference to the indigenous culture, as we saw in the Moorish confession manual and as we will see in the Andes, he does explain the sin's punishment to potential transgressors in terms that suggest his audience was native Amerindian rather than Spanish:

> And if this is a sin, it is even worse if you commit other sins against nature, like a man being with another man, because these men will not just go to hell but will also be burned by the authorities in a very large fire. Therefore, you should be careful not to commit such a great sin, because it was due to this sin that God destroyed the world, drowning it with lots of water. As a consequence, only eight people, who later repopulated the world, survived in a wooden ark. And once again God sent fire from the sky to burn other cities, and he destroyed them because of this sin. And in this way he will destroy you and he will burn you and the authorities will kill you if you commit this sin. And the devil will carry all of you who commit this sin off to hell, where you will be greatly tormented.

> Y si esto es pecado, mucho más lo es si hacen otros pecados contra natura, así como un hombre con otro, porque éstos no solamente irán al infierno, pero también acá los quemará la Justicia en un fuego muy grande. Y por esto os habéis de guardar mucho de cometer tan gran pecado, porque por este pecado destruyó Dios una vez el mundo y lo ahogó con muchas aguas. De tal manera no quedaron sino ocho personas en un arca de madera, de donde se tornó después a poblar el mundo. Y otra vez envió Dios fuego del cielo que quemó otras ciudades, y las destruyó por este pecado. Y así destruirá a vosotros y os quemará y matará la Justicia si este pecado hacéis. Y a todos cuantos hacéis este pecado os llevará el diablo al infierno, y os dará por ello muy grandes tormentos.

> (In Durán, *Monumenta catechetica*, 60–61)

Here, the name of the punished biblical city is not mentioned, perhaps because the native penitents would not have understood the reference to

Sodom and Gomorrah. The emphasis is on relating the divine punishment of burning cities full of sodomites and the burning that the "Justicia," or colonial authorities, would carry out. Because the text is directed to the Amerindian, there is little attention paid to textual precision. Cordoba conflates the Sodom and Gomorrah story with the universal Flood. The hyperbole of the story reaches the extreme of holding same-sex sodomites responsible for the destruction of the world. Punishment, after the earthly burning, culminates in the accused's damnation to hell, led by the devil. Durán clarifies that this mention of the Justicia was in reference to either the Inquisition or the civil authorities (ibid., 61n10). In addition to giving us another impression of how sodomy would be treated in the Americas by the missionaries, this passage also leaves a record of the violent treatment of sodomitical offenders in the Caribbean colonies, a violence that appeared again in the Andes.

PREACHING DAMNATION, CONFESSING SODOMY IN THE ANDES

Monica Barnes has characterized the *Doctrina christiana* as a "distorting mirror" in which the Andeans had to look at their own cultural image reflected back by European discourse. She reports that the Andean penitents had to memorize parts of the catechism and frequently heard the sermons and confession questions in village churches ("Catechisms and Confesionarios," 67). This act of linguistic control over the evangelization process standardized the message that would be emitted to colonial subjects. While the earlier, more diverse voices of morality escaped the totalizing influence of official church doctrine, in this new period of colonial institutional reform it was crucial for the message to be clear and unequivocal. But to achieve these goals, the missionaries and their indigenous and mestizo assistants had to adapt the antecedent models discussed above to the local particularities of the Andean context. Because they had taken the time to learn about indigenous cultural and religious practices, the writers of the Andean *Doctrina christiana* carefully resemanticized indigenous concepts in the translation of Christian doctrine and theology into the native languages of the region. The textual "mirror," therefore, like any transculturated text, reflected a distorting image, in part, as a result of indigenous informants' participation in the writing and translating of the ecclesiastical documents.

The *Catecismo mayor*, written at the third Council of Lima, is the fundamental reference book for the teaching of the Christian doctrine. In the fourth section of the catechism, as we saw in the Spanish catechism directed at the Moors, there is an extended dialogue explaining the Ten Commandments. The dialogue is didactic in form and tone: a *"pregunta"* (question, indicated by the letter *P*) is asked and a *"respuesta"* (answer, indicated by the letter *R*) is given concerning the sins of those who break the commandments. In this version of the catechism, the questions and answers are written in the dominant three languages of the colony.

The theme of sexuality is addressed in the sixth commandment: "Thou shalt not commit adultery." In the catechism, the dialogue is as follows:

> Q: Who breaks the sixth, that is, thou shalt not commit adultery? A: He who commits a filthy act with another's woman, or with a single woman, and even worse if it is with another man, or with a beast; and also he that delights in dishonest words or touching with you or another. And God punishes these evils with eternal fire in the other life, and often in this present life, with serious harm to body and soul.
>
> P: Quien quebranta el sexto, que es, No adulterar?
> R: El que comete fealdad con muger agena, o con soltera, y mucho más si es con otro hombre, o con bestia: y también el que se deleyta en palabras, o tocamientos deshonestos contigo o con otro. Y tales maldades les castiga Dios con fuego eterno en la otra vida, y muchas veces en esta presente, con graves males del cuerpo, y alma.
>
> (*Doctrina christiana,* 143–144)

This brief explanation of the sixth commandment alludes to the hierarchy of sinful sex acts that Lavrin outlines in her study of colonial sexuality in New Spain (*Sexuality and Marriage,* 47–95) and that we have seen in the Spanish catechism discussed above. This differentiation between what was then considered to be "natural" sex acts (i.e., heterosexuality and procreativeness) and "unnatural" sex acts (i.e., homosexuality, bestiality, or masturbation) is followed with a warning about the punishment for such sins. This admonishment is conspicuously the only detailed mention of God's potential wrath in the catechism's dialogue on the Ten Commandments. The exaggerated nature of this divine penalty is a reiteration of earlier versions (analyzed above) and is echoed in other treatments of sexual transgressions in other parts of the *Doctrina christiana.*

By comparing these Catholic descriptions of sins with those sins believed to have been important to the Incas, we can further understand the transculturating nature of the evangelization process. This comparison also provides additional evidence to support the notion that male same-sex activity was not considered sinful in pre-Hispanic times, that this religious prejudice was introduced by the Europeans. The texts suggest that the lengthy explanations and the menacing threats of punishment served to introduce to the Andeans values that were previously foreign to them. The *Doctrina christiana* includes a report written by Juan Polo de Ondegardo, the royalist encomendero and twice-appointed corregidor of Cuzco. This report, *Instrucción contra las cerimonias, y ritos que usan los Indios conforme al tiempo de su infidelidad,* supplied extensive information on Andean religious practices for the second Council of Lima in 1567 (MacCormack, *Religion in the Andes,* 186). Polo de Ondegardo gathered this knowledge while confiscating deified mummies of Inca ancestors and destroying *huacas* (ibid., 187). His report includes a list of the Inca morality laws that supposedly governed the Andes prior to the Spanish invasion:

> The sins they principally accused each other of were, first, to kill someone outside of war. Likewise, to commit adultery. Likewise, to steal. And the most remarkable sins were being negligent in venerating their *huacas,* speaking poorly of the Inca, and failing to obey the Inca. They did not accuse themselves of interior sins or acts.

> Los pecados de que principalmente se acusavan eran. Lo primero, matar uno á otro fuera de la guerra. Item tomar la mujer agena. Item dar yervas, ó hechizos para hacer mal. Item hurtar. Y por muy notable pecado tenían el de cuydo [descuido]en la veneración de sus Huacas, y el quebrantar sus fiestas: y el dezir mal del Inga: y el no obedecerle. No se accusavan de pecados o actos interiores.

> (*Instrucción,* in Polo de Ondegardo, *Informaciones,* 13)

We note that Polo de Ondegardo reports no mention of an Inca proscription of sodomy. As we saw above, in the interviews that Toledan *visita* officials conducted with elderly Andeans in 1571, the question as to whether the Incas punished sodomy and cross-dressing was answered negatively by all but one interviewee. Guaman Poma provides extensive information on the common pre-Columbian punishments administered to Andeans of all social levels, but sodomy is not mentioned (*Primer nueva corónica,* f303–f314:lines 229–236). My research has uncovered no evidence of pre-Hispanic prohibitions of same-sex praxis or transgendering; indeed, as we saw in Chapters 2 and 3, same-sex praxis fulfilled ritual obligations in some circumstances.[38] The missionaries, in their presentation of sins, established a new moral paradigm in the Andes.[39]

Sodomy was not the only sin the catechism writers felt it necessary to explain in some detail. They expanded on those "sins" that did not have corresponding sins in the Andean value systems, going into greater detail when explicating commandments one, five, six, nine, and ten; the others seem to have been more readily understood or accepted by the Andean penitents. For example, the first commandment, "Honor God above all other things" [Honrar a Dios sobre todas las cosas] in the Andes was a difficult request due to the multiplicity of sacred divinities Andeans worshiped (*Doctrina christiana,* 135). The priests were aware of the Andeans' propensity to deify many forces of nature and important topographical sites. Therefore, it was necessary to list the various Andean religious traditions that contradicted this Catholic belief and that led to sin. The trespasser of this commandment was "el que adora qualquiera criatura, o tiene ydolos, o guacas, o da crédito a falsas sectas, y heregias, o sueños, y gueros, que son vanidad, y engaño del Demonio" (ibid., 135–136) [he who worships any creature, or has idols, or *huacas,* or who credits false sects and heresies, or dreams and premonitions, which are all vanity and the devil's deceit]. Of course, all of these were routine Andean practices, many of which were resisting colonial evangelization.[40] They were not sins for the Andeans; on the contrary, they were part of sacred, ritual behavior. We note the writers' use of local cultural practices, like the adoration of "*huacas,*" in their examples to teach the Andeans new behavior.

Other commandments were not accompanied by such narratives. For example, the third commandment, "Honor religious observances" [Sanctificar las fiestas], seems quite similar to the Andean mandate to respect the ritual calendar. No further explanation or divine threat is needed in the Catholic discourse to ensure compliance, for ritual practice was thoroughly ingrained in the Andean conscience. It was merely a question of changing names and symbols. The same applies for the seventh commandment, "Do not steal" [No hurtar]. The Incas had a strict law against stealing; therefore, no further explanation in the catechism was necessary.

Yet, the priests did have to embellish their descriptions and punishments for the sixth commandment. As we have seen, there is no mention of sex-related sins in the pre-Hispanic Andean cultures, except for a differently defined heterosexual adultery and incest. Indeed, those chroniclers who address the issue are appalled by the diversity of sex acts and are confused by the different sexual and gender identities in the indigenous populations. In Chapters 2 and 3 we saw how sexuality related to female political agency and how third-gender ritualists practiced ritual sodomy. By stressing the severe Christian punishments awaiting sodomites and other sexual trans-gressors, the priests leave us another clue as to how these practices were considered by the pre-Hispanic Andeans. Because the catechism must go to the extreme of threatening severe bodily and spiritual punishments, it suggests that the indigenous peoples did not proscribe same-sex acts be-fore the arrival of the Spaniards.

The catechists' insistence on scaring the penitents away from same-sex behavior is amplified in the sermons included in the *Tercero catecismo y ex-posición de la doctrina cristiana por sermones* (1585). Estenssoro recounts how the "word," that is, textual explanations of doctrine, was introduced into the missionary project after the visual mediums of the early years failed ("Descubriendo los poderes de la palabra," 75–80). He goes on to elaborate how Francisco de Ávila followed the 1585 sermons with his own collec-tion of sermons meant to address the persistence of idolatries in the Andes (ibid., 82–83). Indeed, Guaman Poma's drawings and texts leave little doubt of his opinion on the effective transmission of doctrine through sermons, a genre that he would imitate in his own writings. He both critiques and emulates the sermons he heard in his lifetime, providing us with a testi-mony of the indigenous reception of evangelical preaching.[41] One of his drawings depicts his understanding of hell and includes "*luxuria*" as one of the sins that condemns sinners to an eternity of "hunger and thirst and weeping and gnashing of teeth and doubly-sharpened knives, spirits cre-ated to avenge and serpents and worms and scorpions and hammers" [ham-bre y sed y llanto y crujir de dientes y cuchillo dos veces agudos, espiritus criados para venganza, y serpientes, y gusanos, y escorpiones, y martillos] (*Primer nueva corónica*, f942:lines 778–779) (Figure 10).

The twenty-third sermon included in the Andean *Doctrina christiana* ad-dresses the sixth commandment, where we again find the theme of same-sex sexuality:

> Sermon XXIII of the Sixth Commandment. In which it is
> taught how God is greatly angered by adultery, and how he
> punishes it, and how fornication with a single woman, even

FIGURE 10   *City of hell. From Guaman Poma,* Nueva corónica y buen gobierno.

one, is a mortal sin, and how God punishes the nations of Indians for their luxurious ways.

Sermon XXIII del Sexto Mandamiento. En que se enseña quanto enoja a Dios el adulterio, y como lo castiga, y como el fornicar tambien con soltera, aunque sea una sola es pecado mortal, y de las otras maneras de luxuria por las cuales castiga Dios, a la nación de los Indios.

(642)

The sermon is explicitly addressed to the indigenous population, as evidenced by the reference to "nations of Indians" in the sermon's title and to various comments in the text.

Again, we are confronted with a text adapted to the Andean context, for the authors refer to specific cultural practices known to have existed in the Andes. The first part of the sermon explains the sin of adultery in its heterosexual form, using biblical examples of God's wrath toward men who fornicate with the wives of others and with unmarried women. But the writers also refer to the colonial context, glorifying the Christian laws for the protection they afford the "poor Indians": "And look what a great God you have, though you be but a poor Indian, for God does not allow the Spaniard, or the Corregidor, or the Viceroy, not even the Inca himself, if he lived, to touch your wife" [Y mirad quan buen Dios teneys que aunque seays un yndio pobrecito, no da Dios licencia al Español, ni al Corregidor, ni al Virrey, ni al mismo Inga si viviera, que os toque vuestra mujer] (ibid., 643). Along with the colonial administrators, the Inca, "if he lived," would also have to obey the Christian laws against adultery which protect their native women. Of course, we know from Guaman Poma and other sources that women were routinely abused by the Christian colonialists and missionaries.[42] Also prohibited is the Andean premarital relationship known in Spanish as "*amancebamiento*," and as "*sirvinakuy*" in Quechua, in which an Andean man and woman lived together in a "trial marriage, which became one of the most resistant practices of Andean sexual culture."[43]

As if the Christian God's authority were not convincing enough, at one point the authors appeal to the Andeans' memory of pre-Hispanic tradition and authority by invoking the Inca:

The Gospel and the entire sacred scripture says that if you do not believe it you are not a Christian, and you are little more than a beast if you believe that God does not punish such sins.

Your Inca punished with death he who took the wife of his neighbor, killing him in a rage. Therefore, God, king of the heavens, punishes no better than your Inca.

El Evangelio lo dize, y toda la sagrada Scriptura, si no lo creeys no soys Christianos, y aun soys mas que bestia si creeys que Dios no castiga a tales peccados, vuestro Inga castigava con muerte al que tomava la mujer de su proximo y le hazia morir rabiando, pues Dios que es rey del cielo, no castigara mejor que vuestro Inga.

(Ibid., 647)

The sinful, noncompliant Indian, reduced to the status of "beast" in this inflammatory rhetoric, an animal incapable of believing that God would punish trespassers of the sixth commandment, is encouraged to remember the Inca, just as the Moor was to appreciate Mohammad's understanding of original sin in Ayala's confession manual. The logic of the passage is clear: if the penitent does not recognize Christian authority, then perhaps he will remember the Inca's, who reportedly prohibited this form of adultery in the list of Inca morality laws reported by Polo de Ondegardo and other chroniclers. When convenient for the sermon writers, Andean culture became a site of reinforcement of Christian morality.

As we observed in the catechism, however, the Andeans did not prohibit the "nefarious sin"; therefore, in the same sermon there is no appeal to Inca authority as it may have related to same-sex praxis. Instead, European morality relating to sodomy is introduced in the following passage from the pedagogical discourse, as seen in antecedents considered above:

Above all these sins is the nefarious sin we name sodomy, which is when a man sins with a man or with a woman in an unnatural way, and above all this is to sin with beasts, sheep, mares, for this is a great abomination. If there are among you men who commit sodomy sinning with other men, or with boys, or with beasts, know that for this sin fire and brimstone fell from the sky and turned to ash the cities of Sodom and Gomorrah. Know that the just laws of our kings of Spain punish the sin by death penalty and burning.

Sobre todos estos peccados es el pecado que llamamos nefando, y sodomía, que es pecar hombre con hombre, o con muger no por el lugar natural, y sobre todo esto es aun peccar con bestias, con ovejas, o yeguas, que esta es grandisima abominación. Si ay algunos entre vosotros que cometan sodomía peccando con otros hombres, o con muchachos, o con bestias, sepa que por esso baxo fuego y piedra apusre[*sic*] del cielo, y abraso y bolvio ceniza a que las cinco ciudades de Sodoma y Gomorra. Sepa que tiene pena de muerte y ser quemado por las leyes justas de nuestros reyes de España.

(Ibid., 651–652)

The use of first person plural in the first sentence of this passage is notable: "*llamamos.*" With this verb form, the sermon situates the sin squarely in the moral universe of the colonizer. Instead of referring to pre-Hispanic moral authority, this passage must refer to European, Christian tradition, specifically, the biblical story of Sodom and Gomorrah and the Spanish Crown's sodomy laws. The iteration of these tropes, as we will see again below in the official history of Toledo's viceroyalty, become justifications for the violent destruction of the Andeans:

Know that according to the sacred scriptures, because of this sin, God destroys kingdoms and nations. Know that the reason for which God has permitted the Indians to be so afflicted and harassed by other nations is because of that vice that your ancestors had and many of you still have. And know that I tell you on behalf of God that if you do not mend your ways your entire nation will perish and God will finish you off and will scrape you off this earth.

Sepa que por esso dize la sagrada Scriptura, que destruye Dios a los reynos y naciones. Sepa que la causa porque Dios ha permitido que los indios seays tan afligidos y acosados de otras naciones es porque esse vicio que vuestros passados tuvieron y muchos de ustedes todavia teneys. Y sabed que os digo de parte de Dios que si no os emendays que toda vuestra nación perecera y os acabara Dios y os raera de la tierra.

(Ibid., 651–652)

It is remarkable how this explicit justification for the Spanish invasion and destruction of Andean cultures is linked to sodomy and not to the other forms of sexuality. Again, recurring to the Judeo-Christian scriptural tradition, the preachers claim moral authority to punish the errant behavior of the Andeans. Responsibility for the Andeans' suffering is transferred to a segment of Andean society; the omnipotent Christian God permits the afflictions because of the vileness of the "nefarious" sinners. Here we can appreciate a foreshadowing of the "scapegoating" of third-gender subjects perpetrated by Inca Garcilaso, discussed in the next chapter. The passage ends with a threat for further destruction if the sinners do not change their behavior.

If the catechism and sermons were primarily teaching documents designed for didactic purposes, the confession manuals were conceived as the examinations that would give the missionaries feedback on their progress in evangelization, and perhaps as control of penitents' consciences. The confession manual that accompanied the *Doctrina christiana* reflects the same ideology espoused in the other religious documents examined above; however, it represents a more direct contact between colonizer and colonized. The purpose of the confession manual was, as noted in its prologue, "to erase the repugnant errors that the unfaithful have" [quitar los errores contrarios que los Infieles tienen] (ibid., 199). These "repugnant errors" resulted from how "persuaded and convinced of his errors and nonsense the devil had them" [persuadidos y assentados les tenía el Demonio sus disparates y errores] (ibid.). The power of the devil had to be combated with more than just Christian doctrine; the new colonial subjects had to learn of their mistaken ways before the church's ideals could be accepted and practiced.

Harrison, in her extensive research on the Andean confession manuals, has contributed a detailed analysis of the Spanish resemanticization of Quechua words and concepts used in the language of conversion.[44] Her scholarship opens a window on the linguistic mechanics of transculturation, as I will explore below, with a focus on same-sex sexuality. While Harrison's work has also explored the way indigenous sexuality was brought into colonial discourse through the "codifying [of] heterosexual intimacy" in the confession manuals ("Theory of Concupiscence," 139), I suggest that this imposition of normative Christian sexuality, together with the catechism and sermons, also silenced Andean practices of ritual sexuality and left in the colonial ecclesiastical discourse only a Western, pathologized notion of indigenous same-sex erotics.

Serge Gruzinski, in his analysis of confession among the Nahuas of New Spain, explores the effects confessional discourse had on the Nahuas' conceptions of self and society. As he suggests, "Confession can also become an instrument for expressing church-approved forms of individualization and guilt, eroding the traditional ties and interpersonal relations of colonized societies" ("Individualization and Acculturation," 96). The indigenous penitent experiences through confession a process in which he is forced to assimilate a foreign system of morality and at the same time assume two new roles: "as vectors of an embryonic individualism and as ideologically and psychologically dominated subjects of the Catholic confessor" (ibid., 99–100).

Gruzinski's observation that the penitent undergoes a process of individualization when entering the confessional is a provocative way of considering the ecclesiastical discourse's effect on third-gender subjectivity in the Andes. As discussed in Chapters 2 and 3, the Andean third-gender subject was linked to his community through ritual practice. In addition to proscribing profane practices of same-sex sexuality, the confession manuals reflect a treatment of sodomy that decontextualized pre-Columbian male-to-male, ritual sexual behavior, divorcing it from its communal significance. By individualizing the act, the confessor's words repositioned the third-gender ritualist in a secular space, removing him from the liminal, ritual space associated with the feminine, agriculture, and ancestor communication. Not only was sex "put into discourse," as Foucault points out (*History of Sexuality,* 11), but, in the case of the colonial *confesionario,* "sex" as it was conceived by the Andeans, in both its ritual and its profane manifestations, was transculturated. The language of the evangelical documents attempts to transform pre-Columbian Amerindian cognition of sex and gender. I will examine three facets of this transculturation: how the confessional separated the penitent from his or her community; how confession separated him from his ritual practice; and how new notions of acceptable sexual behavior were introduced.

"Sodomy," as it was understood by the Spanish missionaries, was not a translatable concept into the Andean languages until a resemanticization of the signifiers for the Andean perception of sin took place. Harrison's linguistic analysis of the colonial Quechua terms used to translate "sin" suggests that the entire notion of sin in Quechua related to a different moral paradigm ("Cultural Translation," 111–114). While Christian sin (*pecado*) signified a range of possible transgressions in relation to the textual canon of laws and regulation of conduct, the Andean near-equivalent corresponded to an ongoing communal negotiation of reciprocal obligations. Early colonial bilingual dictionaries, such as González Holguín's Quechua dictionary and Bertonio's Aymara dictionary, presented two words as equivalents of sin: *hucha* and *cama.* Perhaps because the word *cama* had a more positive connotation for the Quechua speakers, *hucha* soon became the Quechua word most often used in the religious writing of the sixteenth and seventeenth centuries (ibid., 114). However, as Harrison has written, "*Hucha,* as found in the context of indigenous culture, is often associated with what is owed but has not yet been settled up, sort of a debt to society kept track of on a large balance sheet" (ibid., 112).

This relationship between individual and society implicit in the pre-Hispanic connotation of the Quechua word is further expressed by its use in other circumstances. Gerald Taylor and Tom Zuidema's work on the "societal transactions" that involved ritual responsibilities reveals another instance in which *hucha* would be employed to signify a person's failure to perform or his flawed performance of ritual duties (ibid.). In another example of Andean transgression, the word "emphasized that individual actions subvert the common good; one labors for one's own benefit (*por el suyo*)" (ibid., 113). Harrison ends her explication of the terms by reminding us that the penitent in her example from a seventeenth-century sermon uses *hucha* in her confession, but resists its Catholic resemanticization by expressing her "innocence" ("Cultural Translation," 114, 124).

Lydia Fossa adds to our understanding of *hucha* by exploring its use in Cieza de León's account of the Capacocha ceremony, isolating the ideology that clouded its original meaning. In the context of this annual ritual in which oracles from around Tawantinsuyu gathered in Cuzco to "consult" with the Inca and his high priests, the *hucha* was the *consulta* (meeting or consultation) ("Leyendo hoy a Cieza de León," 39–40). Here, again, is more evidence of the reciprocal nature of a social transaction between Inca and oracle. As we have seen in previous chapters, relationships between *huacas* and Andean ritualists, in both myths and chronicles, were often characterized in sexual terms, both metaphorically and literally, and sometimes through ritual sodomy. Perhaps because these kinds of ritual activities were considered idolatrous, the term *hucha* was adopted by the missionaries as the equivalent of "sin" (ibid., 40) and, as we will see below, was used to translate "sodomy."

The term, acculturated as it was, stayed in the colonial discourse and was continually used to express the different transgressions proscribed by the Catholic missionaries. The indigenous concept is misrepresented, therefore, not only in the dominant, Spanish, discourse, but in the subjugated, Quechua, as well. The discursive transculturation occurs in the Quechua because the written language itself is a product of colonial practice.[45] This notion of sin will be carried into later writing on the Andes, in texts produced in both colonial languages and by various colonial subjects: in Spanish and Quechua and by Spaniards, Creoles, mestizos and ladinos. The use of the term *hucha* to express the Christian idea of sin transformed the indigenous penitents' cognition of transgression from a ritual or communal obligation to individual actions that, on the whole, were not considered offenses in the pre-Columbian Andes.

What has been said about sin in general can now be applied specifically to issues of sexuality and, in this particular case, to sodomy. Harrison has observed that, "increasingly, *huchallicuni* became a synonym for sexual transgression, although there were many other perfectly adequate verbs in Quechua" ("'True' Confessions," 15). She points out that the addition of the suffix *lli* to the noun form *hucha* "compounds the notion of sinfulness, for it denotes that an individual takes on the characteristics indicated by the noun, a transformation brought about by the individual himself or herself (Cusihuamán 1976: 7.11.14, 196). Thus, through the suffixes, the individual's own responsibility for sin could be emphasized in the translation of the Catholic doctrine" (ibid., 15). Here we can see the grammatical mechanics behind the discursive transculturation of the concept of collective transgression into individualized sin. The priest's use of this verb necessarily suggests to the Quechua speaker an intimate relationship between his action and morality. Responsibility to community is deemphasized, and the penitent's individual subjectivity is heightened. Any relationship a sexual act may have had to communal tradition, such as Andean rituality, is severed. The reader may recall the self-conscious comments by the Huarochirí narrator when referring to sexual unions of the *huacas;* in the original Quechua, the word *hucha* is used, indicating how widespread the translation had become by the early seventeenth century.[46]

Indeed, González Holguín's dictionary lists other Quechua words for fornication: "*Yoccuni.* Tener copula hombre o animal con hembra o fornicar hombre [*Vocabulario,* 369]; *Puñuni.* Dormir [296]; *Purini.* Andar caminar [297]; *Huchallicuni.* Pecar" [200] (*Yoccuni.* To copulate man or animal with female or to fornicate; *Puñuni.* To sleep; *Purini.* To walk; *Huchallicuni.* To sin). Only the last verb indicates sinfulness; the others appear to be euphemisms for the sexual act. By choosing *huchallicuni* to signify sinful sexual acts, the priests isolated sexual praxis from its indigenous, communal context.[47] When discussing sodomy, the translators used *Huchallicuni* in combination with other Quechua words descriptive of the sexual act. For example, in the sermon analyzed above, the phrase "Sobre todos estos pecados es el pecado que llamamos nefando, y sodomia, que es pecar hombre con hombre, o con muger no por el lugar natural" (*Doctrina christiana,* 651) [Above all these sins is the nefarious sin we name sodomy,

which is when a man sins with a man or with a woman in an unnatural way] is translated into Quechua as "Cay tucuy huchacunamantapas
hua[ss]a hucharacmi hatunin huchaca, cari pura hua[ss]anacuc mananispa
huarmicta huah[ss]ac, chaymi ancha hatun huchacta huchallicun." The expression, "this is the greatest possible sin" is glossed using *huchallicuni,* while
"sodomy" is rendered using *hucha* in combination with *cari pura* (between
men) and *hua[ss]a,* which is defined in González Holguín's dictionary as
"the hips of a beast" [las anclas (ancas) de la bestia] (ibid., 184).

In addition to divorcing the ritual significance of sodomy from indigenous memory, the semantical maneuvering undertaken by the missionaries and lexicographers leaves us with a void in the colonial lexicon: there
is no recorded word for sodomy in the indigenous languages that does
not reflect Western attitudes.[48] All of these expressions and those of the
dictionaries carry the mark of European ideology, which obfuscates pre-
Columbian conceptions of Andean same-sex sexuality as well as Andean
ritual sodomy.

While the *Doctrina christiana* was directed at the indigenous Andeans, the
official history of the Toledo regime was written for European readers. The
Historia índica marks a key stage in the transculturation of Andean gender
and sexuality, one in which the native informants' agency in protecting
their cultural knowledge continues to contribute to a re-presentation of
the autochthonous culture that belies pre-Hispanic significance. The colonial regime had gathered information on and had begun to regulate the
Andeans' gender and sexuality. Now the story had to be told in a historical
narrative, one which justified the discourses of coloniality that shaped that
narrative's composition. Pedro Sarmiento de Gamboa represents another
step in the transculturation of ritual sexuality and liminal gender subjectivity, which became permanently embedded in Andean literary and historical discourse, as we shall see in Chapter 5.

MAMA HUACO, THE QUEER TYRANT:
ABJECTION OF THE FEMININE IN
SARMIENTO DE GAMBOA

Pedro Sarmiento de Gamboa was an important contribu-
tor to Toledo's collective reply to Las Casas's critique of Spanish colonization. Sarmiento, whom MacCormack groups with Cieza and Betanzos as
"more methodical and reflective" than earlier writers (*Religion in the Andes,*
81), wrote a history of the rise of the Inca empire, *Historia índica* (1572),

compiling the testimony of native informants from the Cuzco region. He interviewed "more than one hundred *khipukamayuqs*" for his history, commissioned by Toledo (Urton, *History of a Myth*, 19), and at the end of the document, forty-two "notables" from the *panaqas* (lineages) of Cuzco, affirmed its veracity by signing their names.[49] Although the information has been judged to be some of the most reliable and original of all the histories (Sánchez, *Literatura peruana*, 145), its narration is charged with Toledan justification ideology, which seeks to depict the Incas as tyrannical usurpers of power and therefore illegitimate rulers of the Andean peoples. At stake was the right of the Spanish monarchs to govern the Andes. In the analysis that follows we shall see how the representation of gender and sexuality became an ideological tool in Sarmiento's justification of Spanish conquest, and how the more complex indigenous notions of third-gender subjectivity were glossed as pathological behaviors.

As Antonio Cornejo Polar has suggested, Andean colonial discourse in the chronicles is characterized by its heterogeneity and is composed of two principal influences: on the one hand, the universe of the conquistadores, missionaries, and colonial authorities; and, on the other hand, the universe of the indigenous Andean peoples.[50] It is the convergence of the two universes, a mixture of textual and oral traditions, that resulted in Sarmiento's *Historia índica*. Cornejo Polar formulated his theory of Peruvian literature, with its roots in the colonial discourse under analysis, by proposing that the producer, the text, and the receptor belonged to one universe (i.e., the Western literary tradition) while the referent of the text belonged to the universe of the Other (i.e., Andean indigenous culture). If we take into account the indigenous informants' participation in the writing of the text, then the producer must be characterized not just as writing from a strictly Spanish/European literary and religious tradition, but also as being influenced by the indigenous culture transmitted from the oral tradition. As I strived to achieve above with my analysis of the *visita* testimonials, I believe it is important to talk again about how the oral tradition of the Andean informants became transculturated in the chronicler's transcription and interpretation of Andean mythohistory.

Sarmiento does not simply ignore the Andean oral tradition, nor does he invent what is convenient for his narrative; instead, he appropriates Andean mythic symbolism to reflect a post-Tridentine gender ideology that justifies conquest and colonization. He opens his chronicle with the requisite preface addressed to his intended reader, King Phillip II, and with praise for his more immediate patron and supervisor, Francisco de Toledo. From these first passages we glean the subtext of his entire history of the

Incas: gathering information from the colonized Andeans that would dis-
prove the allegations of the Lascasians, the defenders of the Amerindians,
those who "began to make a difficulty about the right and title which the
kings of Castille had over these lands" (4) [comenzaron a dificultar sobre
el derecho y título que los reyes de Castilla tenían a estas tierras] (*Historia
índica,* 196).[51] Sarmiento, referring to the sponsorship of Phillip II's father,
Carlos V, of the Valladolid debates (discussed in Chapter 2), questions those
who advocated for the recognition of the Incas as sovereigns of the region
by claiming that their opinions were formed based on inaccurate information gathered by early governors who

> did not use the diligence necessary for ascertaining the truth,
> and also owing to certain reports of the Bishop of Chiapa
> who was moved to passion against certain conquerors in
> his bishopric with whom he had persistent disputes . . . he
> said things on the right to this country gained by the con-
> querors of it, which differ from the evidence and judicial
> proofs which have been seen and taken down by us, and
> from what we who have traveled over the Indies enquiring
> about these things, leisurely and without war, know to be
> facts.
>
> (5)
>
> no hicieron las diligencias necesarias para informar de la ver-
> dad del hecho [and from] ciertas informaciones del obispo
> de Chiapa [Las Casas], que, movido de pasión contra algunos
> conquistadores de su obispado, con quien tuvo pertinancísimas
> diferencias . . . , dijo cosas de los dominios de esta tierra a
> vueltas de los conquistadores de ella, que son fuera de lo que
> las averiguaciones y probanzas jurídicas se ha visto y sacado en
> limpio y lo que sabemos los que habemos peregrinado todas
> las Indias.
>
> (*Historia índica,* 197)

    Implicitly decrying the fact that Las Casas never traveled in Peru, Sar-
miento ignores Las Casas's extensive secondhand knowledge of the Andean
region, which is summarized in "De las antiguas gentes del Peru" (On the
Ancient Peoples of Peru) based on the bishop's readings of Xeres, Astete,
Cieza de León, Molina, and others. Sarmiento's remark illustrates his dis-

cursive strategy of discrediting those chronicles and histories that preceded his own while creating the "need" for new evidence. More subtle, perhaps, is his discursive move to privilege legal discourse over proto-ethnographic knowledge such as that produced by Cieza de León and Las Casas.

Sarmiento juxtaposes the apologists' spurious knowledge and the early governors' lazy, stay-in-Lima attitude with Viceroy Toledo's infamous round of *visitas* throughout the colony. In addition to his firsthand observations, Toledo sent his secretary and interpreter with Dr. Gabriel de Loarte, Toledo's confidante, who was instrumental in establishing the *reducciones* in Huarochirí. They traveled to the valley of Yucay on the *visita* whose questionnaire we just considered and to other regions to interview elderly Andeans in order to gather information on the Incas.[52] As the foregoing analysis illustrates, the questions were worded in such a way as to prove that the Incas had been tyrannical rulers over the valley and, therefore, that the Spanish Conquest was justified. This information forms the basis of Sarmiento's history, and he represents these reports to be truthful portrayals of the pre-Hispanic, tyrannical past:

> Accordingly, in his general visitation, which he is making personally throughout the kingdom, he has verified from the root and established by a host of witnesses examined with the greatest diligence and care, taken from the principal old men of the greatest ability and authority in the kingdom, and even those who pretend to have an interest in it from being relations and descendants of the Incas, the terrible, inveterate and horrible tyranny of the Incas, being the tyrants who ruled in these kingdoms of Peru, and the *curacas* who governed the districts. This will undeceive all those in the world who think that the Incas were legitimate sovereigns, and that the *curacas* were natural lords of the land.

(9)

> Y así en la visita general que por su persona viene haciendo con mucha suma de testigos, con grandísima diligencia y curiosidad examinados, de los más principales ancianos y de más capacidad y autoridad del reino y aun de los que pretenden ser interesados en ello, por ser parientes y descendientes de los ingas, la terrible, envejecida, y horrenda tiranía de los Ingas, tiranos que fueron en este reino del Perú, y de los curacas

particulares de los pueblos de él, para desengañar a todos los
del mundo que piensan que estos dichos Ingas fueron reyes
legítimos y los curacas señores naturales de esta tierra.

(*Historia índica*, 198)

As we saw in the analysis of the *visita* reports, these transcribed testimonies must be read with caution. Urton has established that Sarmiento's
informants were agents in the recording of pre-Hispanic history, narrating
a local version of the Andean creation myth rather than an imperial version. Thus, Paucartambo was established in the literary canon as a site of
Inca origin, which legitimated the later claims of the informants to colonial privileges, such as freedom from tribute obligations (Urton, *History of
a Myth,* 18–40). Having posited that the Incas and the contemporary local
rulers known as *curacas* were tyrants, Sarmiento goes on to list the vices and
customs to which the Andeans were supposedly subjugated, giving credit
to the Spanish monarchs for putting an end to such practices:

> Besides this, there are their tyrannical laws and customs. It will
> be understood that your Majesty has a specially true and holy
> title to these kingdoms of Peru, because your Majesty and your
> most sacred ancestors stopped the sacrifice of innocent men,
> the eating of human flesh, the accursed sin, the promiscuous
> concubinage with sisters and mothers, the abominable use of
> beasts, and their wicked and accursed customs. For from each
> one God demands an account of his neighbor, and this duty
> especially appertains to princes, and above all to your Majesty.
>
> (10)

> Y demás de esto, de sus tiránicas leyes y costumbres se enten-
> derá el verdadero y santo título que Vuestra Majestad tiene,
> especialmente a este reino y reinos del Perú, porque Vuestra
> Majestad y sus antepasados reyes santísmos impidieron sacrifi-
> car los hombres inocentes y comer carne humana, el maldito
> pecado nefando, y los concúbitos indiferentes con hermanas
> y madres, abominable uso de bestias, y las nefarias y malditas
> costumbres suyas; porque a cada uno mandó Dios de su pró-
> jimo, y esto principalmente pertenece a los príncipes, y entre
> todos a Vuestra Majestad.
>
> (*Historia índica*, 199)

Here, the litany of dehumanizing accusations seems to respond directly to earlier apologists' assertions that the Incas had evolved past these "uncivilized" practices. We are reminded of Cieza de León's remarks that tried to set the Incas apart from the unconquered, marginal Andean peoples. Included here is the "accursed sin," and, as we saw in the *Doctrina christiana,* the Toledan discourse repeats the vindication of invasion and colonization by inscribing this practice as sin and ignoring the ritual nature of same-sex praxis and the cross-gendered subjectivity of third genders in Andean tradition. In the continuation of this passage, Sarmiento recurs to European authorities, adopting the natural-law argument, which I analyze in Chapter 2, as the justification for Spain's war against the indigenous Andeans:

> Even if they had been true and natural lords of the soil, it would be lawful to remove them and introduce a new government, because man may rightly be punished for these sins against nature, though the native community has not been opposed to such practices nor desires to be avenged, as innocent, by the Spaniards. For in this case they have no right to deliver themselves and their children over to death, and they should be forced to observe natural laws, as we are taught by the Archbishop of Florence, Innocent, supported by Fray Francisco de Victoria in his work on the title to the Indies.
>
> (10–11)

> Unicamente por lo cual se les pudo hacer y dar guerra y prozeguir por el derecho de ella contra los tiranos, y aunque fueron naturales y verdaderos señores de la tierra y se pudieron mudar señores e introducir nuevo principado, porque por estos pecados contra natura pueden ser castigados y punidos, aunque la comunidad de los naturales de la tierra no contradijesen a tal costumbre ni quieran ser por esto los inocentes vengados por los españoles, porque en este caso no son de su derecho, de tal manera que a sí mismos o a sus hijos pueden entregar a la muerte, porque pueden ser forzados a que guarden ley de naturaleza, como lo enseña el arzobispo de Florencia e Inocencio y lo confirma fray Francisco de Vitoria en la relación que hizo de los títulos de las Indias.
>
> (*Historia índica,* 199)

The reader is left with a truncated notion of Andean gender, a pathologized construct that conflates all indigenous Andeans into a regulatable
category of sinner and barbarian. Because the natives ostensibly permitted
such "barbaric" behavior, which was evidenced in some of the Toledo *visita*
reports, the Spanish are justified in their destruction of Andean society.
Sarmiento recognizes the Andean community's permissive attitude toward
same-sex praxis, reflected in the Toledo *visita* reports, as one reason Spaniards have a duty to intervene and usurp Inca sovereignty. The only acceptable norm was heterosexual, procreative copulation within the confines of
the institution of matrimony. Any deviation from this norm rationalized
punishment.

Sarmiento's expression of Toledan gender ideology is clearer still in his
versions of Andean myths. He mentions making a selection from the oral
narratives he heard while in the southern Andes and only includes a small
number of myths. There are two myths that stand out as clever manipula-
tions of Andean values of gender and sexuality and provide a contrast of
two versions of Andean femininity: one version that represents a Christian, European ideal of women; and another that represents a threat to
that ideal. As the reader will readily realize, Sarmiento reverses the portrayal of the non-Inca and the Inca that we observed in Cieza de León's
chronicle (analyzed in Chapter 2). Just as in the analysis of the sodomite
giants, here again we can appreciate how indigenous myths were manipu-
lated for ideological purposes, a process of transculturation in which indigenous informants and Spanish historians contributed to the creation of
a heterogeneous literary corpus. The inherent queerness—that is, the subversion of the dominant cultural logic in both the originary and the newly
hegemonic domains—of this process is evident. The products of transculturation never precisely resemble their predecessors' cultures.

The first myth, an idealization of heteronormative, patriarchal ideals,
is Sarmiento's retelling of the *"fábula"* [fable] of the "hermanos Cañares"
[Cañari brothers], who survived a flood in the province of Quito, in the
district of Tomebamba. While the two brothers are planting seeds in the
mountaintop that saved them from the rising waters, "some small loaves
of bread and a jar of *chicha"* (30) [unos panecitos y un cántaro de chicha
(*Historia índica*, 207)] mysteriously appear. Upon investigating, the brothers
discover two women preparing them food:

> While they were watching they saw two Cañari women
> preparing the victuals and putting them in the accustomed

place. When about to depart the men tried to seize them, but they evaded their would-be captors and escaped. The Cañaris, seeing the mistake they had made in molesting those who had done them so much good, became sad and prayed to Viracocha for pardon for their sins, entreating him to let the women come back and give them the accustomed meals. The Creator granted their petition. The women came back and said to the Cañaris—"The Creator has thought it well that we should return to you, lest you should die of hunger." They brought them food.

(30–31)

Y estando aguardando, vieron venir dos mujeres Cañares, y guisáronles la comida y pusiéronsela donde solían. Y queriéndose ir, los hombres les quisieron prender; mas ellas se descabulleron de ellos y se escaparon. Y los Cañares, entendiendo el yerro que habían hecho en alborotar a quien tanto bien les hacía, quedaron tristes, y pidiendo al Viracocha perdón de su yerro, le rogaron que les tornase a enviar aquellas mujeres a darles el mantenimiento que solían. Y el Hacedor se lo concedió, y tornando otra vez las mujeres, dijeron a los Cañares: "El Hacedor ha tenido por bien de que tornemos a vosotros, porque no os muráis de hambre." Y les hacían de comer y servían.

(*Historia índica*, 207)

Thus, the Cañari were saved from lonely despair and potentially queer pairings. No excuse for sodomitical giants here. Through a divine gift the women become the helpmates of the men.

While the Huarochirí myths analyzed in Chapter 3 suggest the pre-Hispanic autonomy of women and women's agency in establishing reciprocal, complementary relationships, here the agent of such pairing becomes "Viracocha," who, in the language of the chronicler, comes close to an omnipotent god of a monotheistic society. Here the Andean norm of diversity of deities and an androgynous primordial divinity, present in Huarochirí and other sources, is reduced to "el Hacedor" (the [male] Creator). Very unlike the sexual mores displayed in Huarochirí, here a Christianized discourse represents the women as pure until divine intervention hands them over to the men. In the version of this Cañari myth recounted by Cristóbal de Molina, the saviors of the men are macaws, not women (31). Sarmiento records a myth that establishes a heteronormative code of sexual conduct with the introduction of gender differentiation and, later, procreation:

> Then there was friendship between the women and the Cañari brothers, and one of the Cañari brothers had connexion with one of the women. Then, as the elder brother was drowned in a lake which was near, the survivor married one of the women, and had the other as a concubine. By them he had ten sons.
>
> (31)

> Y tomando amistad las mujeres con los hermanos Cañares, el uno de ellos hubo ayuntamiento con la una de las mujeres. Y como el mayor se ahogase en una laguna, que allí cerca estaba, el que quedó vivo se casó con la una y a la otra la tuvo por manceba. En las cuales hubo diez hijos.
>
> (*Historia índica,* 208)

This representation of the Cañari women as naturally chaste stands in stark contrast with Cieza's depiction of female lasciviousness, which he wrote to defend the "good Incas" in relation to the non-Inca peoples. These "good Indians," the Cañari, we must remember, were conquered by the Incas.

This vision of non-Inca Andean women served as a clever introduction to Sarmiento's depiction of Inca mythohistory. His narration of the founding of Cuzco emphasizes the role of the feminine half of the mythical founding Inca couple, Manco Capac and Mama Huaco, who "began to settle and take possession of the land and water, against the will of the Huallas . . . and they did many unjust things" (56) [comenzaron a poblar y tomarles las tierras y aguas contra la voluntad de los Guallas . . . y hicieron en ellos muchas crueldades" (*Historia índica,* 218)]. The ambiguous figure I discussed in the last chapter, Mama Huaco, comes to subtly personify deviance and tyranny in Sarmiento's history.

I close my discussion of transculturation in the Toledo period with a consideration of how a queer subject such as Mama Huaco emerges from the writing of coloniality, how an indigenous figure, ambiguous in the indigenous and ladino sources, is left in official history as a monstrous Other. In Sarmiento's version of this myth, Manco Capac takes a less-prominent role in certain actions attributed to his partner/wife, Mama Huaco. It is she, "very strong and agile" [fortísima y diestra] who appropriates the mythical golden *vara* (staff of authority) that in other versions is wielded by Manco Capac, though Sarmiento admits the ambiguity (*Historia índica,* 217). It is she who penetrates the valley of Cuzco's fecund earth with the phallic symbol of power and masculine force (ibid., 217). Sarmiento, furthermore, is one of the only historians to give her lines of dialogue, so we hear her voice violently reprimanding her brother Ayar Cachi, whom she and the rest of the clan tricked so as to get rid of the troublemaking sibling: "When Ayar Cachi refused to return, his sister Mama Huaco, raising her foot, rebuked him with furious words, saying: 'How is it that there should be such cowardice in so strong a youth as you are?'" (49) [Y como Ayar Cache rehusase la vuelta, levantóse en pie su hermana Mama Guaco, y con feroces palabras reprehendiéndole dijo: ¡Cómo tal cobardía ha de parecer en un tan fuerte mozo como tú!" (ibid., 215)].

With these images, Sarmiento presents the notion that the illegal usurpations of the Incas were perpetrated by a *mujer varonil,* a transgressively masculinized woman. Culpability for these actions caused by her greater cruelty is assigned more to the feminine than to the masculine gender in a haunting description of Mama Huaco:

> They relate that Mama Occlo [*sic;* should read "Guaco" in the translation as in the original] was so fierce that, having killed one of the Huallas Indians, she cut him up, took out the inside, carried the heart and lungs in her mouth, and with an *ayuinto,* which is a stone fastened to a rope, in her hand, she attacked the Huallas with diabolical resolution. When the Huallas beheld this horrible and inhuman spectacle, they feared that the same thing would be done to them, being simple and timid, and they fled and abandoned their rights. Mama Occlo [Guaco] reflecting on her cruelty, and fearing that for it they would be branded tyrants, resolved not to spare any Huallas, believing that the affair thus be forgotten. So they killed all they could lay their hands upon, dragging infants from their mother's wombs, that no memory might be left of these miserable Huallas.
>
> (56–57)
>
> Y cuentan que Mama Guaco era tan feroz, que matando un indio Gualla le hizo pedazos y le sacó el asadura y tomó el corazón y bofes en la boca, y con un haybinto—que es una piedra atada en una soga, con que ella peleaba—en las manos

se fue contra los Guallas con diabólica determinación. Y como
los Guallas viesen aquel horrendo e inhumano espectáculo,
temiendo que de ellos hiciesen lo mesmo, huyeron, ca simples
y tímidos eran, y así desampararon su natural. Y Mama Huaco
y Manco Capac, visto la crueldad que habían hecho y temiendo
que por ello fuesen infamados de tiranos, parecióles no dejar
ninguno de los Guallas, creyendo que así se encubriría. Y así
mataron a cuantos pudieron haber a las manos, y a las mujeres preñadas sacaban las criaturas de los vientres, por que no
quedase memoria de aquellos miserables Guallas.

(*Historia índica*, 218)

Mama Huaco is represented in diabolical terms in which the feminine
is transformed into something threatening and destructive. The violence
of this foundational act escalates to such a point that the Incas not only ex-
terminate the autochthonous Guallas, but also kill pregnant women and
eat human organs. Infanticide, cannibalism, and tyranny mark the Incas'
identity. With the narrative focus on Mama Huaco, any notion of gender
complementarity is corrupted; the demonic, inhuman woman could literally eat the submissive Cañari portrayed in Sarmiento's first myth.

The implication is that even the Incas' women were depraved and tyrannical, refusing to maintain the traditional roles of the home. This denatu-
ralizing of Mama Huaco goes to the extreme of denying her fecundity in
the founding of the Inca's matriarchal line: Sarmiento attributes Manco
Capac's firstborn to another sister, Mama Ocllo, and not to Mama Huaco.
We are left with the archetypical western image of the Amazon woman:
Mama Huaco as cannibal and nonreproducing, a transgressor of heteronormative patriarchy.

As a primary character in the foundational myth of the Inca civilization,
Mama Huaco functions metonymically to suggest that feminine barbarity
extended throughout the region and represented a threat to the Christian
values of the conquistadores or the proto-Christian Andeans. The implication is that, if the Incas acted in such a manner to found their imperial
city, destroying "good" Indians such as the Cañari (the narrative sequence
suggests relating all pre-Inca peoples as one benevolent *behetría*), then the
Spanish conquest and colonization of the Andes was completely justifiable.
After all, as Sarmiento proves with his rhetorical representation of the Inca
figure, the Incas broke the laws of nature.

What is perhaps most interesting about this narrative, however, is how vestiges of Andean gender culture become mobilized in Sarmiento's rhetoric. It is in these fragments of pre-Hispanic gender culture that we find the heterogeneity of the colonial discourse and we understand better the transculturation of gender and sexuality. Mama Huaco is an excellent example of this phenomenon, for as we saw in the last chapter, she seems to have been an ambiguously gendered archetype in the Andean mythic tradition. Sarmiento takes the fragments from the oral tradition, including voices from conquered non-Incas, and constructs Mama Huaco to serve his ideological purposes, as well as those of some of his local informants. Those elements of what we may consider Mama Huaco's pre-Hispanic subjectivity—her role as warrior woman, her gender liminality as the keeper of the corn during the sterile season, her symbolic positioning as an *ipa*—became, perhaps with the aid of local informants with their own politics in mind, perfect fodder for Sarmiento's presentation of her. The complexity of her position in Inca mythohistory that we appreciate through reconstructing her from multiple sources is simplified and demonized.

A comparison with two of Sarmiento's contemporaries substantiates my point. Juan de Betanzos offers a version of the same events described by Sarmiento in his *Suma y narración de los Incas* (1551), but without demonizing Mama Huaco. Although the two historians extracted their information about the Incas from similar sources, Betanzos had a more intimate relationship with the Cuzco indigenous culture due to his marriage to a cousin of Inca Atahualpa and to his profound knowledge of Quechua.[53] We note a simpler and more direct style in Betanzos's account; as he himself observed, his narrative lacked "graceful style and smooth eloquence" [estilo gracioso y elocuencia suave] (*Suma y narración*, 8). Betanzos explains and justifies this style in a letter of presentation to Viceroy Mendoza, saying he wished to remain a "faithful translator" of the native Andeans (ibid.). It is also important to note that his locus of enunciation is the indigenous *casa* of his Andean family, not the *cabildo* of colonial government. If Sarmiento represents colonial authority in his relationship with Francisco de Toledo, Betanzos is more aligned with Inca culture due to his matrimony to a *ñusta incaica,* the Inca "princess" Cuxirimay Ocllo, baptized with the name of doña Angelina Yupanqui. Since she was Atahualpa's cousin, Betanzos had access to the Inca ruling class, and therefore to the *quipucamayocs* of the Inca Tawantinsuyu. His domination of Quechua, which he learned before arriving in Peru in the indigenous language schools of Santo Domingo and in his first years in the Peruvian colony, served him well in the writing of his history. In Betanzos, there is an absence of the Toledan rhetoric we observe in Sarmiento:

the wife of the one they call Ayar Cachi (the one who got lost
in the cave) named Mama Huaco, gave an Indian of this coca
people a blow with an *ayllos* [pre-Hispanic Andean weapon]
and killed him and opened him and took out his lungs and
heart and in front of the rest of the people she blew air into
the lungs and having seen this the Indians had great fear and
with the dread they had taken on in that hour, they fled the
valley that they call to this day, Gualla.

la mujer de Ayarcache (el que se perdió en la cueva) llamada
Mamaguaco dio a un indio de los deste pueblo de coca un
golpe con unos ayllos y matólo y abrióle de presto y sacóle los
bofes y el corazón y a vista de los demás del pueblo hinchó los
bofes soplándolos y visto por los indios del pueblo aquel caso
tuvieron gran temor e con el miedo que habían tomado luego
en aquella hora se fueron huyendo al valle que llaman el día de
hoy Gualla.

(Ibid., 20)

What Sarmiento portrays as cannibalism, in Betanzos takes on a more
symbolic or ritual character in which the lungs of the defeated Guallas are
inflated, not eaten, a possible reference to Andean divination practices. The
Guallas flee and are not exterminated; no infanticide is reported. The other
significant difference between the two versions is that in Betanzos's Mama
Huaco is paired with Ayar Cachi, Manco Capac's brother. Betanzos's informants did not associate Mama Huaco's power with the Inca patriarch,
but with the Trickster figure, Ayar Cachi. If we understand Ayar Cachi as
the Andean symbol for disorder, as Urbano has suggested (*Wiracocha y Ayar*,
liv), then from this source we could understand Mama Huaco as the feminine counterpart of this figure and the moral cautionary tale the Trickster figure embodies. In this way, the Andean ideal of complementarity is
maintained and the Andean ideal of balance is emphasized. We recall that
her pre-Hispanic archetype was ambiguously gender liminal, because she
represented sterility in the agricultural calendar, that is, the unproductive
time of the year. In Betanzos, it seems her warrior-woman persona is remembered, but is tempered by her divination practice and complementary
position to the Ayar Cachi.

The celebrated mestizo writer Inca Garcilaso de la Vega, whom I will
discuss more thoroughly in Chapter 5, conflates two Andean female figures who are commonly represented as sisters, Mama Huaco and Mama

Ocllo, naming Manco Capac's partner, Mama Ocllo Huaco. In his effort to
harmonize the two cultures of his heritage and recover the Incas' honor
expunged by Toledo and Sarmiento's anti-Inca discourse, Inca Garcilaso
depicts Mama Ocllo Huaco as a symbol of feminine domestic order: she
establishes Hurin Cuzco (the lower *ayllu* division of the imperial city) and
teaches women how to weave (*Comentarios reales,* bk. 2 chap. 2, 59). He goes
as far as to say that the foundational couple taught the locals "natural law"
and other morals given to the Incas by the Sun god, intimating a monotheistic tradition (ibid.). The foundational family, a "king" and a "queen,"
seems to be based on Inca Garcilaso's knowledge of European dynastic
monarchies, more appealing to his European audience than the foreign
Andean traditions. The only mention of the multiple siblings discussed in
earlier colonial and indigenous sources is presented as a "fable" and dis-
missed in favor of the official "history" Inca Garcilaso offers in his apologia
of the Incas (ibid., bk. 1, chap. 18).

Even in the fable, the names for the female counterparts of the four
Ayar brothers are left out, except for Manco Capac's partner, Mama Ocllo
Huaco. There is no mention of Mama Ocllo Huaco's participation in the
military expansion of the Inca state, perhaps a denial of her public, military role, which would have been too transgressive of Renaissance, European gender ideology. Rather than be demonized, as in Sarmiento's version, Mama Ocllo Huaco is presented as an honorable woman. I will return
to Inca Garcilaso's depiction of gender and sexuality in Chapter 5, for as
we shall see, this domestication of the Mama Huaco archetype is but a first
glimpse at the transculturation of gender culture in Garcilaso's *Comentarios
reales.*

For the Andean informants who repeated their oral narratives to the
Spaniards, Mama Huaco may have been an archetype of female military,
religious, or political power, represented by signs of gender liminality to
account for the inherent gender duality of Andean cosmology. In the writings of the Spanish, she became an ambiguous figure, an identity that was
portrayed in the colonial discourse according to the rhetorical needs of
the informant and the writer. For Sarmiento, Mama Huaco served as the
personification of a barbarous and inhumane people in need of civilization and evangelization. The Amazon-like figure transgressed normative
gender categories of the Spanish mind-set and violated the natural laws of
Western tradition.

Mama Huaco, figured prominently as a transgressive, masculinized
woman, became a sign of the abject in Toledo's official chronicle, just as
third-gender subjectivities had become regulated, abject figures in late

sixteenth-century colonial society, from the pulpits to the confessionals, from the bonfires of civil authorities to the rhetorical fires of hell. In addition to justifying the Spanish colonization of the Andes, this characterization of the feminine and the in between clouded future generations' vision of pre-Hispanic Andean gender and sexuality. Perhaps a more direct representation of gender diversity and sexuality would have been too threatening to the Counter-Reformation culture of the post-Tridentine era. As third-gender ritualists went underground and as their transgendered performances were transformed into more subtle representations of liminality and invocations of androgyny, the image of indigenous sodomite became inscribed into the Andean historiographic and literary tradition in the form of Inca "scapegoat" in the monumental foundational text, the *Comentarios reales,* the subject of my next chapter.

Five   SUBALTERN HYBRIDITY?

Inca Garcilaso and the Transculturation
of Gender and Sexuality in the
Comentarios Reales

How many must there be in the world who flee from others
because they do not see themselves.
                                        —*Lazarillo de Tormes*

In this chapter I consider yet another historian writing from
the *chaupi* between two cultures, the Inca Garcilaso de la Vega.[1] I am interested in exploring the "darker side" of his "subaltern" identity and the
complexities of cultural hybridization in his seminal "mestizo" text, *Co-*
mentarios reales de los Incas (1609), while weighing the limitations of recent
theoretical characterizations of one of Latin America's founding fathers of
counterhegemonic colonial writing.[2] The queer neocultures produced
from his *chaupi* are not unique to the hegemonic early-modern gender
and sexual ideology, but are strange to and transgressive of pre-Hispanic
Andean gender culture. We must cross the Atlantic yet again to understand what I consider to be one of the most transculturating of the colonial Andean texts and its representation of the Andean third gender. In
this chapter, we shall appreciate the full implications of transculturation, of
what Moreiras calls the "war machine" and its ideological filtering of cultural practices that produce queer products ("José María Arguedas"). The
tropes of sexuality that originated in Iberia, traveled to the Andes, and misrepresented the unintelligible aspects of Andean gender culture now return to their point of origin in this foundational history of the Incas and
of the Spanish Conquest, written by a mestizo, a culturally queer writing
subject in the hostile years of imperial Spain.[3] As we shall see, the Andean
sexual Other is not only misrepresented, but also completely sacrificed in
Inca Garcilaso's effort to mediate between his two cultures.

In thinking through the myriad possibilities of subject construction in
the mid-to-late sixteenth century, it is provocative to ask what happens
when one "hybrid" subject meets another in rhetorical exchanges between

colonial literatures. Does one recognize himself in the other? This question is not the invention of twenty-first-century scholars, but was also an issue for the early-modern intellectuals on both sides of the Atlantic. The Renaissance Spanish picaresque hero Lazarillo de Tormes melancholically expressed this moral dilemma, reproduced as the epigraph to this chapter, in reference to his half-brother's rejection of his black father, who fled in fear from his own father's racial identity, which he perceived as anathema. In the context of the *pureza de sangre* (blood purity) social dynamics of imperial Spain, the issue of race and ethnicity was at the heart of subject construction.

Inca Garcilaso was aware of the implications of race, as evidenced by his explicit self-positioning in all of his writings. His self-conscious shaping of a discursive identity appears throughout the *Comentarios reales,* first in the "Preface to the Reader," when he declares that his authority to "comment" on other histories and chronicles lies in his being "a native from the city of Cuzco" (4) [natural de la ciudad del Cuzco (5)]. In his "Notes on the General Language of the Indians of Peru" Inca Garcilaso identifies as an Indian —"since I am an Indian" (5) [pues soy indio (7)]—and therefore as expert in the linguistic interpretation that becomes one of his most distinguishing attributes as a revisionist historian. Finally, when discussing the "new generations" of racial combinations in colonial Peru, Inca Garcilaso assumes the name given to him and others of mixed Indian and Spanish blood:

> The children of Spaniards by Indians are called *mestizos,* meaning we are a mixture of the two races. The word was applied by the first Spaniards who had children by Indian women, and because it was used by our fathers, as well as on account of its meaning, I call myself by it in public and am proud of it, though in the Indies, if a person is told, "You are a *mestizo,*" or "He's a *mestizo,*" it is taken as an insult.

(607)

> A los hijos de español y de india o de indio y española, nos llaman mestizos, por decir que somos mezclados de ambas naciones; fue impuesto por nuestros padres y por su significación me lo llamo yo de boca llena, y me honro con él. Aunque en Indias, si a uno de ellos le dicen "sois un mestizo" o "es un mestizo," lo toman por menosprecio.

(Bk. 9, chap. 31, 266)

232 *Decolonizing the Sodomite*

Here, Inca Garcilaso recognizes the queer, precarious position of mestizos in the colonies, but nevertheless assumes the status with pride and sets forth to give voice to his Andean cultural heritage and history.

Nonetheless, race, which is often privileged when characterizing Inca Garcilaso's mestizo subjectivity, is not the only identity marker we should consider when discussing subaltern status in the early-modern period. As I shall argue in this chapter, gender and sexuality must be taken into account in our analysis of Inca Garcilaso's process of subjectivization, given that sexual Otherness was yet another determinant in the construction of early-modern subjectivity. In the case of Inca Garcilaso, gender and sexual anxieties ran parallel to racial preoccupations and informed how and why he disregarded the third-gender Andean subject commonly represented as the "sodomite"—that monstrous figure of early-modern culture referred to as the *efeminado* in Covarrubias's moralist emblem (considered in Chapter 1). While impurity of blood was a pretext for discrimination in early-modern Spain, ambiguous sexuality caused horror and repulsion and was, as we have seen, a target for the moralizing discourse of both religious and civil discourses and led to severe punishment, if not execution. Inca Garcilaso fashions his discursive identity in the *Comentarios reales* in part by sacrificing the native third-gender subjects that threatened the status of the Andean culture in the expanding Spanish empire, thereby continuing a process of transculturation begun with the first European observers of Andean cultural practices. Inca Garcilaso writes against what other scholars have observed to be a rhetorical feminization of the colonized Amerindian body and the invaded American topography.[4] His strategy to vindicate his mother's culture in the eyes of the Europeans, however, at times acculturates those Andean social constructs that were unintelligible to outsiders but ritually vital to insiders, as I note in his representation of Mama Huaco (see Chapter 4).

Inca Garcilaso's rhetorical use of the "sodomites" reflects classic paradigms of what René Girard has called "texts of persecution" (*Girard Reader*, 105), that is, texts that express collective violence against a people's enemies in terms that can become acceptable as foundational history. In this process of mythmaking, Inca Garcilaso returns to the queer tropes of sexuality of early colonial discourse to mobilize the ambiguity of sexual difference in order to frame his retelling of key Inca conquests. As Girard has shown, mythical texts—and one can argue that *Comentarios reales* takes on certain mythical attributes, especially as the foundational history of Tawantinsuyu and colonial Peru—do not explicitly represent acts of sacrificing scapegoats. The acts of violence perpetrated against them are inscribed in a complex corpus of texts and intertexts related to gods, heroes, foundations of social order, and the like (ibid., 97). Nonnormative sexuality, from the Western perspective, becomes a sacrificial victim in Inca Garcilaso's text, not completely erased but left in the foundational history of Peru as a reminder of the Incas' level of civilization compared with that of the barbarous pre-Incas and Inca enemies.

How, then, can we characterize the writer's subjectivity in light of his marginalizing rhetoric? Recent commentary has sought to claim Inca Garcilaso as a subaltern, as a resistant voice that speaks for the subordinate classes of the colonial period. This characterization ignores his erasure of other subalterns and subaltern *conocimiento,* in this case, "insider" knowledge of Andean gender culture. While not anachronistically linking Andean third-gender subjects to modern or postmodern sexual identities, I would like to problematize the treatment of gender and sexuality in colonial discourse within the context of subaltern studies and in the theorization of colonial subjectivity in processes of transculturation. In the words of the "Founding Statement" of the Latin American Subaltern Studies Group, I raise "questions of who represents whom" ("Latin American Subaltern Studies Group Founding Statement," 5), specifically complicating Inca Garcilaso's subjectivization in relation to third gender. In short, I wish to hybridize the "hybrid," to interrogate the critics' tendency to idealize hybrid subaltern identity, and to queer from the margins this idealized hybrid that risks becoming a new center in colonial studies. To *queer,* in this sense, is to reread the canonical text from a position that privileges the complexity of Andean sexual culture; it is to break with an assumed heteronormative paradigm found in some Latin American theorizations of culture, as I discuss in the Introduction.

THEORIZING THE "HYBRID" SUBALTERN

Antonio Gramsci describes the subaltern classes as "not unified and . . . [unable to] unite until they are able to become a 'State': their history, therefore, is intertwined with that of civil society, and thereby with the history of States and groups of States" (*Selections,* 52). This initial theorizing by Gramsci became one of the guiding precepts of the 1990's in the work of the Southeast Asian Subaltern Studies Group, led by Ranajit Guha.[5] Because "subalterns" do not form a unitary political position vis-à-vis the state, their voices commingle with those of the hegemonic discourses of civil society. The "Founding Statement" of the Latin American

Subaltern Studies Group traces the history of Latin American "organic" and traditional intellectuals' preoccupation with the representation of subaltern classes back to the 1960's. This manifesto echoes Guha's location of subalterns in traditionally elitist historiography and institutions: "The insight of Guha was that the subaltern, by definition not registered or registrable as a historical subject capable of hegemonic action (seen, that is, through the prism of colonial administrators or 'educated' native leaders), is nevertheless present in unexpected structural dichotomies, fissures in the forms of hierarchy and hegemony, and, in turn, in the constitution of the heroes of the national drama, writing, literature, education, institutions, and the administration of law and authority" ("Latin American Subaltern Studies Group Founding Statement," 2). Therefore, the issue should not be, "Can the Subaltern Speak?"[6] but, in the colonial or any historical context, how to decipher his or her voice from the multiple utterances that form hegemonic discourse. As Spivak warns, this recovery should avoid essentializing the subjectivity of the subaltern, an admonishment that I bear in mind by discussing "third gender" in performative terms. Phyllis Peres has observed: "Subaltern discourse necessarily incorporates the rhythms and strands of hegemonically approved discourse with the counter rhythms of uniquely subaltern experience" ("Subaltern Spaces," 3). In Inca Garcilaso's case, the challenge will be to distinguish the complex "rhythms" of his canonical text.

As José Antonio Mazzotti has commented, the tendency of traditional Hispanists to claim Inca Garcilaso as an acculturated Renaissance writer is being challenged (*Coros mestizos*, 28–29). In Inca Garcilaso's writings we see both the adoption of colonial discourse and the resistance of the colonized subject to that discourse. From his father's Spanish culture Inca Garcilaso acquired part of his discursive subjectivity by adopting Renaissance rhetoric in writing his corrective history. Margarita Zamora has written extensively on the role of language and rhetoric in the *Comentarios reales*, characterizing the text as a humanist approach to the interpretation, rather than the representation, of Inca civilization (*Language, Authority*, 4). In her insightful essay exploring the relationship between Inca Garcilaso's 1590 translation of León Hebreo's *Dialoghi di amore* (1535) and his discursive strategies in the *Comentarios reales*, Doris Sommer characterizes Inca Garcilaso's position in Spain at the time of his writing as an "internal exile" (*Proceed with Caution*, 62) and highlights the specific stylistics the writer adopted from his experience translating León Hebreo. Inca Garcilaso's philological methodology is in the tradition of European humanists like Erasmus and Lorenzo Valla and is exemplified by his frequent exegesis of Quechua words in order to correct their usage in other Spanish historians' chronicles. Zamora views his writing style as the key to the text's communicability with its intended reader: the royal court of Spain (*Language, Authority*). Sommer calls this technique of self-authorization "supplementing" (*Proceed with Caution*, 73–81), which Inca Garcilaso employed along with the strategies of "unsaying" (ibid., 82) and "inciting expert talk" (ibid., 82–83). His readers were intrigued by these rhetorical devices, perhaps for their "dizzying effects" (ibid., 83), as Sommer argues, or possibly because they were familiar enough and therefore acceptable, as Zamora and Roberto González Echeverría contend.[7] Ultimately, for whatever intangible reasons, Inca Garcilaso's strategies sustained his authority for the rereading of early colonial history from the point of view of a mestizo, an ethnic and cultural hybrid.

Inca Garcilaso's corrective history of the Incas is considered by some to be one of the first anticolonialist texts, conceived and written to articulate a discourse counter to the Spanish historicization of his native land and other parts of the Americas.[8] The originality of his work lies in its challenge to the colonial project by appropriating the colonizer's discourse and the reinterpretation of colonial history. As Sara Castro-Klaren has observed, Inca Garcilaso engaged this discourse "from a subaltern and self-endangering position, [and] managed to produce a critique of European modes of representation when this colonial discourse was in full power/knowledge ascendancy" ("Writing Subalternity," 237). He responds specifically to the Toledan chroniclers of the late sixteenth century, who demonized the Incas to justify the consolidation of Spanish colonial power, and he is classified by Porras Barrenechea's still-useful history of the chroniclers as an "Inca sympathizer" (*Cronistas del Perú*, 19).

Although it took some time, the *Comentarios reales* became a certifiably "subversive" text in the eyes of the Crown late in the eighteenth century. Readings of the text reportedly inspired participants in the uprising of Tupac Amaru, which led to the censure and prohibition of the *Comentarios reales*.[9] From these critical perspectives one can consider Inca Garcilaso a subaltern, relative to Spanish colonialists, to Spanish society, and to the authoritative histories and chronicles of the time.

Nonetheless, what complicates the study of his writings, particularly the text I have chosen to consider, and any characterization of his subjectivity is the locus of enunciation that he constructed for himself in order to assure that his voice was heard in that "internal exile." Inca Garcilaso's rhetoric ultimately positions him in a liminal space between the colonizer and the colonized, in the *chaupi*. This problematic subject position goes beyond the mere identity crisis of a first-generation mestizo whose parents were an Inca mother from the Orejones (Inca elite) lineage and a Spanish hidalgo father. The complication arose when he aspired to write the corrective version of the Spanish occupation of Tawantinsuyu. Considered a bastard, denied an inheritance, and living in a Spain skeptical of if not hostile to Indians, Inca Garcilaso had to adopt the European discursive practices discussed above in order to access a position of legitimacy. Terms such as "bastard," "exile," "Indian," "mestizo," or "Inca," however, do not adequately inform an interpretation of Inca Garcilaso's writing. The reader cannot assume that such identity terms reflect certain ideologies or special knowledge. Inca Garcilaso's subjectivity is less one of these essentialist categories and more the product of a process of identification related to colonial power relations that made being a "mestizo" or an "Inca" significant vis-à-vis colonial discourse.[10]

Understanding Inca Garcilaso's locus of enunciation as it is expressed in the *Comentarios reales* suggests that we foreground its "hybrid" nature. Homi Bhabha has defined a liminal form of cultural identification as "the moment of culture caught in an aporetic, contingent position, in-between a plurality of practices that are different and yet must share the same space of adjudication and articulation" (*Location of Culture*, 57). Bhabha's definition pertains to the colonial condition of the Andes where Inca Garcilaso spent his adolescence and began his process of self-identification. He inhabited a space of multiple cultural influences in which his native language was Quechua and reading the *quipus*, indigenous mnemonic devices, was learned before or while learning to read books. Yet, he was also schooled in the Spanish classics and served as scribe to his father during military campaigns of colonial conquest.[11]

Bhabha directs us away from representation of the referent, which would imply a cultural binarism (subject/object; inside/outside), toward a process of enunciation that "attempts repeatedly to 'reinscribe' and relocate that claim to cultural and anthropological priority (High/Low; Ours/Theirs) in the act of revising and hybridizing the settled, sententious hierarchies, the locale and the locutions of the cultural" (ibid.). This process can be conceived as dialogic in that it "attempts to track the processes of displacement and realignment that are already at work, constructing something different and hybrid from the encounter: a third space that does not simply revise or invert the dualities, but revalues the ideological bases of division and difference" (ibid., 58). Inca Garcilaso speaks from this "third space," what I have called the "*chaupi,*" as a mestizo engaged in anticolonial discourse, a voice that "revalues" the history of his native lands from the margin and therefore "revalues" the colonial project.

Inca Garcilaso's *mestizaje* may be the ultimate representation of the colonial legacy in the construction of this third space. But the biological beginnings of the mestizo are further transformed through the process of identification discussed throughout this book: transculturation, an often-violent process during which the colonized resisted and adapted to the imposition of European cultural expansion. Part of this transculturation is Inca Garcilaso's own contribution to our knowledge of the pre-Columbian Andean culture, to his correcting of the colonial historiography that had materially and discursively conquered his mother's culture. Understanding Inca Garcilaso's hybridity and the liminal position of his text requires the reader to think of Bhabha's concept of hybridity in performative terms, where the writing subject at times invokes his Andean heritage while at others he silences and distorts those aspects of his Andean culture that do not harmonize with European hegemonic discourse. As we will see below, at times Inca Garcilaso "performs" an Inca identity in his historical fiction that presupposes a unitary notion of Andean culture, a simplification of the multiethnic and multicultural pre-Hispanic Andes in order to vindicate his maternal culture. Bhabha's privileging of difference over absolute identity is appropriate for characterizing Inca Garcilaso as a writing subject who negotiates the highs and lows of both his American and his European heritage that inform his corrective commentaries. From an Andean perspective, I would characterize his text as a product of a symbolic *tinkuy* in which European gender ideology wins the rhetorical battle.

The question becomes whose version of history is he correcting? Which aspects does he "supplement" and "unsay" and which does he erase completely? And, perhaps more important for colonial studies, does Bhabha's alternative way of characterizing the colonial subject's identity—hybridity—take into account the influence of Inca Garcilaso's liminal position on other Andean subjectivities? In short, what happens when Bhabha's hybrid and Spivak's subaltern come face to face with not just an ethnically marked Other, but one complicated by gender ambiguities as well? In addition to (or in spite of) his anticolonial message, Inca Garcilaso's "commentaries" continue the transculturation of indigenous gender and sexuality begun in earlier colonial texts. By idealizing the Orejones, Inca Garcilaso homogenizes the Andean region, ignoring or demonizing the Andean non-Inca cultures while setting up a false hope for a return to a utopian state with the restitution of the Inca bloodline.[12]

What some critics appreciate as discursive maneuvers that gave voice to the Amerindian, I question with regard to the text's long-term effect on our conceptualization of pre-Columbian and early colonial Andean realities. Inca Garcilaso's interpretation of the Inca state as a forerunner of the Christian civilization that acted to unite the New and Old worlds distorts Andean cosmology and is part of the colonial legacy present in the text. Zamora (*Language, Authority*) characterizes this tendency as part of the Renaissance ideal of *concordia* and views Inca Garcilaso's construction of Tawantinsuyu as a "*praeparatio evangelico,*" as a corrective response to the contemporary debate in Spain on the Amerindian's essential humanity. But what did that process of identification, which attempted to link the Andean to the European, do to indigenous concepts of Andean reality? Inca Garcilaso's utopian search for the "noble Inca" vis-à-vis a more savage ancestor or contemporary subaltern did indeed give critical space to a certain class of Amerindian, no matter how misrepresented the Amerindian cosmology. But the question remains whether we hear the other subalterns in Inca Garcilaso's writings and how that subaltern voice is represented. In his weaving of a new historical tapestry of Inca civilization, what effect did his *chaupi,* charged with the harmonizing of the two worlds mentioned above, have in the colonial project of discrediting indigenous religious belief? Does he not exclude the possibility of considering Andean religious thought as legitimate and independent of a European cosmology?

These same questions apply to Inca Garcilaso's construction of an elitist position within his Andean culture. Mazzotti's study of what he calls the "Andean sub-text" in the *Comentarios reales* explores "the transformations of the Cuzco imaginary and the use of certain discursive strategies that allow assigning authority to the work from the perspective of an Andean and mestizo reading" (*Coros mestizos,* 30). Understanding Inca Garcilaso's privileging of Cuzco-centered Inca culture is also crucial for my explication of the transculturation of gender and sexuality in his text. Mazzotti insightfully examines Andean as well as European sources and influences in the *Comentarios reales* and coins a new term for the mestizo's polyphonic narrative: "choral writing" (ibid., 33). This approach allows for a reconsideration of colonial subjectivities: "Such a subjectivity, as we will see, manifests itself in the text through characteristics of *chorality* that imply much more complex functions and polarizations than are commonly accepted under the rubric of the 'harmonizing' mestizo so often simplistically applied to

Garcilaso." Mazzotti's willingness to break the harmonious myth of *mestizaje* in Inca Garcilaso opens the text to readings of how his hybrid subjectivity cuts both ways in its transculturating effects, to how his fashioning of a *chaupi* sacrificed the inclusion of Andean diversity.

As I have argued throughout this study, the agency of Andean colonial informants was instrumental in the foundational narratives shared with Spanish chroniclers, narratives that included myths as the basis of official history.[13] It is in this context that we can better appreciate the *Comentarios reales* as a reflection of the construction of Inca Garcilaso's subjectivity. By examining the sources used in the work, we can perceive similar patterns of kinship-based historical antecedents used as foundations for the authority of writing a corrective history, thus giving a voice counter to colonial expansion but, at the same time, excluding the representation of the non-Inca Andeans. An example of this, contributing to the elaboration of his hybrid identity, is one of Inca Garcilaso's principal informants, his maternal "uncle," whom, through ingenious rhetorical strategies, is presented as part of the noble Inca class.[14] The "uncle" not only establishes Inca Garcilaso's royal heritage by legitimizing his maternal lineage, but also serves as an authoritative source and a critical voice, what Sommer calls "expert talk" (*Proceed with Caution,* 82–83). A subtle example of this is found in chapter 15 of book 1, when the "uncle" relates his version of the Andean creation myth. After mentioning that it was considered blasphemy for a non-Inca to utter the words "Our father the sun" [Nuestro padre el sol], Inca Garcilaso's "uncle" pronounces the sacred words, confirming his own locus of enunciation as an Inca, and, by extension, that of his nephew, Inca Garcilaso. Thus, the authority to speak on behalf of the Incas is established, in much the same way Inca Garcilaso appropriates European discourse to acquire an authoritative voice in Spain. To further substantiate his "uncle's" stories, Inca Garcilaso informs us in chapter 19 of book 1 that he also solicited information from his Inca classmates, who, in turn, consulted their family *quipus,* the records of official history and genealogy. If these are Inca Garcilaso's sources, then we must ask, Where is the voice of the Andean non-Inca? Where are the alternative voices that were marginal to the Inca establishment? Instead of assuming a priori that all Andean subjects conform to notions of early-modern normative gender and sexual culture, it is imperative to ask how the authoritative Inca-centered discourse of the *Comentarios reales* marginalizes the sexual subalterns of Andean culture, which Inca Garcilaso deemed unintelligible to his audience and therefore dangerous to his project.

"MACHOFICATION" OF THE INCAS

Inca Garcilaso wrote in a time and place (Spain) when the feminine, as we saw in Chapter 1, was considered inferior, almost less human than the masculine, when the place of women and effeminate men in early-modern European society was marginal to that of "masculine" men. The reader will recall Covarrubias's *emblema moral* of the *efeminado*. Those who broke and crossed the gender binary were considered monstrous and even dangerous. Indeed, these attitudes are reflected in colonial discourse, as has been observed by Hulme, Montrose, and Félix Bolaños, in which the Amerindians were gendered "feminine" in their representation as defeated peoples. The "sodomy trope," as we have seen, was part of this discursive gendering, a rhetoric that also transculturated indigenous notions of the feminine and third-gender subjectivities. So it may not be surprising to observe in Inca Garcilaso's counterdiscourse, efforts to assert the Incas' masculinity, for, as we have seen, his mission was to vindicate the Andean culture, a culture which had been emasculated by conquest and by colonial histories that recounted the conquest. While Inca Garcilaso, as Sommer argues, might have learned to position himself discursively as a feminine interlocutor when he needed to tactically seduce the authoritative informant into talking or the equally powerful reader into appreciating his discursive authority, when it comes to positioning himself in relation to non-Inca subjectivities, Inca Garcilaso projects a decidedly masculine identity for his people.[15]

In this light, Inca Garcilaso's following comments, found in a chapter on the ritualized ceremonies of *huaracu* in which male youths were readied for military service, training that included the use of arms and the ability to fabricate shoes, might seem a bit earnest. Inca Garcilaso reacts to another historian who simply reported that the Inca men spun thread for making clothing, "though he does not say how or why" (369) [sin decir cómo ni para qué" (bk. 6, chap. 25, 57)]. Inca Garcilaso "supplements" these reports with clarifications so as to conform to Spanish gender ideology and notions of masculinity. The spinning of thread by these young men in the process of becoming warriors was for the purpose of making special shoes to be used in combat (bk. 6, chap. 25, 57). Simply reporting that the Incas spun thread was "to the prejudice of the Indians" (369) [perjuicio de los indios (bk. 6, chap. 25, 57)]. Aware of the Spanish prejudice against "effeminate" behavior among men, Inca Garcilaso insists that

generally speaking there were no more manly people, or
prouder of it, among all the pagans than the Incas, nor any
who so scorned feminine pursuits. All of them were high-
minded and they set their thoughts on the greatest matters
they knew: they boasted of being children of the Sun, and this
boast urged them to heroic thoughts.

(369)

por lo cual sea regla general que en toda la gentilidad no ha
habido gente más varonil, que tanto se haya preciado de cosas
de hombres, como los Incas, ni que tanto se aborreciesen
las cosas mujeriles; porque, cierto, todos ellos generalmente
fueron magnánimos y aspiraron a las cosas más altas de las que
manejaron; porque se preciaban de hijos del Sol, y este blasón
levantaba a ser heroicos.

(Bk. 6, chap. 25, 58)

Besides the fact that this attribution of positive qualities to the Incas
and the Sun god leaves aside the important roles women and feminine-
identified gods played in Andean culture and cosmology, Inca Garcilaso
simplifies a much more complex system of gender construction by inscribing a dimorphic opposition that pitted women against men, the feminine
against the masculine, that ignored the important, complementary roles
that women, the feminine, and the third gender played in the Andes.

In the continuation of this narrative, Inca Garcilaso further inscribes the
binary along European notions of gender divisions through his exegesis of
Quechua words, his strategy for claiming authority in writing these corrective commentaries. He explains to his readers the difference between
two Quechua verbs for the fabrication of wool that was used to make
shoes:

This style of twisting wool is called *milluy*. . . . As the work
was performed by men, the verb was not used of spinning by
women, or it would have been suggested that they were men.
Spinning by women was called *buhca*, . . . As this work was
proper for women, the verb *buhca* was never applied to men or
it would have implied they were women.

(369)

> Llaman a esta manera de torcer lana "milluy" . . . y porque
> este oficio era de hombres no usaban de este verbo las mujeres
> en su lenguaje, porque era hacerse hombres. Al hilar de las
> mujeres dicen "buhca" . . . y porque este oficio era propio de
> las mujeres, no usaban del verbo "buhca" los hombres, porque
> era hacerse mujeres.
>
> (Bk. 6, chap. 25, 58)

What is left unsaid in this explanation of the gendered nature of the Que-chua language is what it might mean for a woman to "hacerse hombre" or a man to "hacerse mujer." How do we read this interesting remark, which alludes to potential "gender trouble"? The expressions "hacerse mujeres/hacerse hombres" could be understood in various ways: "to become women/to become men," as in the myths in which men and women trans-formed into opposite genders; to pretend to be one or the other, as in cross-dressing rituals; or in the pejorative sense that they were "acting like" the opposite gender. The notion that uttering a certain verb or performing a particular task could change the perception of one's gender points to the performative nature of gender construction. As Judith Butler has argued, it is through the iteration of phantasms or nonreal images of some "original" gender construct that gender is "performed."[16] Here, in Inca Garcilaso, we see that, even in his masculinist, European counterdiscourse, the Andean construction of gender reflects that it was through the performance of cer-tain tasks and the use of certain language that one's gender was defined. Lost to the reader of the *Comentarios reales,* though, is whether this trans-gendering power of words was actually exercised in daily practice. In other words, the fact that men did occasionally cross the bipolar line drawn by Inca Garcilaso's narrative is not mentioned in his text.

Recalling the mention of gendered language in the reconstructed char-acterization of the third-gender subject, and how some were reported to "talk like a woman" and perform women's work roles, this passage takes on new meaning. Perhaps "*buhca*" was one of the words used by third-gender subjects that marked their subjectivity in the daily life of the Andes or in liminal ritual moments. Less speculative is my assertion that Inca Garcilaso realized that the knowledge of Inca men's performing "womanly activi-ties" placed the conquered Andean people in a precarious position. Recall the comments Cieza de León made in reference to the Cañari women and Ruiz de Arce's reaction to women rulers on the northern coast. Inca Garci-laso was careful, therefore, to gloss the words in a way that insinuates that the transgendering theoretically possible in the Quechua language's distinction between men and women yarn spinners did not occur. His commentary denies that men used the word "*buhca*," though we know from other sources that there were men who used "women's words" purposefully in order to perform third-gender subjectivity.

To his "supplementing," we should add another rhetorical strategy: silencing. While it would be tempting to read the silence here as protective of sacred practices in Andean culture, as I discussed in Chapter 4, this suppression of third gender recurs in other passages of his corrective history with a more violent tone; in fact, as we will see below, third gender is effaced completely, and in its place we find only references to "sodomites," a truncated version of the third-gender subaltern subjectivity other chroniclers and historians recognized to have existed in the Andes.

DISCIPLINING QUEER INDIANS, SACRIFICING *IPAS*

The suppression of third gender is figured in the narrative as part of a pattern of differentiation in which the Cuzco's Inca elite is contrasted to the barbarous Andean Others. Inca Garcilaso learned this rhetorical strategy well from his Spanish masters, for Inca conquest politics was quite different from the Spanish, as Inca Garcilaso himself suggests in his long discussions of the Inca expansion of Tawantinsuyu. There are two aspects repeated throughout the *Comentarios reales* that help us understand why Inca Garcilaso's "Othering" of the third-gender subjects conforms more to Western notions of colonizing practices than to indigenous Andean norms of political expansion. First, in the many accounts of Inca "*reducciones*," or colonizing of non-Inca Andean peoples, Inca Garcilaso emphasizes that paramount to Tawantinsuyu's unity was the peaceful incorporation of the newly conquered peoples. The most extensive discussion of these customs is quoted from his primary source, Blas Valera. In his chapter on how the Incas "conquered and civilized new vassals," Blas Valera describes how the adversary's "idols" were taken to Cuzco and kept safe in a temple until the vanquished learned to worship the Sun and rejected their "false gods" of their own will (bk. 5, chap. 12, 236). The conquered leaders were also treated with dignity:

> They also carried off the leading chief and all his children
> to Cuzco, where they were treated with kindness and favor

so that by frequenting the court they would learn not only its laws, customs, and correct speech, but also the rites, cere- monies, and superstitions of the Incas. This done, the *curaca* was restored to his former dignity and authority, and the Inca, as king, ordered the vassals to serve and obey him as their natural lord. And so the victorious and vanquished warriors should be reconciled and live together in permanent peace and concord, and that any hatred and rancor that had been generated in the course of the war should be buried and forgotten, they ordered great banquets to be held with an abundant supply of good things.

(265)

También llevaban al Cuzco al cacique principal y a todos sus hijos, para los acariciar y regalar, y para que ellos, frecuentando la corte, aprendiesen, no solamente las leyes y costumbres y la propiedad de la lengua, más también sus ritos, ceremonias, y supersticiones; lo cual hecho restituía al curaca en su antigua dignidad y señorío y, como rey, mandaba a los vasallos le sirviesen y obediesen como a señor natural. Y para que los soldados vencedores y vencidos se reconciliasen y tuviesen perpetua paz y amistad y se perdiese y olvidase cualquiera enojo o rencor que durante la guerra hubiese nacido, mandaba que entre ellos celebrasen grandes banquetes, abundantes de todo regalo.

(Bk. 5, chap. 12, 236)

With this report of Inca hospitality and the reportedly low tributes de- manded of the conquered, Blas Valera may have been countering the To- ledan chroniclers' insistence that the Incas were barbarous usurpers of other Andeans' sovereignty, though a few lines later he claims the Toledo reports support his assessment of the Incas as magnanimous civilizers.[17] Inca Garci- laso would have had similar motives for including the passage that so posi- tively represents the Incas as benign domesticators of the non-Incas.

But, in spite of the rhetoric, there remains an Andean perspective that is instructive for our purposes. Craig Morris's research is uncovering ar- cheological evidence that disputes the chroniclers' interpretations of Inca warfare.[18] He has found virtually no physical evidence of war materials in the archeological compounds where one would expect to find garrisons and evidence of armament stockpiles, and he reminds us that no Spanish source observed an actual battle between Andeans. He concludes that reciprocal relations were established based on interregional economic interdependence, offering evidence that suggests that such large-scale regional integrations between the Incas and the Chinchas of the desert coast were peaceful (Morris, "Inka Strategies," 297). The ideology Incas imposed was expressed through ritual and monumental architecture, and reciprocal exchange. The *tinkuy* ritual battles that served to establish the new, postintegration hierarchies, and that continue to be represented in the Andes today, could be the remnants of pre-Columbian rituals of interethnic negotiations (Platt, *Espejos y maíz,* 17–18). As we have seen throughout this study, the Andean ideal of complementarity would require a postvictory reconciliation in which imbalances, even gendered expressions of dominance, were brought back into harmony. At times, Inca Garcilaso communicates these values to his European reader, perhaps as a parallel to Renaissance notions of decorum and harmony, though Blas Valera's narrative borders on the hyperbolic in its insistence that the Incas were more benevolent than any ancient king of the Old World (bk. 5, chap. 12, 238).

The second aspect of Conquest politics that Inca Garcilaso repeats throughout his *Comentarios reales* is the imparting of Inca garments to the vanquished peoples. For example, the Inca Capac Yupanqui colonized much of the area in Collasuyu using this strategy: "He ordered them to be presented with many garments, his own for the chiefs and others of less distinction for their families. He granted them other honors of great value and esteem, and the *curacas* were well content" (166–167) [Mandóles dar mucha ropa de vestir, de la Inca para los caciques, y de la otra no tan subida, para sus parientes; hízoles otras mercedes de mucho favor y estima, con que los caciques quedaron muy contentos (bk. 3, chap. 14, 150)]. And again, after the arduous conquest of the Chinchas, to make amends, Inca Capac Yupanqui "and they also received the highly esteemed garments and jewels from the Incas, at which they were all well satisfied" (354) [les dio de vestir y preseas de las muy estimadas del Inca, con que todos quedaron muy contentos (bk. 6, chap. 19,45)]. Exceptions to this practice were noteworthy enough for Inca Garcilaso to mention, as he does in describing the difficult expansion into the northern province of Huánucu. The Inca warriors reportedly broke the pacific tradition established by Manco Capac and violently attacked the enemy, to which Inca Tupac Inca Yupanqui responded: "the Inca restrained them, bidding them remember the law of the first Inca Manco Capac, who bade them reduce the Indians to their rule with blandishments and presents and not by force of arms" (484) [los aplacó diciéndoles que no olvidesen la ley del primer Inca Manco Capac, que mandaba sujetasen los indios a su Imperio con halagos y regalos, y no con armas y sangre (bk. 8, chap. 4, 159)].

In this context of Inca Garcilaso's insistence that Incas conquered peacefully except as a last resort, the violent reaction to what he calls "sodomites" sticks out as an aberration. I argue that, rather than reflecting pre-Hispanic, Inca conquest politics, these passages respond to Inca Garcilaso's desire to further characterize the Incas as worthy predecessors of Christian civilizers and as macho imperialists capable of disciplining the sexually deviant non-Incas. Inca Garcilaso contributes, therefore, to the transculturation of indigenous notions of sexuality by sacrificing a more complex understanding of Inca civilization and those queer elements that formed part of its cultural reproduction. The suppression of third-gender subjectivity in the text is but another tension in the ambiguous, hybrid narrative, as I will show in three examples.

The first is found in Inca Garcilaso's description of the idolatrous pre-Inca peoples. He draws on Cieza de León's writings, but embellishes and exaggerates the propensity of non-Inca Andeans to human sacrifice, cannibalism, nudity, and incest. His strategy is similar to the Lascasian writings of Cieza, who also posits the pre-Inca peoples as moral barbarians; however, instead of viewing the differentiation between these peoples and the Incas as one of degrees of sophistication in an evolutionlike movement of "progress," Inca Garcilaso figures the Incas' civilizing mission in providential terms. As Zamora has observed, Inca Garcilaso identified a weakness in Las Casas's idealization of the Amerindian and the later Jesuit José de Acosta's blame of Indian idolatries on satanic inspiration. Instead, Inca Garcilaso introduces the concept of divine will as the agent that differentiates between the pre-Inca peoples and the Incas (*Language, Authority,* 115–117). A people prepared to receive the word of Christ could not have permitted such transgressive sexuality as reported by earlier chroniclers. Thus, Domingo de Santo Tomás's text (analyzed in Chapter 2), which Cieza de León included in his chronicle, is incorporated into this first part of the *Comentarios reales,* but altered from the more ethnographic original. The text is reduced, and all mention of third-gender subjectivity is erased:

> In some regions there were sodomites, though not very openly
> nor generally, but only among certain individuals and in secret.
> In some parts they had them in their temples because the Devil
> persuaded them that their gods delighted in such people, thus
> treacherously lifting the veil of shame that the gentiles felt

about this crime and inuring them to commit it in public and in general.

(39)

Hubo sodomitas en algunas provincias, aunque no muy al descubierto ni toda la nación en común, sino algunos particulares y en secreto. En algunas partes los tuvieron en sus templos porque les persuadía el demonio que sus dioses recibían mucho contento con ellos, y haríalo el traidor por quitar el velo de la vergüenza que aquellos gentiles tenían del delito y porque lo usaran todos en público y en común.

(Bk. 1, chap. 14, 35)

What Domingo de Santo Tomás had described as the "vice of sodomy" used by transgendered men in the context of rituals is transformed by Inca Garcilaso into a generalized pathology of aberrant sexuality. The rhetorical move from "in each important temple or house of worship they have a man or two, or more, depending on the idol, who go dressed in women's attire from the time they are children, and speak like them, and in manner, dress, and everything else imitate women" (Domingo de Santo Tomás, quoted in Cieza, *The Incas,* 314) to *"sodomitas,"* refigures the third-gender subjectivity, divorcing it from its more complex cultural significance. The biblical figure is invoked; "sodomite" conjures up, without a lengthy discourse on the sinfulness of the sexual act, the analogy with those who were destroyed by the fires of God. The fragments of sacredness we glean from Domingo de Santo Tomás's description are distorted almost beyond recognition. Inca Garcilaso's hyperbole insinuates that ritual sodomy in the temple was the catalyst that encouraged the widespread, unabashed use of the vice: what had once been practiced secretly now was rampantly used in public and among all the people. His rhetorical silencing of the third-gender practitioners of sodomy effaces any connection same-sex sexuality had to indigenous sacrosanctity, for in his account, sodomy spread from the temple to corrupt the commoners. Left in the text, but not erased, are profane subjectivities that can be demonized; in effect, their sodomitical proclivities are blamed on the devil, and their relation to the biblical phantasm of Sodom assures their place in hell, as well as their destruction on earth.

Following this corrective history of the pre-Inca peoples, sodomites and all, Inca Garcilaso announces in the subsequent chapter the arrival of the Inca saviors:

While these people were living or dying in the manner we have seen, it pleased our Lord God that from their midst there should appear a morning star to give them in the dense darkness in which they dwelt some glimmerings of natural law, of civilization, and of the respect men owe to one another. The descendents of this leader should thus tame these savages and convert them into men, made capable of reason and of receiving good doctrine, so that when God, who is the son of justice, saw fit to send forth the light of his divine rays upon those idolaters, it might find them no longer in their first savagery, but rendered more docile to receive the Catholic faith and the teaching and doctrine of our Holy Mother the Roman Church.

(40)

Viviendo o muriendo aquellas gentes de la manera que hemos visto, permitió Dios Nuestro Señor que de ellos mismos saliese un lucero del alba que en aquellas oscurísimas tinieblas les diese alguna noticia de la ley natural y de la urbanidad y respetos que los hombres debían tenerse unos a otros, y que los descendientes de aquél, procediendole bien en mejor cultivasen aquellas fieras y las convertiesen en hombres, haciéndoles capaces de razón y de cualquiera buena doctrina, para que cuando ese mismo Dios, sol de justicia, tuviese por bien enviar la luz de sus divinos rayos a aquellos idólatras, los hallase, no tan salvajes, sino más dóciles para recibir la fe católica y la enseñanza y doctrina de nuestra Santa Madre Iglesia Romana.

(Bk. 1, chap. 15, 36)

Thus the Incas are introduced as the proper governors and teachers of the barbarous Andean Others, including the sodomites, as we will see below. The preceding passage is replete with the rhetorical tropes associated with the Conquest and colonization: above all, the Western imposition of "natural law," a privileging of rationality, and adherence to Christian doctrine. Each of these cultural imports is anathema to third-gender subjectivity: natural law for its gender ideology, which privileges the masculine at the expense of the feminine and elides gender ambiguity; reason for its resistance to shamanic, mystical practices; and Christian doctrine for its sexual ideology. Inca Garcilaso extends the metaphoric light from the bi-

cultural Sun (a symbolic image resonant in both Western and Andean cultures) to discipline the "sodomites" identified among the *fieras* (beasts) of
the non-Inca peoples. Inca Garcilaso ends his introduction of the providential role the Incas played by referring to the state of the contemporary
"barbarians," even after seventy years of Spanish domination, stating that
those Indians under Inca control prior to the Spanish Conquest were more
capable of receiving the Gospel, thus reenforcing the author's subject position: Inca Garcilaso distances himself and his family's kinship group from
those elements in pre-Columbian Andean culture that were transgressive
of Western norms.

Inca Garcilaso details the Inca punishment of third-gender sexual transgressions throughout his account of the Incas' rise to power. He draws
a distinction between punishing and conquering, for, as we saw above,
Inca conquest was idealized as a primarily pacific enterprise. My first two
examples of these punishments are related to the peoples of the Chinchaysuyu region, specifically, the peoples of the northern coastal zone of
present-day Peru, the same region, in Inca terms, where the Moche and,
later, the Huarochirí prospered. The first area, various valleys of the Yunca,
were integrated into Tawantinsuyu in the traditional "peaceful" manner by
Inca Capac Yupanqui's "general," Auquititu, who reported back to the Inca
about his success and about the idolatrous customs of the locals, including
the statement that "there were a few sodomites" [había algunos sodomitas]
(bk. 3, chap. 13, 146). The Inca responded with the following instructions:

> In particular he ordered that the sodomites should be sought
> out with great care and when found burnt alive in the public
> square, not only those proved guilty but those convicted on
> circumstantial evidence, however slight. Their houses should
> be burnt and pulled down, and the trees on their fields pulled
> up by the roots and burnt so that no memory should remain
> of so abominable a thing, and it would be proclaimed as an
> inviolable law that thenceforward none should be guilty of
> such a crime, or the sin of one would be visited on his whole
> town and all the inhabitants would be burnt just as single ones
> were now being burnt.
>
> (162)
>
> Y en particular mandó que con gran diligencia hiciesen pes-
> quisa de los sodomitas, y en pública plaza quemasen vivos los
> que hallasen no solamente culpados sino indicados, por poco

que fuese; asimismo quemasen sus casas y las derribasen por
tierra y quemasen los árboles de sus heredades, arrancándolos
de raíz, por que en ninguna manera quedase memoria de cosa
tan abominable, y pregonasen por ley inolvidable que de allí
en adelante se guardasen de caer en semejante delito, so pena
de que por el pecado de uno sería asolado todo su pueblo y
quemados su moradores en general, como entonces lo eran en
particular.

(Bk. 2, chap. 13, 146–147)

Inca Garcilaso, having lived in Spain since 1560, was most likely aware
of the civil code and inquisitional laws regarding sodomy. The punishment
for sodomy in sixteenth-century Spain, as we saw in Chapter 1, was a public auto de fé in which the guilty were burned at the stake. A comparison of
the language used in the laws of the Catholic kings reveals striking similari-
ties with Inca Garcilaso's description of the Incas' supposed punishments:
the law reads that the convicted sodomite "be burned in the flames of fire
on the spot . . . without any other evidence . . . along with his possessions
and properties" (in Carrasco, *Inquisición,* 41). In Spain, the guilty sodomite
lost not only his life, burned in the place of conviction, but his possessions
as well.[19]

Inca Garcilaso adds the final threat to those who would repeat the sinful behavior, an echo from medieval laws and sixteenth-century sermons
and catechisms, in which total destruction of the village harks back to
Sodom and Gomorrah's fate. As I show in Chapter 4, other historians' lists
of Inca punishments do not mention sodomy as a sin or a punishable offense, which substantiates that this reported Inca punishment of sodomy is
Inca Garcilaso's own invention. By drawing on the rhetorical traditions of
civil and ecclesiastical Iberia, Inca Garcilaso further delineated his Incas as
being in the same mold as the Christians, thereby establishing in his readers' minds an image of propriety based on differentiation.

In fact, his hyperbole seems to grow with each additional layer of imaginative detail he adds to the description of the moralizing Incas, whose
discipline was reportedly warmly welcomed by the natives:

This was done as the Inca directed, to the great wonder of
the natives of those valleys that this unspeakable crime should
be dealt with in this new fashion. It was indeed so hated by
the Incas and their people that the very name was odious to

them and they never uttered it. Any Indian from Cuzco, even
though not an Inca, who used it as a term of abuse when
roused to anger in dispute with another was automatically
regarded as disgraced and looked upon for many days by the
rest of the Indians as something vile and filthy for having let
the word pass his lips.

(162–163)

Lo cual todo se cumplió como el Inca lo mandó, con gran-
dísima admiración de los naturales de todos aquellos valles
del nuevo castigo que se hizo sobre el nefando; el cual fue
tan aborrecido de los Incas y de toda su generación, que aún
el nombre solo les era tan odioso que jamás lo tomaron en
la boca, y cualquiera indio de los naturales de Cuzco, aunque
no fuese de los Incas, que con enojo, riñendo con otro, se lo
dijese por ofensa, quedaba el mismo ofensor por infame, y por
muchos días le miraban los demás indios como a cosa vil y
asquerosa, porque había tomado tal nombre en la boca.

(Bk. 2, chap. 13, 147)

Here the "sin that dare not speak its name," the medieval Christian trope
discussed in previous chapters, has found its way into the Incas' moral vocabulary, only to be silenced yet again. Inca Garcilaso would have us believe
that the Incas had a similar distrust for the mere naming of the offense. Of
course, Inca Garcilaso has subtly anchored this morality in the heart of his
kin group, Cuzco, where, supposedly, there was the most concern for not
naming the sin. As we saw in previous chapters, words used to signify third
gender, names for these subjects, were pronounced by Andean informants
without mention of a prohibition. In this case, Inca Garcilaso's strategy of
"supplementing" was employed a bit sloppily, for, later in his history, he
forgets to add this horrendous offense to the list of the Incas' laws. The extensive laws attributed to Inca Pachacuti, for example, whose source is Blas
Valera, include only the sexual offense of adultery, which can be found in
other Andean historians' accounts. The laws pertaining to marriage, which
most likely accounted for incest, are lost (bk. 7, chap. 36, 82–83). Later,
Inca Garcilaso reports Inca Roca's laws, which also fail to mention sodomy
(bk. 4, chap. 19, 203).

Finally, the Inca punishments for other crimes recorded in his history
reflect what might have been a more Andean penal system than the auto

de fé Inca Garcilaso records here. For example, when a rival ethnic group killed the Inca Pachacuti's "ministers," his vengeance was limited to extracting the offenders' front teeth (bk. 9, chap. 3, 214).

Indigenous chronicler Guaman Poma de Ayala offers an extensive recounting of Inca discipline, some of which he represents graphically in his drawings (*Primer nueva corónica*, f. 303–314:lines 229–239). He enumerates seventeen "*castigos*," descriptions ranging from details of what constituted a crime to the punishment to the penal facilities. Burning is not included on his list. Instead, according to him, Andean punishments consisted of underground jails, "*zancay*," in which were found poisonous snakes and ferocious felines. Other offenders were assigned to work details, "*chacnay thocllauan chipnay uillaconanpac*," while adulterers were sentenced to stoning in a place called Uinpillay or, if for forced adultery, into exile to the dreaded land of the Chuncos. Those who dishonored a "*doncella*" (virgin) were strung up and hung by their hair, "*arauay*." Only the offenders who committed the crime of killing by using enchantment or poisoned potions were said to be killed along with their family and not buried, so that the buzzards would eat their bodies. This last punishment is the only one described by Guaman Poma that is similar to Inca Garcilaso's assertion that the sodomites' families were also destroyed by the Incas.

In chapter 11 of book 6, Inca Garcilaso continues to narrate the Inca conquests carried out by Inca Capac Yupanqui, the mythic founder of the Inca empire of Tawantinsuyu. The passage I analyze here follows a long narrative accounting of other conquests the Incas had carried out. Here, interethnic rivalry is figured in terms of the sodomy trope:

> In the province of Huaillas he inflicted very severe punishment
> on some perverts who very secretly practiced the abominable
> vice of sodomy. As no case of this crime has ever been heard
> of until then among the Indians of the mountains (though
> it was known among the coastal Indians, as we have said),
> its occurrence among the Huaillas caused great scandal, and
> gave rise to a saying among the Indians which is still used
> as a stigma on that tribe. It is "Astaya Huaillas," "Go hence,
> Huaillas," implying that they still stink of their ancient sin,
> though it was little practiced and in great secrecy, and was well
> punished by Inca Capac Yupanqui.

(337–338)

Y en la provincia de Huaillas castigó severísimamente algunos
sométicos, que en mucho secreto usaban el abominable vicio
de la sodomía. Y porque hasta entonces no se había hallado
ni sentido tal pecado en los indios de la sierra, aunque en
los llanos sí, como ya dejamos dicho, escandalizó mucho al
haberlos entre los Huaillas, del cual escándalo nació un refrán
entre los indios de aquel tiempo, y vive hasta hoy en oprobio
de aquella nación, que dice: Astaya Huaillas, que quiere decir
"Apártate allá, Huaillas," como que se hiedan por su antiguo
pecado, aunque usado entre pocos y en mucho secreto, y bien
castigado por el Inca Cápac Yupanqui.

(Bk. 6, chap. 11, 30–31)

As in the examples above, "sodomite" is employed as a sign for transgressive sexual acts by barbarous non-Incas and, as such, erases any notion of
third-gender subjectivity that may have existed in the conquered culture.
Inca Garcilaso continues to inscribe a Christian morality in his description of the Inca conquest of the Andes. The moralizing discourse is introduced in the narrative through the insertion of coded words such as "vice,"
"sin," "scandal," and "crime" to characterize same-sex sexuality.[20] The presence of these words in Inca Garcilaso's description betrays any notion of a
pre-Hispanic, indigenous version of events and values. His introduction of
Christian values in the retelling of Inca history thereby marginalizes the
Incas' potential or former rivals in the eyes of European readers and also
distorts Andean values of gender and sexuality.

Inca Garcilaso continues the established pattern of "Othering" by emphasizing characteristics of the Indians' practice of sodomy: that it was
practiced secretly and that the sodomitical Indians were punished by Inca
Capac Yupanqui. The "sodomite" had to be represented as an aberration,
as someone who would hide himself and "in secret" would practice his
"vice," commit his "sin." The narrator needed to separate sodomites from
society in general to continue his representation of the Incas as the "noble
savage."[21] One difference in this account is that Inca Garcilaso is now accusing highlanders of the sin, a discovery he depicts as a "scandal," since
these practices were found in the virile sierra. To find "sodomites" in the
highlands was indeed scandalous because of the area's nearness to the center and birthplace of the Incas. Until then, the chroniclers had insisted that
the "moral perversions" existed only in the coastal plains, though, as I have

shown in Cieza de León's chronicle, this, too was a colonial fiction, one which Inca Garcilaso reconciles here, as did his original source, Cieza de León. Inca Garcilaso's ideology of privileging the Inca dynasty required him to distance them from any so-called uncivilized behavior and, in turn, to distance himself from any possible implication in sodomitical activity. Inca Garcilaso, a mestizo positioning himself for royal favors in Europe, and perhaps to remain above reproach, again stages the conquest of this "other" Andean culture as a disciplinary action: Inca Capac Yupanqui reportedly punishes this errant behavior.

But again, any reading of this passage is complicated even further if we regard this section of Inca Garcilaso's history as an Inca justification of the conquest of the Huaillas people. There are multiple discourses in the chronicles that we must consider: the historian, Inca Garcilaso in this case, surely had his discursive needs in transcribing the oral Inca history, but so did the native informants. These informants were often, according to Inca Garcilaso, the official historians of the Inca empire. It was their responsibility to justify the actions of the Incas for the collective memory of the people. In this context, the refrain mentioned by Inca Garcilaso, "stay away from there, Huaillas," could be understood as an echo of the "official" history of the Inca conquest of Huaillas. The refrain seems to be an insult, "shaming that nation," a memory of the Othering of the Huaillas by the Incas.[22]

In Inca Garcilaso's text, however, the refrain must be subtly framed to justify the incorporation of the Huaillas into the Inca empire. That is, not all Huaillas practiced the "sin," only a discreet few and in secret, and they were punished by the civilizing Incas. Represented in this way, the "sodomites" could not be seen as contaminating the "noble savages" who would form part of the Inca empire. In effect, Inca Garcilaso was willing to "sacrifice" the subjectivities of what might have been third genders and relegate them to the position of deviant sexual practitioners. Erased is any notion of third-gender subjectivity or ritual same-sex praxis as discussed above; all ways of life other than the intelligible "sinful" ones are left in the commingled and unrecorded discourses of other subaltern Andean cultures.

Inca Garcilaso's third account of the Incas' castigation of sodomy seems to be embedded in an indigenous discourse of interethnic rivalry between the Incas and the Chinchas, who reportedly boasted of being holdouts in the Inca conquest of their territories. The *Comentarios reales* contains several chapters on Chincha resistance, which Inca Garcilaso attributes to the Incas' patience and preference for peaceful conquest (bk. 6, chap. 18, 43). He insists on the Incas' power and ability to have conquered them at any

point and praises their peaceful resolve to wait out the Chinchas and to
pursue them through gift giving and negotiation (bk. 6, chap. 19, 45).

Then the narrative turns more aggressive, and Inca Garcilaso begins to
"contradict" the Chincha claims of cultural superiority and ferocity, accusing them of being cowardly and lazy. Finally, Inca Capac Yupanqui is
said to have ordered the burning of a group of Chincha sodomites. The
language is almost identical to the description considered above:

> In dealing with the new laws and customs that were to be
> implanted in Chincha, the Inca learned that there were a large
> number of sodomites among them. He had them arrested and
> burned them all alive on the same day, giving instructions that
> their houses should be pulled down, their fields laid waste and
> their trees uprooted, so that no memory should remain of
> anything the sodomites had planted with their hands: women
> and children would have been burnt for the sin of their fathers,
> if this had not appeared inhumane, for the vice was one that
> the Incas abominated exceedingly.
>
> (355)

> y tratando en Chincha de las nuevas leyes y costumbres que
> habían de tener, supo [el Inca] que había algunos sométicos, y
> no pocos, los cuales mandó prender, y en un día los quema-
> ron vivos todos juntos y mandaron derribar sus casas y talar
> sus heredades y sacar los árboles de raíz, porque no quedase
> memoria de cosa que los sodomitas hubiesen plantado con sus
> manos, y las mujeres e hijos quemaron por el pecado de sus
> padres, si no pareciere inhumanidad, porque fue un vicio éste
> que los Incas abominaron fuera de todo encarecimiento.
>
> (Bk. 6, chap. 19, 45)

Again the hyperbole grows until, finally, the wives and children of the sodomites are burned. Could this be a justification for the violence the Incas
perpetrated against their coastal rivals? As we will see below, the rivalry between the Yuncas and the Incas of the sierra took on even more explicitly
sexual metaphors to express a deep resentment between the two regions,
one that lives on to this day.

As we have seen in this study, the gendering of the Incas as virile and
dominant is a colonial trope that distorted indigenous conceptions of

gender and sexuality, in which gender duality was negotiated and harmonized through mediation. The complexities of the negotiation, the *yanantin,* like that portrayed in the Huarochirí myths, for example, are simplified here, and the tension between regions is displaced onto the "sodomites." Here, Inca Garcilaso embeds this gendered opposition in Peru's foundational text and gives birth to a trope that will evolve into part of the nationalist discourse of indigenism.[23] The language he uses in this account of immoral coastal sodomites is lifted from European discourse on transgressive sexuality and is used to distance the Incas from "barbarous" behavior. Pre-Columbian interethnic rivalries are the raw material for this discursive strategy, but, ultimately, they are left distorted in Peruvian cultural discourse, a colonial legacy that continues to influence Peruvian narrative today.[24]

COMPLICATING HYBRID SUBALTERNITY

To characterize Inca Garcilaso as a "subaltern writer," as several contemporary critics have done, is to oversimplify his complex locus of enunciation and process of identification. By privileging his subaltern position as a mestizo writer in a Spanish-dominated world and as a supposedly reliable voice of the Andean subaltern, other voices are misrepresented or effaced. A more nuanced characterization and understanding of his subjectivity and motives is necessary to avoid essentializing both the subaltern and the subalternizer. Considering the treatment of third-gender subjectivities in colonial texts reminds us to think of the subaltern as what John Beverly calls a "relational identity."[25] Furthermore, by rereading colonial texts with an ear for those subaltern voices muffled by the prejudices of both the colonial period and contemporary scholarship, we may find important differences in indigenous gender constructions and ideologies that otherwise are conflated with the European attitudes informing hegemonic colonial discourse. Inca Garcilaso wrote from the *chaupi* between two worlds, two civilizations; at times, he positioned himself "outside" his Andean world in order to be heard in the world of his other ancestry. Taken as a rhetorical device in a counterdiscourse, is this "betrayal" any more acceptable to the overall community? We must recognize that this "outside" locus of enunciation was constructed "in order to remain inside" a certain community that had established power relations vis-à-vis the rest of the Andean region, that is, the Inca establishment.[26] Inca Garcilaso's subjectivity is inside and outside, privileged and marginal, dominant and subaltern.

The *Comentarios reales* leaves us with what I would call a hybrid, subaltern writing subject, one who represents the Cuzco Inca Other in relation to the Spanish empire and whose counterdiscourse transculturates other Andean subalterns, specifically, the third-gender subjectivity behind the sodomy trope. But is his counterdiscourse indeed "a will to claim one's own otherness—regardless of its contents and circuitry," as Castro-Klaren suggests?[27] No doubt, Inca Garcilaso recognized his Otherness, as we see in his proud self-definition as an Indian; but this recognition was carefully selective, and what is left for us to appreciate is reduced according to his understanding of what he could make intelligible and acceptable to his European readers. In the process of transculturation, Inca Garcilaso sacrificed what he perceived to be distasteful, unspeakable even, to the hegemonic culture: that same-sex sexuality and transgendering could have a role in the reproduction of Andean culture. Ironically, in the same theoretical "third space" that the third-gender subjects occupied to negotiate reciprocity and complementarity, Inca Garcilaso chose to destroy rather than to create. The sexually queer is scapegoated by the culturally queer. The instability of the masculine Spanish subject, first encountered in Spanish medieval epic poetry, rears its head again, this time absorbed into a "hybrid" subaltern subject's portrayal of the Other that is partly himself. Inca Garcilaso's abjection of that part of himself that was the founding repudiation of the feminine in the Spanish literary tradition finds itself constituting the new mestizo subject, as well.

In rereading the "heroes of national drama, writing, literature," as the subaltern studies "Founding Statement" challenges us to do, we learn how to "listen" to subaltern voices and how to characterize subaltern subjectivity. In the process, we may learn to think of all subjects as relational identities in processes of identification, which, at times, positions them as marginal to certain hegemonic discourses while often privileging them relative to other subalterns. This approach is also instructive for the recovery of alternative forms of cultural reproduction that the transculturation "war machine" erases.

In conclusion, I would like to return to this chapter's epigraph. Lazarillo de Tormes's keen observation of our tendency to run away before we see ourselves in the Other might suggest an interesting missed opportunity: What if Inca Garcilaso had read and taken to heart Lazarillo de Tormes's remark? It seems, instead, that he understood the dangers of being sexually different in intransigent early-modern Spain, which the fictional "*tercero*" from the moralist's emblem warned against. Lazarillo de Tormes's message, from one subaltern to another, might have resonated and produced a different representation of third-gender and same-sex sexuality in the Andes. Perhaps Inca Garcilaso could have seen himself in all the manifestations of Andean culture, including those unintelligible to Western cultural norms, yet in danger of the inquisitional fires of intolerance. These imagined "what if" encounters of recognition are still possible in the readings that we contemporary critics perform using inclusive theoretical models of interpretation that listen to the voices of all subaltern subjects as they emerge from the transculturated tropes and rhetoric of colonial discourse.

EPILOGUE

Dancing the Tinkuy, *Mediating Difference*

"I am sure that in the cantina, after you and I leave, all sorts of queer things go on," Lituma said. "Don't you think?"

"It grosses me out so much that I hate going there," replied his deputy. "But you could die of sorrow closed up in the station, without taking a drink from time to time. Of course all kinds of barbarisms go on when Dionisio gets them drunk to his liking and, later, they probably all fuck each other in the ass. You know what I say, sergeant? It doesn't bother me a bit when the Shining Path executes a faggot."

—MARIO VARGAS LLOSA, *Lituma en los Andes*

Tinkuy mediates and produces difference out of the union of complementary opposites. It is tempting, therefore, to celebrate Inca Garcilaso's *Comentarios reales* as an example of a *tinkuy* consciousness, as a hybrid bridge between subaltern Andean and hegemonic Spanish cultures. The consequences of the transculturation of Andean gender and sexuality, however, cannot be appreciated without reading the entire corpus of Andean colonial historiography from the queer margins of Renaissance hegemony. This reading reveals what was sacrificed from Inca Garcilaso's understanding of Andean culture, that which he was unwilling to embrace as a new subject of miscegenation who had crossed the ocean into the center of the Spanish empire. It is as if Inca Garcilaso was attempting a *tinkuy* negotiation between the two cultures, yet the phallic symbolic order of Spanish patriarchal culture pulled him out of balance in certain moments of his textual commentary. The symbolic androgyne was obscured in his urgency to articulate a narrative counter to some voices of Spanish colonial discourse, analogous, perhaps, to the resistant strands of discourse I identify in the Huarochirí myths. Inca Garcilaso's *tinkuy* self-fashioning shed those cultural clothes that did not complement a Renaissance, decorous subject,

especially one modeled after the ideal man of arms and letters. As crossings go, Inca Garcilaso's was to a space of relative hegemony, at least as his
subjectivity related to gender and sexuality of early-modern Spain and its
empire.

The preceding pages are my attempt to reconsider a marginalized subjectivity while meeting a significant challenge: to discuss possible readings
of these tropes and their corresponding claims of representation of indigenous referents without falling into well-worn patterns of trying to make
intelligible to a Western audience something that does not correspond to
Western notions of subjectivity. In previous scholarship on this topic, these
subjects have been pathologized as degenerates, posited as analogous contemporaries of the European and Middle Eastern sodomites, and, more recently, as forerunners of modern homosexual identity. I asked myself, Is
there not another way of rendering intelligible same-sex desire and same-
sex praxis in non-Western contexts? I have attempted to refocus the study
of subjectivity, concluding that we can render colonial subjects intelligible
to our readers, students, and colleagues only by focusing on the discursive
practices that interpellated them in the first place, the tropes that claim to
represent them in colonial historiography. The result is an "alternative fiction" written from the margins of heteronormative discourse.[1] The ideologically charged tropes of sexuality, once decolonized, became accessible
knowledge of cultural difference.

Not taking masculinity as a naturalized notion, I have traced the unstable, contested nature of masculinity in Spanish discourse, noting how
the feminine became the abject outsider that formed the heart of the
masculinist discourse. In a similar fashion, I have traced the performative
nature of femininity in Andean discourse, a cultural value that was symbolically complementary to an equally important masculinity. Although
Conquest politics, particularly in the later stages of Inca expansion, figured the local inhabitants as feminine in a symbolic marriage with the
outside masculine, careful reading of Andean myths detects a counterdiscourse that privileges preunion feminine autonomy through sexual metaphors. In this context, I have been able to understand a third-gender category related to the magical, ritual, agricultural sphere of Andean culture,
a liminal subject that joins the symbolically opposing male- and female-
gendered spheres of culture in an invocation of the Andean androgyne. I
have shown how colonial discourse mobilized certain medieval artifacts in
its representation of third-gender subjects. From the fragments of the same
discourse, I have pieced together a possible understanding of how gender

liminality fit into pre-Columbian Andean society, under the sanction of a sacred understanding of the feminine and the androgyne.

We have witnessed how the third gender was misrepresented by the Toledan chroniclers and from colonial interrogations of indigenous informants, whose resistant silencing of the sacred nature of ritual sodomy aided in the transformation of the hegemonic discourse's representation of the subjects. By underscoring the agency of the indigenous peoples who came into contact with coloniality, we better understand how transculturation was implicated in the re-presentation of their culture to both native and outside readers. The colonial project's protoethnographic research not only informed the viceroyalty's laws and punishments, but also found its way into the ecclesiastical literature, a pedagogical discourse that reflected back to the natives a distorted vision of their own history and customs. Among the disfigured reflections were the moralized treatment of same-sex and other forms of sexuality. Finally, I have observed how the neocultures of indigenous sexual subjects, the tropes that were shaped and reshaped by multiple agents in a stream of reiterations from the first chronicles and *relaciones* to the later histories and evangelizing tools, found their way into the hybrid text of the "father" of Peruvian literature.

The history of queer tropes of sexuality does not end with the conclusion of the *Comentarios reales.* As we have learned in this study, the meaning and value of subjectivities change over time and through complex processes in which their performances adapt to new realities. As my project continues to evolve, it will become important to explore how far the echoes of Inca Garcilaso's text resonate in Peruvian literature. As gender studies opens a critique on patriarchal and heterosexist contemporary Andean society, this research invites interpretations of how the tropes of sexuality powerfully refigure subjectivity in other contexts.

Armed with a methodology that approaches tropes of colonial discourse as accessible knowledge of transculturated subjectivities, scholars can gain a new understanding of the heterogeneous gender culture in colonial contact zones, and thereby better consider subsequent reiterations of those figures in the national literatures of the Andes and beyond. How does the neo-Inca aestheticist movement of the nineteenth century figure gender and sexuality in its search for an expression of national identity and unity? Does gender diversity survive the homogenizing discourse of nation building? In the *indigenistas'* appeal for a new representation of "the Indian," what happens to the once-autonomous but complementary feminine sphere of Andean culture? Finally, in the Andean novels of the Latin American van-

guard and later "Boom," what role does the sexual Other play and what relationship does he or she have with the past?

In the passage that serves as epigraph to this Epilogue, we see a reiteration of the sexual Other in the characterization of the sexually ambiguous Dionisio from Mario Vargas Llosa's 1993 novel, *Lituma en los Andes.*
What forms of transculturation are at play in the representation of these
attitudes? Here, the conflictive Andean space of the 1980's emits a fear
and loathing of gender and sexual diversity from both poles of power in
contemporary Peru: the Maoist revolutionaries and the nationalist military. And the Quechua community? What does go on in the cantinas after
the *chicha* runs out? Would the Quechua people characterize those liminal moments of carnivalesque excess as "barbaric," as does the coastal offi-
cer in Vargas Llosa's novel? Or are those now near-clandestine moments
echoes of phantasmagoric, original ritual performances of alternative sexuality that mediated between the absolute opposites of Andean culture? The
metaphoric connotations of characters and themes in the novel suggest a
resonance from colonial times in which an outsider faces a seemingly unintelligible Other. Difference in the novel is represented through queer
tropes of sexuality, tropes informed by Western and Andean mythologies.
Andean society is figured as barbarous, uncivilized: labyrinths, bacchana-
lia, fratricide, human sacrifice, cannibalism, and sodomy come together in
an apocalyptic vision of the end of the twentieth century, of the fragmen-
tation of Peruvian society. Queer tropes of sexuality endure.

Lituma en los Andes is ultimately an "outsider's" coming-to-terms with
a heterogeneous and unintelligible culture in dynamic processes of cultural transformation in which the abject must be repudiated for the sake
of both personal and national survival. The continuity between colonial
and contemporary tropes of sexuality in hegemonic discourse invites the
question of whether there is, in indigenous and mestizo ritual performances, a similar "survival" of that which was scapegoated and sacrificed
in colonial times. Contemporary performances of Andean culture, from
indigenous and mestizo "insiders," continue to negotiate transculturation
through tropes of the body. Recent ethnographic research on sexuality and
ritual dance in the Peruvian highlands confirms how gender and sexuality
continue to figure prominently in community ceremonies, as we appreciated in Chapter 3.

The *danza,* for example, is a contemporary iteration of the pre-Hispanic
taqui (song-dance genre performed in public ceremonies), which we considered in Chapters 3 and 4. We saw how the body was enacted in the descriptions of Huarochirí rituals and how *taquis* manifested as an irrational

threat to colonial hegemony in the form of Taqui Onqoy, an anticolonial performance of bodily difference. The *taqui,* in the contemporary form of *danzas,* continues to express the negotiation of difference that we have considered in this book.[2] These performances have not been immune to societal changes; indeed, they respond to change by expressing new relationships in their ever-changing societies, as Zoila Mendoza has so insightfully shown in her study of mestizo ritual *danzas* in a Cuzco community, San Jerónimo (*Shaping Society through Dance*). These *danzas,* I propose, afford us one last perspective on the workings of transculturation and the *tinkuy* negotiation of sexual difference and demonstrate the endurance of third-gender performance in the Andes.

We have seen, in Chapter 3, how third-gender subjectivity is performed in different ways in several contemporary indigenous rituals, but those ethnographies do not directly address ritual gender and sexual liminality. Research is still needed on why, for example, the *waylakas* cross-dress in the contemporary *mujonomiento* ceremony of Chincheros. We are certain to find innovative reinterpretations of performances that continue to change as their cultural contexts are altered through transculturation. Mendoza's study of mestizo ritual dance in the southern Andes provides a model for future interpretations of the effects of transculturation on contemporary public performances of subjectivity. Her research demonstrates how gender and sexuality were implicated in the transformations of the *danzas* as a Cuzco community metamorphosed. In a finding that is relevant to my study, for example, she discovered that since the 1940's the female Dama character in the San Jerónimo Majeños dance, which traditionally was performed by a cross-dressed man, has been danced by a woman. She concludes that "the reconstruction of the role of the *Dama* may be seen as an effort by the Majeños to link the principles of masculinity and propriety that the *comparsa* advocated. Giving the role to a real woman made the *danza* more decent because, according to the Majeños, no respectable townsmen (as opposed to peasants), not even in ritual, should dress like a woman" (ibid., 158). Mendoza links this transformation to the Majeños' increased power in the region and the increased class and ethnic distinctions being negotiated in part through ritual, public performances. The transformations of public indigenous performances that began in the colonial period (see Dean, *Inca Bodies*) continue to express the negotiations of power along lines of class, ethnicity, and gender. Where do third-gender subjects fit into these performances of Andean religiosity and social relations?

Fritz N. Villasante Sullca has considered the role of sexuality in contemporary Andean ritual. His "De fiestas y rituales" focuses on the "fiesta de la Mamacha de Carmen" in Paucaratambo, Peru.³ In the annual festival in honor of the Virgin, "Mamacha de Carmen," *danzas* dedicated to the Virgin reveal complex social relationships and the ongoing reproduction of culture, including the negotiation of sexual difference. According to Villasante, traditionally, the Virgin was the only female presence in the ritual space, and the dance groups were symbolically gendered male ("De fiestas y rituales," 5). All the female roles in the *danzas,* therefore, were performed by cross-dressed men. Were they vestiges of the phantasmagorical original performance of gender liminality needed in the mediation between the masculine (male dancers) and the feminine (Mamacha Carmen)? We do not have an answer, but the traditional cross-dressing began changing in the 1980's as societal alterations pressured dance groups to reconfigure their offerings to the Virgin. Villasante's ethnography reveals the ongoing transculturation of ritual festival dances, with particular emphasis on the changing attitudes toward the cross-dressing dancers.

As in the more urban perspectives of San Jerónimo, Cuzco, where the transvestite figure had begun to disappear much earlier, in the more-distant Paucaratambo, attitudes are also changing. Men have become reluctant to dance the transvested roles due to peer pressure that has begun to question their masculinity, pressure attributed to "homophobic" attitudes imported from the cities (ibid., 16). Traditionally, by cross-dressing, the male dancers were "feminized" (ibid., 7) in performances that moved them along the gender spectrum to symbolically enact an in-between position. This new reluctance to dance cross-dressed is more pronounced in the dances associated with an increasing mestizo identity, whereas the *danzas* with stronger and more pronounced "ethnic" identity continue to perform more explicit gender liminality through the incorporation of "homosexuals" into those roles (ibid., 16).

Even in the instances in which women have begun to dance the traditional cross-dressed roles, a sense of third gender remains: the women chosen are characterized as "masculinized" in order not to compete with the Virgin in her sacred space, to have the physical endurance necessary to dance, and perhaps to recall the originary third gender (ibid., 23). Villasante's rich ethnography is a step toward understanding the contemporary meanings behind age-old performances.⁴ Andean society changes, while ancient, gendered performances are reiterated, in new contexts, in response to contemporary needs, discourses of power, and desires.

By returning to the *chaupi,* that mediating space where sacred *conocimiento* is revealed, performed, and enacted, we have gained a better understanding of colonial hybrid texts and their authors and of more contemporary ritual representations of Andean culture. Reading from the *chaupi* enables us to invoke the *chuqui chinchay* and the third space in the *tinkuy* reproduction of Andean culture, not as a romanticization of the exotic Other, but as a paradigm that privileges the mediation and not the erasure of difference. Along the way we have learned how Andeans negotiate Otherness, bridge *pachacutis,* and resist cultural homogenization. The product of this *tinkuy* may not, ultimately, be revealed only in the written texts of Andean literature and historiography, but also in the continual performances of ritual *danzas* and ceremonies in the mountain villages of the Andes and the coastal plains of the Pacific. These *danzas* are social texts, performative, *tinkuy* products of centuries of transculturation in which queer subjects continue to resist the cultural "war machine" by donning the Other's clothes, by invoking the sacred Andean androgyne, and by moving their bodies in gendered performances of alterity and union.

NOTES

INTRODUCTION

1. It is important to understand the physical and cultural spaces and peoples represented in this book as the Andes, Andeans, and Andean culture. Tawantin-suyu, the Inca empire encountered by the Spanish in 1532, was a multiethnic, multilingual region that stretched along the Andes mountains from today's southern Colombia to northern Argentina; it included territories that spread from the highlands eastward to the Amazonian jungle basin and westward to the Pacific Ocean. The Incas were but one of the many ethnic groups in this region, a group that began an imperial expansion in the middle of the fifteenth century. They quickly established reciprocal governing relationships between their southern, highland capital and their place of origin, Cuzco, and other ethnic centers throughout the Andes. This rise to power was accomplished in an eighty-year period; therefore, many non-Inca cultures retained much of their identity and language. As I discuss Tawantinsuyu and the subsequent Spanish invasion and colonization, I will strive to differentiate the distinct cultural areas. Indeed, I will argue that the diversity of ethnicities presented unique challenges for the Spanish chroniclers' portrayal of the Inca and Andean cultures in the sixteenth century and may help explain why and how the subjects of this study, third genders, were objects of transculturation.

2. This anecdote is found in ladino writer Santa Cruz Pachacuti's *Relación de antigüedades.* I will analyze this passage in greater detail in Chapter 3.

3. I am referring to three seminal works in Latin American colonial studies: Irving Leonard's *Books of the Brave;* Ángel Rama's *La ciudad letrada;* and Walter Mignolo's *The Darker Side of the Renaissance.*

4. When I speak of "locus" or "place of enunciation," I refer to Walter Mignolo's use of the term to mean something that "invites a change of orientation and allows us to think of identification rather than identity, as a process of location related to the place of speaking rather than a description which will capture the correspondence between what one is and what one is supposed to be according to some preexisting cultural realities" (*Darker Side of the Renaissance,* 11).

5. These Aymara (*ipa*) and Quechua (*orua*) language terms meaning "third gender" are explicated in Chapters 3 and 4.

6. Marjorie Garber's *Vested Interests* is an early recognition of the role that cultural manifestations of "third" positions can have in discourse and the crisis of
anxiety they can produce. She emphasizes, in her analysis of cross-dressing, that
"'third' is a mode of articulation, a way of describing a space of possibility. Three
puts into question the idea of one: of identity, self sufficiency, self-knowledge" (11).

7. A ladino is an indigenous person who has learned to read and write colonial languages and has been evangelized in the teachings of Catholicism.

8. William Leap has characterized the queer movement, both in its "nationalist" and its "theoretical" modes, as a "claim to space" (*Word's Out,* 103–104). "Under
this formulation, 'queer' is no longer the status of 'the other,' as defined by the
conventions of the mainstream. Queer is now the starting point for a queer's own
social critique, and the mainstream is now positioned, in spite of its objections,
within the margin" (ibid., 104). For a discussion of "queer theory" and its application to literature, see "What Does Queer Theory Teach Us about X," by Lauren
Berlant and Michael Warner: "Queer publics make available different understand-
ings of membership at different times, and membership in them is more a matter of aspiration than it is the expression of an identity or a history" (344). Another early contribution to queer theory is Alexander Doty's *Making Things Perfectly
Queer.* Doty parts from the idea that queer positions in mass culture are constructed in specific historical contexts and that the reader has the possibility to
adopt a receptive strategy that privileges a "queer" reading of any text. This approach liberates the reader to use his or her imagination in order to reconstruct
a history that has been denied for sociohistorical reasons. The "queer" reader re-
claims a marginal space from which he or she can read the text. Teresa de Lauretis,
in "Queer Theory," characterizes this strategy as "a form of resistance to cultural
homogenization" in order to explore "other constructions of the Subject" (iii). Max
Kirsch, in *Queer Theory and Social Change,* cautions scholars about the social implications of embracing queer theory, because of its tendency to stress the individual,
thereby furthering the ends of advanced capitalism and its alienation and discour-
agement of community action. My study stresses how queer subjectivity can actually build community through the example of third-gender presence in ritual actions of community. Reclaiming the historical place of queer subjects, without
romanticizing or ignoring the material reality of their existence, is an important
step toward understanding alternative possibilities in cultural reproduction and social interaction.

To avoid any possible misunderstanding of my position, the reader of this study
should keep in mind that I am not suggesting that the third-gender subjects discussed below are equivalent to or forefathers of modern gay, lesbian, bisexual, or
transgender identities. What they may share with today's queer subjects is a similar history of marginalization. I made this same distinction in an earlier version of

my research ("Third Gender," 31n1). I address the issue of romanticizing the subject of gender liminality below.

9. In this study I understand "culture" as a "contested space" in which subjects reproduce meanings and values in turbulent streams of change, in which the aesthetic products of their reproduction are but narrow windows through which both outsiders and insiders may view the lived experience of the culture producers. As Homi Bhabha has observed, implicit in this understanding of culture is a notion of struggle for survival; he encourages us "to engage with culture as an uneven, incomplete production of meaning and value, often composed of incommensurable demands and practices, produced in the act of social survival" ("Postcolonial Criticism," 438). While Bhabha theorizes culture in the context of postcolonial realities, his insights are applicable to the colonial moment as well, especially if we consider the colonial "contact zone," as defined by Mary Louise Pratt: "social spaces where disparate cultures meet, clash, and grapple with each other, often in highly asymmetrical relations of domination and subordination" (*Imperial Eyes*, 4). Out of these contested cultural spaces come new forms to be processed and understood by the producers and the receptors of cultural signs. This way of comprehending culture is crucial for this study, for, in Bhabha's words, "The great, though unsettling, advantage of this position is that it makes you increasingly aware of the construction of culture and the invention of tradition" ("Postcolonial Criticism," 438). My analysis takes a similar position in relation to Andean culture and focuses on how the gender and sexual culture is reconstructed in the newly contested space of the first hundred years after the arrival of the Spanish conquistadores.

10. Ángel Rama's *Transculturación narrativa en América Latina* is most responsible for the diffusion of the term transculturators in literary criticism, a project he began with his analysis of Arguedas and extended to other transculturators that negotiated the complex "neoculturations" of the Americas, bridging gaps between oral, native traditions and literary, European and North American cultural production. Latin American critics have adopted the term *transculturation* to describe the literary and discursive practices of the late twentieth century and, in the process, have adjusted Ortiz's original use of the word. José María Arguedas, for example, adapted Ortiz's term to the Andean region by emphasizing the continual presence and influence of the indigenous cultures, an influence that in Cuba had been virtually eliminated by the colonial enterprise. Both his ethnographic and his literary works are marked by a deeply felt identification with the transculturated people of Peru and a commitment to giving voice to the unique neocultured character of the region. Antonio Cornejo Polar's work since 1980 has also carefully developed a similar notion of the region's cultural production, culminating in his final book, *Escribir en el aire*. Cornejo Polar problematizes the issues of discourse, the subject, and representation from the perspective that Latin America's cultural production, since the colony, has been formed by a heterogeneous group of voices (17). While cultural and sexual heterogeneity have been obscured by the *hispanizante* tenden-

cies of Peruvian and other Latin American critics, less-prejudiced and more-subtle readings are opening the way for revisions of our characterizations of Andean cultural production, in particular, and Latin American cultural production, in general. See, for example, the collection about issues of transculturation edited by Mabel Moraña, *Ángel Rama y los estudios latinoamericanos.*

11. I follow Peter Hulme's definition of colonial discourse as one that is "an ensemble of linguistically-based practices unified by their common deployment in the management of colonial relationships, an ensemble that could combine the most formulaic and bureaucratic of official documents . . . with the most non-functional and unprepossessing of romantic novels" (*Colonial Encounters,* 2).

12. For this trend in anthropology, see Clifford and Marcus, *Writing Culture;* Boone and Mignolo, *Writing without Words;* and Behar and Gordon, *Women Writing Culture.*

13. José Rabasa's *Inventing America* also posits European historiography as "inventing" the notion of the Americas that is inscribed in the lettered discourse of European consciousness.

14. I will distinguish between opposite-sex sodomy and same-sex sodomy when the referent is ambiguous.

15. Part of the challenge in working with the colonial scriptural economy is sifting through the fragments left from what Walter Mignolo has called the "darker side of the Renaissance." We are left with the "*huellas,*" or "tracks," of indigenous oral discourse, vestiges that Martín Lienhard has identified as integral to an "alternative literature" (*La voz y su huella*). Indeed, Mignolo's theorization of "colonial semiosis" also encourages us to open our interpretations to more than just the privileged writing of the moment and to take into consideration other forms of cultural signifiers (*Darker Side of the Renaissance,* 7–8). My inclusion of pre-Columbian ceramics and iconography as well as my consideration of nonliterary texts such as the catechisms, confession manuals, and sermons, is a step in that direction. Regina Harrison has long advocated the recognition of the "clash" between not only linguistic systems but also different cultural codes of expression ("Modes of Discourse"). Her *Signs, Songs, and Memory in the Andes* instructs us on how a "cultural translation" must delve into deeper meanings of both cultural systems (32–54) and includes non-Western cultural production as an object of study. Gustavo Verdesio's "Todo lo que es sólido se disuelve en la academia" and "En busca de la materialidad perdida" call for more attention to the material record in postcolonial and subaltern studies so as to restore agency to the subaltern and to begin truly to treat subalterns as subjects and producers of knowledge.

16. This textualization of the body began to be appreciated as part of colonial, postcolonial, and neocolonial writings as gender and sexuality increasingly became theorized as discursive constructs, in the fields of both anthropology and literary criticism. Beginning with a revision of anthropology's treatment of women predicated on a critique of structuralist tendencies that constituted totalizing theories based on binary oppositions and hierarchies of gender, scholars began to ques-

tion traditional representation of women as passive objects related to "nature," and of men posited as political and social agents associated with "culture." In addition to destabilizing customary assumptions of equality in so-called primitive cultures, anthropologists began to explore multiple gender categories in societies they studied. Anthropology and literary criticism's traditional Eurocentrism has begun to be broken as greater attention is paid to cultural specificity in gender studies. Notions of power and status as they relate to gender are now understood as culturally determined, which has led to a questioning of naturalized categories of "man" and "woman." This ultimately suggests a reconsideration of biological determinism's role in the categorization of gender. This revision is localized on the body, following Clifford Geertz's reelaboration of Simone de Beauvoir's notion that bodies (sexes) are born, but people (genders) are constructed in given contexts. The body is marked by the gender ideologies of its society, ideologies that change according to historical contexts. Because the differentiation of bodies is cultural and not universal, anthropologists observe how the body relates to power in the culture under consideration in order to understand that society's gender ideology through the study of language, myth, and ritual in the reproduction of gender culture. Literary criticism has undergone a parallel transformation in the ways gender and sexuality are interpreted, given that both fields share an intellectual connection to the feminist and civil rights movements of the 1960's, to poststructuralist theory, and, more recently, to postmodern and postcolonial critiques.

17. I have developed my understanding of *tinkuy* from both colonial accounts and modern ethnographies. Catherine Allen has presented one of the most succinct and insightful definitions of *tinkuy* based on her fieldwork in the highland indigenous community of Sonqo: "Through *tinkuy*, social unity is created dialectically and expressed in terms of complementary opposition. Although *tinkuy* refers to ritual dance-battles, the word has wider applications. It is not easily translated into English ('dialectic' conveys a similar meaning but is far too abstract). When streams converge in foaming eddies to produce a single, larger stream, they are said to *tinkuy*, and their convergence is called *tinku* (or *tingu*). *Tinkus* are powerful, dangerous places full of liberated and uncontrollable forces" (*The Hold Life Has,* 205). Bolin's *Rituals of Respect* emphasizes how *tinkuy* creates a sense of solidarity among the participants in the ritual dance-battles, bringing together the opposing sides (96–100), and deepens our understanding of this ideology in other rituals, such as marriage ceremonies. Her research aids my characterization of third gender's participation in the joining of gendered opposites, discussed in Chapters 2 and 3. Isbell, Platt, and Franquemont (Franquemont cited in Paul, *Paracas Ritual Attire*) also add to my theorization of *tinkuy*. It should be noted that my use of *tinkuy* as a metaphor does not ignore the contentious nature of the ritual negotiation, for as Allen alludes to in her definition, the actual practice invokes imagery of "battles," that is, of struggle and competition that eventually is worked out in union.

18. Cereceda recognizes these patterns throughout the Andean highlands, including in Puno, Arequipa, and Cuzco ("Semiology of Andean Textiles," 150).

19. *Chaupi,* a Quechua term, is similar to *chhima. Chaupi* was defined by Diego González Holguín in 1608 in *Vocabulario de la lengua general de todo el Perú* as "half, or the middle of things or places or time or work" [mitad, o el medio de las cosas o lugares o tiempo o obra] (99).

20. González Holguín defines *chhullu:* "a thing without its companion among things that are paired" [una cosa sin compañera entre cosas pareadas] (ibid., 119).

21. By studying the tradition of parallel inheritance that afforded women property rights within the kinship-based *ayllu* system, the complementary roles of males and females in the basic family unit, the corresponding gender duality of Andean deities, and the religious institutions run by women, Silverblatt concludes that, prior to the Inca ethnic group's political ascension in the region, "women and men in the Andean *ayllu* apprehended a world criss-crossed by bonds of gender" (*Moon, Sun, and Witches,* 39). The Inca, as they increased their political power in the region, took advantage of these complementary linkages between men and women to ideologically reproduce the *ayllu* structure on a larger, interethnic scale. As a result, Silverblatt argues, women rose parallel to men in the emerging "conquest politics" of the Incas' regional expansion. Integral to this politics was the re-creation of pre-Inca gendered "prestige hierarchies" based on relationships established between "conquering" outsiders, conceptualized as male, and original inhabitants, conceptualized as female (ibid., 68). The male "conquerors" were aligned with a male deity, Illapa, who was said occasionally to impregnate women, thereby legitimizing exogamic unions and producing "children of Illapa," who became intermediaries between the divinity and humans. While these local prestige hierarchies served the purpose of ordering and classifying in the *ayllus,* and the "conquered" did not lose access to productive resources nor were they subjugated by force (ibid., 72), the Incas would later repeat the symbolic patterns in order to dominate other ethnic groups. The new political order established by the Incas, in which Inca rulers were figured as stand-ins for the male Sun god, created alliances with subjugated territories by taking local chieftains' virgin daughters as *acllas,* or "wives," of the Sun/Inca (ibid., 87). The Incas' sexual control over these young women, by which they maintained their virginity and which endowed them with semidivine status, was one of the primary means by which Tawantinsuyu was governed (ibid., 107).

22. Trying to avoid Western paradigms of gender and sexuality, Roscoe and other anthropologists and historians have worked hard to develop ethnographies that describe third genders from the perspective of the native people's culture. Roscoe's model, as first presented in "Gender Diversity in Native North America," includes several components. The first dimension to analyze is the role of third gender in society, specifically, "productive specialization," "supernatural sanction," and "gender variation" ("Gender Diversity," 65). Next, we must ask if the third genders were "accepted and integrated members of their communities" (ibid., 66). Finally, by analyzing how the berdache fit into the society's larger gender culture, we can determine whether the Andean berdache is indeed a third gender. A uni-

fied analysis of the gender diversity in a society, as suggested by Roscoe, would take into consideration the sociocultural processes that construct gender in a society and would address the cultural meanings of social relationships, the power relationships among genders, and how historical discourses have affected the subject positions in question (ibid., 70).

23. A collection of essays edited by Sue-Ellen Jacobs, Wesley Thomas, and Sabine Lang, *Two-Spirit People,* is a unique collaborative effort between anthropologists and contemporary Two-Spirit–identified people. ("Two-Spirit People" is the preferred name of the Native American gay, lesbian, and third-gender community [*Two-Spirit People,* 6], who seek to disavow the colonial term *berdache* used by most social scientists.) The essays, focused entirely on North American native ethnic groups, bring into dialogue Native American Two-Spirit People and anthropologists in order to clarify points of contention and misunderstanding.

24. For a critique of Roscoe's scholarship and the subject of gender and power in the Pueblo Indians, see Gutiérrez, "Must We Deracinate Indians" and "A Gendered History." Trexler also critiques Roscoe's work in "Gender Subordination."

25. Pete Sigal's *From Moon Goddesses to Virgins* is an example of how cultural specificity yields in-depth understanding of the complexities of gender and sexuality in colonial contexts.

26. For critiques of Trexler's book, see Mason, "Sex and Conquest," and Roscoe, *Changing Ones.* I first engaged Trexler's research in "Third Gender, Tropes of Sexuality" and "Toward an Andean Theory of Ritual Same-Sex Sexuality." In this book I continue to address the problem of his overemphasis on masculine subjugation as the defining characterization of berdache in the Andean context.

CHAPTER 1

1. While I depend on Foucault's history of sexuality for general trends, readers wishing to explore this topic further should consider more recent and in-depth studies, such as Craig Williams's *Roman Homosexuality,* the most comprehensive treatment of the subject to date. Winkler's *The Constraints of Desire* provides a nuanced account of sexuality in Ancient Greece.

2. Foucault studies the process of "subjectivation," or "the manner in which the individual could form himself as the ethical subject of his actions," in the turbulent transition from the Greek city-states to the Roman empire (*Care of the Self,* 95). These antecedents can best be understood as "a male ethics," that is, a system of thought developed by and for the free men of the Greek city-states, in which the highest virtue was moderation (Foucault, *Use of Pleasure,* 22). Moderation in the "use of pleasure" was based on a relationship between the individual and himself, without the interdiction of civil or religious authorities. While there were no rules of conduct to be applied to the general population, there was much attention paid to the ethical issues revolving around the ideal relationship that a free man

should have with himself, his wife, and potential young male lovers. Summarizing, the relationship between a free man and himself was one of austere self-regulation (ibid., 93); that between a free man and his wife was a "political" one in which the man dominated and guided the woman (ibid., 84); and that between a free man and a boy was an erotic, reciprocal one in which the boy exchanged his physical beauty for the elder's wisdom in the framework of an evolution toward platonic friendship (ibid., 245).

3. This intensification of personal ethics occurred in the context of the first centuries AD, during "a weakening of the political and social framework within which the lives of individuals used to unfold" (Foucault, *Care of the Self,* 41), for the expansiveness of the Roman empire produced circumstances in which the individual required more self-regulation. John Boswell also discusses the "ruralization" of Roman culture as a possible influence on the changing sexual ethics (*Christianity,* 119–121).

4. See Boswell, *Christianity,* especially pages 66–70, for his analysis of the lack of Roman laws related to sexuality.

5. The first laws to address same-sex sexuality as transgression seemed to be applied to the passive participant, most important, to the passive male prostitute, in the sixth century (ibid., 171).

6. Trexler (*Sex and Conquest,* 44–45) proposes that Visigoth proscriptions of sodomy related to political concerns that the secular, active perpetrators of sodomy were gaining power through the groups of passive males they kept as concubines and that the clergy exercised power over the passive students who boarded with them.

7. Jordan, *Invention of Sodomy,* 1.

8. Foucault, *History of Sexuality,* 101.

9. Bailey (*Homosexuality*) and Boswell (*Christianity*) have argued this point.

10. For studies of cannibalism in colonial discourse, see Hulme's *Colonial Encounters;* Félix Bolaños (*Barbarie y canibalismo en la retórica colonial*); and Freccero ("Cannibalism, Homophobia, Women"). Freccero makes explicit the connection between the tropes of cannibalism and homophobia in Montaigne, while Bolaños and Hulme develop critical readings of the tropes in the colonial Americas.

11. For foundational studies in this new field, consult Brittan (*Masculinity and Power*), Brod (*Making of Masculinities*), Gilmore (*Manhood in the Making*), Hadley (*Masculinity in Medieval Europe*), Lees (*Medieval Masculinities*), Murray (*Male Homosexuality*), and Sedgwick (*Between Men; Epistemology of the Closet*). For evocative and often personal accounts of current Latino writers' confrontations with masculinity issues, see Ray González's anthology, *Muy Macho.*

12. Other queer studies of the Hispanic tradition, including Mohillo and Irwin (*Hispanisms and Homosexualities*), Chávez-Silverman and Hernández (*Reading and Writing the Ambiente*), and Foster and Reis (*Bodies and Biases*), begin later, with readings of Renaissance texts.

13. Recent scholarship in queer studies includes Berlant and Warner ("What

Does Queer Theory Teach Us about X"), Butler (*Bodies That Matter;* "Critically Queer"; *Gender Trouble*), de Lauretis ("Queer Theory"), Doty (*Making Things Perfectly Queer*), Kirsch (*Queer Theory and Social Change*), Leap (*Word's Out*), and Sedgwick (*Between Men; Epistemology of the Closet*).

14. The Hispano-Arab literature reflects the Muslim shift from the rural customs of the Visigoths to the urban culture of the legendary Islamic cities. Boswell has reviewed the variety of sources that treat same-sex desire with indifference in the Hispano-Arabic tradition (*Christianity,* 194–200). During the Muslim occupation of the peninsula there were no Christian laws passed regarding sodomy (ibid., 198). This is not to imply, as Boswell does, that there was unbridled acceptance of homosexuality in the period. As Hutcheson has commented, Arabic authors of the times, while citing a full range of sexual practices, also instill a notion of heteronormativity in their writings ("Sodomitic Moor," 107).

15. Hutcheson, in "The Sodomitic Moor," argues that this image is more a product of the early-modern age, exacerbated by later historians, also in denial about the peninsula's multiple heterodoxies. His insightful essay cautions us to understand that Christians were often accused of lascivious behavior as a rebuke for their loss of the peninsula to the invading Moors (103). As we will see in my analysis of the Cid, the hyperbolic emphasis on his performance of masculinity is rooted in this need to enact austere, and therefore not lascivious, signs of sexuality as a mode of differentiation.

16. For a complete history of the text, see Celso Rodríguez Fernández's introductory study to his Spanish translation of the original Latin manuscript, especially pages 17–19 (*Pasión de S. Pelayo*). All cited passages are taken from this edition. Mark Jordan's insightful essay on this figure, in *Invention of Sodomy* and reproduced in Blackmore and Hutcheson, *Queer Iberia,* emphasize how Pelagius is represented in Raguel's narrative, in the later writings by Saxon canoness Hrotswitha, and in the liturgy associated with the saint's cult. Jordan argues that the homoerotic desire associated with the martyrdom of Pelagius was necessarily sublimated over time to allow for his eventual canonization as a cult figure in orthodox Christianity. Hutcheson also comments on Pelagius in "Sodomitic Moor."

17. Jordan comments on the etymology of the adverb employed to modify the kind of touching the king purportedly did to Pelagius, *joculariter:* "It could mean something like 'humorously,' but that meaning hardly fits here. In Ovid, who may well be on Raguel's mind, the root verb, *joco,* is used as a metaphor for copulation. So *tangere joculariter* may mean at least 'to touch sexually' and perhaps even 'to fondle' in the quite sexual sense" (*Invention of Sodomy,* 12).

18. Again, Jordan's etymology is enlightening. "Effeminate" could signify, as in the general sense of the times, the relationship between "sexual self-indulgence and womanliness" or could refer to the Vulgate's "condemnation of the reign of Roboam, [in which] the 'effeminate' are those who commit 'all the abominations of the gentiles, which God destroyed before the face of the sons of Israel'" (ibid., 13).

19. Hutcheson points out, in his consideration of the place of the "sodomitic

Moor" in Reconquest narratives, that this binary was a common trope in European texts of the times and expressed, more than an anachronistic notion of heterosexuality versus homosexuality, a contrast between evil Muslims and good Christians ("Sodomitic Moor," 101). The Moor's sexuality was suspect because he embodied difference in relationship with the Christian, and therefore was "already suspect to the spontaneous conflation in medieval moralistic discourse of idolatry, sorcery, treachery, and sexual perversion" (ibid., 102).

20. As Judith Butler reminds us in *Bodies That Matter,* "the subject is constituted through the force of exclusion and abjection, one which produces a constitutive outside to the subject, an abjected outside, which is, after all, 'inside' the subject as its own founding repudiation" (3).

21. See also Burshatin's review of the critical literature on the figure of the Moor in premodern Spanish literature in "The Docile Image."

22. Trexler's chaps. 1 and 2 (*Sex and Conquest*) provide a similar view of the relationship between power and the figuring of sexuality in the peninsula, as he traces the historical evidence from same-sex rape of vanquished enemies in "antiquity" to early-modern public sexualized punishments.

23. For an explanation of the political and economic structure of the society represented in the poem, see Juan Ramón Resina, "Honor y las relaciones feudales."

24. I choose the epic poem instead of the historiography in order to understand these issues as they were represented in the popular forms of cultural production. Future research might fruitfully trace the tropes analyzed below into the peninsular historiographic tradition, above all, in the chronicles of Reconquest.

25. I am not interested in the Cid's historical persona in this study; therefore, my attention will be limited to the literary character as represented in the epic poem. For a study of the relationship between the poem's character and the historical figure, see Ramón Menéndez Pidal, *El Cid Campeador,* and Richard Fletcher, *The Quest for El Cid.*

26. See Boswell's *Christianity,* 29–30n55, for references from Greek classical literature.

27. Foucault gleans this information from Plato's *Protagoras* in order to emphasize the importance of timing in the love of boys, for "the razor that shaved it (first beard) must sever the ties of love" (*Use of Pleasure,* 199).

28. Boswell explains that this Jewish law was not universally adopted by the Romans, because of the early Christians' ambivalence toward Jewish laws; however, beards came into favor under the Roman emperor Hadrian. See *Christianity,* 102.

29. All textual references are taken from the modernized edition prepared by Francisco López Estrada (Anonymous, *Poema del Cid*). Most translations are from W. S. Merwin's verse translation (Anonymous, *The Poem of the Cid*). I occasionally offer a more precise translation of the epithets that refer to the beard. Traditional scholarship has tended to read these epic epithets as formal devices that completed the hemistiches of the verse, maintaining the syllabication of the *mester de juglaría*

(the verse form of the medieval troubadours). As my analysis proposes, these epithets also function as figures of speech whose refrain signifies important elements of the hero's character.

30. Carmen Benito-Vessels has noted how the wife of the Cid is more submissive than other women represented in the *Estoria de Espanna,* one of the most important and extensive historical chronicles of Spain's early history ("La mujer," 56).

31. For the critical history and his own opinion of the Cid's status as Alfonso's vassal in the poem, see Nicolás Marín Granada's "Señor y vasallo."

32. "¡Dios, sí que se muestra alegre/el Cid de barba florida/al decirle Álvar Fáñez/que ya pagó las mil misas" (930–931) [God, how he rejoices/he, bearded handsomely,/because Álvar Fáñez/had paid the thousand masses (64)]. I have chosen to translate the epithets more literally in my analysis than does the poet-translator W. S. Merwin, in order to underline the increasing hyperbole of the poem's original language.

33. See discussion of the beard in the Bible in Peloubet, *Peloubet's Bible Dictionary,* 77.

34. To this day there remain flattering colloquialisms like "Un hombre con toda la barba" (a man with a full beard), demonstrating the longevity of these cultural concepts.

35. For theoretical development of homosocial behavior, see Sedgwick's *Between Men.*

36. Benito-Vessels, "La mujer," 58–59.

37. "Nunca mostró las costumbres nin las cosas que pertenecien a mugeres" [She never displayed the customs or the things that pertained to women] (ibid., 58).

38. Since Joan Kelly-Gadol asked her famous question, "Did Women Have a Renaissance?" early-modern studies have increasingly focused on gender issues in keeping with the transition from a "Renaissance"-focused study of high culture to approaches that have "set aside the implicitly hierarchical agenda of 'Renaissance' in its traditional sense for a more prosaic, level mode of analysis that strives for greater cultural inclusiveness." For more discussion of the significance of the evolution and recent changes in the discipline, see Leah S. Marcus's "Renaissance and Early Modern Studies," from which the foregoing quote is taken, p. 43.

39. I am indebted to Carmen Benito-Vessels for reminding me of Dorothy Severin's reading of Calisto as a parody of Leriano, the courtly lover in Diego de San Pedro's classic Spanish sentimental romance, *Cárcel de Amor.* See Severin's *Tragicomedy and Novelistic Discourse in Celestina,* 26.

40. For an excellent explanation of Seneca's influence in *La Celestina,* see Louise Fothergill-Payne's *Seneca and Celestina;* for *voluptas,* see pages 47–48.

41. "O mundo, mundo . . . me pareces un laberinto de errores, un desierto espantable, una morada de fieras, juego de hombres que andan en coro, laguna llena de cieno, región llena de espinas, monte alto, campo pedregoso, prado lleno de serpientes, huerto florido y sin fruto, fuente de cuidados, río de lágrimas, mar de miserias" (338) [Oh world, world! . . . It is a labyrinth of errors, a frightful desert,

a den of wild beasts, a game in which men run in circles, a lake of mud, a thorny thicket, a dense forest, a stony field, a meadow full of serpents, a river of tears, a sea of miseries (Rojas, *The Celestina,* 159)].

42. For background information on Saint John of the Cross and a canonical critical reading of his poetry, see Dámaso Alonso's *La poesía de San Juan de la Cruz.*

43. Translations are from Ken Krabbenhoft, *Poems of St. John of the Cross.* The reader should note that the gender of the lover and of the poetic voice is not marked in this English translation, as it is in the Spanish original.

44. This English translation suggests that both the lover and the beloved are transformed, while in the original, because of the gender markings, it is the "feminine" soul that is transformed by the "masculine" divine agent.

45. Dombrowski's account is a summary of work done by Jurgen Moltmann and Gerda Lerner (76).

46. McKendrick, *Women and Society,* 16.

47. I refer to the series of oppositions outlined in Ian Maclean's *Renaissance Notion of Woman:* passive/active, matter/form, potency/act, imperfection/perfection, incompleteness/completion, deprivation/possession.

48. For a more recent study of the role played by women's bodies in early-modern Spain and Spanish America, see Georgina Dopico Black's *Perfect Wives, Other Women.*

49. Carrasco notes that in 1567 there was approximately one *familiar* for every thirty-four neighbors in the small villages and rural areas of Valencia (*Inquisición y represión sexual,* 14).

50. Inquisition trial records reflect the witnesses', and often the accused's, knowledge of the church's teachings on sodomy (ibid., 16–19). In addition, Carrasco suggests that the confessional dialogue often seemed to prefigure the trial confessions gained from the accused (ibid., 17). We should also take into account issues of peer pressure and church power over the witnesses when considering the attitudes of those giving testimony.

51. The first sodomite was burned by the Inquisition in 1572 (ibid., 45).

52. See Antonio Gramsci's *Selections from the Prison Notebooks,* 1921–1935.

53. Quoted in Carrasco (*Inquisición y represión sexual,* 41), from *Siete partidas,* Ley I y II, Tít. XXI, Setenta Partida.

54. Quoted in ibid., from *Novísima recopilación de las leyes de España,* Ley I, Tít. XXX, Lib. XII, facs. ed. of *Boletín oficial del estado,* Madrid, 1976, vol. 5: 427–428.

55. See Goldberg's introduction to *Reclaiming Sodom,* in which he reviews the scholarship on the English Renaissance by Alan Bray and on the North American colonies by Jonathan Katz.

56. Carrasco (*Inquisición y represión sexual,* 42–43) evaluates the formal conditions necessary for heresy during the period and concludes that it was an easy rhetorical move to assimilate sodomy into heresy, though this was never officially carried out by the church.

57. See Burshatin's study of the life of Eleno de Céspedes, a hermaphrodite from sixteenth-century Spain ("Written on the Body").

58. For a thorough treatment of Covarrubias's lexicography, see Calvo Pérez's *Sebastián de Covarrubias*. For Covarrubias's ideology, see especially pages 142–149.

59. For a fuller treatment of this topic, in which López Baralt discusses the influence of hermetic and neoplatonist philosophies in the development of the moral emblems, see "La cultura literaria de la imagen del Siglo de Oro" in *Icono y conquista*. Calvo Pérez offers the following definition of the emblematic genre: "Emblemática: insignias, taraceados, jeroglíficos, pegmas, etc., que representan algún concepto moral que debe ser comúnmente glosado con cierta estrofa de versos y un monte o lema motivador" (*Sebastián de Covarrubias,* 37).

60. Covarrubias Orozco, "Emblema 64," *Emblemas morales* (published 1610).

61. The reference is to the famous "bearded lady," Brígida del Río, whose portrait Fray Juan Sánchez Cotán painted. Her celebrity went beyond portraits. As Sherry Velasco notes, "regardless of the various ways in which Brígida del Río was interpreted by her contemporaries, according to early-modern documents these anomalies were marketable, as the 'barbuda de Peñaranda' received twelve *reales* for exhibiting her 'freakish' appearance in Valencia (Pérez Sánchez 68)" ("Marimachos, hombrunas, barbudas," 74). Velasco provides an insightful discussion of the *mujer varonil* (manly woman) motif in Cervantes.

62. Elizabeth Perry, in her history of gender in early-modern Spain, comments that effeminacy and transvestism were grounds for suspicion of homosexual sodomy (*Gender and Disorder,* 132). Cross-dressing, prohibited in Deuteronomy, chap. 22, inspired moralists to warn that "transvestism leads to lasciviousness" (133).

CHAPTER 2

1. As I discuss in Chapter 1, Jordan explains the process through which sodomy became an ecclesiastical trope of the Middle Ages and labels the trope an "artifact," defined as "any structure or changed appearance produced by processing" (*Webster's New World Dictionary,* 78).

2. Ibid.

3. With this prelude to the analysis that follows, I wish to accentuate the methodological challenge involved in my project: how to discuss the transculturation process without first positing the subjectivity that will become transformed. For, as we will see, the reconstruction of this subjectivity is taken from the same sources whose rhetoric fragmented the subject in the first place.

4. I appreciate Rolena Adorno's generosity in supplying me with a copy of Hanke's transcription of the questionnaire from his 1935 dissertation. Helen Rand Parish of Beverly, California, brought the document to Adorno's attention (personal communication, April 9, 2000).

5. Goldberg uses Richard Eden's early English translation (1533) of *Decades* to emphasize how the episode was mobilized in the early-modern European imagination ("Sodomy in the New World," 46).

6. Goldberg goes on to argue that this scene becomes a "mirror in which Europeans might find themselves" (46). For a similar argument about the noble savage figure, see Hayden White's *Tropics of Discourse*.

7. See Trexler (*Sex and Conquest*) for a discussion of how, in his Pan-American history, the berdache came into being as dependent and abject subjects in their own culture. I discuss this issue as it relates to the Andes below and in Chapter 3.

8. For analysis of the sodomy issue in other parts of the Americas, see Goldberg ("Sodomy in the New World"), Guerra (*Precolumbian Mind*), Gutiérrez ("Must We Deracinate Indians"), Kimball ("Aztec Homosexuality"), Poirier ("French Renaissance Travel Accounts"), Sigal (*From Moon Goddesses to Virgins*), and Trexler (ibid.).

9. Lewis Hanke's *La lucha por la justicia en la conquista de América* continues to be the definitive study of this issue. See also Margarita Zamora's summary in chap. 5 of *Language, Authority and Indigenous History*.

10. Miguel Molina Martínez provides a succinct overview of this history in "El concepto del indio" in *La leyenda negra* (83–112).

11. The other causes were based on a people's idolatry, to disseminate Christianity, and to protect the weak among the barbarians. See Hanke's summary, *La lucha*, 346–373.

12. "Solamente Oviedo, que presumió de escribir historia de lo que nunca vió, no cognosció, ni vido algunas déstas, las infamó de deste vicio nefando, diciendo que eran todos sodomitas, con tanta facilidad y temeridad como si dijera que la color dellas era un poco fusca o morena más que la de los de España" (*Historia de las Indias,* 231) [Only Oviedo, who was presumptuous enough to write history from what he never saw, never met or saw one of these, but he defamed them with this nefarious vice, saying that they were all sodomites, with such ease and recklessness as if he were saying their color was a bit dark or more brown than that of the Spaniards (231)].

13. "Pudo ser que por alguna causa, aquel o otros, si quizá los había, se dedicase a hacer oficios de mujeres y trujese de aquel vestido, no para el detestable fin, de la manera que refiere Hipocras y Galeno, que hacen algunas gentes cithia, los cuales, por andar mucho a caballo, incurren cierta enfermedad, y para sanar de ella, sángranse de ciertas venas, de donde finalmente les proviene a que ya no son hombres para mujeres, y cognosciendo en sí aquel defecto, luego mudan el hábito, y se dedican, ofrecen y ocupan en los oficios que hacen las mujeres, y no para otro mal efecto. Así pudo ser allí o en otras partes destas Indias donde aquéllos se hallasen, o por otras causas, según sus ritos y costumbres, y no para fin de aquellas vilezas" (ibid., 231–232) [It could be that for some reason, they or others (third gender), if there were some of these, they took on roles of women and adopted their dress, not for the detestable purpose (sodomy), but in the way that Hipocras and Galeno refer to it, like some of the Scythian peoples, who for riding a lot on horseback, de-

veloped a certain disease that they cured by bloodletting from certain veins which eventually left them as women, and understanding that defect, they then began to wear women's clothes and adopt women's roles, but not with any bad purposes. It could be for this reason in these or other parts of the Indies where they (third gender) are found, or for other reasons, according to their rituals and customs, and not for the purpose of that vileness" (231–232)].

14. Luis Alberto Sánchez, *Literatura peruana*, 72. For other favorable opinions, see Cieza de León, *Discovery and Conquest*, 27.

15. I cite from the Spanish editions of Cieza's *Crónica del Perú*, which was divided into three parts and published by the Pontificia Universidad Católica del Perú in three volumes. Translations from parts 1 and 2 are mine unless noted, in which case, they come from Harriet de Onís's English translation (*Incas of Pedro de Cieza de León*). The reader should be aware that the Onís translation, edited by Victor Wolfgang von Hagen, while useful, alters the original texts by interlacing chapters from the two parts and by omitting "repetitions," as the editor notes in his preface (ix). These omissions required that I translate several passages from the original.

16. For a thorough yet concise biography of Cieza and his relationship with the encomienda system in what is today Colombia, see the Cooks' introduction to their translation of part 3 of the *Crónica del Perú* (*Discovery and Conquest*). Cieza was awarded an encomienda for his services in the founding of Arma, but then lost his grant because of the changing political fortunes of his patron (ibid., 10–11). He departed Colombia for Peru in order to join the loyalist "reconquest" of Peru after the fall of the Pizarros.

17. Some have commented that this strategy was related to Cieza's practical need to receive patronage from the Crown through the support of la Gasca. Franklin Pease points out in his introduction to *La crónica del Perú* that there is some doubt about whether Cieza received his patronage from la Gasca during the writing of the first two parts of the *crónica* (xxix). Pease shares an interesting observation told to him by Enrique Carrión of the narrative's official denomination as "chrónica" or "coronista," the latter being the designation assigned to the third part of his *crónica*, but not the first. While some take the two words to be synonyms, *chrónica* comes from the Greek *khronos*, referring to time, while *coronista* derives from the Latin *corona* (crown). Cieza's use of "coronista" with the third part of his work, the part pertaining to the civil wars, which we know la Gasca asked him to chronicle for his government, suggests that his earlier writings, *La primera parte* and *La segunda parte*, were not realized in his official capacity as "cronista de Indias."

18. Franklin Pease links this use of the term *behetría* to medieval historiography, which in turn was derived from the ethnocentric Greek and Roman traditions (*Crónica del Perú*, xxxvi). The connotation is of free, but unorganized, populations.

19. Cook and Cook document his use of native informants, including *quipucamayocs* (keepers of the *quipu*), whom he interviewed in Cuzco (*Discovery and Conquest*, 9, 15).

20. Cook and Cook relate a comment made by Cieza concerning his boyhood encounter and his early fascination with the Andean Others and their riches: "I cannot stop thinking about those things, when I remember the opulent pieces that were seen in Seville, brought from Cajamarca, where the treasure that Atahualpa promised the Spanish was collected" (ibid., 6).

21. Peter Hulme's outstanding exploration of Columbus's discursive use of anthropophagy, and the explorer's coining of the term *cannibal* from the name of the Caribs, inhabitants of the Caribbean islands, illustrates the instability of the word. See especially chap. 1 of *Colonial Encounters.*

22. For a thorough treatment of the *mamaconas,* see Silverblatt's *Moon, Sun, and Witches,* 80–108 passim.

23. See José Rabasa's "Utopian Ethnography in Las Casas's *Apologética*" and his discussion of these tropes' utopian and critical elements in *Inventing America,* 173.

24. See Goldberg ("Sodomy in the New World"), Williams (*Spirit and the Flesh*), and Chapter 5 here.

25. See Pease's introduction, *Crónica del Perú,* xxiv–xxv.

26. Marshall Saville, in *Antiquities of Manabi, Ecuador,* surveys the archeological remains in the area represented in the myth, reporting that, indeed, there are large wells measuring six feet in diameter and ten feet in depth cut into the solid rock surface of the earth (81–82). He also records the presence of large, symmetrically shaped "tombs" cut into the rock, reaching depths of ten to twelve feet (ibid., 83–84).

27. *Huacas* were sacred sites in Andean religious practice, often the places of ritual ceremonies. Frank Salomon defines *huaca* in his introduction to the Huarochirí manuscript as "any material thing that manifested the superhuman: a mountain peak, a spring, a union of streams, a rock outcrop, an ancient ruin, a twinned cob of maize, a tree split by lightning. Even people could be *huacas*" (*Huarochirí Manuscript,* 17).

28. See Mannheim, *Language of the Inca,* 140.

29. See Arboleda ("Representacionces artísticas"), Harrison ("'True' Confessions"), and Trexler (*Sex and Conquest*).

30. Fossa Falco, "Leyendo hoy a Cieza de León," 34.

31. Bertonio recruited indigenous informants from the Juli area and trained them in Christian doctrine and in writing in Aymara (*Vocabulario,* xxxi). From these writings the linguist selected words to be defined in his dictionary. Xavier Albó has expressed the value of Bertonio's dictionary as a source of ethnographic information: "His acuity and fidelity as an observer, researcher, and systemizer provides us an important archive of facts of Aymara life and culture from his times" (*Vocabulario,* liv).

32. This comment leads us to understand that there was both a profane and a sacred use of sodomy in the Lake Titicaca region. Evidently, shepherds were known to indulge in same-sex erotics.

33. Here I wish to emphasize my use of "third" as metonymic, as I discuss in the Introduction and in my dissertation. I evidently did not make this theoretical point clear enough, given Trexler's questioning of my equating eunuchs with what he calls "berdache" ("Gender Subordination," n39). See Ringrose ("Living in the Shadows") for a discussion of eunuchs in Byzantium as third gender.

34. For the idolatry campaigns carried out in the colonial Andes, see Griffiths (*Cross and the Serpent*) and Mills (*Idolatry and Its Enemies*). Duviols's *La destrucción de las religiones andinas* continues to be an authoritative account of the campaigns, as well.

35. For more on ecclesiastical literature's treatment of sodomy in the Andes, see Harrison's "'True' Confessions." I dedicate part of Chapter 4 to this topic, as well.

36. I feel compelled to repeat clearly that my intention is not to romanticize in any way historical sacrificial or ritual sexual practices. Trexler's critique of my dissertation explicitly misrepresents both my intentions and some aspects of my argument. His ad hominem linkage of my argument with NAMBLA is fundamentally unfounded and offensive, given the insinuation. In reference to this section of my dissertation, in which I rehearse alternative interpretations of Domingo de Santo Tomás's report of temple sodomy, and evidently in reference to Roscoe's *Changing Ones,* Trexler's note 44 reads, "In both these utterances, the reader recognizes the language not of the scholar of juvenile development, but, *inter alia,* of NAMBLA, the North American Man/Boy Love Association" ("Gender Subordination," 96).

37. See Benson and Cook's collection of essays on ritual sacrifice in the Andes, *Ritual Sacrifice.*

38. For an exploration of young male participants' roles and attitudes in ritual same-sex fellatio in the highlands of New Guinea, see Gilbert Herdt's *Guardians of the Flutes.* Roscoe discusses Mohave children's paths to berdache status, noting that "Mohaves credited a combination of predestination, occupational preferences, social influences, and, above all, dreams" ("How to Become a Berdache," 365). Williams reports that dreams and visions were common methods of self-identification among berdache of many North American native ethnicities, including the Papagos, Yumas, Yaqui, Yokuts, Lakota, and Omaha (*Spirit and the Flesh,* 25–30).

39. In *Sex and Conquest,* Trexler recognizes this passage from Blas Valera, a mestizo Jesuit writing in the Andes at the end of the sixteenth century, but still concludes that the temple sodomites were "sexual subordinates" who served to signify their lords' higher status (117). In his critique of my dissertation, "Gender Subordination," Trexler analyzes this passage at greater length, arguing that I misunderstood the source. I have clarified my argument here.

40. Trexler insists that I uncritically grouped the eunuch priests with what he understands to be berdache subjects ("Gender Subordination," 78). I stand behind my argument here that this reference by Blas Valera provides another fragment of knowledge for understanding Andean and, in this case, specifically Inca attitudes toward gender liminality. This source links the participation of eunuch priests as third-gender subjects, as defined above, to the Incas' power structure by providing

284   *Notes to Pages 110–116*

ethnographic information on the priests' "religious" roles in the culture, including the prayers offered on behalf of the Incas.

41. I am indebted to Regina Harrison for suggesting this possibility to me.

42. Godenzzi and Vengoa, *Runasimimanta Yuyaychakusun*, 116.

43. Silverblatt analyzes this story in greater detail, highlighting how the sacrificed girl's tomb became an important *huaca* in her region. The younger brothers who became her priests seemed to channel her voice from beyond (*Moon, Sun, and Witches*, 99), thus speaking like women. This raises the question of whether the transgendered priests described here were always associated with female-identified *huacas*.

CHAPTER 3

1. *Guacos* are ceramic objects often found in the ceremonial burial grounds of the Andes, not to be confused with *huacas*, which are the sacred superhuman identities and shrines discussed below. The *guaco* to which I refer is displayed in the Rafael Larco Herrera Museum's Sala Erótica, display case number four. Golte recognizes that the braids in Moche iconography emphasize femininity (*Iconos y narraciones*, 53). The Larco Hoyle collection also has a vessel in the shape of a human hermaphrodite from the Virú culture.

2. See Bolaños (*Barbarie y canibalismo*), Hulme (*Colonial Encounters*), Montrose ("Work of Gender").

3. My goal is to provide an alternative version of the gender culture that became transculturated as the Spanish chroniclers began their interpretations and "inventions" of the Andes. While I believe it is impossible to recover an "authentic," "trustworthy" version of pre-Columbian reality, given the biased nature of our literary sources and the fragmentary quality of our anthropological and archeological records, we must start at least with a strategically essentialized and reconstructed notion of indigenous gender and sexuality in order to understand the processes of transculturation that I describe in the rest of this book. Here I refer to Diana Fuss's notion of "nominal essence," discussed in the Introduction.

4. The physical environment of the north coast was an important determinant in the region's cultural development and provides for many explanations of the mythological tradition represented by Moche iconography. While the Moche peoples depended for their sustenance primarily on the Pacific Ocean, in which they fished from reed and balsa boats, the valleys created from the highland rivers' drainage proved to be important oases in the coastal desert plain that runs the length of the Peruvian coast. The twelve valleys between the Piura and the Huarmey rivers became varied social centers interconnected through trade in what Rostworowski has called a "horizontal economy" (Bawden, *The Moche*, 47).

5. The great forces of nature that inspired the awe of the Moche and shaped their metaphysical relationships ranged from the cyclical influences of the Niño

ocean current in the Pacific to the powerful earthquakes that periodically and un-
expectedly shook the highlands. The integration of the natural world in Moche
culture is evidenced by the quantity and quality of artistic representations of animals, topography, and humans. The presence of the mountains and the sea in the
rituals depicted on Moche ceramics leads us to understand the great importance of
the natural world in Moche cosmology.

6. The two archeologists in charge of excavations in San José de Moro,
Jequetepeque, Christopher Donnan and Luis Jaime Castillo Butters, have commented that their research is confirming these coincidences ("Excavaciones de
tumbas," 415).

7. The following is a summary of Gero's research presented at the symposium "Recovering Gender in Pre-Hispanic America," Dumbarton Oaks, Washington, D.C., October 12–13, 1996. Gero's presentation was titled "Field Knots and
Ceramic Beaus: Recovering Gender in the Peruvian Early Intermediate Period."

8. Cordy-Collins hypothesizes that trade with the Maya may have introduced
the bloodletting Moon cult to the Moche ("Blood and the Moon Priestesses," 47).

9. As Cordy-Collins notes, the Maya men sometimes cross-dressed for bloodletting ceremonies. For more on the Maya Moon goddess and transvestism, see
Sigal's *From Moon Goddesses to Virgins.*

10. For research on the place of women in spheres of power in the Moche culture and region, see Donnan and Castillo ("Excavaciones de tumbas") and Gero
("Field Knots and Ceramic Beaus"). For a comprehensive review of the feminist-
inspired study of gender in archeology, see Conkey and Gero's "Programme to
Practice."

11. For a brief review of the literature on this subject, see Manuel Arboleda,
"Representaciones artísticas." Trexler reviews this topic as well, analyzing Larco
Hoyle's *Checan,* 111–114.

12. All quoted passages are taken from Frank Salomon and George L. Urioste's
translation and critical edition of *Huarochirí Manuscript.*

13. See Salomon's introduction, especially pages 24–28, for a summary of research conducted by Antonio Acosta, Karen Spalding, Pierre Duviols, and Gerald Taylor on Ávila's career and possible motive for compiling the myths in the
manuscript.

14. Frank Salomon suggests that the note in the manuscript's margin, "from the
hand and pen of Thomas" (24) and the poor Spanish grammar of the transcriber
are evidence that he was a village scribe or other minor native functionary.

15. For an excellent history of the term *ladino* and the subject position ladinos
occupied in the colonial Americas, see Adorno, "Images of Indios Ladinos."

16. For a nuanced analysis of the Quechua discourse employed, see the translation notes to the preface in *Huarochirí Manuscript* (41–42).

17. We have the names of the four male *quipucamayocs* from the 1542 document
known as the "Chronicle of the *Khipukamayuqs*" (Urton, *History of a Myth,* 43). Exclusively male informants' names are also included in Viceroy Francisco de Toledo's

visita reports. Harrison, however, has shown that Andean women did use *quipus* to help them remember the sins they were to confess in Catholic confession ("Cultural Translations in the Andes"). Gary Urton (*Signs of the Inca Khipu*) remarks that the construction of the *quipu* may be marked by gender; women seem to spin the thread one way and men in the other direction (66), which would suggest that there may have been female *quipucamayocs*, though they were not officially interviewed and recorded by the Spaniards.

18. For a concise history of European body paradigms from the classical age through the Renaissance and beyond, see Anthony Synnott's *The Body Social*, especially chap. 1.

19. If we consider the Trickster to be a residual representation of a prior masculine deity, for example, Con, the masculine force that preceded the pre-Incan deity Pachacamac in the region, then we see that the female forces were not merely protected by the current primary male *huaca*, Pachacamac, but that they acted as agents in the reciprocity-building process of Andean culture. Pachacamac is absent from the narrative except as father to Urpay Huachac's two daughters.

20. See Salomon's note 106, page 56, for a clarification of this term in the context of the story. Salomon suggests that the narrator used the word *adultery* in order to communicate the notion of a sexual transgression, though not necessarily that of unfaithfulness to one's spouse.

21. For theory on homosociality and its links to patriarchal gender and sexual relations, see Sedgwick's *Between Men*.

22. Platt translates the term based on its etymology and uses in context as "helper and helped united to form a unique category," while he reports that the Macha gloss the word as "pair" or "man-and-woman" ("Mirrors and Maize," 245).

23. This pattern is repeated later in the manuscript (chap. 30) in the story of two other *huacas*, the male Anchi Cara and the female Huayllama. In this concise story, characterized by Salomon as an allegory of "a rivalry over a high lake coveted by the Allauca of Checa and by Surco" (134n734), the female *huaca* initially holds back water from the male *huaca*, but they end up "sinning together" and uniting in stone forever (134). Again, feminine autonomy is displayed, negotiation ensues, and complementary union is achieved.

24. Isbell, *To Defend Ourselves*, 55.

25. Harrison explains that the difference between good and bad *supay* was indicated by qualifying adjectives *alli* or *mana alli*. She goes on to explain the semantic transculturation that the term had suffered by the time González Holguín's dictionary of 1608 rendered the notion of demon as strictly *supay*, and the word for "angel" entered into the Quechua language as the signifier for what once was understood as "good *supay*" (*Signs, Songs and Memory*, 47–48). Silverblatt also explains how the term became resemanticized in colonial discourse to signify malevolence, thereby losing its pre-Hispanic semantic complexity (*Moon, Sun, and Witches*, 177–178).

26. Salomon ("Nightmare Victory," 64n165) explains the ritual significance of

quishuar wood, which was used by the Andeans to construct temples, such as to the Inca Quishuar Cancha at Cuzco.

27. Salomon explains that "the *huacas'* main duty was to impersonate the great *huacas* in festivals and reenact their myths" (ibid., 18).

28. Salomon explains: "The premise is that different human groups receive their life-energy and specific powers from different *huacas*" (ibid., 77).

29. For an excellent overview of the androgyne in world mythology, see Jean Libis's *El mito del andrógino*. The first part explicates the relationship between the androgyne and the divine in various cultures and times (23–72).

30. Frank Salomon has responded to Isbell's argument in "'Conjunto de nacimiento' y 'Línea de esperma' en el manuscrito quechua de Huarochirí (ca. 1608)," cautioning that her interpretation of the *yuriy* and the *yumay* may be too overreaching. Salomon emphasizes the political use of these terms in the context of ethnic divisions of the Yauyo and the Yunca. He concludes by reminding the reader that the manuscript represents a "colonial synthesis" of these conflicts that privileges the masculine versions of the myths ("'Conjunto de nacimiento,'" 321–322). His understanding of the role the indigenous informants and narrators, most certainly all men, play in the composition confirms the idea discussed here that the dominant narratives privileged the masculine "líneas de esperma" (lineages of sperm) while the feminine equivalents were suppressed.

31. This definition of the Andean cultural concept *tinkuy* is based on Tristan Platt, "Mirrors and Maize." For an explanation of the concept in Aymara culture, which is similar, see Bouysse-Cassagne and Harris, "*Pacha.*"

32. The manuscript was found, along with the Huarochirí manuscript and other important documents related to Spanish observation of native traditions, in Ávila's papers (Duviols, "Estudio y comentario," 15).

33. All references are from Duviols and Itier, *Relación de antigüedades.*

34. I do not mean to insinuate that Santacruz Pachacuti identified with or even practiced same-sex sexuality. By occupying the *chaupi* as a ladino writing subject, he was culturally queer vis-à-vis the majority of his contemporaries, much like the Huarochirí narrator. As I explain in the Introduction, I am using the word *queer* as a way of figuring difference in the processes of transculturation.

35. In my earlier explication of this myth ("Toward an Andean Theory") I interpreted the siblings as both male, based on the Urbano-Sánchez transcription of the manuscript, which reads, "Y el dicho Manco Capac como su hermano tardó tanto embió a su hermano para que lo llamase" (185). I have consulted the facsimile edition prepared by Duviols and Itier, and the original writing is smudged and nearly impossible to decipher. Later in the story, however, both transcriptions represent the siblings as brother and sister. Therefore, I have revised my interpretation to assume that the second sibling is a sister.

36. I take this interpretation of *ojeado* from Ana Sánchez's edition of the *relación*. Her explanation is based on the Andean folk belief in the *mal de ojo* (evil eye). See Santa Cruz Pachacuti Yamqui, *Relación de antigüedades,* 185n28.

37. The ambiguity about the number of siblings and their gender can be observed in the Spanish version's use of a singular direct object pronoun, "lo" while the narrator speaks of "brother and sister."

38. I am indebted to Henrique Urbano for calling my attention to this passage.

39. In Chapter 4 I analyze in greater detail the ideological context in which Pedro Sarmiento de Gamboa wrote *Historia índica* (1572), a history of the Andean region drafted for the colonial viceroy, Francisco de Toledo. There is no clear evidence that Santacruz Pachacuti had access to this history, but the versions of the foundational myth are strikingly similar.

40. Santacruz Pachacuti identifies the *otorongo* (jaguar) as the deity of the hermaphrodites, as I discuss below.

41. The González Holguín Quechua-Spanish dictionary (1608) further confirms the notion of "pairing" in the Quechua term *tinquichi:* "*Tinquini:* Hermanar dos o muchas cosas o parerlas" (vol. 1, 343) [to bring together two or many things or to pair them].

42. At this point, a reader unfamiliar with the Andes might ask how important these reflections of symmetry could really be to a culture? For the highlanders, it seems that it is central to their entire world view. A brief look at the textile tradition, and stone carving as well, reveals an incredible attention to symmetrical design, especially to geometrical doublings. The remarkable samples of textiles that have survived the ravages of time, for example, from the time of the confluence of the Nazca and the Huari cultures, show the importance of reflected images. The weaving technique named "Sprang" is characterized by the mirror effect, in which the image in the upper half of the piece is the exact reflection of the lower half. The two sides come together in a central dividing line, just as the cosmic divisions are separated by *kay pacha* and the ecological zones by *chawpirana* (Iriarte, "Textilería andina"). For other studies of Andean textiles and their cultural significance, see Cereceda ("Semiology of Andean Textiles") and Paul (*Paracas Ritual Attire*). Cereceda's study of the dual division of the *talega* bags and their center dividing space is suggestive of the kinds of symbolic symmetry I am discussing here ("Semiology of Andean Textiles," 155–156).

43. Here I will briefly note the ideological difference between the two dictionaries. Santo Tomás's 1560 *Lexicon* was written by a Dominican sympathizer with the indigenous population in the early years of the Conquest; González Holguín's *Vocabulario,* compiled forty-eight years later, was written by a Jesuit missionary implicated in the process of efficient evangelization and colonization. The first carries no moral judgment in its definition, while the second glosses the Quechua with a moralizing rhetoric, equating same-sex praxis with demonical idolatry and sin. González Holguín's first gloss, "servirse un hombre de otro," seems to echo the Spanish conception of same-sex sexuality in which the relationship is a prostitution of the passive. Of course, another possible reading of these entries would be that the same-sex praxis of women posed less of a threat to patriarchal mascu-

linity than did the male same-sex activity implied by González Holguín's entry, thus Santo Tomás's nonjudgmental entry.

44. Considering such cultural practices in this way does not imply a romanticization of the subjects performing ritual duties. It is clear that ritual sexuality implies symbolic posturing of fundamentally unequal relationships as it mirrors the mythical relationships between deities and superhuman subjects, as we saw in Santacruz Pachacuti's rendering of the Ayar siblings' foundational journey.

45. Duviols argues that Guaman Poma was influenced by the Spanish Corpus Christi processions and linked the Tarasca figure, represented by a female and a dragonlike being, to produce the image he presents of Mama Huaco ("De la Tarasca a Mama Huaco").

46. Duviols recognizes the connection between this scene of corn planting and the original conquest and settlement of the Cuzco valley by the Incas (ibid., 338), as does Brian Bauer, who has also written on the relationship between conquest and agriculture in these myths and rituals ("Legitimization of the State," 330–333). Bauer emphasizes the singing of *haylli*, "songs of triumph," during this ceremony, as seen in Guaman Poma's comments (ibid., 328).

47. Silverblatt follows her observation of gender duality in the characterization of Mamayutas with an example of an elderly woman serving as the priestess who guarded the offerings that women brought to the deity (*Moon, Sun, and Witches,* 35). An alternative reading of the figure in the Guaman Poma drawing would be that she is simply an old woman, who would have been "sterile" because of her advanced age, and therefore "masculinized." This explanation, however, would not account for the transgendering reported in the ethnography, nor would it fully explain the "manly" depictions of Mama Huaco as a warrior woman, discussed below.

48. "*Memillaatha o memillachatha:* disfrazar a uno en hábito de muchacha, commo si fuesen en danzas o máscaras" [to masquerade in the dress of a girl, as if he were in a dance or wearing masks] (*Vocabulario,* 221).

49. Jan Szeminski has translated the dance's name, "huarmi auca," in this passage from the Quechua as either "mujer guerrera" [warrior woman] or "enemigo de mujeres" [women's enemy] (vol. 3, 198). His translation makes it seem that the men in this ritual dance were paying homage to women warriors, an image that appears in other chronicles, or, as in the second gloss, the transgendered men were somehow women's enemies. Although there are reports of tension between women and third-gender subjectivities in the historiography, I believe the second gloss to be nonsensical in the context of this ritual dance, given that, in both the text and the accompanying drawing, the cross-dressed men are dancing hand-in-hand with women. Trexler builds his case for native Andean women's scorn for the third-gender subjectivity on one comment in Montesinos's *Memorias antiguas,* whose goal it was to show how the Incas entered into moral decline because of the implicitly effeminate influence of lowland invaders (*Sex and Conquest,* 151).

50. In an earlier analysis of this drawing of the *huarmi auca* dance ("Toward an

Andean Theory"), I suggested that the dance's name, "*huarmi auca,*" could be related to Ayar Auca and represent third-gender subjectivity related to Andesuyo, agriculture, and shamanistic magic. After reading Duviols's comments, however, I tend to agree with his explanation of the dance's significance. Whether the dancing, cross-dressed men were third-gender subjects related to Ayar Auca, or the ceremony is a vestige from celebrations of warrior women, the suggestive connection between myth, ritual, magic, and gender liminality deserves more research.

51. For a summary of Lehmann Nitsche's analysis, see Duviols's introductory study to his edition of the *Relación,* especially pages 103–106. Duviols disregards the Viracocha–as–"cosmic egg" theory on the basis of his argument that the oval in the drawing comes from Christian architecture's church façades. However, such a refutation does not address the presence of the egg as progenitor in the other Andean myths Lehmann Nitsche identified. I do not believe that one interpretation excludes the other, for Santacruz Pachacuti's text and drawings are hybrid compositions, influenced by both Christian and native Andean traditions.

52. Henrique Urbano, in his structuralist study of Andean mythology (*Wiracocha*), identifies three principal cycles of myths that survived transcription into the colonial historiography of the southern Andes. In each of the cycles, which he designates Viracocha, Ayar, and Chanca, there are corresponding sociopolitical functions as well as heroes that personify those functions, including the priestly ritual function and the agricultural and magic-curative function (*Wiracocha,* lvii–lix). In the Viracocha cycle, Urbano finds the hero Tocapo's activities to be related to the production of textiles by weaving (ibid., lviii). Although almost all Andeans at some point in their lives worked in some part of the textile-producing process, we know that certain fabrics were destined for ritual use, and these special fabrics were produced under highly regulated conditions in exclusively female and third-gender spaces, the *acllawasi,* where the *acllas* or *mamaconas* lived in seclusion (Silverblatt, *Moon, Sun, and Witches,* 82). In the Ayar cycle, the ritual function was symbolized by the younger brother known as Ayar Ucho, described above as the Inca "sodomized" by a *huaca* in the foundational story (*Wiracocha,* lviii). For the Chancas, this purpose was fulfilled by Yanavilca and Teclovilca, who expressed their functions through ritual use of colors associated with the sun and moon (ibid.). In the Viracocha sequence, Imaymana displays knowledge of the specific curative qualities of different plants (ibid., lix). In the Ayar cycle, Ayar Auca serves a magical-agricultural function in which his role is that of "lord and protector of the agricultural fields." Finally, in the Chanca cycle, it is Malma and Irapa who perform the agricultural and curative function, "with markedly feminine activities" (ibid.).

CHAPTER 4

1. Butler clarifies her theory of performativity and the constitution of gendered subjects in *Bodies That Matter:* "performativity must be understood not as a

singular or deliberate 'act,' but, rather, as the reiterative and citational practice by which discourse produces the effects that it names" (2).

2. See Stern, *Peru's Indian Peoples,* 72–73, and Matienzo, *Gobierno del Perú.*

3. See Gálvez Peña's discussion of this change and his comment that the censure began in 1570 ("Prólogo," xxvii, xli–xlvii).

4. See Stern, *Peru's Indian Peoples,* 27–50.

5. See James Lockhart's *Spanish Peru 1532–1560,* especially chap. 2, for more information on the social structure of the encomiendas. Lockhart defines "encomienda" as "a royal grant, in reward for meritorious service at arms, of the right to enjoy the tributes of Indians within a certain boundary, with the duty of protecting them and seeing to their religious welfare. An *encomienda* was not a grant of land" (9).

6. Stern has argued convincingly that the weakness of this early system of alliances was that "the colonial economy continued to depend for goods and labor almost wholly upon an Andean social system, managed and controlled by Andean social actors, relationships and traditions" (*Peru's Indian Peoples,* 40).

7. The Inquisition was forbidden by the Spanish Crown to be applied to the indigenous peoples, "on the grounds of their simplicity and poor understanding" (Griffiths, *Cross and the Serpent,* 31).

8. See Duviols, "La destrucción de las religiones andinas," xxviii.

9. *Sumario del concilio de 1567,* 21.

10. For another study of the impact colonization had on gender relations in the Andes, with a focus on seventeenth-century Lima, see Maria Emma Mannarelli's *Pecados públicos,* especially chap. 1. Ana Sánchez has compiled a selection of the idolatry trials carried out in seventeenth-century Chancay (see *Amancebados).* Two of the Andean ritualists prosecuted were women.

11. Toledo instituted broad reforms in the crisis-stricken colony, implementing many of the reformist ideas first proposed by Matienzo. Stern has summarized Toledo's viceroyalty's accomplishments as follows: "During his twelve years of rule (1569–1581), Toledo's government conducted oral inquiries on Inca tyranny which supported the morality of Spanish conquest; invaded the neo-Inca kingdom and publicly executed its militant ruler, Tupac Amaru; undertook a massive inspection of the entire viceroyalty; 'reduced' the natives into Hispanic style settlements under the control of Spanish *corregidores* and Indian functionaries; set up a system of tribute and rotating forced labor, the colonial *mita;* organized a prosperous mining economy fueled by the *mita* labor system; tied the colonial elite's economic well-being to the institutions of a revitalized state; and left behind a huge corpus of legislation to govern the politics and economics of the reorganized regime" (*Peru's Indian Peoples,* 76).

12. Adorno discusses this reading strategy in "Discurso jurídico," in which she uses the examples of Felipe Guaman Poma de Ayala and Álvar Núñez Cabeza de Vaca as writers of both scriptural forms.

13. For the history of the *Relaciones geográficas de Indias* and their antecedents, see Marcos Jiménez de la Espada's "Antecedentes" (5–117).

14. These texts have been published in Toledo, "Informaciones acerca del señorio y gobierno de los Incas."

15. See Foucault's *History of Sexuality,* 92–95.

16. Harrison's analysis is based on grammarian Antonio G. Cusihuamán's *Gramática quechua.*

17. To take the erotic appeal into account is to recognize that the same-sex act of sodomy was not exclusively a power relationship based on subjugation of a weaker partner.

18. Greenberg, *Construction of Homosexuality,* 183–185. This book offers examples of how anthropology has consistently misread the ethnography on third gender in Native North American tribes. Greenberg calls for anthropologists to reconsider third-gender relationships with kinship groups in the same way they analyze structured patterns in indigenous heterosexual relationships. As he points out, third genders were expected to follow the same social taboos relating to kinship and mating; for example, they could not commit incest with anyone in their kinship group if that tribe or sodality practiced exogamy. Furthermore, ridicule must be interpreted within the context of joking relationships, and anthropologists must take care in distinguishing between attitudinal bias of the ethnographers and misunderstandings of offhand remarks.

19. Victoria Reifler Bricker has studied the use of humor in highland Chiapas, noting the participation of "female impersonators" and "homosexuals" in ritual occasions (*Ritual Humor,* 185–186).

20. Charles Briggs's study of the Mexicano (of the southwestern United States) oral tradition considers oral narrative, such as these testimonies, as performances in the sense of repeated texts that "embed textual elements in an ongoing interaction" (*Competence in Performance,* 4). Briggs emphasizes the importance of the context in the speakers' structure of oral narrative and elaborates that "the study of contextualization reveals the status of interpretation as an emergent, interpersonal activity that relies on such features not solely for patterning form and content, but also for structuring the process for negotiating a shared frame of reference" (ibid., 15).

21. Walter Williams (*Spirit and the Flesh*), working with contemporary North American Indians, has shown how the "Two-Spirit People" (third gender) and their communities have guarded their special identity from outsiders for fear of persecution.

22. Harrison cites these passages from Duviols and Guaman Poma in "Pérez Bocanegra's *Ritual formulario,*" 274.

23. It should also be noted that Toledo was responsible for at least one public execution of a prominent colonial figure charged with committing sodomy. Ironically, the accused was the very same interpreter who translated the *visita* testimonies, Jiménez.

24. Rostworowski, "Algunos comentarios," 119.

25. The mention of female-to-male cross-dressing raises an interesting question: Were there women who cross-dressed, and, if there were, why? While this study has focused on the "male" third gender, it is worth noting the existence, as mentioned in Chapter 2, of some evidence that women took on roles that were considered men's and that some early mythology seems to create a space for the "*marimacho*," or masculinized female. We will see below, in the case of Sarmiento's representation of Inca mythology, the ambiguous figure of Mama Huaco, gendered as a *marimacho*-like subject.

26. The linguistic impediment to evangelization will be discussed below in the context of the translations in the *Doctrina christiana*. Further evidence of this challenge has been explored in William P. Mitchell and Barbara H. Jaye's study of the use of pictographs in the representation of the catechism's lessons in the Andes ("Pictographs in the Andes"). Although there is no evidence of a colonial use of this technology in the Andes, pictographic representation of the Christian message was widespread in the nineteenth and twentieth centuries throughout the region.

27. Dominican friar Domingo Santo Tomás included a bilingual Quechua-Spanish sermon, "Plática para todos los indios," in his *Grammatica o arte de la Lengua general de los indios de los reynos del Peru* (1560).

28. This requirement came out of the Laws of Burgos, passed in 1512 as the result of intense debate initiated by Montesinos's sermons, and called for justice in the American encomienda system. See Hanke, *La lucha,* 23–24.

29. As Durán reminds us in the thorough introduction to his Spanish edition of the texts, *Monumenta catechetica hispanoamericana* (340), these documents were the definitive evangelical tools used during the entire colonial and half of the republican periods, until 1899. The third Council of Lima was the direct result of legislation passed at the Council of Trent (1561–1563), which required periodic church councils to review church regulations related to discipline, faith, and customs (Durán, *El catequismo,* 65). Along with this proclamation from the metropolis came another from the Spanish Crown; indeed, the reforms of Trent depended on the participation of the king of Spain and other royal houses of Europe (ibid., 67). In 1568, Felipe II convoked the Junta Magna de Indias to reorganize the civil and ecclesiastical government of the colonies. From the Junta, in which Francisco de Toledo participated, came the order to hold the church council in Lima. Although the third Council of Lima was convened in 1572 after the General Visita had begun, it was postponed until 1582, when Archbishop Mogrovejo inaugurated it (ibid., 71).

30. Barnes ("Catechisms and Confesionarios"), Durán (*El catequismo*), Harrison ("Confesando el pecado en los Andes"; "The Language and Rhetoric of Conversion"; "The Theory of Concupiscence"), Mannheim (*Language of the Inca*), and Vargas Ugarte (*Historia de la iglesia*) discuss the translations in the *Doctrina christiana*.

31. According to the *Declaración* that accompanies the Quechua version of the *Doctrina christiana,* the translators were Juan Balboa, first Creole graduate of the Universidad de San Marcos in Lima and professor of Quechua; Alonso Martínez, a Cuzco canon lawyer and speaker of Quechua; and Bartolomé de Santiago, Jesuit

mestizo born in Arequipa between 1548 and 1549. Santiago lived in Cuzco from the time he became a Jesuit, in 1574, accompanied by Blas Valera, and was a confessor and preacher to the Indians. Francisco Carrasco, a mestizo born in Cuzco, was *párroco de indios* (priest of an Indian parish) in his native city (Durán, *El catequismo*, 256–259). Of the six censors and editors, Blas Valera, also a mestizo and Quechua speaker, is named by Durán and seems to have been in charge of the Aymara translation, as well. From this list of contributors, three of whom were mestizos, we can appreciate the knowledge of indigenous culture they represented. Who better to write the guides to evangelization?

32. Dean devotes the rest of her book to the unique ways the Inca descendants, and the non-Incas as well, appropriated Spanish triumphal signs and preserved their own cultural signs in the evolving pageantry of Corpus Christi.

33. Don Juan de Ribera's prologue to the 1599 edition of the text, from which I take the selections analyzed below, provides this biographical information (Ayala, *Catecismo*, 2).

34. For official language-policies in the conversion of the Andeans, see Harrison's "Language and Rhetoric of Conversion." Harrison shows how Amerindian language dictionaries responded to the need to evangelize and impose a language hegemony in the Andes. Her study also highlights the resistance implicit in some of the Quechua-language entries in the dictionaries.

35. Although we should note that the *quipu*, woven tapestries, *keros* (painted ceremonial vases), and ceramics with iconography are increasingly being considered as forms of "writing" systems in the pre-Hispanic Andes. See, among others, Boone and Urton, *Signs of the Inca Khipu*.

36. Harrison has observed, however, that in the Andes some confessors continued to ask detailed questions, as is the case of Pérez Bocanegra's 1631 confession manual (143–144). One might speculate that, in his case, given that he wrote his monumental confession manual and catechism in the multiple languages of his somewhat remote parish, being on the periphery gave him license to delve deeper into his parishioners' sex lives. As I argue here, the manuals dedicated to the conversion of cultural Others tend to be more explicit than standard peninsular versions.

37. For examples of sodomy reported by these chroniclers, see Guerra's *Pre-Columbian Mind*. Trexler's *Sex and Conquest* also discusses some chroniclers' reports of sodomy among the Caribs and Arawaks (65).

38. Ward Stavig's *Amor y violencia sexual* places too much faith in the Inca Garcilaso's insistence that the Incas punished sodomy in Tawantinsuyu (31). I reserve comment on Inca Garcilaso until Chapter 5.

39. See also Harrison's comparison of Polo de Ondegardo's list of Andean sins with a list obtained in the seventeenth-century's extirpation campaigns ("'True' Confessions," 10–11). Although further removed from the Toledo era, this document indicates that the indigenous concept of "sin" did not include sexual transgressions.

40. For a history of the indigenous resistance to the extirpation-of-idolatrous practices, see Mills's *Idolatry and Its Enemies.*

41. For more development of Guaman Poma's relationship with colonial sermons, see Adorno's *Guaman Poma.* We should remember, of course, that Guaman Poma was not a "typical" Andean penitent, for he was literate and a Christian convert, a ladino. Much of his information on the religious practices and other elements of Andean and Inca culture came from the experience he had as an assistant to Albornoz, whom he praises in his chronicle as a good extirpator of idolatries.

42. See Silverblatt's *Moon, Sun, Witches,* 138–147, for a summary of Guaman Poma's critique of colonial officials', including priests', abuse of women.

43. Harrison has studied how the pastoral documents treated this delicate subject ("'True' Confessions," 16–18).

44. See ibid.; "Confesando el pecado"; "Cultural Translation"; "Language and Rhetoric of Conversion"; and "Theory of Concupiscence."

45. See Mannheim (*Language of the Inca*), who has shown this to be the case in his study of colonial Quechua.

46. For example, in chap. 30 of the *Huarochirí Manuscript,* when two *huacas* "sinned together," in Quechua the term used is "*huchallicorcancu.*" Salomon comments in his note on the translation that this is the narrator's use of a "shame-oriented colonial term" (134n741).

47. Harrison has explored this same phenomenon with the issue of trial marriage, demonstrating that by pursuing and prohibiting this Andean practice, the missionaries displaced the *ayllu*'s extended-family structure with the Western notion of a nuclear family predicated on the institution of marriage ("'True' Confessions," 18).

48. The dictionaries and ecclesiastical documents analyzed in this study reflect the spoken language of certain geographic regions of the Andes at certain times, and not necessarily those regions or times where and when same-sex praxis occurred. For example, González Holguín's *Vocabulario* was composed from his linguistic experiences in Cuzco, where he lived for a short time between 1581 and 1586, before moving on to other missions. Therefore, he gathered his vocabulary some fifty years after the European invasion and during the period of more intense evangelization. His lexicon was written with the expressed purpose of aiding missionaries in the evangelization process and in the extirpation of idolatries, a movement that began just as his vocabulary was published. A Jesuit, his ideology was quite different from that of his Dominican predecessor, Domingo de Santo Tomás, though later in life he began defending Amerindians in other missions from harsh Spanish work regimes. As Harrison reminds us, "Even the linguists of the colonial period who were most enlightened and sympathetic to the plight of the Andean Indians wrote dictionaries that served to hegemonically incorporate the natives within European systems of epistemology and ethics" ("Language and Rhetoric of Conversion," 3).

González Holguín's prologue to the second volume of his dictionary gives us a clue to how selective his lexicon was. He admits that he left out of his dictionary words he deemed "curious" or "ostentatious" (*Vocabulario,* 376). This reference to ostentatious speech may have been to the court language of the Incas, which was a mixture of words incorporated by the Inca elite from many regions, the same speech avoided by the writers of the *Doctrina christiana* (Mannheim, *Language of the Incas,* 179). Could this have been the cultural space in which words for ritual sodomy would have been found? Would an indigenous word for ritual sodomy be interpreted as merely curious? Would such a word seem antiquated, given that the Spanish had established hegemony over the Cuzco region by the time of the lexicographer's arrival, therefore limiting opportunities for him to witness sodomy rituals? These questions are impossible to answer, but they leave us with the reminder that dictionaries are far from perfect sources of cultural information.

49. See Urton's *History of a Myth,* 65–66. Also see Sir Clements Markham's introduction to his translation of the text (*History of the Incas*).

50. See Cornejo Polar, *Escribir en el aire,* especially chap. 1.

51. English translations are taken from Markham's translation of the text (*History of the Incas*), except where noted. The reader is cautioned that the Markham translation has several mistakes that can lead to misunderstandings. I have corrected those passages when I felt the translation affected the meaning and interpretation of the original.

52. See Arthur Franklin Zimmerman, *Francisco de Toledo,* 91–106.

53. Lydia Fossa's work, presented at the Latin American Studies Association conference in Guadalajara, Mexico, in April 1997, highlights the Quechua substrate of Betanzos's narrative.

CHAPTER 5

1. I will refer to the author of the *Comentarios reales* as "Inca Garcilaso," though other scholars shorten his name to Garcilaso. I maintain the double name in order to honor his cultural hybridity. He was born with the name Gómez Suárez de Figueroa and renamed himself years later to honor both sides of his family: his father, Capt. Garcilaso de la Vega, nephew of the great Spanish poet Garcilaso de la Vega; and his mother, Chimpu Ocllo, daughter of Huallpa Tupac and Cusi Chimu, granddaughter of Inca Tupac Inca Yupanqui, niece of the penultimate Inca, Huayna Capac, and cousin to the last Incas in power, Huáscar and Atahualpa (Miró Quesada, "Prólogo," x). For a more nuanced explication of Inca Garcilaso's name changes, see Fernández, *Inca Garcilaso: Imaginación, memoria e identidad.*

2. All citations are taken from Aurelio Miró Quesada's edition, *Comentarios reales de los Incas.* The translations are taken from Harold V. Livermore's translation, *Royal Commentaries.* I follow José Antonio Mazzotti's lead in referring to the text by the author's original name: *Comentarios reales,* for the first part; *Segunda parte de*

los Comentarios reales for the second part. For Mazzotti's clarification of the text's original name, see *Coros mestizos,* 24n2.

3. The reader will recall that I use the term "queer" to mean "eccentric, odd, strange" in relation to the cultural hegemony of the writer's locus of enunciation.

4. Peter Hulme's "Polytropic Man" and Louis Montrose's "Work of Gender" are excellent analyses of the gendered nature of colonial discourse.

5. See Guha's preface and article, "On Some Aspects of the Historiography of Colonial India," in *Selected Subaltern Studies.*

6. I refer to the title of Gayatri Chakravorty Spivak's infamous critique of Western intellectuals' attempts to recover the "subaltern voice."

7. See González Echeverría's "Imperio y estilo en el Inca Garcilaso" and Zamora's *Language, Authority,* especially chaps. 2 and 3.

8. See José Rabasa, "On Writing Back."

9. For this interesting history, see José Durand, "Presencia de Garcilaso Inca."

10. For a summary of the material conditions of mestizos in the Spanish empire, see Mazzotti, *Coros mestizos,* 23–24.

11. See Garcilaso de la Vega, *Comentarios reales,* ix–xii, for background on the author's formative years.

12. Alberto Flores Galindo has explored this topic in *Buscando un Inca.*

13. Urton's study of the descendants of an Inca nobility, specifically, their claim to special privileges under Spanish rule based on their pre-Conquest position of power, reminds us that the Andeans "were not passive, inert objects in these new historical and political processes; rather, they were active participants in the production of their own histories through their engagement of the Spaniards at all levels of sociopolitical integration (i.e., from that of the descendants of Inca nobility in Cuzco to the various local terrains controlled by the ethnic lords" (*History of a Myth,* 126).

14. For a thorough discussion of how the uncle figures into the "*coralidad*" of the text, see Mazzotti, *Coros mestizos,* 107–118.

15. Sommer's suggestive reading of Inca Garcilaso's lessons taken from the *Diálogos de amor* includes her observation that Garcilaso seems to have "learned to double as Sophia when he learned, in his own work, to maneuver around a privileged and powerful reader who could be taught to desire and defer to the guide" (*Proceed with Caution,* 90). Her equally insightful observation on Inca Garcilaso's "effeminized" positioning as listener to "expert talk" is found in her discussion of the narrator's deference to his uncle, discussed above.

16. Butler clarifies her theory of performativity and the constitution of gendered subjects in *Bodies That Matter:* "performativity must be understood not as a singular or deliberate 'act,' but, rather, as the reiterative and citational practice by which discourse produces the effects that it names" (2).

17. Porras Barrenechea includes Blas Valera among the post-Toledan chroniclers sympathetic to the Incas (*Cronistas del Perú,* 19).

18. Morris is the dean of anthropology and archeology at the American Museum of Natural History, New York. Morris's research is summarized in "Inka Strategies of Incorporation and Governance."

19. Inca Garcilaso's reference to the uprooting of trees in sodomites' fields seems more likely to be a reference to Iberian punishments than to Andean ones.

20. I interpret "sodomy" as a reference to "same-sex sexuality" rather than to other forms of "unnatural sex," because Inca Garcilaso tends to discuss other forms of sexual transgressions involving women without employing the term *sodomy*. As we saw in Chapter 4, the term evolved toward this narrower definition over the course of the early-modern period.

21. See Hayden White's explanation of the colonial noble savage trope in *Tropics of Discourse*.

22. The reader may recall my discussion of the myth of Mama Huaco's role in the mythic conquest and settlement of the Cuzco valley by the original founding couple. The autochthonous peoples that Manco Capac and Mama Huaco violently displaced from the valley were said to be the Huallas. Could Inca Garcilaso be echoing remnants of interethnic tensions between the invading Incas and the local Huallas, who, fleeing after the Incas' arrival, settled in the northern area where Inca Capac Yupanqui conquered them yet again? Perhaps by figuring the Huaillas as sodomites, Inca Garcilaso is justifying the foundational violence perpetrated against the original valley dwellers, as well as this later conquest. Brian Bauer has examined the mythical Inca conquest of Cuzco and suggests that the Mama Huaco episode is symbolic of the Incas' uprooting of the Hualla peoples and establishing the valley as the mythical beginnings of corn agriculture ("Legitimization of the State"). I have been unable to confirm whether the Huaillas in Inca Garcilaso's text are the same as the Huallas of the mythic conquest of Cuzco. González Holguín's Quechua dictionary defines *huaylla* as "the green meadow, not dry, the good grass" [el prado verde no agostado, o el buen pasto] (*Vocabulario*, 192). According to Bauer, the Huallas of the foundational myth grew coca in what was then a semitropical valley, that is, a "green meadow."

23. For Inca Garcilaso's influence in Peru's nationalist literary and cultural movements, see Flores Galindo's *Buscando un Inca*.

24. As Mario Vargas Llosa has observed, the *indigenistas* of the Peruvian literary tradition have commonly gendered the Peruvian coast feminine and the sierra masculine, positing the Inca civilization as a macho defender of patrimony while the coastal cultures quickly succumbed to the invading Spanish (*Utopía arcaica*, 75–76). In Chapter 3, I discuss the local representation of highland-lowland rivalry in the Huarochirí myths.

25. Here I credit John Beverley for his move to think of us all as having potential or partial subaltern subjectivities. In *Against Literature*, Beverley discusses this concept in relation to testimonial literature and mentions that "subaltern is in any case a relational identity" (104).

26. Doris Sommer coined the term "outsider" in her analysis of so-called resis-

tant texts. In considering Rigoberta Menchú's "subaltern speech," the term foregrounds the "irony of betraying norms of [her] community in order to preserve it, becoming an outsider in order to stay inside." These ideas first appeared in "Resisting the Heat" and have been refined and expanded in *Proceed with Caution* (8–9).

27. See Castro-Klarén's "Writing Subalternity," in which she perceptively elaborates how Inca Garcilaso and Guaman Poma interrogate hegemonic colonial culture from subaltern positions. The quotation in my text is taken from Castro-Klarén's discussion of the two subjects' writings as "a praxis of agency designed to achieve a shift in the positions of domination and subordination. It is 'un no dejarse'" (238). While I recognize the virtuosity of such maneuvers on the part of both colonial subjects, as I have argued throughout this chapter, this "praxis of agency" has its consequences in the representation of other Andean subjectivities.

EPILOGUE

1. José Rabasa characterizes his study of the formation of Eurocentrism and its discursive "invention" of America as "an alternative history, a fiction that undermines the universality of European history and subjectivity—not with factual contradiction, but rather by elaborating a narrative that maps out blind spots and opens areas for counterdiscourse while decolonizing our present picture of the world" (*Inventing America*, 212).

2. While an in-depth analysis of contemporary ritual dance is beyond the scope of this study, I hope these final comments inspire further research into the intersection between sexuality, gender liminality, and public performance in the Andes and their connections to pre-Hispanic and colonial performances of third gender.

3. My citations are taken from Villasante Sullca's manuscript of this title, presented at the international symposium "De Amores y Luchas: Diversidad Sexual, Derechos Humanos y Ciudadanía," Universidad Nacional de San Marcos, Lima, September 13, 2000. I appreciate the author's permission to cite from this manuscript.

4. Villasante provides many details on specific dancers and their reputations, sexual identities, and contributions to the *danzas,* as well as information on the community's attitudes toward issues of gender and sexuality.

BIBLIOGRAPHY

Acosta, José de. *Historia natural y moral de las Indias*. 1590. In *Obras*. Biblioteca de Autores Españoles, vol. 73. Madrid: Ediciones Atlas, 1954.

Acosta Rodríguez, Antonio. "Los clérigos doctrineros y la economía colonial, 1600–1630." *Allpanchis* 16, no. 19 (1982): 117–149.

Adorno, Rolena. "Discurso jurídico, discurso literario: El reto de leer en el siglo XX los escritos del XVI." In *Memorias de las jornadas andinas de literatura latinoamericana*. La Paz: Plural Editores–Facultad de Humanidades y Ciencias de la Educación, 1995.

———, ed. *From Oral to Written Expression: Native Andean Chronicles of the Early Colonial Period*. Syracuse, NY: Syracuse University, 1982.

———. *Guaman Poma: Writing and Resistance in Colonial Peru*. Austin: University of Texas Press, 1986.

———. "Images of Indios Ladinos in Early Colonial Perú." In *Transatlantic Encounters: Europeans and Andeans in the Sixteenth Century*. Edited by Kenneth J. Andrien and Rolena Adorno. Berkeley & Los Angeles: University of California Press, 1991.

———. "Literary Production and Suppression: Reading and Writing about Amerindians in Colonial Spanish America." *Dispositio* 11, nos. 28–29 (1986): 1–25.

———. "Reconsidering Colonial Discourse for Sixteenth and Seventeenth Century Spanish America." *Latin American Research Review* 28, no. 3 (1993): 135–145.

———. "El sujeto colonial y la construcción cultural de la alteridad." *Revista de Crítica Literaria Latinoamericana* 14, no. 28 (1988): 55–68.

———. "Textos imborrables: Posiciones simultáneas y sucesivas del sujeto colonial." *Revista de Crítica Literaria Latinoamericana* 41 (1995): 33–49.

Adorno, Rolena, and Patrick Charles Pautz. *Álvar Núñez Cabeza de Vaca: His Account, His Life, and the Expedition of Pánfilo de Narváez*. Vol. 3. Lincoln: University of Nebraska Press, 1999.

Allen, Catherine J. *The Hold Life Has: Coca and Cultural Identity in an Andean Community*. Washington, DC: Smithsonian Institution Press, 1988.

Alonso, Dámaso. *La poesía de San Juan de la Cruz*. Madrid: Aguilar, 1966.

Alter, Robert. "Sodom as Nexus: The Web of Design in Biblical Narrative." In *Reclaiming Sodom.* Edited by Jonathan Goldberg. New York: Routledge, 1994.

Andrien, Kenneth J., and Rolena Adorno, eds. *Transatlantic Encounters: Europeans and Andeans in the Sixteenth Century.* Berkeley & Los Angeles: University of California Press, 1991.

Anghiera, Pietro Martire de. *The Decades of the Newe Worlde or West India.* 1555. Ann Arbor, MI: University Microfilms, 1966.

Anonymous. *Lazarillo de Tormes.* Edited by Francisco Rico. Madrid: Cátedra, 1987.

Anonymous. *Poema del Cid.* Edited by Francisco López Estrada. Madrid: Editorial Castalia, 1984.

Anonymous. *The Poem of the Cid.* Translated by W. S. Merwin. London: J. M. Dent and Sons, 1959.

Anzaldúa, Gloria. *Borderlands/La Frontera: The New Mestiza.* San Francisco: Aunt Lute Books, 1987.

———. *Entrevistas.* Edited by Ana Louise Keating. London: Routledge, 2000.

Arboleda, Manuel. "Representaciones artísticas de actividades homoeróticas en la cerámica moche." *Boletín de Lima,* Vols. 16, 17, 18, special ed. (1981): 98–107.

Arciniegas, Germán. *America in Europe: A History of the New World in Reverse.* New York: Harcourt Brace Jovanovich, 1986.

Arguedas, José María. *Formación de una cultura nacional indoamericana.* Mexico City: Siglo XXI, 1975.

Arnold, Denise Y., ed. *Más allá del silencio: Las fronteras de género en los Andes.* La Paz: ILCA/CIASE, 1997.

Arriaga, Pablo José de. *La extirpación de la idolatría del Perú.* 1621. In *Crónicas peruanas de interés indígena.* Edited by Francisco Esteve Barba. Biblioteca de Autores Españoles, vol. 209. Madrid: Ediciones Atlas, 1968.

Atkinson, Jane Monnig, and Shelly Errington, eds. *Power and Difference: Gender in Southeast Asia.* Stanford, CA: Stanford University Press, 1990.

Ayala, Martín de. *Catecismo para instrucción de los nuevamente convertidos de moros.* Valencia: Casa de Pedro Patricio Mey, 1599.

Azpilcueta Navarro, Martín de. *Manual de confesores y penitentes.* Madrid: Ferrer, 1554.

Bailey, Derrick Sherman. *Homosexuality and the Western Christian Tradition.* London: Longmans, 1955.

Barker, Francis; Peter Hulme; Margaret Iversen; Diana Loxley, eds. *Europe and Its Others.* Vol. 2. Colchester, Eng.: University of Essex, 1985.

Barnes, Monica. "Catechisms and Confesionarios: Distorting Mirrors of Andean Societies." In *Andean Cosmologies through Time.* Edited by Robert V. H. Dover, Katherine E. Seibold, and John H. McDowell. Bloomington: Indiana University Press, 1992.

Bauer, Brian S. "Legitimization of the State in Inca Myth and Ritual." *American Anthropologist* 98, no. 2 (1996): 327–337.

Bawden, Garth. *The Moche.* Cambridge, MA: Blackwell, 1996.

Behar, Ruth, and Deborah A. Gordon. *Women Writing Culture*. Berkeley & Los Angeles: University of California Press, 1995.

Bendezú, Edmundo. "Ruptura epistemológica del discurso del Inca Garcilaso." *Cuadernos Americanos* 3, no. 18 (1989): 190–199.

Benito-Vessels, Carmen. "La mujer en *La estoria de Espanna:* Desde el rapto y el amancebamiento hasta la autoafirmación política." *Exemplaria Hispánica* 10, nos. 1–2 (1988): 41–48.

Benson, Elizabeth P., and Anita G. Cook, eds. *Ritual Sacrifice in Ancient Peru*. Austin: University of Texas Press, 2001.

Berlant, Lauren, and Michael Warner. "What Does Queer Theory Teach Us about X?" *PMLA* 10, no. 3 (1995): 343–349.

Bertonio, P. Ludovico. *Vocabulario de la lengua aymara.* 1612. Cochabamba, Bol.: Centro de Estudios de la Realidad Económica y Social, 1984.

Betanzos, Juan de. *Suma y narración de los Incas.* 1551. Madrid: Ediciones Atlas, 1987.

Beverley, John. *Against Literature.* Minneapolis: University of Minnesota Press, 1993.

Bhabha, Homi K. *The Location of Culture.* London: Routledge, 1994.

———. "Postcolonial Criticism." In *Redrawing the Boundaries: The Transformation of English and American Literary Studies.* Edited by Stephen Greenblatt and Giles Gunn. New York: Modern Language Association, 1992.

Blackmore, Josiah, and Gregory S. Hutcheson, eds. *Queer Iberia: Sexualities, Cultures, and Crossings from the Middle Ages to the Renaissance.* Durham, NC: Duke University Press, 1999.

Blackwood, Evelyn, ed. *The Many Faces of Homosexuality.* New York: Harrington Park Press, 1986.

Bleys, Rudi C. *The Geography of Perversion.* New York: New York University Press, 1995.

Bolaños, Álvaro Félix. *Barbarie y canibalismo en la retórica colonial: Los indios pijaos de Fray Pedro Simón.* Bogotá: CEREC, 1994.

Bolin, Inge. *Rituals of Respect: The Secret of Survival in the High Peruvian Andes.* Austin: University of Texas Press, 1998.

Boon, James A. *Other Tribes, Other Scribes: Symbolic Anthropology in the Comparative Study of Cultures, Histories, Religions, and Texts.* Cambridge, NY: Cambridge University Press, 1982.

Boone, Elizabeth, and Walter Mignolo, eds. *Writing without Words: Alternative Literacies in Mesoamerica and the Andes.* Durham, NC: Duke University Press, 1994.

Boswell, John. *Christianity, Social Tolerance, and Homosexuality.* Chicago: University of Chicago Press, 1980.

Bouysse-Cassagne, Thérèse, and Olivia Harris. "*Pacha:* En torno al pensamiento aymara." In *Tres reflexiones sobre el pensamiento andino.* Edited by Thérèse Bouysse-Cassagne and Olivia Harris. La Paz: Hisbol, 1987.

Bredbeck, Gregory W. *Sodomy and Interpretation: From Marlowe to Milton.* Ithaca, NY: Cornell University Press, 1991.

Bricker, Victoria Reifler. *Ritual Humor in Highland Chiapas.* Austin: University of Texas Press, 1973.

Briggs, Charles. *Competence in Performance: The Creativity of Tradition in Mexicano Verbal Art.* Philadelphia: University of Pennsylvania Press, 1988.

Brittan, Arthur. *Masculinity and Power.* Oxford: Basil Blackwell, 1989.

Brod, Harry, ed. *The Making of Masculinities.* Winchester, MA: Allen & Unwin, 1987.

Brotherston, Gordon. *Book of the Fourth World.* Cambridge: Cambridge University Press, 1992.

Burshatin, Israel. "The Docile Image: The Moor as a Figure of Force, Subservience, and Nobility in the *Poema de Mio Cid.*" *Romance Quarterly* 31, no. 3 (1984): 269–280.

———. "The Moor in the Text: Metaphor, Emblem, and Silence." *Critical Inquiry* 12, no. 1 (1985): 98–118.

———. "Written on the Body: Slave or Hermaphrodite in Sixteenth-Century Spain." In *Queer Iberia: Sexualities, Cultures, and Crossings from the Middle Ages to the Renaissance.* Edited by Josiah Blackmore and Gregory S. Hutcheson. Durham, NC: Duke University Press, 1999.

Butler, Judith. *Bodies That Matter: On the Discursive Limits of "Sex."* New York: Routledge, 1993.

———. "Critically Queer." In *Playing with Fire: Queer Politics, Queer Theories.* Edited by Shane Phelan. New York: Routledge, 1997.

———. *Gender Trouble: Feminism and the Subversion of Identity.* New York: Routledge, 1990.

Bynum, Caroline Walker. *Gender and Religion.* Boston: Beacon Press, 1986.

Cadena, Marisol de la. "'Las mujeres son más indias': Etnicidad y género en una comunidad del Cusco." *Revista Andina* 9, no. 1 (1991): 7–47.

Calvo Pérez, Julio. *Sebastián de Covarrubias o la fresca instilación de las palabras.* Cuenca, Spain: Diputación Provincial de Cuenca, 1991.

Carrasco, Rafael. *Inquisición y represión sexual en Valencia (1565–1785).* Barcelona: Laertes, 1985.

Castañeda Delgado, Paulino. "La política española con los caribes durante el siglo XVI." In *Homenaje a D. Ciriaco Pérez-Bustamante,* vol. 2. Madrid: Consejo Superior de Investigaciones Científicas, 1970.

Castro-Klaren, Sara. "Writing Subalternity: Guaman Poma and Garcilaso, Inca." *Dispositio* 46 (1996): 229–244.

Cereceda, Verónica. "The Semiology of Andean Textiles: The Talegas of Isluga." In *Anthropological History of Andean Polities.* Edited by John V. Murra, Nathan Wachtel, and Jacques Revel. Cambridge: Cambridge University Press, 1986.

Cevallos, Francisco J. "La retórica historiográfica y la aculturación en tres cronistas peruanos." *Revista de Estudios Hispánicos* 20, no. 3 (1986): 55–66.

Chávez-Silverman, Susana, and Librada Hernández, eds. *Reading and Writing the Ambiente: Queer Sexualities in Latino, Latin American and Spanish Culture.* Madison: University of Wisconsin Press, 2000.

Cieza de León, Pedro de. *La crónica del Perú. Primera parte.* 1553. Lima: Fondo Editorial de la Pontificia Universidad Católica del Perú, 1995.

———. *Crónica del Perú. Segunda parte.* Edited by Francesca Cantú. Lima: Pontificia Universidad Católica del Perú, 1986.

———. *The Discovery and Conquest of Peru.* Translation of *La crónica del Perú. Tercera parte.* Edited and translated by Alexandra Parma Cook and Noble David Cook. Durham, NC: Duke University Press, 1998.

———. *The Incas of Pedro de Cieza de León.* Translation of *La crónica del Perú. Primera parte.* Edited by Victor Wolfgang von Hagen. Translated by Harriet de Onís. Norman: University of Oklahoma Press, 1959.

Classen, Constance. *Inca Cosmology and the Human Body.* Salt Lake City: University of Utah Press, 1993.

Clifford, James, and George Marcus. *Writing Culture: The Poetics and Politics of Ethnography.* Berkeley & Los Angeles: University of California Press, 1986.

Cobo, Bernabé. *History of the Inca Empire.* Edited and translated by Roland Hamilton. Austin: University of Texas Press, 1979.

———. *Inca Religion and Customs.* Edited and translated by Roland Hamilton. Austin: University of Texas Press, 1990.

Columbus, Christopher. "Diario del primer viaje." In *Textos y documentos completos.* Edited by Consuelo Varela and Juan Gil. Madrid: Alianza Editorial, 1995.

———. *The Voyages of Christopher Columbus.* Translated by Cecil Jane. London: Argonaut Press, 1930.

Concilios Limenses. (1551–1772). 2 vols. Edited by Rubén Vargas Ugarte. Lima, 1952.

Conkey, Margaret W., and Joan M. Gero. "Programme to Practice: Gender and Feminism in Archeology." *Annual Review of Anthropology* 26 (1997): 411–437.

Cordy-Collins, Alana. "Blood and the Moon Priestesses: Spondylus Shells in Moche Ceremony." *Ritual Sacrifice in Ancient Peru.* Edited by Elizabeth P. Benson and Anita G. Cook. Austin: University of Texas Press, 2001.

Cornejo Polar, Antonio. *Escribir en el aire: Ensayo sobre la heterogeneidad socio-cultural en las literaturas andinas.* Lima: Editorial Horizonte, 1994.

Corr, Rachel. "Reciprocity, Communion, and Sacrifice: Food in Andean Ritual and Social Life." *Food and Foodways* 10 (2002): 1–25.

Costa Lima, Luis. *Control of the Imaginary.* Minneapolis: University of Minnesota Press, 1988.

———. *The Darker Side of Reason: Fictionality and Power.* Stanford, CA: Stanford University Press, 1992.

Covarrubias Orozco, Sebastián de. *Emblemas morales.* Madrid: Luis Sánchez, 1610.

Cruz, Anne J., and Mary Elizabeth Perry, eds. *Culture and Control in Counter-Reformation Spain.* Minneapolis: University of Minnesota Press, 1992.

Cruz, San Juan de la. *The Poems of St. John of the Cross.* Translated by Ken Krabbenhoft. New York: Harcourt Brace, 1999.

———. *Poesías completas.* Edited by Pedro Salinas. Buenos Aires: Cruz del Sur, 1947.

Cusihuamán, Antonio G. *Gramática quechua, Cuzco callao.* Lima: Ministerio de Educación/Instituto de Estudios Peruanos, 1976.

Dean, Carolyn. *Inca Bodies and the Body of Christ.* Austin: University of Texas Press, 1999.

De Beauvoir, Simone. *Second Sex.* Translated by H. M. Parshley. New York: Bantam, 1961.

de Certeau, Michel. *Heterologies: Discourse on the Other.* Minneapolis: University of Minnesota Press, 1986.

————. *The Practice of Everyday Life.* Berkeley & Los Angeles: University of California Press, 1984.

de Lauretis, Teresa. "Queer Theory: Lesbian and Gay Sexualities, An Introduction." *Differences* 3, no. 2 (1991): iii–xviii.

Díaz del Castillo, Bernal. *Historia verdadera de la conquista de Nueva España.* Mexico City: Editorial Porrúa, 1970.

Doctrina christiana y catecismo para instrucción de indios. 1584–1585. Facsimile of edition prepared by Antonio Ricardo. Madrid: Consejo Superior de Investigaciones Científicas, 1985.

Dombrowski, Daniel. *St. John of the Cross: An Appreciation.* Albany: State University of New York Press, 1992.

Domínguez Faura, Nicanor. "Juan de Betanzos y las primeras cartillas de evangelización en la lengua general del Inga (1536–1542)." In *La venida del reino: Religión, evangelización, y cultura en América, siglos XVI–XX.* Compiled by Gabriela Ramos. Cuzco: Centro de Estudios Regionales Bartolomé de Las Casas, 1994.

Donnan, Christopher B. *Moche Art and Iconography.* Los Angeles: University of California, Los Angeles Latin American Center Publications, 1976.

Donnan, Christopher B., and Luis Jaime Castillo Butters. "Excavaciones de tumbas de sacerdotisas moche en San José de Moro, Jequetepeque." In *Moche: Propuestas y perspectivas: Actas del Primer Coloquio sobre la Cultura Moche, Trujillo, 12 al 16 de abril de 1993.* Edited by Santiago Uceda and Elías Mujica. Trujillo: Universidad Nacional de la Libertad, Instituto Frances de Estudios Andinos, Asociación Peruana para el Fomento de las Ciencias Sociales, 1994.

Dopico Black, Georgina. *Perfect Wives, Other Women: Adultery and Inquisition in Early Modern Spain.* Durham, NC: Duke University Press, 2001.

Doty, Alexander. *Making Things Perfectly Queer: Interpreting Mass Culture.* Minneapolis: University of Minnesota Press, 1993.

Dover, Robert V. H.; Katherine E. Seibold; and John H. McDowell, eds. *Andean Cosmologies through Time.* Bloomington: Indiana University Press, 1992.

Durán, Juan Guillermo. *El catequismo del III Concilio Provincial de Lima y sus complementos pastorales, 1584–1585.* Buenos Aires: Facultad de Teología, Universidad Católica Argentina, 1982.

————. *Monumenta catechética hispanoamericana (siglos XVI–XVIII).* Vols. 1 and 2. Buenos Aires: Ediciones de la Facultad de Teología, Universidad Católica Argentina, 1990.

Durand, José. "Presencia de Garcilaso Inca en Tupac Amaru." *Cuadernos Americanos* 3, no. 18 (1989): 209–227.

Duviols, Pierre. "De la Tarasca a Mama Huaco: La historia de un mito y rito cuzqueño." In *Religions des Andes et langues indigènes: Équateur, Pérou, Bolivie, avant et après la conquête espagnole*. Edited by Pierre Duviols. [Aix-en-Provence]: Université de Provence, 1993.

———. *La destrucción de las religiones andinas (conquista y colonia)*. Translated by Albor Maruenda. Mexico City: Universidad Nacional Autónoma de México, 1977. (*La lutte contre les religions autochtones dans le Pérou colonial* [*L'extirpation de il idolatrie entre 1532 et 1660*]. Lima: Institut Français d'Études Andines, 1971.)

———. "Estudio y comentario etnohistórico." In *Relación de antigüedades deste reyno del Perú*. Edited by Pierre Duviols and César Itier. 1613. Cuzco: Centro de Estudios Regionales Andinos Bartolomé de Las Casas, 1993.

———, and César Itier, eds. *Relación de antigüedades deste reyno del Perú*. 1613. Cuzco: Centro de Estudios Regionales Andinos Bartolomé de Las Casas, 1993.

El Saffar, Ruth. "The Evolution of Psyche under Empire: Literary Reflections of Spain in the 16th Century." In *Cultural and Historical Grounding for Hispanic and Luso-Brazilian Feminist Literary Criticism*. Edited by Hernán Vidal. Minneapolis: Institute for the Study of Ideologies and Literature, 1989.

Estensorro Fuchs, Juan Carlos. "Descubriendo los poderes de la palabra: Funciones de la prédica en la evangelización del Perú (siglos XVI–XVII)." In *La venida del reino: Religión, evangelización y cultura en América, siglos XVI–XX*. Compiled by Gabriela Ramos. Cuzco: Centro de Estudios Regionales Bartolomé de Las Casas, 1994.

Fernández, Christian. *Inca Garcilaso: Imaginación, memoria e identidad*. Lima: Fondo Editorial Universidad Nacional Mayor de San Marcos, 2004.

Fletcher, Richard. *The Quest for El Cid*. Oxford: Oxford Unversity Press, 1989.

Flores Galindo, Alberto. *Buscando un Inca*. Havana: Casa de las Américas, 1988.

Fossa Falco, Lydia. "Leyendo hoy a Cieza de León: De la Capacocha a la Capac Hucha." *Boletín de Lima* 73 (January 1991): 33–41.

Foster, David William, and Roberto Reis, eds. *Bodies and Biases: Sexualities in Hispanic Cultures and Literatures*. Minneapolis: University of Minnesota Press, 1996.

Fothergill-Payne, Louise. *Seneca and Celestina*. Cambridge: Cambridge University Press, 1988.

Foucault, Michel. *The Care of the Self: The History of Sexuality*. Vol. 3. 1984. Translated by Robert Hurley. New York: Vintage Books, 1990.

———. *The History of Sexuality: An Introduction*. 1976. Translated by Robert Hurley. New York: Vintage Books, 1990.

———. *The Order of Things*. 1966. New York: Vintage Books, 1973.

———. *The Use of Pleasure: The History of Sexuality*. Vol. 2. 1984. Translated by Robert Hurley. New York: Vintage Books, 1990.

"Founding Statement, Latin American Subaltern Studies Group." *Dispositio* 19, no. 46 (1996):1–11.

Freccero, Carla. "Cannibalism, Homophobia, Women: Montaigne's 'Des canni-bales' and 'De l'amitié.'" In *Women, Race, and Writing in the Early Modern Period*. Edited by Margo Hendricks and Patricia Parker. London: Routledge, 1994.

Fuss, Diana. *Essentially Speaking: Feminism, Nature, and Difference*. London: Routledge, 1989.

Gálvez Peña, Carlos M., ed. "Prólogo." In *Historia del reino y provincias del Perú*. By Giovanni Anello Oliva. Lima: Pontificia Universidad Católica del Perú, Fondo Editorial, 1998.

Garber, Marjorie. *Vested Interests: Cross Dressing and Cultural Anxiety*. New York: Harper Perennial, 1992.

García, Juan Carlos. *Ofensas a Dios*. Cuzco: Centro de Estudios Regionales Andinos Bartolomé de Las Casas, 1994.

Garcilaso de la Vega, Inca. *Comentarios reales de los Incas*. 2 vols. Edited by Aurelio Miró Quesada. 1608. Caracas: Biblioteca Ayacucho, 1985.

—————. *Royal Commentaries of the Incas and General History of Peru*. Translated by Harold V. Livermore. Austin: University of Texas Press, 1966.

Geertz, Clifford. *The Interpretation of Cultures*. New York: Basic Books, 1973.

Gero, Joan M. "Field Knots and Ceramic Beaus: Recovering Gender in the Peruvian Early Intermediate Period." Paper presented at Pre-Columbian Studies Symposium "Recovering Gender in Pre-Hispanic America," Dumbarton Oaks, Washington, DC, October 12, 1996.

Gilmore, David D. *Manhood in the Making: Cultural Concepts of Masculinity*. New Haven, CT: Yale University Press, 1990.

Girard, René. *The Girard Reader*. New York: Crossroad Publishing, 1996.

Godenzzi, Juan Carlos, and Janet Vengoa Zúñiga. *Runasimimanta Yuyaychakusun: Manual de lingüística quechua para bilingües*. Cuzco: Centro de Estudios Regionales Andinos Bartolomé de Las Casas, 1994.

Goldberg, Jonathan. "Bradford's 'Ancient Members' and 'A Case of Buggery . . . amongst Them.'" In *Nationalisms and Sexualities*. Edited by Andrew Parker, Mary Russo, Doris Sommer, and Patricia Yaeger. New York: Routledge, 1992.

—————, ed. *Reclaiming Sodom*. New York: Routledge, 1994.

—————, ed. *Sodometries: Renaissance Texts, Modern Sexualities*. Stanford, CA: Stanford University Press, 1992.

—————. "Sodomy in the New World: Anthropologies Old and New." *Social Text* 9 (1991): 45–56.

Golte, Jürgen. *Iconos y narraciones: La reconstrucción de una secuencia de imágenes moche*. Lima: Instituto de Estudios Peruanos, 1994.

González, Ray, ed. *Muy Macho: Latino Men Confront Their Manhood*. New York: Anchor Books, 1996.

González Echeverría, Roberto. "Humanism and Rhetoric in *Comentarios reales* and *El carnero*." In *In Memory of Willis Knapp Jones*. York, SC: Special Literatures Publishing, 1987.

———. "Imperio y estilo en el Inca Garcilaso." *Discurso Literario* 3, no. 1 (1985): 75–80.

———. *Myth and Archive: A Theory of Latin American Narrative.* Cambridge: Cambridge University Press, 1990.

González Holguín, Diego. *Vocabulario de la lengua general de todo el Perú, llamada lengua quichua, o del Inca.* 1608. Edited by Ruth Moya. Quito: Corporación Editora Nacional, 1993.

González Stephan, Beatriz, and Lúcia Helena Costigan, comps. *Crítica y descolonización: El sujeto colonial en la cultura latinoamericana.* Caracas: Academia Nacional de la Historia, 1992.

Gordon, Deborah A. "Conclusion: Culture Writing Women: Inscribing Feminist Anthropology." In *Women Writing Culture.* Edited by Ruth Behar and Deborah A. Gordon. Berkeley & Los Angeles: University of California Press, 1995.

Graff, Gerald, and Bruce Robbins. "Cultural Criticism." In *Redrawing the Boundaries: The Transformation of English and American Literary Studies.* Edited by Stephen Greenblatt and Giles Gunn. New York: Modern Language Association, 1992.

Gramsci, Antonio. *Selections from the Prison Notebooks.* Edited by Quintin Hoare and Geoffrey Nowell Smith. New York: International Publishers, 1971.

Greenberg, David F. *The Construction of Homosexuality.* Chicago: University of Chicago Press, 1988.

Greenblatt, Stephen. *Marvelous Possessions: The Wonder of the New World.* Chicago: University of Chicago Press, 1991.

———. *New World Encounters.* Berkeley & Los Angeles: University of California Press, 1993.

Greenblatt, Stephen, and Giles Gunn, eds. *Redrawing the Boundaries: The Transformation of English and American Literary Studies.* New York: Modern Language Association, 1992.

Griffiths, Nicholas. *The Cross and the Serpent: Religious Repression and Resurgence in Colonial Peru.* Norman: University of Oklahoma Press, 1996.

Gruzinski, Serge. "Individualization and Acculturation: Confession among the Nahuas of Mexico from the Sixteenth to the Eighteenth Century." In *Sexuality and Marriage in Colonial Latin America.* Edited by Asunción Lavrin. Lincoln: University of Nebraska Press, 1989.

Guaman Poma de Ayala, Felipe. *El primer nueva corónica y buen gobierno.* 1615. Edited by Franklin Pease G. Y. Translated by Jan Szeminski. 3 vols. Mexico City: Fondo de Cultura Económica, 1993.

Guerra, Francisco. *The Precolumbian Mind.* New York: Seminar Press, 1971.

Guha, Ranajit, and Gayatri Spivak, eds. *Selected Subaltern Studies.* New York: Oxford University Press, 1988.

Gutiérrez, Ramón. "A Gendered History of the Conquest of America: A View from New Mexico." In *Gender Rhetorics: Postures of Dominance and Submission in History.* Edited by Richard C. Trexler. Binghamton, NY: Center for Medieval and Early Renaissance Studies, 1994.

———. "Must We Deracinate Indians to Find Gay Roots?" *Outlook* 1, no. 4 (1989): 61–67.

———. *When Jesus Came, the Corn Mothers Went Away: Marriage, Sexuality, and Power in New Mexico, 1500–1846.* Stanford, CA: Stanford University Press, 1991.

Gutiérrez de Santa Clara, Pedro. *Quinquenarios o Historia de las guerras civiles del Perú.* 1580. Biblioteca de Autores Españoles, vols. 165–167. Madrid: Editorial Atlas, 1963.

Hadley, D. M. *Masculinity in Medieval Europe.* New York: Longman, 1999.

Hanke, Lewis. *La lucha por la justicia en la conquista de América.* Madrid: Ediciones Istmo, 1988.

———. "Studies in the Theoretical Aspects of the Spanish Conquest of America." PhD diss., Harvard University, 1935.

Harrison, Regina. "Confesando el pecado en los Andes: Del siglo XVI hacia nuestros días." *Revista Crítica de Literatura Latinoamericana* 19, no. 37 (1993): 169–185.

———. "Cultural Translation in the Andes: The Pregnant Penitent." *Latin American Indian Literatures Journal* 11, no. 2 (Fall 1995): 108–128.

———. "The Language and Rhetoric of Conversion in the Viceroyalty of Peru." *Poetics Today* 16, no. 1 (1995): 1–27.

———. "Modes of Discourse: The Relación de antigüedades deste reyno del Perú by Joan de Santa Cruz Pachacuti Yamqui Salcamaygua." In *From Oral to Written Expression: Native Andean Chronicles of the Early Colonial Period.* Edited by Rolena Adorno. Syracuse, NY: Maxwell School of Citizenship and Public Affairs, Syracuse University, 1982.

———. "Pérez Bocanegra's *Ritual formulario:* Khipu Knots and Confession." In *Narrative Threads: Accounting and Recounting in Andean Khipu.* Edited by Jeffrey Quilter and Gary Urton. Austin: University of Texas Press, 2002.

———. *Signs, Songs, and Memory in the Andes: Translating Quechua Language and Culture.* Austin: University of Texas Press, 1989.

———. "The Theory of Concupiscence: Spanish-Quechua Confessional Manuals in the Andes." In *Encoded Encounters: Race, Gender, and Ethnicity in Colonial Latin America.* Edited by Francisco Javier Cevallos, Jeffery A. Cole, Nina M. Scott, and Nicomedes Suárez-Araúz. Amherst: University of Massachusetts Press, 1994.

———. "'True' Confessions: Quechua and the Spanish Cultural Encounters in the Viceroyalty of Peru." Latin American Studies Center Series, no. 5. College Park: University of Maryland, 1992.

Hastorf, Christine A. *Agriculture and the Onset of Political Inequality before the Inca.* Cambridge: Cambridge University Press, 1993.

Herdt, Gilbert. *Guardians of the Flute: Idioms of Masculinity.* Chicago: University of Chicago Press, 1994.

———, ed. *Third Sex, Third Gender: Beyond Sexual Dimorphism in Culture and History.* New York: Zone Books, 1994.

Hocquenghem, Anne Marie. *Iconografía mochica.* Lima: Fondo Editorial de la Pontificia Universidad Católica del Perú, 1987.

Horswell, Michael J. "Third Gender, Tropes of Sexuality, and Transculturation in Colonial Andean Historiography." PhD diss., University of Maryland, College Park, 1997.

―――. "Toward an Andean Theory of Ritual Same-Sex Sexuality and Third Gender Subjectivity." In *Infamous Desire: Male Homosexuality in Colonial Latin America.* Edited by Pete Sigal. Chicago: University of Chicago Press, 2003.

Howard-Malverde, Rosaleen. *The Speaking of History: Willapaakushayki or Quechua Ways of Telling the Past.* London: University of London, Institute of Latin American Studies, 1990.

The Huarochirí Manuscript. 1608. Edited and translated by Frank Salomon and George L. Urioste. Austin: University of Texas Press, 1991.

Huarte Navarro, Juan de Dios. *Examen de los ingenios.* 1604.

Hulme, Peter. *Colonial Encounters: Europe and the Native Caribbean, 1492–1797.* London: Methuen, 1986.

―――. "Polytropic Man: Tropes of Sexuality and Mobility in Early Colonial Discourse." In *Europe and Its Others.* Edited by Francis Barker, Peter Hulme, Margaret Iversen, and Diana Loxley. Colchester, Eng.: University of Essex, 1985.

Hunt, Lynn, ed. *Eroticism and the Body Politic.* Baltimore: Johns Hopkins University Press, 1991.

Hutcheson, Gregory S. "The Sodomitic Moor: Queerness in the Narrative of *Reconquista.*" In *Queering the Middle Ages.* Edited by Glenn Burger and Steven F. Kruger. Minneapolis: University of Minnesota Press, 2001.

Iriarte, Isabel. "Textilería andina." Paper presented at the Colegio Andino, Centro Bartolomé de Las Casas, Cuzco, July 23, 1996.

Isbell, Billie Jean. "De inmaduro a duro: Lo simbólico femenino y los esquemas andinos de género." In *Más allá del silencio: Las fronteras del género en los Andes.* Edited by Denise Y. Arnold. La Paz, Bol.: ILCA/CIASE, 1997.

―――. "La otra mitad esencial: Un estudio de complementariedad sexual andina." *Estudios Andinos* 5 (1976): 37–56.

―――. *To Defend Ourselves: Ecology and Ritual in an Andean Village.* Austin: University of Texas Press, 1978.

Jacobs, Sue-Ellen; Wesley Thomas; and Sabine Lang. *Two-Spirit People: Native American Gender Identity, Sexuality, and Spirituality.* Urbana: University of Illinois Press, 1997.

Jara, René, and Nicholas Spadaccini. *1492–1992: Rediscovering Colonial Writing.* Hispanic Issues, no. 4. Minneapolis: Prisma Institute, 1989.

Jiménez de la Espada, Marcos. "Antecedentes." In *Relaciones geográficas de Indias—Perú. Biblioteca de Autores Españoles.* Edited by José Urbano Martinez Carreras. Madrid: Atlas, 1965.

Jordan, Mark D. *The Invention of Sodomy in Christian Theology.* Chicago: University of Chicago Press, 1997.

Kaliman, Ricardo. "La palabra que produce regiones: El concepto de región desde la teoría literaria." Tucumán, Arg.: Universidad Nacional de Tucumán, Instituto de Historia y Pensamiento Argentinos, 1994.

———. "Sobre los sentidos del concepto de lo Andino." Unpublished, 1995.

Kauffman Doig, Federico. *Sexual Behavior in Ancient Peru.* Lima: Kompahtos, 1979.

Kelly-Gadol, Joan. "Did Women Have a Renaissance?" In *Becoming Visible: Women in European History.* Edited by Joan Kelly-Gadol. Boston: Houghton-Mifflin, 1977.

Kimball, Geoffrey. "Aztec Homosexuality: The Textual Evidence." *Journal of Homosexuality* 26 (1993): 7–24.

King, Margaret L. *Women in the Renaissance.* Chicago: University of Chicago Press, 1991.

Kirsch, Max H. *Queer Theory and Social Change.* New York and London: Routledge, 2000.

Krabbenhoft, Ken. *The Poems of St. John of the Cross.* New York: Harcourt Brace, 1999.

Kristal, Efraín. "Fábulas clásicas y neoplatónicas en los *Comentarios reales de los Incas.*" In *Homenaje a José Durand.* Edited by Luis Cortest. Madrid: Editorial Verbom, 1993.

Kristeva, Julia. *Powers of Horror: An Essay on Abjection.* Translated by Leon S. Roudiez. New York: Columbia University Press, 1982.

Lagos, Cora. "Confrontando imaginarios: Oralidad, pintura y escritura en México colonial." PhD diss., University of Michigan, 1997.

Laqueur, Thomas. *Making Sex: Body and Gender from the Greeks to Freud.* Cambridge, MA: Harvard University Press, 1990.

Larco Herrera, Rafael. *Checan.* Geneva: Nagel Publications, 1965.

Larson, Catherine. "Reforming the Golden Age Dramatic Canon: Women's Writing, Women's Voice, and the Question of Value." *Gestos* 14 (1992): 117–125.

Las Casas, Bartolomé de. *Apologética historia sumaria.* 2 vols. Edited by Edmundo O'Gorman. Mexico City: Universidad Nacional Autónoma de México, 1967.

———. *Brevísima relación de la destrucción de las Indias.* 1552. Edited by Manuel Ballesteros Gaibrois. Madrid: Fundación Universitaria Española, 1977.

———. *De las antiguas gentes del Perú.* In *Colección de libros españoles raros o curiosos.* Edited by D. Marcos Jiménez. Madrid: Manuel G. Hernández, 1892.

———. *Historia de las Indias.* 1547. Edited by Agustín Millares Carlo. Mexico City: Fondo de Cultura Económica, 1965.

Lavrin, Asunción, ed. *Sexuality and Marriage in Colonial Latin America.* Lincoln: University of Nebraska Press, 1989.

Leacock, Eleanor. "Women's Status in Egalitarian Societies: Implications for Social Evolution." *American Ethnologist* 13 (1986): 118–130.

Leap, William L. *Word's Out: Gay Men's English.* Minneapolis: University of Minnesota Press, 1996.

Lees, Clare A. *Medieval Masculinities: Regarding Men in the Middle Ages.* Minneapolis: University of Minnesota Press, 1994.

León, Luis de. *La perfecta casada y poesías selectas*. Edited by Florencia Grau. Barcelona: Editorial Iberia, n.d.

Leonard, Irving A. *Books of the Brave: Being an Account of Books and the Men in the Spanish Conquest and Settlement of the Sixteenth-century New World*. New York: Gordian Press, 1964.

Lévi-Strauss, Claude. *Elementary Structures of Kinship*. Translated by James Harle Bell and John Richard von Sturmer. Edited by Rodney Needham. Boston: Beacon Press, 1969.

Libis, Jean. *El mito del andrógino*. Madrid: Ediciones Siruela, 2001.

Lienhard, Martín. *La voz y su huella: Escritura y conflicto étnico-social en América Latina, 1492–1988*. Hanover, NH: Ediciones del Norte, 1991.

Lockhart, James. *The Men of Cajamarca: A Social and Biographical Study of the First Conquerors of Peru*. Austin: University of Texas Press, 1972.

———. *Spanish Peru 1532–1560: A Colonial Society*. Madison: University of Wisconsin Press, 1968.

López Baralt, Mercedes. *Icono y conquista: Guaman Poma de Ayala*. Madrid: Hyperión, 1988.

MacCormack, Sabine G. "Children of the Sun and Reason of State Myths, Ceremonies and Conflicts in Inca Peru." Latin American Studies Center Series, no. 6. College Park: University of Maryland, 1990.

———. *Religion in the Andes*. Princeton, NJ: Princeton University Press, 1991.

Maclean, Ian. *The Renaissance Notion of Woman: A Study in the Fortunes of Scholasticism and Medical Science in European Intellectual Life*. Cambridge: Cambridge University Press, 1980.

Mannarelli, María Emma. *Pecados públicos: La ilegitimidad en Lima, siglo XVII*. Lima: Ediciones Flora Tristán, 1994.

———. "Sexualidad y desigualdades genéricas en el Perú del siglo XVI." *Allpanchis* 35–36, no. 1 (1990): 225–248.

Mannheim, Bruce. *The Language of the Inca since the European Invasion*. Austin: University of Texas Press, 1991.

Marcus, Leah S. "Renaissance and Early Modern Studies." In *Redrawing the Boundaries: The Transformation of English and American Literary Studies*. Edited by Stephen Greenblatt and Giles Gunn. New York: Modern Language Association, 1992.

Marín-Granada, Nicolás. "Señor y vasallo." *Romanische Forschungen* 86 (1974): 451–461.

Martín, Luis. *Daughters of the Conquistadores: Women of the Viceroyalty of Peru*. Dallas: Southern Methodist University Press, 1983.

Mason, Peter. *Deconstructing America: Representations of the Other*. New York: Routledge, 1990.

———. "Sex and Conquest: A Redundant Copula." *Anthropos* 92 (1997): 577–582.

Matienzo, Juan de. *El gobierno del Perú*. Buenos Aires, 1910.

Maus, Katherine Eisaman. "A Womb of His Own: Male Renaissance Poets in the

Female Body." In *Sexuality and Gender in Early Modern Europe: Institutions, Texts, Images.* Edited by James Grantham Turner. Cambridge: Cambridge University Press, 1993.

Mazzotti, José Antonio. *Coros mestizos del Inca Garcilaso: Resonancias andinas.* Lima: Fondo de Cultura Económica, 1996.

McDowell, John H. "Exemplary Ancestors and Pernicious Spirits." *Andean Cosmologies through Time.* Edited by Robert V. H. Dover, Katherine E. Seibold, and John H. McDowell. Bloomington: Indiana University Press, 1992.

McKendrick, Melveena. *Woman and Society in the Spanish Drama of the Golden Age: A Study of the "Mujer Varonil."* Cambridge: Cambridge University Press, 1974.

Medina, José Toribio. *Historia del tribuna de la Inquisición de Lima.* Santiago de Chile: Fondo Histórico y Bibliográfico J. T. Medina, 1956.

Mendoza, Zoila S. *Shaping Society through Dance: Mestizo Ritual Performance in the Peruvian Andes.* Chicago: University of Chicago Press, 2000.

Menéndez Pidal, Ramón. *El Cid Campeador.* Madrid: Espasa-Calpe, 1950.

Mignolo, Walter. *The Darker Side of the Renaissance: Literacy, Territoriality, and Colonization.* Ann Arbor: University of Michigan Press, 1995.

———. "Decires fuera de lugar: Sujetos dicentes, roles sociales y formas de inscripción." *Revista de Crítica Literaria Latinoamericana* 41 (1995): 9–31.

———. *Local Histories/Global Designs: Coloniality, Subaltern Knowledges, and Border Thinking.* Princeton, NJ: Princeton University Press, 2000.

Millones, Luis. "Nuevos aspectos del Taqui Onqoy." In *Ideología mesiánica del mundo andino.* Edited by Juan M. Ossio. Lima, 1973.

———. "Reflexiones en torno al romance en la sociedad indígena: Seis relatos de amor." *Revista de Crítica Literaria Latinoamericana* 8, no. 14 (1981): 7–29.

Millones-Figueroa, Luis. "El demonio en la *Crónica del Perú* de Cieza de León." *Cuadernos Americanos* 61 (1997): 179–185.

Mills, Kenneth R. *Idolatry and Its Enemies: Colonial Andean Religion and Extirpation 1640–1750.* Princeton, NJ: Princeton University Press, 1997.

Miró Quesada, Aurelio. "Prólogo." In *Comentarios reales.* By Garcilaso de la Vega. 2 vols. Edited by Aurelio Miró Quesada. Caracas: Biblioteca Ayacucho, 1985.

Mirrer, Louise. *Women, Jews, and Muslims in the Texts of Reconquest Castile.* Ann Arbor: University of Michigan Press, 1996.

Mitchell, William P., and Barbara H. Jaye. "Pictographs in the Andes: The Huntington Free Library Quechua Catechism." *Latin American Indian Literatures Journal* 12, no. 1 (1996): 1–42.

Mohillo, Silvia, and Robert McKee Irwin, eds. *Hispanisms and Homosexualities.* Durham, NC: Duke University Press, 1998.

Molina Martínez, Miguel. *La leyenda negra.* Madrid: Editorial Nerea, 1991.

Montesinos, Fernando. "Memorias antiguas historiales y políticas del Perú." 1644. *Colección de libros españoles raros y curiosos,* vol. 16. Madrid: Miguel Ginesta, 1882.

Montiel, Edgar. "El Inca Garcilaso en el laberinto de la soledad." *Cuadernos Americanos* 3, no. 18 (1989): 200–210.

Montrose, Louis. "The Work of Gender in the Discourse of Discovery." In *New World Encounters*. Edited by Stephen Greenblatt. Berkeley & Los Angeles: University of California Press, 1993.

Moraña, Mabel, ed. *Ángel Rama y los estudios latinoamericanos*. Pittsburgh: Instituto Internacional de Literatura Iberoamericana, 1997.

Moreiras, Alberto. "José María Arguedas y el fin de la transculturación." In *Ángel Rama y los estudios latinoamericanos*. Edited by Mabel Moraña. Pittsburgh: Instituto Internacional de Literatura Iberoamericana, 1997.

Morris, Craig. "Inka Strategies of Incorporation and Governance." In *Archaic States*. Edited by Gary M. Feinman and Joyce Marcus. Santa Fe, NM: School of American Research Press, 1998.

Murra, John V. *Formaciones económicas y políticas del mundo andino*. Lima: Instituto de Estudios Peruanos, 1975.

Murra, John V.; Nathan Wachtel; and Jacques Revel, eds. *Anthropological History of Andean Politics*. Cambridge: Cambridge University Press, 1986.

Murray, Stephen O. *Male Homosexuality in Central and South America*. San Francisco: Instituto Obregón, 1987.

Oliva, Giovanni Anello, S.J. *Historia del reino y provincias del Perú*. Edited by Carlos M. Gálvez Peña. Lima: Pontificia Universidad Católica del Perú, Fondo Editorial, 1998.

Ortiz, Fernando. *Cuban Counterpoint: Tobacco and Sugar*. Translated by Harriet de Onís. Durham, NC: Duke University Press, 1995.

Ortner, Sherry. "Is Female to Male as Nature Is to Culture?" In *Women, Culture, and Society*. Edited by Michelle Rosaldo y Louise Lamphere. Stanford, CA: Stanford University Press, 1974.

Osorio, Alejandra. "Seducción y conquista: Una lectura de Guamán Poma." *Allpanchis* 35–36, no. 1 (1990): 293–330.

Parker, Andrew; Mary Russo; Doris Sommer; and Patricia Yaeger, eds. *Nationalisms and Sexualities*. New York: Routledge, 1992.

Pastor Bodmer, Beatriz. *The Armature of Conquest: Spanish Accounts of the Discovery of America, 1492–1589*. Stanford, CA: Stanford University Press, 1992.

Paul, Anne. *Paracas Ritual Attire: Symbols of Authority in Ancient Peru*. Norman: University of Oklahoma Press, 1990.

Pease, Franklin. "Inka y kuraka: Relaciones de poder y representación histórica." Latin American Studies Center Series, no. 8. College Park: University of Maryland, 1990.

Peloubet, F. N., ed. *Peloubet's Bible Dictionary*. Chicago: John C. Winston, 1925.

Peres, Phyllis. "Subaltern Spaces in Brazil." *Dispositio* 6 (1996): 113–126.

Pérez de Tudela Bueso, Juan. "Estudio preliminar." In *Crónicas del Perú. Biblioteca de Autores Españoles*. Madrid: Real Academia Española, 1963.

Pérez Fernández, Isacio. *Bartolomé de Las Casas en el Perú*. Cuzco: Centro de Estudios Rurales Andinos Bartolomé de Las Casas, 1986.

316   *Decolonizing the Sodomite*

Perry, Mary Elizabeth. *Gender and Disorder in Early Modern Spain.* Princeton, NJ: Princeton University Press, 1990.

Platt, Tristan. *Espejos y maíz: Temas de estructura simbólica andina.* Cuadernos de Investigación CIPCA, no. 10. La Paz: Centro de Investigación y Promoción del Campesinado, 1976.

———. "Mirrors and Maize: The Concept of *Yanantin* among the Macha of Bolivia." In *Anthropological History of Andean Polities.* Edited by John V. Murra, Nathan Wachtel, and Jacques Revel. Cambridge: Cambridge University Press, 1986.

Poirier, Guy. "French Renaissance Travel Accounts: Images of Sin, Visions of the New World." *Journal of Homosexuality* 25, no. 3 (1993): 215–229.

Polo de Ondegardo, Juan. 1559. *Informaciones acerca de la religión y gobierno de los Incas.* Colección de Libros y Documentos Referentes a la Historia del Perú, vols. 3 and 4. Lima: Sanmartí, 1916.

Porras Barrenechea, Raúl. *Los cronistas del Perú (1528–1650) y otros ensayos.* Edited by Franklin Pease G. Y. Lima: Biblioteca Clásica del Perú, 1986.

Pratt, Mary Louise. *Imperial Eyes: Travel Writing and Transculturation.* London: Routledge, 1992.

Rabasa, José. *Inventing America: Spanish Historiography and the Formation of Eurocentrism.* Norman: University of Oklahoma Press, 1993.

———. "On Writing Back: Alternative Historiography in *La Florida del Inca.*" *Latin American Identity and Constructions of Difference.* Edited by Chanady Amaryll. Minneapolis: University of Minnesota Press, 1994.

———. "Utopian Ethnography in Las Casas's *Apologética.*" In *1492/1992 Re/Discovering Colonial Writing.* Edited by René Jara and Nicholas Spadaccini. Hispanic Issues, no. 4. Minneapolis: Prima Institute, 1989.

Rama, Ángel. *La ciudad letrada.* Hanover, NH: Ediciones del Norte, 1984.

———. *Transculturación narrativa en América Latina.* Mexico City: Siglo XXI, 1982.

Ramos, Gabriela, comp. *La venida del reino: Religión, evangelización y cultura en América, siglos XVI–XX.* Cuzco: Centro de Estudios Regionales Bartolomé de Las Casas, 1994.

Reiter, Rayna. *Toward an Anthropology of Women.* New York: Monthly Review Press, 1975.

Resina, Juan Ramón. "El honor y las relaciones feudales en 'El poema de mio Cid.'" *Revista de Estudios Hispánicos* 18, no. 3 (1984): 417–428.

Ringrose, Kathryn M. "Living in the Shadows: Eunuchs and Gender in Byzantium." In *Third Sex, Third Gender: Beyond Sexual Dimorphism in Culture and History.* Edited by Gilbert Herdt. New York: Zone Books, 1994.

Rodríguez Fernández, Celso. *La pasión de S. Pelayo: Edición crítica, con traducción y comentarios.* Monografías de Universidad de Santiago de Compostela, vol. 160. Santiago de Compostela: Universidad de Santiago de Compostela, 1991.

Rojas, Fernando de. *La Celestina.* Edited by Dorothy S. Severin. Madrid: Cátedra, 1997.

————. *The Celestina: A Novel in Dialogue.* Translated by Lesley Byrd Simpson. Berkeley & Los Angeles: University of California Press, 1955.

Roscoe, Will. *Changing Ones: Third and Fourth Genders in Native North America.* New York: St. Martin's Press, 1998.

————. "Gender Diversity in Native North America: Notes toward a Unified Analysis." In *A Queer World.* Edited by Martin Duberman. New York: New York University Press, 1997.

————. "How to Become a Berdache: Toward a Unified Analysis of Gender Diversity." In *Third Sex, Third Gender: Beyond Sexual Dimorphism in Culture and History.* Edited by Gilbert Herdt. New York: Zone Books, 1994.

————. "Mapping the Perverse." *American Anthropologist* 98, no. 4 (1996): 860–862.

————. *The Zuni Man-Woman.* Albuquerque: University of New Mexico Press, 1991.

Rostworowski de Diez Canseco, María. "Algunos comentarios hechos a las ordenanzas del doctor Cuenca." *Historia y Cultura* 9 (1975): 119–154.

————. *Pachacamac y el señor de los milagros.* Lima: Instituto de Estudios Peruanos, 1992.

————. "Visión andina pre-hispánica de los géneros." In *Otras pieles: Género, historia, y cultura.* Compiled by Maruja Barrig and Narda Henríquez. Lima: Pontificia Universidad Católica del Perú, 1995.

Ruiz de Arce, Juan. *Relación de servicios en Indias.* 1545. *Boletín de la Real Academia de Historia* 102 (1933): 327–384.

Ruiz de Navamuel, Álbaro. *Informaciones de las idolatrías de los Incas e indios y de cómo se enterraban, etc.* 1574. *Colección de documentos inéditos relativos al descubrimiento, conquista y organización de las antiguas posesiones españolas.* Madrid: Imprenta de Manuel G. Hernández, 1874.

Said, Edward. *Culture and Imperialism.* New York: Vintage, 1993.

————. *Orientalism.* New York: Vintage, 1978.

————. *The World, the Text, the Critic.* Cambridge, MA: Harvard University Press, 1983.

Salles-Reese, Verónica. "Yo Don Joan de Santacruz Pachacuti Yamqui Salcamaygua . . . digo." *Revista Iberoamericana* 61 (1995): 170–171; (1995): 107–118.

Salomon, Frank. "'Conjunto de nacimiento' y 'Línea de esperma' en el manuscrito de Huarochirí (ca. 1608)." In *Más allá del silencio: Las fronteras de género en los Andes.* Edited by Denise Y. Arnold. La Paz: ILCA/CIASE, 1997.

————. "Nightmare Victory: The Meaning of Conversion among Peruvian Indians (Huarochirí, 1608?)." *Latin American Studies Center Series,* no. 7. College Park: University of Maryland, 1990.

Sánchez, Ana. *Amancebados, hechiceros y rebeldes (Chancay, siglo XVII).* Cuzco: Centro de Estudios Regionales Andinos Bartolomé de Las Casas, 1991.

Sánchez, Luis Alberto. *La literatura peruana.* Vol. 2. Buenos Aires: Editorial Guarania, 1950.

Santa Cruz Pachacuti Yamqui, Juan de. *Relación de antigüedades deste reyno del Pirú.*

1613. *Varios: Antiguidades del Perú.* Edited by Henrique Urbano and Ana Sánchez. Madrid: Historia 16, 1992.

———. *Relación de antigüedades deste reyno del Perú.* 1613. Edited by Pierre Duviols and César Itier. Cuzco: Centro de Estudios Regionales Andinos Bartolomé de Las Casas, 1993.

Santo Tomás, Domingo de. *Gramática o Arte de la lengua general de los indios de los reynos del Peru.* Madrid, 1994.

Sarmiento de Gamboa, Pedro. *Historia índica.* 1572. Biblioteca de Autores Españoles, vol. 135. Madrid: Ediciones Atlas, 1965.

———. *History of the Incas.* Translated by Sir Clements Markham. Mineola, NY: Dover, 1999.

Saville, Marshall Howard. *The Antiquities of Manabi, Ecuador.* New York: Irving Press, 1910.

Schlegel, Alice. "Gendered Meanings: General and Specific." In *Beyond the Second Sex: New Directions in the Anthropology of Gender.* Edited by Peggy Sanday and Ruth Goodenough. Philadelphia: University of Pennsylvania Press, 1990.

Sedgwick, Eve. *Between Men: English Literature and Male Homosocial Desire.* New York: Columbia University Press, 1985.

———. *Epistemology of the Closet.* Berkeley & Los Angeles: University of California Press, 1990.

Sepúlveda, Juan Ginés de. *Tratado sobre las justas causas de la guerra contra los indios.* 1547. Mexico City: Fondo de Cultura Económica, 1987.

Severin, Dorothy Sherman. *Tragicomedy and Novelistic Discourse in Celestina.* Cambridge: Cambridge University Press, 1989.

Sigal, Pete. *From Moon Goddesses to Virgins: The Colonization of Yucatecan Maya Sexual Desire.* Austin: University of Texas Press, 2000.

———, ed. *Infamous Desire: Male Homosexuality in Colonial Latin America.* Chicago: University of Chicago Press, 2003.

Silverblatt, Irene. *Moon, Sun, and Witches: Gender Ideologies and Class in Inca and Colonial Peru.* Princeton, NJ: Princeton University Press, 1987.

Smith, Paul Julian. *The Body Hispanic: Gender and Sexuality in Spanish and Spanish American Literature.* New York: Oxford University Press, 1989.

Sommer, Doris. *Proceed with Caution when Engaged by Minority Writing in the Americas.* Cambridge, MA: Harvard University Press, 1999.

———. "Resisting the Heat." *Cultures of United States Imperialism.* Edited by Amy Kaplan and Donald Pease. Durham, NC: Duke University Press, 1993.

Spitta, Sylvia. *Between Two Waters: Narratives of Transculturation in Latin America.* Houston: Rice University Press, 1995.

Spivak, Gayatri Chakravorty. "Can the Subaltern Speak?" In *Marxism and the Interpretation of Culture.* Edited by Cary Nelson and Lawrence Grossberg. Chicago: University of Illinois Press, 1988.

Stavig, Ward. *Amor y violencia sexual: Valores indígenas en la sociedad colonial.* Lima: Instituto de Estudios Peruanos/ University of South Florida, 1996.

Stern, Steve J. *Peru's Indian Peoples and the Challenge of Spanish Conquest.* Madison: University of Wisconsin Press, 1982.

Stoler, Ann Laura. *Race and the Education of Desire.* Durham, NC: Duke University Press, 1995.

Sumario del concilio de 1567. In *Organización de la iglesia y órdenes religiosas en el virreinato del Perú en el siglo XVI: Documentos del Archivo de Indias,* vol. 2: 154–233. Edited by Roberto Levillier. Madrid: Sucesores de Rivadeneyra, 1919.

Surtz, Ronald E. *Writing Women in Late Medieval and Early Modern Spain: The Mothers of Teresa de Ávila.* Philadelphia: University of Pennsylvania Press, 1995.

Synnott, Anthony. *The Body Social: Symbolism, Self and Society.* London: Routledge, 1993.

Taussig, Michael T. *The Devil and Commodity Fetishism in South America.* Chapel Hill: University of North Carolina Press, 1980.

Todorov, Tzvetan. *The Conquest of America: The Question of the Other.* Translated by Richard Howard. New York: Harpers, 1987.

Toledo, Francisco de. "Informaciones acerca del señorio y gobierno de los Incas hechas por mandado de Don Francisco de Toledo Virey del Perú 1570–1572." *Colección de Libros Españoles Raros o Curiosos,* vol. 16, 131–259. Madrid: Miguel Ginesta, 1882.

Towle, Evan B., and Lynn M. Morgan. "Romancing the Transgender Native: Rethinking the Use of the 'Third Gender' Concept." *GLQ* 8, no. 4 (2002): 469–497.

Trexler, Richard C. "Gender Subordination and Political Hierarchy in Pre-Hispanic America." In *Infamous Desire: Male Homosexuality in Colonial Latin America.* Edited by Pete Sigal. Chicago: University of Chicago Press, 2003.

———. *Sex and Conquest: Gendered Violence, Political Order, and the European Conquest of the Americas.* Ithaca, NY: Cornell University Press, 1995.

Ugarteche, Oscar. *Historia, sexo, y cultura en el Perú.* Lima: Abraxas Editorial, 1993.

Urbano, Henrique. "El escándalo de Chucuito y la primera evangelización de los Lupaqa (Perú). Nota en turno a un documento inédito de 1574." *Cuadernos para la Historia de la Evangelización en América Latina* 2 (1987): 203–228.

———. "Historia de la iglesia y etnología religiosa en el sur andino." *Cuadernos para la Historia de la Evangelización en América Latina* 1 (1986): 249–269.

———. "Huayna Cápac y sus enanos: Huellas de un ciclo mítico andino prehispánico." *Historia y Cultura* 20 (1990): 281–293.

———. *Wiracocha y Ayar: Héroes y funciones en las sociedades andinas.* Cuzco: Centro de Estudios Regionales Bartolomé de Las Casas, 1981.

Urton, Gary. *At the Crossroads of the Earth and the Sky: An Andean Cosmology.* Austin: University of Texas Press, 1981.

———. *The History of a Myth: Pacariqtambo and the Origin of the Inkas.* Austin: University of Texas Press, 1990.

———. *Signs of the Inka Khipu.* Austin: University of Texas Press, 2003.

Valera, Blas. *De las costumbres antiguas de los naturales del Perú. Varios: Antiguidades del*

Perú. 1590. Edited by Henrique Urbano and Ana Sánchez. Madrid: Historia 16, 1992.

Valverde, Fray Vicente. *Carta relación de Fray Vicente Valverde a Carlos V sobre la conquista del Perú*. 1539. Edited by Juan José Vega. Lima: Ediciones Universidad Nacional de Educación, 1969.

van Deusen, Nancy E. "Los primeros recogimientos para doncellas mestizas en Lima y Cuzco, 1550–1580." *Allpanchis* 35–36, no. 1 (1990): 249–292.

Vargas Llosa, Mario. *Lituma en los Andes*. Barcelona: Editorial Planeta, 1993.

———. *La utopía arcaica: José María Arguedas y las ficciones del indigenismo*. Mexico City: Fondo de Cultura Económica, 1996.

Vargas Ugarte, Rubén. *Historia de la iglesia en el Perú 1511–1568*. 2 vols. Lima: Imprenta Santa María, 1953.

Velasco, Sherry. "Marimachos, Hombrunas, Barbudas: Masculine Women in Cervantes." *Bulletin of the Cervantes Society of America* 20, no. 1 (2000): 69–78.

Verdesio, Gustavo. "En busca de la materialidad perdida: Un aporte crítico a los proyectos de recuperación de las tradiciones aborígenes propuestas por Kush, Dussel y Mignolo." *Revista Iberoamericana* 192 (2000): 625–638.

———. "Revisando un modelo: Ángel Rama y los estudios coloniales." In *Ángel Rama y los estudios latinoamericanos*. Edited by Mabel Moraña. Pittsburgh: Instituto Internacional de Literatura Iberoamericana, 1997.

———. "Todo lo que es sólido se disuelve en la academia: Sobre los estudios coloniales, la teoría poscolonial, los estudios subalternos y la cultura material." *Revista de Estudios Hispánicos* 35 (2001): 633–660.

Vidal, Hernán. *Socio-historia de la literatura colonial hispanoamericana: Tres lecturas orgánicas*. Minneapolis: Institute for the Study of Ideologies and Literature, 1985.

Villasante Sullca, Fritz N. "De fiestas y rituales, al juego, humor, erotismo, sexualidad y la vida cotidiana." Paper presented at "De Amores y Luchas: Diversidad Sexual, Derechos Humanos y Ciudadanía," Symposium, Universidad Nacional de San Marcos, Lima, September 13, 2000.

Villegas, Juan. *Aplicación del Concilio de Trento en Hispanoamérica, 1569–1600: Provincia eclesiástica del Perú*. Montevideo: Instituto Teológico de Uruguay, 1975.

White, Hayden. *The Content of the Form*. Baltimore: Johns Hopkins University Press, 1987.

———. *Tropics of Discourse: Essays in Cultural Criticism*. Baltimore: Johns Hopkins University Press, 1978.

Williams, Craig. *Roman Homosexuality: Ideologies of Masculinity in Classical Antiquity*. Oxford: Oxford University Press, 1999.

Williams, Walter L. *The Spirit and the Flesh: Sexual Diversity in American Indian Culture*. Boston: Beacon Press, 1986.

Winkler, John J. *The Constraints of Desire: The Anthropology of Sex and Gender in Ancient Greece*. New York: Routledge, 1990.

Zamora, Margarita. "Filología humanista e historia indígena en los *Comentarios reales*." *Revista Iberoamericana* 53, no. 140 (1987): 547–558.

————. *Language, Authority, and Indigenous History in the Comentarios Reales de los Incas.* Cambridge: Cambridge University Press, 1988.

Zárate, Agustín de. *Historia del descubrimiento y conquista del Perú.* Edited by Franklin Pease G. Y. and Teodoro Hampe Martínez. Lima: Pontificia Universidad Católica del Perú, Fondo Editorial, 1995.

Zuidema, R. Tom. *Inca Civilization in Cuzco.* Translated by Jean-Jacques Decoster. Austin: University of Texas Press, 1990.

INDEX

community, 107–112; and subjectivity and sexuality, 144–151; summary characterization of, 165; theory of, 20–23; in *visita* report, 178–186; *waylaka* as, 156–157. *See also* berdache, sodomites
third space, 2, 6, 8, 69, 82, 123, 236–237
Thomas, Wesley, 273n23
tinkuy, 17, 18, 26, 27, 259, 265, 271n17; and Inca Garcilaso, 237; as reading strategy, 137–139, 141; and *tinquichi,* 146, 288n41; and *yanantin,* 146–149
Titu Cusi Yupanqui, 172–173
Toledo, Francisco de, 27, 71, 103, 166, 171, 175, 216, 291n11
Topaynga, 86
Towle, Evan, 22, 23
transatlantic, 4, 5
transculturation, 28, 69, 82, 88, 91, 96, 116, 269n10; distinguished from *tinkuy,* 139; and *Doctrina Christiana,* 196, 211; and Inca Garcilaso, 230–258; and indigenous informants, 189; of indigenous myths, 91–101, 221–223, 226; as protonational, gendered process, 169; as queer process, 8, 125, 141, 221, 233; theorization of, 4–12; and third gender, 22–26, and tropes of sexuality, 12–17; as "war machine," 11, 196, 230
transgender, 23, 64, 72; in creation myth, 164; Quechua vocabulary for, 112, 242; in ritual, 154; transgendered work roles, 86, 242. *See also* cross-dressing, third gender
transsexual, 21
transvestism, 71, 94–95, 106, 107, 154
Trexler, Richard, 23, 24, 106–108, 121, 183, 273nn24,26, 276n22, 280n7, 282n36, 283nn33,39,40
tropes of sexuality, 3, 4, 8, 12–17, 29, 82; troping, 13. *See also* sodomy trope

Túmbez, 82
Tupac Amaru, 173, 235
tupu, 117, 157
two-spirit, 21, 272n23

Urbano, Henrique, 158, 227, 290n52
Urioste, George L., 123, 131
Urton, Gary, 161, 178, 219, 285n17

Valera, Blas, 109–110, 183, 243–245
Vargas Llosa, Mario, 251, 259, 262, 293n31
Vellasco, Sherry, 279n61
Verdesio, Gustavo, 270n15
Vilcabamba, 173
Villasante Sullca, Fitz, 22, 184, 263–264, 299nn3,4
Viracocha: as androgynous, 164–165; in Cañari myth, 222
visitas, 167, 168, 175; and Sarmiento de Gamboa, 218; and third gender, 176–186
Vitoria, Francisco de, 75

Warner, Michael, 268n8
White, Hayden, 12, 13
Williams, Craig, 273n1
Williams, Walter, 21, 183, 292n21
Winkler, John J., 273n1

yanantin, 17, 27, 130, 134, 136; etymologies of, 147, 149; as gendered symmetry, 147; in Inca mythology, 142–143; and same-sex sexuality, 149–150; and third gender, 146–151
Yauyos, 128–129
Yungas (also Yuncas), 102, 116, 128–129

Zamora, Margarita, 234–235, 238, 246
Zuazo, Alonso de, 71
Zuidema, Tom, 111, 158, 162, 213

Lightning Source UK Ltd.
Milton Keynes UK
UKHW010952280422
402152UK00001B/35